Android Application Development for the Intel® Platform

Ryan Cohen, Lead Project Editor
Tao Wang, Lead Contributing Author

Android Application Development for the Intel® Platform

Ryan Cohen & Tao Wang

Publisher: Heinz Weinheimer
Associate Publisher: Jeffrey Pepper
Lead Editors: Steve Weiss (Apress); Stuart Douglas and Paul Cohen (Intel)
Coordinating Editor: Melissa Maldonado
Cover Designer: Anna Ishchenko

Distributed to the book trade worldwide by Springer Science+Business Media New York, 233 Spring Street, 6th Floor, New York, NY 10013. Phone 1-800-SPRINGER, fax (201) 348-4505, e-mail orders-ny@springer-sbm.com, or visit www.springeronline.com.

For information on translations, please e-mail rights@apress.com, or visit www.apress.com.

About ApressOpen

What Is ApressOpen?

- ApressOpen is an open access book program that publishes high-quality technical and business information.

- ApressOpen eBooks are available for global, free, noncommercial use.

- ApressOpen eBooks are available in PDF, ePub, and Mobi formats.

- The user-friendly ApressOpen free eBook license is presented on the copyright page of this book.

Contents at a Glance

About the Lead Project Editor... xvii

About the Lead Contributing Author... xix

About the Technical Reviewer xxi

Introduction xxiii

■Chapter 1: Overview of Embedded Application Development
for Intel Architecture.. 1

■Chapter 2: Intel Embedded Hardware Platform........................... 19

■Chapter 3: Android Application Development Processes
and Tool Chains for Intel® Architecture.. 47

■Chapter 4: Real Device Environment Installation 85

■Chapter 5: The Android OS.. 131

■Chapter 6: Customization and Installation of Android............... 191

■Chapter 7: GUI Design for Android Apps, Part 1:
General Overview 203

■Chapter 8: GUI Design for Android Apps, Part 2:
The Android-Specific GUI... 235

■Chapter 9: GUI Design for Android Apps, Part 3:
Designing Complex Applications... 271

■Chapter 10: GUI Design for Android Apps, Part 4:
Graphic Interface and Touchscreen Input.................................. 305

Chapter 11: Performance Optimization for Android
Applications on x86 335

Chapter 12: NDK and C/C++ Optimization 391

Chapter 13: The Low-Power Design of Android Application
and Intel Graphics Performance Analyzers (Intel GPA):
Assisted Power Optimization 445

Index 483

Contents

About the Lead Project Editor xvii

About the Lead Contributing Author xix

About the Technical Reviewer xxi

Introduction xxiii

■Chapter 1: Overview of Embedded Application Development
for Intel Architecture 1

Introduction to Embedded Systems 1

    Mobile Phones 3

    Consumer Electronics and Information Appliances 3

Definition of an Embedded System 4

    Limited Resources 4

    Real-Time Performance 4

    Robustness 5

    Integrated Hardware and Software 5

    Power Constraints 5

    Difficult Development and Debugging 5

Typical Architecture of an Embedded System 6

    Typical Hardware Architecture 6

    Microprocessor Architecture of Embedded Systems 9

    Typical Software Architecture 15

Special Difficulties of Embedded Application Development 17

Summary 18

■**Chapter 2: Intel Embedded Hardware Platform**............................ **19**

Intel Atom Processor **19**

Intel Atom Processor Architecture 20

Features of the Intel Atom Processor 24

Other Technologies Used by the Intel Atom Processor 28

Intel Embedded Chipset **29**

Intel System on Chip (SoC) **30**

Medfield.. 31

Bay Trail 32

64-Bit Android OS on Intel Architecture............................... **32**

64 Bits vs. 32-bit Android 32

Memory and CPU Register Size 33

Reference Platform for Intel Embedded Systems **34**

Internet of Things (IoT) and Next Unit of Computing (NUC)..................... 34

Smartphones 36

Tablets 39

In-Vehicle Infotainment 42

Other Application Platforms and Fields 42

Robotics 43

Summary... **45**

■**Chapter 3: Android Application Development Processes
and Tool Chains for Intel® Architecture**......................................**47**

Android Application Development **47**

Development Environment of Android Applications................................. 48

The Android Application Development Process 51

Debugging and Simulation of Android Systems 55

Typical Development Tool Chains 60

  Editor 62

  Compiler and Linker 62

  Debugger 63

  Build Manager 63

  Makefile Auto Generation Tool 63

  Optimizing Tools -- gprof 64

Overview, Installation, and Configuration of Android Application
Development Tool Chains on Intel® Architecture 65

Intel Environment Setup for Android (OS X Host) 72

Android Development on Linux-based Host Machines 73

Intel® Integrated Native Developer Experience beta 73

  Tools and Libraries 74

  Setup 75

  Intel INDE Installation 75

Summary 83

Chapter 4: Real Device Environment Installation 85

Mobile Phone Setting 85

  Installing the USB Driver on the Host Machine 85

  Interaction between the Host Machine and the Target Machine 88

  Developing Android Applications 88

  Debugging Android Applications 110

Intel Auxiliary Tools for Android Application Development 124

  Intel C++ Compiler (Intel ICC) 125

  Intel Graphics Performance Analyzers for Android OS 126

  Intel System Studio 127

  Intel Project Anarchy: a Free Mobile Game Engine by Havok 129

  Intel Performance Libraries 129

Summary 130

Chapter 5: The Android OS 131

Android Overview 131

Android Architecture 133

Basic Android Functionality from a Programming Perspective 134

Android System Interface 134

Common Linux Commands and Operations 140

Using the Android Development and Auxiliary Tools 151

Using the Emulator 151

Accept "yes" for custom hw and choose x86 for hw.cpu.arch propertyUsing
the Help File 156

Using DDMS 160

Using adb at Command Prompt 177

Using Android Commands 183

Using Telnet for Emulator Commands 186

Summary 190

Chapter 6: Customization and Installation of Android 191

Tailoring and Customization of an Embedded OS 191

Overview of Android Customization 192

ROM Package/Image 193

Overview of Android Image Customization 196

Example of Android Image Customization 196

Installation/Reflash of the Android Image 199

Image Installation Example 200

Intel Build Tools Suite 201

Summary 202

■Chapter 7: GUI Design for Android Apps, Part 1:
General Overview 203

Overview of GUIs for Embedded Applications 203

Characteristics of Interaction Modalities of Android Devices 204

UI Design Principles for Embedded Systems 208

Considerations of Screen Size 208

Size of Application Windows 209

Considerations Arising from Touch Screens and Styluses 210

Keyboard Input Problems 213

Software Distribution and Copyright Protection Problems 214

Android Application Overview 214

Application File Framework 214

Component Structure of Applications 228

Content Provider 231

Android Emulator 231

Introducing Android Runtime (ART) 232

Summary 233

■Chapter 8: GUI Design for Android Apps, Part 2:
The Android-Specific GUI 235

State Transitions of Activities 235

Activity States 235

Important Functions of Activities 237

The Context Class 240

Introduction to Intent 243

The Main Roles of Intent 244

Intent Resolution 244

xi

The Relationship between Applications and Activities 247

The Basic Android Application Interface 247

    GuiExam Application Code Analysis..248

    Using Layouts as Interfaces 253

    Using the View Directly as an Interface..255

    Component ID 257

Buttons and Events 259

    Inner Class Listener..260

    Using ImageView 262

    Exit Activities and Application...266

Summary... 269

■Chapter 9: GUI Design for Android Apps, Part 3:
Designing Complex Applications 271

Applications with Multiple Activities 271

    Triggering an Explicit Match of Activities with No Parameters............................272

    Triggering Explicit Matching of an Activity with Parameters of Different
    Applications..281

    Implicit Matching of Built-In Activities..292

    Implicit Match that Uses a Custom Activity 297

Summary... 304

■Chapter 10: GUI Design for Android Apps, Part 4:
Graphic Interface and Touchscreen Input................................... 305

Display Output Framework... 305

Drawing Framework for Responding to Touchscreen Input 310

Multi-Touch Code Framework 313

Responding to Keyboard Input 317

Dialog Boxes in Android 322

Using an Activity's Dialog Theme 322

Using a Specific Dialog Class 323

Using Toast Reminders 323

Dialog Box Example 323

Application Property Settings 328

Summary 333

■ Chapter 11: Performance Optimization for Android
Applications on x86 335

Principles of Performance Optimization 335

Reducing Instructions and Execution Frequency 336

Selecting Faster Instructions 336

Improving the Degree of Parallelism 337

Using the Register Cache Effectively 337

Performance Optimization Methodology 338

Performance Optimization Approaches 338

Intel Graphics Performance Analyzers (Intel GPA) 341

Introduction to Intel GPA 341

Installing Intel GPA 344

Using Intel GPA on Android 345

Android Multithreaded Design 355

Android Framework of a Thread 356

Thread Synchronization 367

Thread Communication 370

Principles of Multithreaded Optimization for the Intel Atom Processor 372

Case Study: Intel GPA-Assisted Multithreaded Optimization for an
Android Application 373

Original Application and Intel GPA Analysis 374

Optimized Application and Intel GPA Analysis................................... 381

Summary 390

■Chapter 12: NDK and C/C++ Optimization 391

Introduction to JNI 391

Java Methods and C Function Prototype Java................................... 394

Introduction to NDK 397

Installing NDK and Setting Up the Environment 401

Installing CDT.. 401

NDK Examples 403

Using the Command Line to Generate a Library File 403

Generating a Library File in the IDE 411

Workflow Analysis for NDK Application Development 417

NDK Compiler Optimization 419

Machine-Independent Compiler Switch Options 420

Intel Processor-Related Compiler Switch Options 422

Optimization with Intel Integrated Performance Primitives (Intel IPP) 426

NDK Integrated Optimization Examples... 427

C/C++: Accelerating the Original Application 427

Extending Compiler Optimization 436

Comparing Compiler Optimizations 441

Summary 443

■Chapter 13: The Low-Power Design of Android Application
and Intel Graphics Performance Analyzers (Intel GPA):
Assisted Power Optimization.. 445

Overview of Low-Power Design 445

The Basics of Consumption 446

Power Consumption Control Technology 447

Linux Power-Control Mechanism 454

Tickless Idle... 454

PowerTOP 455

Intel Power-Optimization Aids 456

Low-Power Considerations in Application Design............................... 459

The Most Basic Principle of Low-Power Optimization............................ 459

General Recommendations: High Performance = Low Power Consumption........ 460

Use Low-Power Hardware as Much as Possible to Achieve the Task.................. 460

Polling Is the Enemy of Low-Power Optimization.................................... 460

Event-Driven Programming 462

Reduce Periodic Operations Similar to Polling in Application Programs 462

Low-Power Recommendations for Data Acquisition and Communications.......... 463

Establishing a Power-Aware Program 463

Case Study 1: Intel GPA Assisted Power Optimization for an Android
Application 463

Original Application and Intel GPA Power Analysis 464

Optimized Applications and an Intel GPA Power Analysis....................... 470

Case Study 2: Timer Optimization and Intel GPA Power Analysis 475

Book Summary... 481

Index... 483

About the Lead Project Editor

Ryan Cohen is the contributing editor responsible for leading the international team of content contributors who created this Intel learning resource; he's also an Android enthusiast and Portland State graduate. Ryan has been following Android since 2011 when he made the switch from Apple iOS. When he is not writing about Android, he spends his time researching anything and everything new in the world of Android.

About the Lead Contributing Author

Tao Wang came to the United States as a Ph.D. student to study at Oregon State University in 1993. He has been a software engineer with Intel Corporation since 2002. Tao began blogging and writing about Android in 2008; and, since 2011, he has served as a technical collateral manager for the Intel Android Developer Zone, the developer resource for all things Android at Intel. In his spare time, Tao also runs his own mobile app/client education startup called E-k12. He follows closely the latest progress in application development, as well as testing/debugging/performance optimization for mobile devices and Android on x86 platforms. Tao is skilled in many platforms, including Android SDK and NDK; Intel Android tools, game engines such as Cocos2D-x, AndEngine, and libgdx; OpenGL ES; RenderScript; and Android Runtime. His other areas of interest include mobile Internet technologies such as online content management, cloud-based mobile technologies, embedded devices, robotics, and mobile learning on the go.

About the Technical Reviewer

Xavier Hallade is Developer Evangelist for the Intel Software and Services Group in Paris, France. Since 2012 and the public release of the first Android smartphone based on an Intel platform, he has been helping Android developers improve their support for new hardware and technologies made or supported by Intel.

Introduction

The number of Android devices running on Intel processors has gradually increased ever since Intel and Google announced, in late 2011, that they would be working together to optimize future versions of Android for Intel Atom processors. Today, Intel processors can be found in Android smartphones and tablets made by some of the top manufacturers of Android devices, such as Samsung, Lenovo, and Asus.

The increase in Android devices featuring Intel processors has created a demand for Android applications optimized for Intel architecture. This book was written to help introduce developers of all skill levels to the tools they need to develop and optimize applications for the Intel platform.

Chapter 1

This chapter discusses principles for embedded systems, the architecture of SoC, and some pros and cons of platforms such as ARM and x86/x64.

Chapter 2

This chapter goes into detail about specific Intel hardware platforms. It covers Intel Atom processors, Intel SoCs, and retail devices.

Chapter 3

This chapter introduces Android application development on Intel hardware platforms. It also covers installing the development environment tools for an emulator target machine by showing each tool and application and how to download and install them.

Chapter 4

This chapter discusses how to set up and configure the application development software on a host system and install USB drivers for a real Android device, so that you can build the connection between the device and host system to allow testing and debugging of applications. It also discusses how to use the Intel emulator and the steps required to accelerate the emulator and work with it.

Chapter 5

This chapter covers the Android OS and helps build your understanding for subsequent development of embedded applications.

Chapter 6

This chapter discusses customization in an embedded OS and then explains how to customize Android, specifically.

Chapter 7

This chapter introduces the general GUI design method for desktop systems and then shows how designing the UI and UX for embedded systems is different. It also discusses general methods and principles of GUI design for Android applications.

Chapter 8

This chapter introduces Android interface design by having you create a simple application called GuiExam. You learn about the state transitions of activities, the Context class, intents, and the relationship between applications and activities. Finally, the chapter shows how to use the layout as an interface by changing the layout file activity_main.xml, and how the button, event, and inner event listeners work.

Chapter 9

In this chapter, you learn how to create an application with multiple activities. This application is used to introduce the explicit and implicit trigger mechanisms of activities. Next, you see an example of an application with parameters triggered by an activity in a different application, which will help you understand of the exchange mechanism for the activity's parameters.

Chapter 10

This chapter introduces the basic framework of drawing in the view, how the drawing framework responds to touchscreen input, and how to control the display of the view as well as the multi-touch code framework. Examples illustrate the multi-touch programming framework and keyboard-input responses. You also learn how to respond to hardware buttons on Android devices, such as Volume +, Volume –, Power, Home, Menu, Back, and Search. After that, you see the three different dialog boxes for Android, including the activity dialog theme, specific dialog classes, and toast reminders. Finally, you learn how to change application property settings.

Chapter 11

This chapter introduces the basic principles of performance optimization, optimization methods, and related tools for Android application development.

Chapter 12

This chapter introduces the Android NDK for C/C++ application development, along with related optimization methods and optimization tools. It talks about how the Intel mobile hardware and software provide a basis for low-power design and how the Intel Atom processor provides hardware support for low power, which is a major feature of the Android operating system.

Chapter 13

This chapter provides an overview of and introduction to low-power design, followed by a discussion of Android power-control mechanisms. Finally, it covers how to achieve the goal of low-power application design.

The hope is that this book will help developers to create amazing Android applications that are optimized for the Intel platform. You can find further information on developing applications for Intel architecture at the Intel Developer Zone web site (https://software.intel.com/en-us/android).

CHAPTER 1

■ ■ ■

Overview of Embedded Application Development for Intel Architecture

Embedded systems, an emerging area of computer technology, combine multiple technologies, such as computers, semiconductors, microelectronics, and the Internet, and as a result, are finding ever-increasing application in our modern world. With the rapid development of computer and communications technologies and the growing use of the Internet, embedded systems have brought immediate success and widespread application in the post-PC era, especially as the core components of the Internet of Things. They penetrate into every corner of modern life from the mundane, such as an automated home thermostat, to industrial production, such as in robotic automation in manufacturing. Embedded systems can be found in military and national defense, healthcare, science, education, and commercial services, and from mobile phones, MP3 players, and PDAs to cars, planes, and missiles.

This chapter provides the concepts, structure, and other basic information about embedded systems and lays a theoretical foundation for embedded application development, of which application development for Android OS is becoming the top interest of developers.

Introduction to Embedded Systems

Since the advent of the first computer, the ENIAC, in 1946, the computer manufacturing process has gone from vacuum tubes, transistors, integrated circuits, and large-scale integration (LSI), to very-large-scale integration (VLSI), resulting in computers that are more compact, powerful, and energy efficient but less expensive (per unit of computing power).

After the advent of microprocessors in the 1970s, the computer-using world witnessed revolutionary change. Microprocessors are the basis of microcomputers, and personal computers (PCs) made them more affordable and practical, allowing many private users to own them. At this stage, computers met a variety of needs: they were sufficiently versatile to satisfy various demands such as computing, entertainment, information sharing, and office automation. As the adoption of microcomputers was

1

occurring, more people wanted to embed them into specific systems to intelligently control the environment. For example, microcomputers were used in machine tools in factories. They were used to control signals and monitor the operating state through the configuration of peripheral sensors. When microcomputers were embedded into such environments, they were prototypes of embedded systems.

As the technology advanced, more industries demanded special computer systems. As a result, the development direction and goals of specialized computer systems for specific environments and general-purpose computer systems grew apart. The technical requirement of general-purpose computer systems is fast, massive, and diversified computing, whereas the goal of technical development is faster computing speed and larger storage capacity. However, the technical requirement of embedded computer systems is targeted more toward the intelligent control of targets, whereas the goal of technical development is embedded performance, control, and reliability closely related to the target system.

Embedded computing systems evolved in a completely different way. By emphasizing the characteristics of a particular processor, they turned traditional electronic systems into modern intelligent electronic systems. Figure 1-1 shows an embedded computer processor, the Intel Atom N2600 processor, which is 2.2 × 2.2 cm, alongside a penny.

Figure 1-1. *Comparison of an embedded computer chip to a US penny. This chip is an Intel Atom processor*

The emergence of embedded computer systems alongside general-purpose computer systems is a milestone of modern computer technologies. The comparison of general-purpose computers and embedded systems is shown in Table 1-1.

Table 1-1. *Comparison of General-Purpose Computers and Embedded Systems*

Item	General-purpose computer systems	Embedded systems
Hardware	High-performance hardware, large storage media	Diversified hardware, single-processor solution
Software	Large and sophisticated OS	Streamlined, reliable, real-time systems
Development	High-speed, specialized development team	Broad development sectors

Today, embedded systems are an integral part of people's lives due to their mobility. As mentioned earlier, they are used everywhere in modern life. Smartphones are a great example of embedded systems.

Mobile Phones

Mobile equipment, especially smartphones, is the fastest growing embedded sector in recent years. Many new terms such as *extensive embedded development* and *mobile development* have been derived from mobile software development. Mobile phones not only are pervasive but also have powerful functions, affordable prices, and diversified applications. In addition to basic telephone functions, they include, but are not limited to, integrated PDAs, digital cameras, game consoles, music players, and wearables.

Consumer Electronics and Information Appliances

Consumer electronics and information appliances are additional big application sectors for embedded systems. Devices that fall into this category include personal mobile devices and home/entertainment/audiovisual devices.

Personal mobile devices usually include smart handsets such as PDAs, as well as wireless Internet access equipment like mobile Internet devices (MIDs). In theory, smartphones are also in this class; but due to their large number, they are listed as a single sector.

Home/entertainment/audiovisual devices mainly include network television like interactive television; digital imaging equipment such as digital cameras, digital photo frames, and video players; digital audio and video devices such as MP3 players and other portable audio players; and electronic entertainment devices such as handheld game consoles, PS2 consoles, and so on. Tablet PCs (tablets), one of the newer types of embedded devices, have become favorites of consumers since Apple released the iPad in 2010.

The affordability of consumer electronics truly reflects the cost-effectiveness of embedded system design.

Definition of an Embedded System

So far, you have a general understanding of embedded systems from the examples given. But what is the embedded system? Currently, there are different concepts for *embedded system* in the industry.

According to the Institution of Engineering and Technology (IET), embedded systems are devices used to control, monitor, or assist the operation of equipment, machinery, or plants. Smartphones, as an important sector of embedded systems, have the following characteristics:

Limited Resources

The majority of embedded systems have extremely limited resources. On one hand, the resources referred to here are hardware resources, including computing speed and processing capability of the CPU, size of the available physical memory, and capacity of the ROM or flash memory that stores code and data. On the other hand, resources are also the functions provided by the software. Compared with general operating systems, embedded operating systems have comparatively simple functions and structure. Embedded systems' resource constraints lead to designs that are sufficient, instead of powerful.

Real-Time Performance

The real-time aspect of embedded systems means tasks must usually be executed in a certain, predictable amount of time, and maximum execution time limits must be ensured.

Real time is divided into *soft real time* and *hard real time*. Soft real time has less-stringent requirements; even if the time limit cannot be met in some cases, it won't have a fatal impact on the system. For example, a media player system is soft real time. The system is supposed to play 24 frames in one second, but it is also acceptable when the system fails in some overloaded conditions. Hard real time has strict requirements. The execution of tasks must be absolutely ensured in all situations; otherwise the consequences will be catastrophic. For example, aircraft autopilot and navigation system are hard real-time systems. They must accomplish a specific task within the certain time limit; otherwise a major accident, collision, or crash could occur.

Many embedded systems (mobile phones, game consoles, and so on) do not need real-time guarantees. But real time is the key for some embedded systems, such as a steel-rolling system in a large steel mill and the real-time alarm system in a large electrical substation. In these applications, the system must respond to a specific signal at a given time.

Robustness

Some embedded systems require high reliability. Reliability is also known as *robustness*, which is the ability to continue operating in abnormal or dangerous situations. For example, when an embedded system encounters input errors, network overload, or intentional attacks, the system must be robust enough that it doesn't hang or crash, but operates as usual.

Integrated Hardware and Software

General-purpose computers install software dynamically. The software can be installed and uninstalled according to the users' demands. But for embedded systems, software and hardware are often integrated and sold as a package. This trend is shifting for devices that are always connected via the Internet, such as smartphones and the Internet of Things (wearables, for example). In these cases, original device manufacturers (ODMs) can do regular software updates.

Embedded software is usually built into the hardware ROM and runs automatically when the system is started. Under normal circumstances, the user cannot easily modify or delete the software without the aid of special tools to ensure the integrity of the embedded system. Due to the integration of hardware and software, embedded systems usually do not have the intellectual property rights issues that general computer systems have to address. For example, software piracy on consumer electronics such as mobile phones and digital cameras is almost impossible due to the way the software is installed. However, this feature also leads to slow upgrading of system software, because it is difficult to do so.

Power Constraints

General-purpose computers are often directly connected to AC power. Therefore, general-purpose computer hardware and software designers can assume that the power supply is inexhaustible. But for embedded systems that cannot be directly connected to AC power—for example, mobile phones, electric toys, and cameras—the only power source is the battery. This means their power consumption is constrained, and so energy efficiency is important. Cooling is another key factor. In general, more power consumption within a certain time period causes more heat to be generated, which can cause problems in some cases such as battery fires, malfunctioning components due to overheating, and quick losses of electricity.

Difficult Development and Debugging

Compared to hardware and software development of general-purpose computers, embedded system development has higher technical requirements. For example, developers of embedded software often must understand the working principles and mechanisms of the hardware and hardware layers during the development stage. To debug the code, these developers often must use online simulations, ROM monitors, and ROM programming tools, which don't occur in the desktop development.

Typical Architecture of an Embedded System

Figure 1-2 shows a configuration diagram of a typical embedded system consisting of two main parts: embedded hardware and embedded software. The embedded hardware primarily includes the processor, memory, bus, peripheral devices, I/O ports, and various controllers. The embedded software usually contains the embedded operating system and various applications.

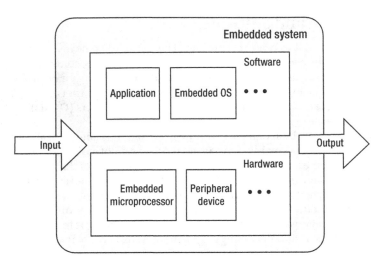

Figure 1-2. *Basic architecture of an embedded system*

Input and output are characteristics of any open system, and the embedded system is no exception. In the embedded system, the hardware and software often collaborate to deal with various input signals from the outside and output the processing results through some form. The input signal may be an ergonomic device (such as a keyboard, mouse, or touch screen) or the output of a sensor circuit in another embedded system. The output may be in the form of sound, light, electricity, or another analog signal, or a record or file for a database.

Typical Hardware Architecture

The basic computer system components—microprocessor, memory, and input and output modules—are interconnected by a system bus in order for all the parts to communicate and execute a program (see Figure 1-3).

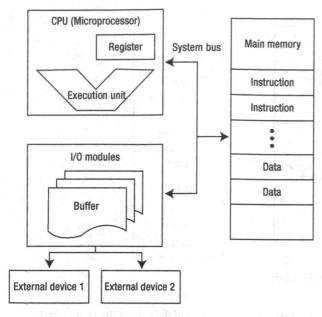

Figure 1-3. Computer architecture

In embedded systems, the microprocessor's role and function are usually the same as those of the CPU in a general-purpose computer: control computer operation, execute instructions, and process data. In many cases, the microprocessor in an embedded system is also called the CPU. Memory is used to store instructions and data. I/O modules are responsible for the data exchange between the processor, memory, and external devices. External devices include secondary storage devices (such as flash and hard disk), communications equipment, and terminal equipment. The system bus provides data and controls signal communication and transmission for the processor, memory, and I/O modules.

There are basically two types of architecture that apply to embedded systems: Von Neumann architecture and Harvard architecture.

Von Neumann Architecture

Von Neumann architecture (also known as Princeton architecture) was first proposed by John von Neumann. The most important feature of this architecture is that the software and data use the same memory: that is, "The program is data, and the data is the program" (as shown in Figure 1-4).

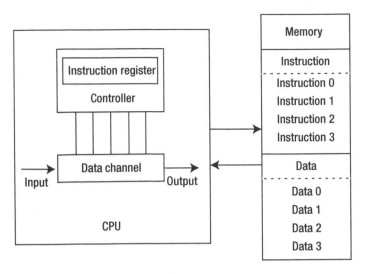

Figure 1-4. *Von Neumann architecture*

In the Von Neumann architecture, an instruction and data share the same bus. In this architecture, the transmission of information becomes the bottleneck of computer performance and affects the speed of data processing; so, it is often called the *Von Neumann bottleneck*. In reality, cache and branch-prediction technology can effectively solve this issue.

Harvard Architecture

The Harvard architecture was first named after the Harvard Mark I computer. Compared with the Von Neumann architecture, a Harvard architecture processor has two outstanding features. First, instructions and data are stored in two separate memory modules; instructions and data do not coexist in the same module. Second, two independent buses are used as dedicated communication paths between the CPU and memory; there is no connection between the two buses. The Harvard architecture is shown in Figure 1-5.

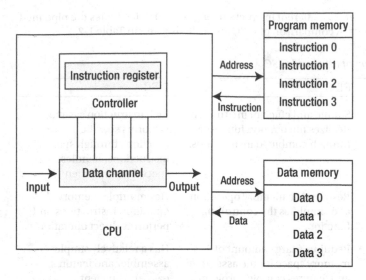

Figure 1-5. *Harvard architecture*

Because the Harvard architecture has separate program memory and data memory, it can provide greater data-memory bandwidth, making it the ideal choice for digital signal processing. Most systems designed for digital signal processing (DSP) adopt the Harvard architecture. The Von Neumann architecture features simple hardware design and flexible program and data storage and is usually the one chosen for general-purpose and most embedded systems.

To efficiently perform memory reads/writes, the processor is not directly connected to the main memory, but to the cache. Commonly, the only difference between the Harvard architecture and the Von Neumann architecture is single or dual L1 cache. In the Harvard architecture, the L1 cache is often divided into an instruction cache (I cache) and a data cache (D cache), but the Von Neumann architecture has a single cache.

Microprocessor Architecture of Embedded Systems

The microprocessor is the core in embedded systems. By installing a microprocessor into a special circuit board and adding the necessary peripheral circuits and expansion circuits, a practical embedded system can be created. The microprocessor architecture determines the instructions, supporting peripheral circuits, and expansion circuits. There are a wide range of microprocessors: 4-, 8-, 16-, 32-, and 64-bit, with performance from MHz to GHz, and ranging from a few pins to thousands of pins.

In general, there are two types of embedded microprocessor architecture: *reduced instruction set computer (RISC)* and *complex instruction set computer (CISC)*. The RISC processor uses a small, limited, simple instruction set. Each instruction uses a standard word length and has a short execution time, which facilitates the optimization of the instruction pipeline. To compensate for the command functions, the CPU is often equipped with a large number of general-purpose registers. The CISC processor features a powerful instruction set and different instruction lengths, which facilitates the pipelined execution of instructions. A comparison of RISC and CISC is given in Table 1-2.

Table 1-2. *Comparison of RISC and CISC*

	RISC	CISC
Instruction system	Simple and efficient instructions. Realizes uncommon functions through combined instructions.	Rich instruction system. Performs specific functions through special instructions; handles special tasks efficiently.
Memory operation	Restricts the memory operation and simplifies the controlling function.	Has multiple memory operation instructions and performs direct operation.
Program	Requires a large amount of memory space for the assembler and features complex programs for special functions.	Has a relatively simple assembler and features easy and efficient programming of scientific computing and complex operations.
Interruption	Responds to an interrupt only at the proper place in instruction execution.	Responds to an interruption only at the end of execution.
CPU	Features fewer unit circuits, small size, and low power consumption.	Has feature-rich circuit units, powerful functions, a large area, and high power consumption.
Design cycle	Features a simple structure, a compact layout, a short design cycle, and easy application of new technologies.	Features a complex structure and long design cycle.
Usage	Features a simple structure, regular instructions, simple control, and easy learning and application.	Features a complex structure, powerful functions, and easy realization of special functions.
Application scope	Determines the instruction system per specific areas, which is more suitable for special machines.	Becomes more suitable for general-purpose machines.

RISC and CISC have distinct characteristics and advantages, but the boundaries between RISC and CISC begin to blur in the microprocessor sector. Many traditional CISCs absorb RISC advantages and use a RISC-like design. Intel x86 processors are typical of them. They are considered CISC architecture. These processors translate x86 instructions into RISC-like instructions through a decoder and comply with the RISC design and operation to obtain the benefits of RISC architecture and improve internal operation efficiency. A processor's internal instruction execution is called *micro operation*, which is denoted as *micro-OP* and abbreviated *mu-op* (or written *m-op* or *mop*). In contrast, the x86 instruction is called *macro operation* or *macro-op*. The entire mechanism is shown in Figure 1-6.

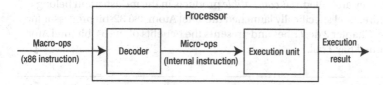

Figure 1-6. *Micro and macro operations of an Intel processor*

Normally, a macro operation can be decoded into one or more micro operations to execute, but sometimes a decoder can combine several macro operations to generate a micro operation to execute. This process is known as x86 *instruction fusion* (macro-ops fusion). For example, the processor can combine the x86 CMP (Compare) instruction and the x86 JMP (Jump) instruction to produce a single micro operation—the compare and jump instruction. This combination has obvious benefits: there are fewer instructions, which indirectly enhances the performance of the processor execution. And the fusion enables the processor to maximize the parallelism between the instructions and consequently improve the implementation efficiency of the processor.

Currently, microprocessors used in most embedded systems have five architectures: RISC, CISC, MIPS, PowerPC, and SuperH. The details follow.

RISC: Advanced RISC Machines (ARM) Architecture

Advanced RISC Machines (ARM) is a generic term for a type of RISC microprocessor. ARM is designed by the British company ARM Holdings. The company specializes in the design and development of RISC chips. As a supplier of intellectual property, the company itself does not manufacture its chips, but licenses its designs to other partners to produce them. The world's major semiconductor manufacturers buy ARM microprocessor cores designed by ARM, add the appropriate external circuits as per different application sectors, and create their own ARM microprocessor chips.

CISC: x86 Architecture

The x86 series CPUs are the most popular CPUs for desktop PCs. The x86 architecture is considered CISC. The instruction set was specially developed by Intel for its first 16-bit CPU (i8086), which was adopted by IBM when it launched the world's first PC in 1981. As Intel launched the i80286, i80386, i80486, Pentium, and other products, it continued to use the x86 instruction set to ensure that legacy applications could be run and protect and integrate diversified software resources. Therefore, those CPUs are called the *x86 architecture*.

In addition to Intel, AMD, Cyrix, and other manufacturers have also produced CPUs based on the x86 instruction set. Those CPUs can run a variety of software developed for Intel processors, so they are called *x86-compatible* products in the industry and belong to the x86 architecture. Intel specifically launched the Intel Atom x86 32-bit processor for embedded systems. Chapter 2 describes and presents the benefits of the 64-bit Intel Atom processor, code-named Bay Trail.

■ **Note**   IA-32, IA-64, Intel 64, IA-32, IA-64, and Intel64 are Intel's architecture types, which apply to its processors as well as compatible CPUs.

IA-32 (Intel Architecture-32) means Intel's 32-bit architecture processor. The number 32 is the working width of a processor; it can process 32 bits of binary data at a time. If other processors (for example, the AMD 32-bit CPU) are compatible with this architecture, they belong to the IA-32 architecture.

IA-64 (Intel Architecture-64) is Intel's 64-bit architecture. With the 64-bit working width, its microarchitecture is completely different from the x86 architecture. IA-64 is not compatible with x86 software, so the x86 software must use various forms of emulation to run on IA-64, often leading to low efficiency. The architecture is created by HP and co-developed by HP and Intel. Intel Itanium is a typical IA-64 processor.

Intel64 is a 64-bit x86 architecture with a 64-bit working width. After it was introduced by AMD, Intel launched a compatible processor named EM64T, officially renamed Intel64. Almost all Intel CPUs are now Intel64: Xeon, Core, Celeron, Pentium, and Atom. Contrary to the IA-64 architecture, it can also run x86 instructions.

MIPS Architecture

Microprocessor without Interlocked Piped Stages (MIPS) is also a RISC processor. Its mechanism is to make full use of the software to avoid data issues in the pipeline. It was first developed by a research team led by Professor John Hennessy of Stanford University in the early 1980s and later was commercialized by MIPS Technologies.

Like ARM, MIPS Technologies provides MIPS microprocessor cores to semiconductor companies through intelligence property (IP) cores and allows them to further develop embedded microprocessors in the RISC architecture. The core technology is a multiple-issue capability: split the idle processing units in the processor to virtualize as another core and improve the utilization of processing units.

PowerPC Architecture

PowerPC is a CPU in the RISC architecture. It derives from the POWER architecture, and its basic design comes from the IBM PowerPC 601 microprocessor Performance Optimized with Enhanced RISC (POWER). In the 1990s, IBM, Apple, and Motorola successfully developed the PowerPC chip and created a PowerPC-based multiprocessor computer. The PowerPC architecture features scalability, convenience, flexibility, and openness: it defines an instruction set architecture (ISA), allows anyone to design and manufacture PowerPC-compatible processors, and freely uses the source code of software modules developed for PowerPC. PowerPC has a broad range of applications from mobile phones to game consoles, with wide application in the communications and networking sectors such as switches, routers, and so on. The Apple Mac series used PowerPC processors for a decade until Apple switched to the x86 architecture.

SuperH

SuperH (SH) is a highly cost-effective, compact, embedded RISC processor. The SH architecture was first developed by Hitachi and was owned by Hitachi and ST Microelectronics. Now it has been taken over by Renesas. SuperH includes the SH-1, SH-2, SH-DSP, SH-3, SH-3-DSP, SH-4, SH-5, and SH-X series and is widely used in printers, faxes, multimedia terminals, TV game consoles, set-top boxes, CD-ROM, household appliances, and other embedded systems.

Typical Structure of an Embedded System

The typical hardware structure of an embedded system is shown in Figure 1-7. A microprocessor is the center of the system, with storage devices, input and output peripherals, a power supply, human-computer interaction devices, and other necessary supporting facilities. In an actual embedded system, the hardware is generally tailor-made for the application. To save cost, the peripherals may be quite compact, and only the basic peripheral circuits are retained for the processor and applications.

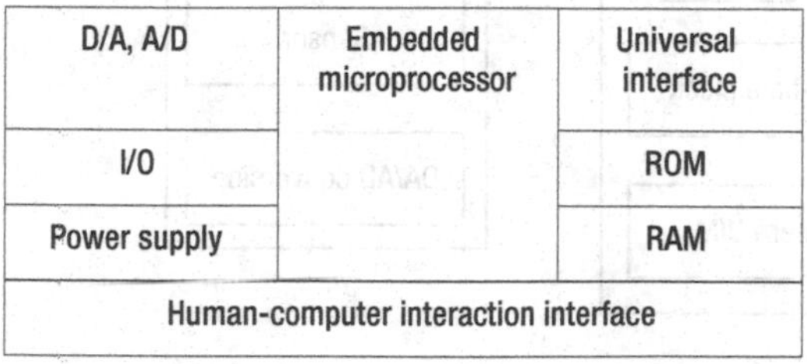

D/A, A/D	Embedded microprocessor	Universal interface
I/O		ROM
Power supply		RAM
Human-computer interaction interface		

Figure 1-7. Typical hardware structure of an embedded system

With the development of integrated circuit design and manufacturing technology, integrated circuit design has gone from transistor integration, to logic-gate integration, to the current IP integration or system on chip (SoC). The SoC design technology integrates popular circuit modules on a single chip. SoC usually contains a large number of peripheral function modules such as microprocessor/microcontroller, memory, USB controller, universal asynchronous receiver/transmitter (UART) controller, A/D and D/A conversion, I2C, and Serial Peripheral Interface (SPI). Figure 1-8 is an example structure of SoC-based hardware for embedded systems.

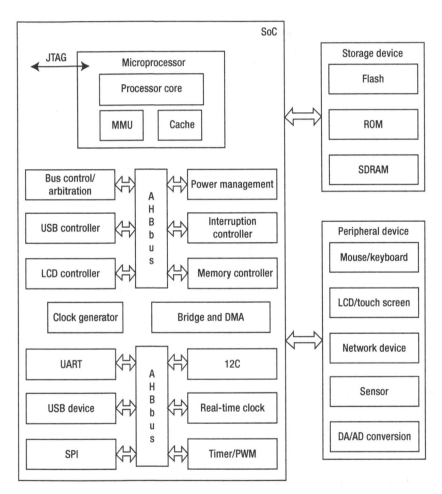

Figure 1-8. *Example of an SoC-based hardware system structure*

A system on a programmable chip (SoPC) advocates that an electronic system be integrated onto a silicon chip with programmable logic technology. Therefore, SoPC is a special type of SoC, in that the main logic function of the entire system is achieved by a single chip. Because it is a programmable system, its functions can be changed via software. It can be said that the SoPC combines the benefits of the SoC, programmable logic device (PLD), and field-programmable gate array (FPGA).

One of the development directions of embedded system hardware is centered on SoC/SoPC, where a hardware application system through the minimum external components and connectors is built to meet the functional requirements of applications.

Typical Software Architecture

Like embedded hardware, embedded software architecture is highly flexible. Simple embedded software (such as electronic toys, calculators, and so on) may be only a few thousand lines of code and perform simple input and output functions. On the other hand, complex embedded systems (such as smartphones, robots, and so on) need more complex software architecture, similar to desktop computers and servers. Simple embedded software is suitable for low-performance chip hardware, has very limited functionality, and requires tedious secondary development. Complex embedded systems provide more powerful functions, need more convenient interfaces for users, and require the support of more powerful hardware. With the improvement of hardware integration and processing capabilities, the hardware bottleneck has gradually loosened and even broken, so embedded system software now tends to be fully functional and diversified. Typical, complete embedded system software has the architecture shown in Figure 1-9.

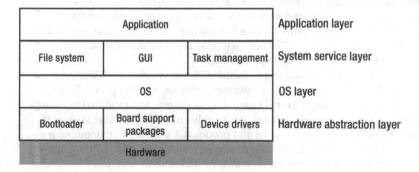

Figure 1-9. Software architecture of an embedded system

An embedded software system is composed of four layers, from bottom to top:

1. Hardware abstraction layer

2. Operating system layer

3. System service layer

4. Application layer

Hardware Abstraction Layer

The hardware abstraction layer (HAL), as a part of the OS, is a software abstraction layer between the embedded system hardware and OS. In general, the HAL includes the bootloader, board support package (BSP), device drivers, and other components. Similar to the BIOS in PCs, the bootloader is a program that runs before the OS kernel executes. It completes the initialization of the hardware, establishes the image of memory space, and consequently enables the hardware and software environment to reach an appropriate state for the final scheduling of the system kernel. From the perspective of end users, the bootloader is used to load the OS. The BSP achieves the abstraction of the hardware operation, empowering the OS to be independent from the hardware and enabling the OS to run on different hardware architectures.

A unique BSP must be created for each OS. For example, Wind River VxWorks BSP and Microsoft Windows CE BSP have similar functions for an embedded hardware development board, but they feature completely different architectures and interfaces. The concept of a BSP is rarely mentioned when various desktop Windows or Linux operating systems are discussed, because all PCs adopt the unified Intel architecture; the OS may be easily migrated to diversified Intel architecture-based devices without any changes. The BSP is a unique software module in embedded systems. In addition, device drivers enable the OS to shield the differences between hardware components and peripherals and provide a unified software interface for operating hardware.

Operating System Layer

An OS is a software system for uniformly managing hardware resources. It abstracts many hardware functions and provides them to applications in the form of services. Scheduling, files synchronization, and networking are the most common services provided by the OS. Operating systems are widely used in most desktop and embedded systems. In embedded systems, the OS has its own unique characteristics: stability, customization, modularity, and real-time processing.

The common embedded OS contains embedded Linux, Windows CE, VxWorks, MeeGo, Tizen, Android, Ubuntu, and some operating systems used in specific fields. Embedded Linux is a general Linux kernel tailored, customized, and modified for mobile and embedded products. Windows CE is a customizable embedded OS that Microsoft launched for a variety of embedded systems and products. VxWorks, an embedded real-time operating system (RTOS) from Wind River, supports PowerPC, 68K, CPU32, SPARC, I960, x86, ARM, and MIPS. With outstanding real-time and reliable features, it is widely used in communications, military, aerospace, aviation, and other areas that require highly sophisticated, real-time technologies. In particular, VxWorks is used in the Mars probes by NASA.

System Service Layer

The system service layer is the service interface that the OS provides to the application. Using this interface, applications can access various services provided by the OS. To some extent, it plays the role of a link between the OS and applications. This layer generally includes the file system, graphical user interface (GUI), task manager, and so on. A GUI library provides the application with various GUI programming interfaces, which enables the application to interact with users through application windows, menus, dialog boxes, and other graphic forms instead of a command line.

Application Layer

The application, located at the top level of the software hierarchy, implements the system functionality and business logic. From a functional perspective, all levels of modules in the application aim to perform system functions. From a system perspective, each application is a separate OS process. Typically, applications run in the less-privileged processor mode and use the API system schedule provided by the OS to interact with the OS.

Special Difficulties of Embedded Application Development

As mentioned earlier in this chapter, embedded systems are generally resource constrained, real time, and robust. These characteristics make application development on embedded systems more difficult than development on general-purpose computers.

The resource-constrained nature of embedded systems means they have fewer resources, lower CPU operation speed and processing, and less RAM than general-purpose systems. Embedded systems store code and data in ROM or flash instead of on hard drives and have less capacity than hard disks. Most dedicated-purpose embedded systems, especially embedded operating systems, also feature very simple functions compared to general-purpose computers. These resource constraints require developers of embedded hardware to select more rational configurations for chips and peripherals. They must consider resource utilization more carefully than they would when developing for the desktop environment.

The embedded interaction poses special requirements for application development. General desktop computers use the GUI windows, icons, menus, and pointers (WIMP), including common interactive elements such as buttons, toolbars, and dialog boxes. WIMP has strict requirements for interactive hardware; for example, it requires the display to be a certain resolution and size, and the mouse or similar devices must support the pointing operation. However, the interactive hardware of many embedded systems does not meet WIMP's requirements. For example, an MP3 player's display is too small, with inadequate resolution; ABS has no display; and most embedded systems do not have a mouse or touch screen to complete the pointing operation (for example, basic mobile phones do not have touch screens). Because the interaction for embedded applications is very special, we cannot completely adopt the WIMP interface.

The special user experience and reliability features of embedded systems add to the difficulty of the application development. For example, users expect the startup time for embedded systems to be much shorter than for general-purpose computers. Compared with general-purpose computer systems, it is also more difficult for embedded systems to ensure reliability. When a task problem occurs, embedded systems do not have the Task Manager, Kill command, or similar tools to terminate the faulty process. Obviously, embedded systems have less tolerance for errors than general systems.

Embedded systems generally do not support native code development. Software development on general-purpose computers usually has native development, compiling, and operation. It is not suitable for embedded systems because they do not have enough resources to run development and debugging tools. Therefore, embedded system software usually uses cross-compile development, which generates execution code on another hardware platform.

The cross-compile development environment is built on the host, whereas the embedded system is called the *target machine*. The cross-compile, assemble, and link tools on the host create the executable binary code, which is not executable on the host: only on the target machine. The executable file is downloaded to the target machine. The development environment on the host doesn't completely reflect the environment on the target machine, so debugging and fault diagnosis of the target machine can be time consuming. The nonnative development model of embedded systems leads to certain challenges for application development.

Summary

This chapter discussed principles for embedded systems, the architecture of SoC, and some pros and cons of platforms such as ARM and x86/x64. Application developers for PCs often ignore the hardware and focus completely on their software, because the two entities are quite independent. However, developers cannot ignore embedded system hardware. Due to the unique features of SoC, constrained resources, and integration of hardware and software, developers need to understand the working principles and mechanisms of the hardware and hardware layers in order to design efficient applications for the SoC (for example, ARM and x86 have different hardware). The next chapter presents a detailed discussion on the Intel embedded hardware platform including the Intel Atom processor, the Intel embedded chipset, SoC, and the reference platform.

CHAPTER 2

■ ■ ■

Intel Embedded Hardware Platform

Application developers on general-purpose computers can often ignore the hardware and focus completely on their software because the two entities have become quite independent. However, developers cannot ignore embedded system hardware. Due to the embedded system's specialized features, constrained resources, and integration of hardware and software, you need to understand the working principles and mechanisms of the hardware and hardware layers in order to design efficient applications for the embedded environment.

As the world's leader in silicon innovation, Intel has been designing high-performance processors and related hardware for general-purpose computers and embedded systems. This chapter focuses on Intel technologies for embedded systems, paving the way for the subsequent application development.

Intel Atom Processor

Intel specifically designed Intel Atom processors for embedded and mobile devices starting in 2008. As the smallest and lowest-power processor, it uses an entirely new microarchitecture for embedded devices to reduce power consumption and yet maintain instruction-set compatibility with Intel Core 2 processors.

The Intel Atom processor is the current Intel-based architecture for embedded systems. It is compatible with Intel architecture instruction software. Compared to Intel processors for desktop systems, its size, power consumption, and other features are more suitable for embedded applications.

Today's generation of Intel Atom processors delivers energy-efficient performance to power a range of computing devices. Thin and light smartphones and tablets. Intelligent cars. Innovative healthcare devices. Smart city infrastructure monitoring. High-performance microservers for the cloud. These are just some of the ways Intel Atom processor innovation drives higher performance at ultra-low power—connecting people, enriching lives, and fueling the Internet of Things.

The Intel Atom processor E3800 product family (formerly Bay Trail) offers a range of multi-core system-on-chip (SoC) options. Based on industry-leading 22 nm process technology, these SoCs integrate the Intel architecture core, graphics, memory, and I/O interfaces into a one-chip solution that delivers outstanding compute, graphics, and media performance.

Intel Atom Processor Architecture

Until the Intel Atom Clover Trail platform, the Intel Atom processor is based on a microarchitecture code-named Saltwell that applies the two-issue wide and in-order pipeline; it also supports Intel Hyper-Threading Technology. The microarchitecture is shown in Figure 2-1.

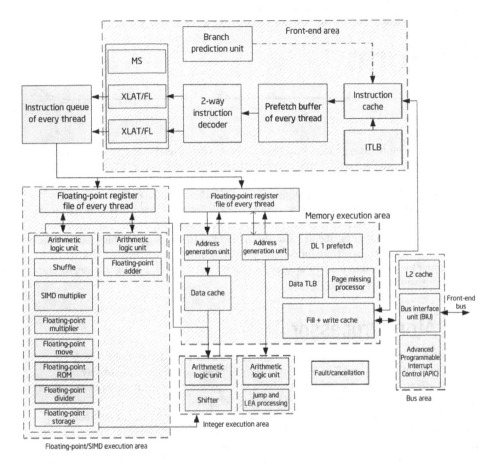

Figure 2-1. *Intel Atom architecture*

The front-end area is an optimized pipeline, including

- 32 KB, 8-way set-associative, L1 Cache

- Branch-prediction unit and instant translation look-aside buffer (ITLB)

- Two instruction decoders, each of which decodes two instructions at most per cycle

In each cycle, the front end may transmit two instructions at most to the instruction queue for scheduling. Also in each cycle, the scheduler may transmit two instructions at most to the integer or SIMD/floating-point execution area through the two-way port. (Single instruction, multiple data [SIMD]) is introduced in the next section.)

The ports for the integer or SIMD/floating-point areas have the following binding features:

Integer execution area

1. Port 0: Arithmetic logic unit 0 (ALU0), shift/rotate unit, and load/store unit.

2. Port 1: Arithmetic logic unit 1, bit-processing unit, jump unit, and LEA.

3. Effective waiting time of "load-to-use" in cycle 0.

SIMD/floating-point execution area

4. Port 0: SIMD arithmetic logic unit, shuffle unit, SIMD/ floating-point multiplication unit, and division unit.

5. Port 1: SIMD arithmetic logic unit and floating-point adder.

6. In the SIMD/floating-point execution areas, the SIMD arithmetic logic unit and shuffling unit are 128 bits wide, but the 64-bit integer SIMD calculation is limited to port 0.

7. The floating-point adder can perform Add packed single-precision (ADDPS)/ Subtract packed single-precision (SUBPS) in the 128-bit data path, whereas other floating-point addition operations are performed in the 64-bit data path.

8. The security-instruction-recognition algorithm of floating-point/SIMD operations can directly execute new, shorter integer arithmetic instructions without waiting for old floating-point/SIMD instructions (which may cause some abnormality).

9. The floating-point multiplication pipeline also supports the storage load.

10. The floating-point addition instruction with load/store reference is distributed through two ports.

The instruction queue conducts the static partition in order to schedule the execution instructions from the two threads. The scheduler can select an instruction from two threads and assign them to port 0 or port 1 for the execution. The hardware selects the pre-fetch/decode/dispatch on the two threads and performs the next execution based on the readiness of each thread.

Silvermont: Next-Generation Microarchitecture

Intel's Silvermont microarchitecture was designed and co-optimized with Intel's 22 nm SoC process using 3D tri-gate transistors. By taking advantage of this industry-leading technology, Silvermont microarchitecture includes

- A new out-of-order execution engine that enables best-in-class, single-threaded performance.

- A new multi-core and system fabric architecture scalable up to eight cores and enabling greater performance for higher bandwidth, lower latency, and more efficient out-of-order support for a more balanced and responsive system.

- New Intel architecture instructions and technologies bringing enhanced performance, virtualization, and security management capabilities to support a wide range of products. These instructions build on Intel's existing support for 64-bit and the breadth of the Intel architecture software installed base.

- Enhanced power-management capabilities including a new intelligent burst technology, low-power C states, and a wider dynamic range of operation taking advantage of Intel's 3D transistors. Intel Burst Technology 2.0 support for single- and multi-core offers great responsiveness scaled for power efficiency.

The microarchitecture is shown in Figure 2-2.

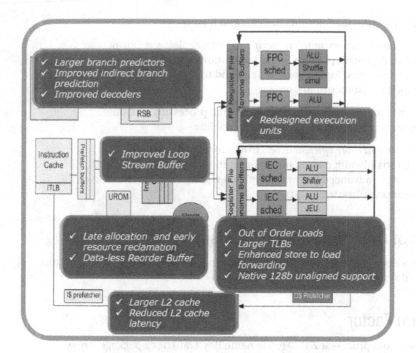

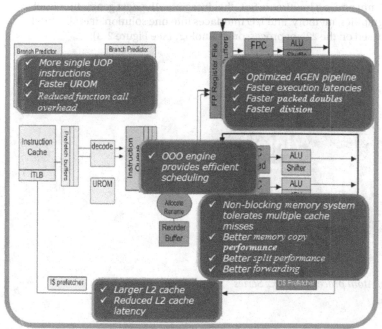

Figure 2-2. Silvermont microarchitecture

Silvermont provides the following benefits and features:

- *High performance without sacrificing power efficiency:* Out-of-order execution pipeline, macro-operation execution pipeline with improved instruction latencies and throughput, and smart pipeline resource management

- *Power and performance:* Efficient branch processing, accurate branch predictors, and fast-recover pipeline

- *Faster and more efficient access to memory:* Low latency, high-bandwidth caches, out-of-order memory transactions, and multiple advanced hardware prefetchers, balanced-core, and memory subsystems

Features of the Intel Atom Processor

Intel Atom processors have features for mobile Internet device (MID), netbook, nettop, and embedded systems, as outlined in this section.

Small Form Factor

The latest Intel Atom processor Z3740 (code name Bay Trail) has a package size of only 17 mm × 17 mm and is a multi-core SoC that integrates the next generation Intel processor core, graphics, memory, and I/O interfaces into one solution. It is also Intel's first SoC that is based on the 22 nm processor technology (see Figure 2-3).

Figure 2-3. Intel Atom processor Z3xxx Series

Low Power Consumption

As mentioned earlier, embedded systems are power constrained. The Intel Atom processor features energy-saving technologies such as Enhanced Intel SpeedStep Technology (EIST),[1] low thermal design power, dynamic cache sizing, and deeper sleep. Devices with Intel Atom processors feature very limited heat dissipation, much less than common "full power" devices.

It should be noted that different Intel Atom processor series have different low-power processing strategies. For example, the N series does not support EIST, nor does it conduct automatic frequency reduction in standby state.

Dynamic Low-Voltage Technology for Mobile and Embedded Devices

Many mobile and embedded systems are powered by battery; so the voltage doesn't have the stability of systems with AC power supplies, for which the voltage maintains a certain range. Intel Atom processors also have adopted the technology to dynamically adjust operating voltage per processor activity states and support the Intel Mobile Voltage Positioning (IMVP)-6 standard for mobile and embedded systems.

High Performance

The Intel Atom processor is an embedded microprocessor, delivers the performance of traditional general-purpose processors, and provides a performance similar to Intel Pentium 4 processors. The high performance is mainly reflected in the following aspects:

- Quad core supports four-core / four-thread out-of-order processing and 2 MB of L2 cache, which makes the device run faster and more responsively by allowing multiple apps and services to run at the same time.

- Intel Burst Technology 2.0 lets the system tap extra cores when necessary, which allows CPU-intensive applications to run faster and more smoothly

- Performance improved by using the 22 nm processor technology:

  - Maximizes current flow during ON state for better performance

  - Minimizes leaks during OFF state, leading to more energy efficiency

---

[1]See the Processor Spec Finder at http://ark.intel.com, or contact your Intel representative for more information.

- 64-bit OS capable

- Supports dynamic power sharing between the CPU and IP (graphics), allowing for higher peak frequencies

- Total SoC energy budget is dynamically assigned according to application needs

- Supports fine-grained low-power states, which provides better power management and leads to longer battery life

- Supports cache retention during deep sleep states, leading to lower idle power and shorter wakeup times

- Offers more than 10 hours of active battery life

SSE3 Instruction Set Enhances the Processing Power of Digital Media

Software applications like CAD tools, 3D/2D modeling, video editing, digital music, digital photography, and games all require massive floating-point parallel computing. They are called *floating-point-intensive applications*. For example, video processing often requires multiplication of two data sets of n length, so the common arithmetic instruction has to operate n times (n cycle). To that end, the SIMD architecture was created. Compared with traditional processors, SIMD processors have more arithmetic units, which are controlled by a controller, while conducting the same data operation in each data set (also known as *vector data*) to achieve spatial parallelism. In the example shown in Figure 2-4, if the CPU uses the eight processing elements, the $n/8$ SIMD instructions can complete the calculation so the operation time is shortened to 1/8 of the original time, and the speed is increased 8 times. The essence of SIMD is to transfer from *one* data process to a data *set* process.

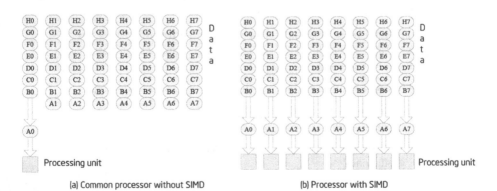

Figure 2-4. Realization procedure of SIMD instructions

Streaming SIMD Extensions (SSE) in Intel processors accelerate the streaming floating-point calculations and greatly improve the performance in floating-point-intensive applications. Intel Atom processors support SSE3 and SSSE3 (Supplemental Streaming SIMD Extension 3; Supplement SSE 3). The version history of the SSE instruction set is shown in Table 2-1.

Table 2-1. *Development History of the SSE Instruction Set*

Version	SSE	SSE2	SSE3	SSSE3	SSE4	AVX
Date	1999	2000	2004	2006	2007	2008
Instructions	70	144	13	32	47	256
Enhancement	Single-precision vector • Flow operation	Dual-precision vector • 128-bit vector integer	Complex arithmetic	Decoding	Video acceleration • Graphics module • Coprocessor acceleration	SSE extension float-point operations

Intel Virtualization Technology (Intel VT)

Intel Atom processors support Intel VT, which is a kind of CPU virtualization technology. Intel VT allows one CPU to simulate the parallel operation of multiple CPUs, lets a platform run multiple operating systems, and enables applications to run independently in separate spaces, thereby increasing application efficiency.

Intel Hyper-Threading Technology (Intel HT Technology) and Multi-Core Technologies

The new Intel Z3xxx Atom processors support Intel HT Technology, which produces an overhead of less than 10% additional power consumption. Meanwhile, the N series adopted the dual-core architecture. Intel HT Technology and multi-core technologies enable processors to execute two instruction threads in parallel and provide thread-level concurrent applications to improve performance and system response in today's multitasking environment. Intel HT Technology and multi-core technologies found in Intel Atom processors create higher execution efficiency than a single-thread microprocessor.

Other Technologies Used by the Intel Atom Processor

In addition, Intel Atom processors use a few other technologies that often go unnoticed but that increase processor performance:

> *Smart cache:* Intel Atom processors use the more intelligent, more efficient cache and bus technologies to effectively support data sharing and provide enhanced performance, response, and energy-saving capability.
>
> *Power-optimized FSB:* Intel Atom processors support up to 1910 MHz frequency (E3845) to meet the needs of demanding applications. In addition, the Intel architecture instruction (macro-ops) fusion technology allows faster execution of instructions in the low-power state.
>
> *Enhanced data pre-fetch technology:* This technology can effectively predict which data will specifically be used and automatically load it into the L2 cache in advance.
>
> *Burst mode:* Burst mode, as enhanced hardware technology, is used in Intel Atom processors after the Z5xx series. It automatically sets the processor performance level based on system load without compromising the thermal design so that the user can select processor performance on demand.
>
> *Low cost:* To meet the needs of embedded systems, Intel Atom processors use low-cost design strategies, one of which is applying the in-order execution of Intel architecture. Compared with the out-of-order execution of general desktop processors, the in-order execution design in Intel Atom processors can reduce the number of transistors and manufacturing costs, but results in lower performance. To compensate for the lower performance involved, Intel Atom processors use the higher operating frequency.

In addition to these features, Intel Atom processors have some unique benefits compared to other embedded processors. Because they are based on Intel architecture, Intel Atom processors have a huge number of compatible Intel architecture-based software applications. Many of these applications can be easily and seamlessly migrated to Intel Atom processor-based devices.

In general, low-power consumption, small size, low cost, low thermal coefficient, and high performance enable Intel Atom processors to be more suitable for embedded system applications. Due to the low-power, lead-free, halogen-free manufacturing process, Intel Atom processors are also very eco-friendly.

Intel Embedded Chipset

A *chipset*, one of the core components of computer motherboards, maximizes the integration of complex circuits and components within a few chips. The chipset determines the functions, level, and grade of the motherboard. If it fails to work correctly with the CPU, the chipset seriously affects overall performance and can even cause hardware failure. If the CPU or microprocessor is the brain, the chipset is the nervous system of the device.

A typical example of a computer system structure is shown in Figure 2-5. The CPU is connected to the main memory RAM, graphics, and other components through FSB, which has high frequency. The network adapter and other components are connected to a medium-speed bus (PCI bus with much lower frequency than FSB). North Bridge (the host bridge chip) realizes the connection of high-speed FSB and the medium-speed bus. Low-speed devices, such as COM, LPT, and USB, as well as the lower-speed ISA bus, are connected to the low-speed bus through South Bridge (the standard bus bridge chip).

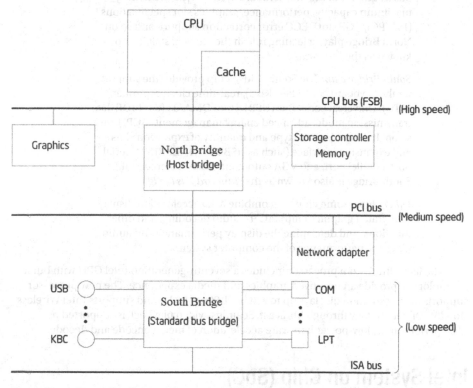

***Figure 2-5.** Example of computer system architecture*

Variations on this architecture include, for example, computers with no ISA bus. North Bridge and South Bridge are integrated in some Intel Atom series of processors, as specified in subsequent sections. The system architecture in Figure 2-5 can help you understand the main components of the chipset and their functions.

■ **Tip   PCI and ISA** The two types of PC bus standards are PCI and ISA. Peripheral Component Interconnect (PCI) is the standard for the local bus and was launched by Intel in 1992. PCI buses are either 32-bit or 64-bit, and 33 MHz or 66 MHz in speed. A 32-bit, 33 MHz PCI bus has a bandwidth of 32/8 × 33 MHz = 132 MB/s. Industry Standard Architecture (ISA) is based on the IBM PC bus and is the bus standard developed in the early 1980s. The bus has a width of 8/16 bits and an operating frequency of 8 MHz, which are far below PCI. Most new computers do not support the ISA bus.

The main chips in the chipset and their functions are as follows:

North Bridge chip: Determines the type of CPU, clock speed, bus frequency of the motherboard system, type of memory, maximum capacity, performance, graphics slot specifications (ISA/PCI/AGP slot), ECC error correction support, and so on. North Bridge plays a leading role in the chipset, so it is also known as the *host bridge*.

South Bridge chip: The South Bridge chip provides the support for the keyboard controller (KBC), real-time clock controller (RTC), Universal Serial Bus (USB), Ultra DMA/33 (66) EIDE data transmission mode, advanced energy management (ACPI), and so on. It determines the type and quantity of expansion slots and expansion interface (such as USB2.0/1.1, IEEE1394, serial port, parallel port, and VGA output interface of a notebook). South Bridge is also known as the *standard bus bridge*.

Other chips: Some chipsets combine a 3D acceleration display (integrated graphics chip), AC'97 audio decoding, and other functions, and determine the display performance and audio playback performance of the computer system.

The latest Intel Atom processor includes a seventh-generation Intel GPU with burst technology to provide an improved graphics and media experience. The new processor supports high-resolution displays up to 2,560 × 1,600 at 60 Hz and supports Intel Wireless (Intel WiDi) technology through Miracast. Seamless video playback is supported by high-performance, low-power hardware acceleration of media encode and decode.

Intel System on Chip (SoC)

Unlike desktop devices, the processor, chipset, graphics, motherboard, and other components cannot be independently manufactured, configured, and then assembled in embedded systems due to constraints of volume and space; otherwise, they would be too large, consume too much power, have impractically complex designs, and have unstable layouts similar to desktops. Therefore, most current embedded systems adopt SoC designs. By integrating peripheral function modules of microprocessor/microcontroller, memory, bus, frequency generator, and A/D or D/A conversion on a single chip, SoC provides the benefits of small size, energy efficiency, high reliability, and simple peripheral circuit design. Intel has gradually embarked on SoC as the development direction for Intel Atom processors. A description of the recent designs follows.

Medfield

Medfield, released in 2012, is Intel's first SoC processor for smartphones. The core of the Medfield platform is the SoC chip (code-named Penwell). In fact, the previous Moorestown platform requires a two-chip solution to achieve the same functionality. As a true SoC, Medfield is different from the single-chip layout of Intel Atom processors but is equivalent to previous chipsets. As a result, it becomes a more compact, energy-efficient processor. The Medfield SoC processor adopts package on package (POP), and the entire chip area is about 12 × 12 mm. The internal architecture of Medfield SoC is shown in Figure 2-6.

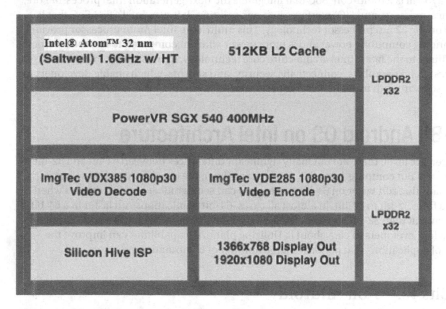

Figure 2-6. Internal architecture of Penwell SoC

The first Medfield SoC, built for smartphones, has an Intel Atom processor Z2460. The plan is to use the latest Intel Atom processors in future Medfield SoCs. For example, the plan for the second Medfield SoC is to adopt the Intel Atom processor Z2610 and has applications for mainstream tablets. Medfield SoC uses a 32 nm processor; integrates a single-core Intel Atom processor, 512 KB L2 cache, PowerVR SGX540 GPU by Imagination Technologies, and dual-channel LPDDR2 memory controller; and supports 30 fps 1080p video decoding. The highest frequency of Intel Atom processors is limited to 1.6 GHz.

The Z2460 may reduce the minimum frequency to 100 MHz, features 1.3 GHz standard operating frequency, and only operates in 1.6 GHz during acceleration mode. As the second Medfield SoC core, the Z2610 maintains operation at 1.6 GHz clock speed.

The Intel Atom processor Z2460 consumes 50 mW of power at 100 MHz clock speed (lowest frequency); 175 mW at 600 MHz clock speed; 500 mW at 1.3 GHz clock speed (standard frequency); and 750 mW at 1.6 GHz clock speed (highest frequency). Compared with desktop processors, the Z2460 has very low power consumption.

Today, the Android OS completely supports Medfield. Intel works with Google to develop software for compiling applications for ARM and Intel architectures.

Bay Trail

Bay Trail, the new Intel multi-core SoC built on the Silvermont architecture, is from Intel's powerful processor family for mobile and desktop devices. Bay Trail is manufactured on Intel's industry-leading tri-gate 22 nm process technology.

Bay Trail is a multi-core SoC that integrates the next-generation Intel processor core, graphics, memory, and I/O interfaces into one solution. It is also Intel's first SoC that is based on the 22 nm processor technology. This multi-core Intel Atom processor provides outstanding computing power and is more power efficient compared to its predecessors. In addition to the latest Intel architecture core technology, it provides extensive platform features such as graphics, connectivity, security, and sensors, which enable developers to create software with unlimited user experiences.

64-Bit Android OS on Intel Architecture

On a generic level, there are not many significant differences between 64-bit and 32-bit processors. But compute-intensive applications (later, the chapter discusses software workloads that run faster on 64-bit processors) can see significant improvements when moved from 32-bit to 64-bit. In almost all cases, 64-bit applications run faster in a 64-bit environment than 32-bit applications in a 64-bit environment, which is a good enough reason for developers to care about it. Utilizing platform capabilities can improve the speed of applications that perform a large number of computations.

64 Bits vs. 32-bit Android

A 64-bit architecture means the width of the integer registers and pointers is 64 bits. The three main advantages of a 64-bit operating system are as follows:

- Increased number of registers
- Extended address space
- Increased RAM

It's not hard to imagine Android phones with 64-bit chips in the not-too-distant future. Because the Android kernel is based on a Linux kernel, and Linux has supported 64-bit technology for years, the only thing Android needs to fully support 64-bit processing is to make the Dalvik VM 64-bit compatible. A Dalvik application (written only in Java) will work without any changes on a 64-bit device because the bytecode is platform independent.

Native application developers can take full advantage of the capabilities offered by the underlying processor. For example, Intel Advanced Vector Extensions (Intel AVX) has been extended to support a 256-bit instruction size on 64-bit processors.

Memory and CPU Register Size

Memory is extremely slow compared to the CPU, and reading from and writing to memory can take a long time compared to how long it takes the CPU to process an instruction. CPUs try to hide this with layers of caches, but even the fastest layer of cache is slow compared to internal CPU registers. More registers means more data can be kept purely CPU-internal, reducing memory accesses and increasing performance.

Just how much difference this makes depends on the specific code in question, as well as how good the compiler is at optimizing the code to make the best use of available registers. When the Intel architecture moved from 32-bit to 64-bit, the number of registers doubled from 8 to 16, and this made for a substantial performance improvement.

Sixty-four-bit pointers allow applications to address larger RAM address spaces: typically, on a 32-bit processor, the addressable memory space available to a program is between 1 and 3 GB because only 4 GB is addressable. Even if 1–3 GB is available, a single program cannot use all the memory that is addressable unless it resorts to a technique like splitting the program into multiple processes, which takes a lot of programming effort. On a 64-bit operating system, this is of no concern because the addressable memory space is pretty large.

Memory-mapped files are becoming more difficult to implement on 32-bit architectures because files over 4 GB are increasingly common. Such large files cannot be memory-mapped easily to 32-bit architectures—only part of the file can be mapped into the address space at a time. To access such a file, the mapped parts must be swapped into and out of the address space as needed. This is a problem because memory mapping, if properly implemented by the OS, is one of the most efficient disk-to-memory methods.

Sixty-four-bit pointers also come with a substantial downside: most programs use more memory because pointers need to be stored and they consume twice as much memory. An identical program running on a 64-bit CPU takes more memory than on a 32-bit CPU. Because pointers are very common in programs, this can increase cache sizes and have an impact on performance.

Register count can strongly influence performance of an application. RAM is slow compared to on-CPU registers. CPU caches help to increase the speed of applications, but accessing cache does result in a performance hit.

The amount of the performance increase is dependent on how well the compiler can optimize for a 64-bit environment. Compute-intensive applications that are able to do the majority of their processing in a small amount of memory see significant performance increases because a large percentage of the application can be stored on the CPU registers.

Contrast this with an unoptimized application that might see a decrease in computer performance because 64-bit pointers require twice the bandwidth. However, in a mobile environment, the OS and installed applications should be engineered to avoid this. A famous example of a large program that runs slower on a 64-bit environment is the Oracle JVM.

Both ARM and Intel 64-bit CPUs have a 32-bit compatibility mode. Although 32-bit applications will run on 64-bit processors, compiling with a 64-bit optimizing compiler allows them to take advantage of the architectural benefits of a 64-bit environment.

Reference Platform for Intel Embedded Systems

The so-called *reference platform* for Intel embedded systems is a wide range of hardware devices that use the Intel Atom processor and SoC. This hardware combination features compact size, low power consumption, high performance, low cost, and an excellent chipset for graphics processing and other specialized sectors. Thus it can be widely used in diversified embedded devices such as netbooks, nettops, tablets, mobile phones, and MIDs.

Internet of Things (IoT) and Next Unit of Computing (NUC)

The Internet of Things (IoT) and Next Unit of Computing (NUC) are recent application sectors for Intel Mobile processors. The Intel NUC Kit DE3815TYKHE, shown in Figure 2-7, is built with an Intel Atom processor for intelligent systems and is a pint-sized unit for value-conscious businesses and organizations. This low-cost, low-power solution introduces many firsts to the Intel NUC form factor: a fanless thermal solution for the ultimate silence and reliability, onboard flash storage for small-footprint software solutions, internal flat-panel display connectivity for built-in screens, a video graphics array (VGA) port for monitor compatibility in legacy installations, a serial ports header for peripherals requiring the robustness of hardware handshaking, a watchdog timer for resilient system availability, and inter-integrated circuit (I2C) and pulse-width modulation (PWM) signals for interfacing with sensors and other embedded devices enabling the IoT. And with its three-year supply availability, the Intel NUC Kit DE3815TYKHE will be around to support long development and production ramp cycles.

Figure 2-7. Intel NUC Kit DE3815TYKHE

With its vertical industrial design and support for Linux and Windows embedded operating systems, this Intel NUC was designed as the essential building block to power the thin-client market. A fanless kit with flash storage built in, USB3 support, and audio headset support, this Intel NUC fits right at home in schools, call centers, and other locations with a large installed base of VGA monitors.

Powered by the Intel Atom processor E3815, the Intel NUC Kit DE3815TYKHE also provides an ideal combination of power consumption, performance, affordability, and software compatibility to drive light digital signage, point-of-sale, and kiosk solutions, among other usages. With 4 GB of embedded MultiMediaCard (eMMC) storage built in, many embedded applications will benefit from a lower overall system-level BOM cost. The high-availability resilience can also be enabled for these and other unattended solutions via the built-in watchdog timer, providing protection against downtime. This Intel NUC provides a discrete Trusted Platform Module device onboard for hardware-based data encryption—a must-have for applications where confidential information is at stake.

Intel Galileo Development Kit for IoT

The Intel Galileo development board, shown in Figure 2-8, is Intel's first product in a new family of Arduino-compatible development boards featuring Intel architecture. The platform is easy to use for new designers and for those looking to take designs to the next level.

Figure 2-8. *The Intel Galileo board*

The Intel Galileo board is a microcontroller board based on the Intel Quark SoC X1000 application processor, a 32-bit Intel Pentium brand SoC. It is the first board based on Intel architecture designed to be hardware and software pin-compatible with shields designed for the Arduino Uno R3.

This platform provides the ease of Intel architecture development through support for the Microsoft Windows, Mac OS, and Linux host operating systems. It also brings the simplicity of the Arduino integrated development environment (IDE) software.

The Intel Galileo board is also software-compatible with the Arduino software development environment, which makes usability and introduction a snap. In addition to Arduino hardware and software compatibility, the Intel Galileo board has several PC industry standard I/O ports and features to expand native usage and capabilities beyond the Arduino shield ecosystem. A full-sized mini-PCI Express slot, a 100 Mb Ethernet port, a Micro-SD slot, an RS-232 serial port, a USB host port, a USB client port, and 8 MB NOR Flash come standard on the board.

The genuine Intel processor and surrounding native I/O capabilities of the SoC provides for a fully featured offering for both the maker community and students alike. It will also be useful to professional developers who are looking for a simple and cost effective development environment to the more complex Intel Atom processor and Intel Core processor-based designs.

Smartphones

As smartphones have become ubiquitous, customer demands for top-of-the-line devices have increased, with design and usability growing in importance.

Lenovo K900

The Lenovo K900, shown in Figure 2-9, is the first large-screen smartphone that is powered by the Intel Atom processor. The K900 is one of the first smartphones in the world to combine a 5.5-inch IPS display with 1,080-pixel full high-definition resolution performance at 400+ pixels per inch, all under the latest, touch-capacitive Gorilla Glass 2.

Figure 2-9. Lenovo K900 smartphone

The Lenovo K900 runs on the Intel Atom Z2580 processor, a dual-core chip, which runs up to 2.0 GHz and utilizes Intel Hyper-Threading Technology to boost performance efficiency. The Intel-powered device also features an Intel Graphics Media Accelerator engine running a PowerVR SGX 544MP2 GPU. Lenovo has equipped the K900 with a large-aperture f1.8 lens, making it the first smartphone to offer such a wide aperture on its camera. Combined with its other specifications, the K900 is now a legitimate stand-in for a digital camera in a smartphone.

Vexia Zippers Phone

The Vexia Zippers phone, shown in Figure 2-10, runs on Android 4 OS and is powered by the Intel Atom processor. It also packs dual SIM and a 5 MP camera so you can take photos and capture video in high definition. Its Zippers interface makes this smartphone unique, and you can personalize it to suit your lifestyle.

Figure 2-10. Vexia Zippers phone

ZTE Grand X2*

The ZTE Grand X2, shown in Figure 2-11, provides instant performance with its advanced dual-core Intel Atom Processor Z2580 with hyper-threading running on the Android OS. Users can enjoy faster web-page loads, application launch times, and content download times, as well as graphics capabilities and responsive multitasking.

Figure 2-11. *ZTE Grand X2 Smartphone*

ZTE's new flagship smartphone is also equipped with an 8 MP socially smart camera with one of the shortest shot-to-shot times on the market, capable of up to 24 frames per second and no shutter lag. It secures a high image quality in challenging environments with real-time 2x axis stabilization, and face and smart scene recognition.

Tablets

Tablets are one of the major application sectors for Intel Atom processors. As a complete computer with a flat touch screen, tablets don't have common keyboard and mouse input devices, but instead have stylus, digital pen, and finger input on the touch screen. Tablets have commanded a huge share of the market since Apple released the iPad in 2010. A few notable tablets featuring Intel Atom processors are detailed next.

Samsung Galaxy Tab 3 10.1

The Samsung Galaxy Tab 3 10.1, shown in Figure 2-12, was announced by Samsung at Computex 2013 and launched in the United States in July of 2013. Its screen is 10.1 inches and has a resolution of 1,280 × 800. The Tab 3 10.1 features an Intel Atom Z2560 dual-core processor clocked at 1.6 GHz and 1 GB RAM, and comes with 16 GB of storage. The tablet has a 3.2 MP rear camera and a 1.3 MP front-facing camera. It also has an SD card slot. At the time of this writing, the device runs Android 4.2.2.

Figure 2-12. *Samsung Galaxy Tab 3 10.1*

Dell Venue 7/8" Tablet

The Dell Venue 7, shown in Figure 2-13 and launched in early 2014, features a 7" screen with a resolution of 1,280 × 800. It runs on the Intel Atom Z2560 dual-core processor, clocked at 1.6 GHz, and includes 2 GB RAM and 16 GB of internal storage. The device includes an SD card slot for expandable storage and has a 3 MP rear-facing camera as well as a VGA front-facing camera. At the time of this writing, the tablet runs Android 4.3.

Figure 2-13. Dell Venue 7/8" Tablet

Acer Iconia A1-830*

The Acer Iconia A1-830 has a 7.9" display with a resolution of 1,024 × 768 and was launched in early 2014. It features the Intel Atom Z2560 dual-core processor, clocked at 1.6 GHz. The device has 1 GB RAM and 16 GB of internal storage. It includes an SD card slot for expandable storage. The front-facing camera is 5 MP and the rear-facing camera is 2 MP. At the time of this writing, the tablet runs Android 4.4.2.

ASUS MeMO Pad FHD 10*

ASUS MeMO Pad FHD 10, shown in Figure 2-14, delivers vivid visuals with the latest Intel Atom Z2560 processor (1.6 GHz), 2 GB memory, a 178° wide view angle, 1920 × 1200 full HD IPS display, and 10-point multi-touch display for an improved gaming experience. The ASUS MeMO Pad FHD 10 weighs 580 g and has a thin 9.5 mm profile. It has a microSD expansion slot.

Figure 2-14. ASUS Memo Pad

With Intel's and Google's partnership, more and more Android-based tablets with Intel Atom processors are released every year.

In-Vehicle Infotainment

In-Vehicle Infotainment (IVI) systems are devices that deliver navigation, entertainment, and networked computing services in vehicles such as cars, trucks, and planes. Automotive manufacturers in particular are increasingly viewing IVI systems as a key differentiator in their products. Drivers and passengers are coming to expect to see in their vehicles the same type of innovations they see in other devices, such as mobile computers and handsets. BMW, Infiniti, Nissan, and certainly others already announced platforms using Intel Atom. Undoubtedly, the Intel Atom processor will be a key player in this promising sector.

Other Application Platforms and Fields

In addition to the sectors described previously, Intel Atom processors and corresponding chips can be applied in a wide range of sectors, platforms, and devices.

Cloud Computing

In cloud computing mode, content and infrastructure are resident in the cloud (network). Cloud content consumers need only a lightweight, thin-client viewer device to participate. The essence of cloud computing is that if infrastructure cost is amortized over a sufficiently large population, many more people can participate and benefit from cloud content and services. With their relatively low price points, devices based on Intel Atom processors will be suitable for the clients of cloud computing.

Devices powered by Intel Atom processors will also contribute to expansion of cloud-content consumer audiences due to their ability to use the Intel architecture code base. The second generation 64-bit Intel Atom C2000 product family of SoC is designed for microservers and cold-storage platforms (code-named Avoton) and for entry networking platforms (code named Rangeley). These new SoCs are the company's first products based on the Silvermont microarchitecture, the new design in the leading 22 nm tri-gate SoC process delivering significant increases in performance and energy efficiency.

Intel also introduced the Intel Ethernet Switch FM5224 silicon, which, when combined with the Wind River Open Network Software suite, brings software-defined networking (SDN) solutions to servers for improved density and lower power.

Robotics

Robotics is the acknowledged key to improve production processes, promote the production capability of customized products, and ensure product quality. Robotic automation has historically been extremely costly, with very long term cost-benefit payback and significant barriers to entry. Fortunately, high-performance Intel Atom processors satisfy most of the automation calculation requirements of robotics and boast a leadership in robotics applications due to their cost-effective and low-power features. Lab tests have shown that with a battery life of up to eight hours for unconnected operation, devices based on Intel Atom processors can easily work a full shift powering mobile robotic devices.

Smith Childs Farms, Inc. in Wisconsin has empowered robot tractors powered by Intel Atom processors. Several of these smaller, more agile tractors can work a field at one time, controlled by a farmer sitting at a desk. They use GPS navigation equipment, onboard sensors, and a series of complex algorithms while sampling the soil and dispensing the precise amount of seed and fertilizer needed. Dennis Smith, owner of Smith Childs Farms, Inc. said, "During prime planting season, you can even see farmers working during the night hours without worrying about available light because sensors on the tractors can 'see' quite clearly in the dark."

Wireless Sensor Networks

Intel Atom processors are used to create intelligent wireless sensor networks, a major application sector of embedded systems.

Intel has deployed a wireless sensor network in its Chandler, Arizona plant. Many battery-powered wireless sensor nodes monitor power consumption and environmental parameters such as temperature, humidity, illumination, and space in the laboratory. The large number of small wireless sensors form a self-configuring, dynamic routing network. These sensors communicate with the server-router that intelligently processes and analyzes the sensor data. Each server-router is a small wireless computing platform with processor, memory, flash memory, I/O, and radio components based on the Intel Atom processor, which processes network data from up to 40 sensors.

This flexible, self-configuring network architecture is easy and cost-effective to install. It can also be easily expanded across office buildings, commercial facilities, and factories or changed per the floor area. The system gives Intel facility managers a new perspective, helping them to minimize electricity costs.

Learning

Intel Atom processors and related hardware enable the production of low-power, cost-effective, and eco-friendly mini/micro computing devices that are readily being adopted in developing countries and markets that have been underserved in the past. These systems support localized and distance learning to contribute to the national education in these countries and regions.

Backpack Journalism and Portable Video Recording

Devices based on Intel Atom processors featuring long battery life, sufficient storage capacity, and convenient Internet connectivity are the ideal devices for the new generation of amateur and ad hoc video journalists to deliver live coverage (such as online webcasts of sporting events, speech and debate contests, and special topic seminars). Editing and processing of recorded video cannot be implemented directly on such devices but can easily be transferred to back-end desktop or servers through the outstanding Internet connectivity of Intel Atom processors, thus realizing rapid and economic video recording using a distributed processing solution.

RFID Field Tools

Radio-frequency ID (RFID) is a promising industry. Used for inventory control and chain-of-custody tracking, such tagging will play a significant role in healthcare, pharmaceutical management and delivery, and the transportation industry. One of the advantages of RFID tags over traditional barcodes is that a tag interrogator can both read and write a tag from a distance of tens of meters or more. To date, tag interrogators have been custom devices that require costly, vendor-specific integration with back-end inventory systems. Devices with Intel Atom processors not only could provide the mobility and connectivity of handheld interrogators but also offer seamless compatibility with Intel architecture back-end inventory and management systems, considerably lowering cost of ownership for these systems.

Summary

Chapters 1 and 2 discussed the history of the embedded platform, the SoC architecture and hardware platform with different categories available for system and application developers. Starting with the next chapter, this book introduces Android application development on Intel hardware platforms. Developing Android system applications requires some special development, debugging, and performance analysis tools. Before developing Android applications, you need to learn about the development process of Android system applications, and so that is where you begin.

■ ■ ■

Android Application Development Processes and Tool Chains for Intel® Architecture

This chapter introduces Android† application development on Intel hardware platforms. Developing Android system applications requires some special development, debugging, and performance analysis tools, and the development environment and object formats are different from those of general-purpose desktop computers. Before developing Android applications, we need to learn about the development process of Android system applications.

Android provides a whole set of tool chains (toolsets) for application development. Early versions of the Android OS supported ARM hardware platforms and started supporting Intel® Atom™ hardware platforms from Android 2.3 (Gingerbread). To support application development on Intel Atom architecture, Intel has added important plug-ins, libraries, and other auxiliary modules to work in conjunction with Android tool chains. In addition, to help developers to get the performance advantages of Intel hardware, Intel has made available development tools such as compilers and Intel® Graphic Performance Analyzer.

This chapter describes the general processes and methods for Android application development on Intel Atom platforms. The methods to achieve optimized performance and low energy consumption using special Intel tools will be introduced in subsequent chapters.

Android Application Development

The following sections describe the development environment, development process, debugging, and simulation of Android systems.

Development Environment of Android Applications

As we mentioned earlier, software development for general-purpose computers is always achieved through native compilation or development. In general, embedded systems are not compatible with the local development environment and so software development is usually done with cross-development.

Cross-Development

The typical cross-development configuration is shown in Figure 3-1. The cross-development environment is built on the development, or host, machine. Usually the host machine is a general-purpose computer such as a PC. The corresponding embedded system is called the target machine. Target machines can be any of the numerous kinds of embedded devices such as mobile phones, tablets, and so on. They may also be special evaluation boards or software-based emulators for development provided by embedded system manufacturers. During development, cross-compilation, assembly, and linking tools on the host machine are used to produce binary code that is executable on the target machine; then the executable files are downloaded and run on the target machine. The cross-development method is not only required for compilation but also for debugging.

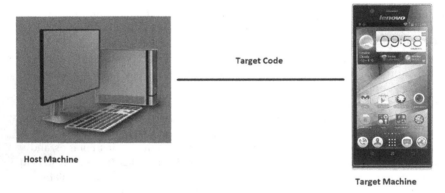

Figure 3-1. Cross-development configuration of embedded systems

The main reason why cross-development was adopted for embedded systems is that native compilation usually cannot be done effectively on the target machine. First, the hardware of the target machine is often unavailable or unstable during the development process. Second, there is a lack of complete native compilation tools on the target machine platform. Third, the performance of the target machine is insufficient, resulting in slow compilation. Software compilation on embedded systems is more time consuming than on desktop computers because it requires not only compilation of applications but also compilation of library dependencies and OS kernels. For example, compiling a Linux† kernel on an Intel® Pentium® 4 processor-based PC takes more than 10 minutes. The main hardware factors determining the compiling speed include CPU speed, memory capacity, and file system I/O speed. On these factors, embedded systems usually perform worse than PCs. This results in low efficiency of native compilation on target machines. The cross-development method is always adopted for embedded systems, such as cross-compilation (including cross-linking) and cross-debugging.

Because of the differences between the host machine and the target machine in their configurations, functions, system structure, and operating environments, they are usually connected via serial port, parallel port, USB, or Ethernet connection cables. Toolsets, including encoder, compiler, connector, debugging tool, and software configuration management tool, are installed on the host machine.

Generally, the host machine and the target machine are different in the following aspects:

- Different structure: usually, the host machine is an Intel architecture system while the target machine might be Intel or non-Intel architecture system structure such as ARM or MIPS.

- Different processing capacities: usually, the processing speed and storage capacity of the host machine are better than those of the target machine.

- Different operating systems: usually, a general OS runs on the host machine while an Android OS runs on the target machine.

- Different output methods: compared with the host machine, the input and output functions of the target machine are less capable.

For some Android systems, these characteristics may not exist or are insignificant. Take the development of an Intel Atom system for example. The host machine and the target machine use the same system Intel architecture structure. Of course, the instruction sets might be different. For example, the host machine (such as the Intel® Core™ 2 Duo processor) might be compatible with SSE4, while the Intel Atom processor only supports SSE3 .We should consider the instruction set for the target machine during compilation. Considering the limited resources of most Intel Atom systems, we recommend the cross-development method.

Programming Languages

During the past four decades, dozens of programming languages have been developed for general-purpose computer applications. From FORTRAN, C/C++, ADA, and Java† to C#NET. Many factors determine a programming language's suitability. Each has its own characteristics, and comprehensive comparisons are impossible. Each language's performance depends on the execution environment. Considering multiple factors and actual development status, the common languages for Android systems include C/C++, Java, and Python†, and occasionally assembly language is used. A combination of languages is needed for programming a sophisticated Android system. The common programming languages are shown in Table 3-1.

Table 3-1. *Commonly Selected Programming Languages*

Level	Common Programming Languages
Application software	C/C++, Java, .NET, script, Python
OS level	C/C++, Assembly
Driver program level	C/C++, Assembly
Boot code, Hardware Abstract Layer (HAL)	Assembly, C/C++

Java, launched by Sun Microsystems in May 1995, is a cross-platform object-oriented programming language and includes the Java programming language and Java platforms (JavaSe, JavaEE, JavaME). Java's style is very similar to that of C and C++. It is a pure object-oriented programming language that has inherited the core contents of the object-oriented C++ and abandoned the pointer (replaced by reference), operator overloading, and multiple inheritance (replaced by interface) in the C++ language, which caused frequent errors. The added Garbage Collector is used for collecting memory occupied by unreferenced objects so the programmer does not need to worry about memory management. In the Java 1.5 version, Sun added other language features such as generic programming, type-safe enum class, variable-length augment, and autoboxing/auto-unboxing.

Java is different from ordinary compilation and execution computer languages in that it is an interpretive computer language. The Java compiler produces binary byte code instead of machine code, which can be executed directly and locally. Compiled Java programs are interpreted into directly executable machine code via Java virtual machine (JVM). The JVM can interpret execution byte code on different platforms to realize the cross-platform feature of "one-time compilation for all executions." However, it takes some time to interpret byte code, which will to some degree reduce the running efficiency of Java programs. To reduce this burden, Google introduced Android Run Time (ART) in 2014 as a Dalvik version 2, which first became available as a preview feature in KitKat (Android 4.4). Future 64-bit Android will be based on ART. In general, Java is a simple, object-oriented, distributed, interpretive, and stalwart. It is an implantable, high-performance, multi-threaded and dynamic programming language. Considering various advantages of Java, it is the first choice for Android application development.

Having chosen a language, you may not necessarily use all of its functions. Although we have selected Java as the development tool for Android, the development process for Android systems is different from traditional (desktop) Java SDK. The Android SDK uses most of the Java SDK, but has abandoned some portions. For example, for the interface, the java.awt package is only referenced by java.awt.font. If a Java game is migrated to the Android platform, it might need to be ported.

We have mentioned that Java is a cross-platform interpretive computer language. This feature has enabled the high migration capability regardless of platform, but it also has some drawbacks, one of which is that the developer cannot use platform- or architecture-related features or potential. But this can be achieved by machine-related target code by compiling C/C++ and assembly languages. This is more obvious during performance optimization. To use the features of the machine hardware and tap into their performance potential, we usually need to use C/C++ and assembly languages for writing optimized applications. Although such code accounts for a small proportion of all code, the programming complexity is much higher than Java. Therefore, such code is only used in some rare cases. We'll see that Android application development has adopted a mixed programming mode based mainly on improved Java and supported by C and assembly languages.

We're going to discuss this programming method in two parts. For developing general functions of Android applications, we are going to use Java. But for performance optimization, we're going to use a mixed-language programming approach.

The Android Application Development Process

Generally speaking, developing Android software requires the same steps as general-purpose software: designing, encoding, compiling, linking, packaging, deploying, debugging, and optimizing. For some Android systems, testing and verification steps are also required. In terms of process, it can be divided into five stages: encoding, construction, deployment, debugging, and tuning. The typical development process is shown in Figure 3-2.

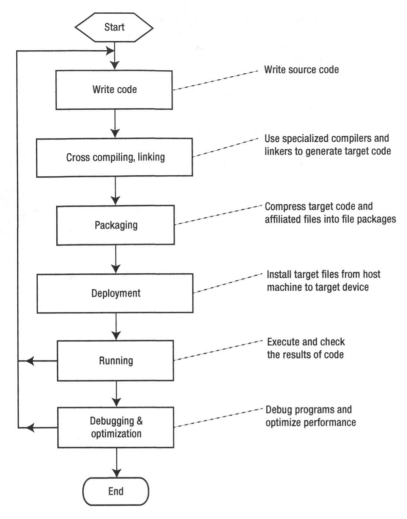

Figure 3-2. *Development process for Android software*

Encoding

Encoding is the first step in the software development process. Software source code can be written using various editors. During Android development, this work is mainly editing .java code and .xml source files.

Construction

The task during the construction stage is to convert code into executable programs on Android hardware. This stage includes sub-steps such as compiling, linking, and packaging as shown in Figure 3-3.

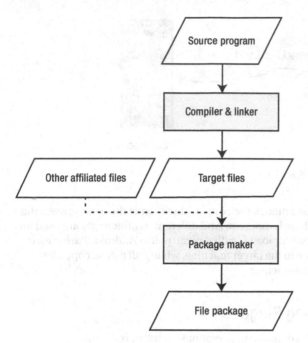

Figure 3-3. Software construction stage

The first step of construction is the build, which means to translate all source code files into target files. Some target files are machine-related such as C/C++ target files that correspond to the execution instructions of the machine. But some are not specific to the machine, such as Java target source code that is not machine-executable instructions. During Android application development, these files usually have the suffix *.class*. On Android, .classes are translated to .dex files.

The second step is packaging. The purpose of packaging is to combine and install all target files and affiliated files into one folder on the target machine. As for Android, .dex files and resource files are all packaged into an .apk file that can be stored outside the target machine. The packaging operation is usually done with special packaging tools.

Deployment

Deployment, the last stage of software development, is where the installation package is copied from the host machine, decompressed, and installed into the memory of the Android device.

Android has adopted USB cable-based ISP deployment. As shown in Figure 3-4, the host machine is connected to the target machine via USB cable. The Android OS runs on the target machine while the Windows† or Linux OS runs on the host machine. The file packages generated (.apk) are copied to one directory of the file system in the target machine before being decompressed and installed to finish deployment. The process can be done using command line terminals or the DDMS inside Eclipse.

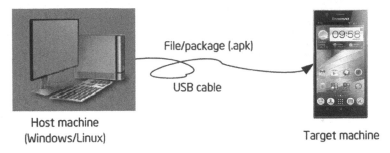

Figure 3-4. Android application deployment

Under the online programming model, the copying direction of the files between the host machine and the target machine is different. And different terminologies are used for file copying. For example, download/upload is called push/pull in Android. *Push* means to copy files from the host machine to the target machine, while *pull* means copy files from the target machine to the host machine.

Debugging and Optimizing Stage

This stage is mainly debugging and optimizing operations on software.

Even the most experienced software engineers cannot totally avoid mistakes in their programs. Mastering debugging techniques is critical for software development. Debugging Android software code is not very efficient because even if you only need to change one line of code, you still need to go through all the build, packaging, and deployment procedures. PC users might be okay with one crash per day. But just imagine the severe consequences if a bug exists in the final Android system product on ATMs, medical operation systems, or satellites.

There are many debugging technologies and techniques for Android software discussed in subsequent sections. Many of the methods are rarely used in general-purpose computer software.

The minimum target for a software product is to ensure its normal running. But this target is not good enough for Android software, which is resource-constrained and has more stringent space and performance requirements than desktop systems. To satisfy these requirements, Android software has to ensure normal running in a performance-optimized way. These goals might be contradictory and developers can hardly realize all of them. So they make compromises usually highlighting the performance requirement.

Improving the performance of an application program is a time-consuming process. It is usually not obvious which functions are consuming most of the execution time. So we need to use specialized tools to analyze the code to accurately understand the performance bottlenecks and advise us on improvements. This process is usually called code profiling, and the tool used is called a *profiler* or *performance analyzer*.

The principle of using a profiler for improving performance is to optimize the frequently called portions of the software. For example, if 50 percent of the time is spent on string functions and we optimize such functions by 10 percent, then we can reduce the execution time of the software by about 5 percent. By using a profiler you can accurately measure the various portions of time spent during the execution process to understand which areas can be optimized. Some profilers can bring about improvement suggestions specific to the type of processor. For example, the Intel® Vtune™ Amplifier identifies hotspots in the code that can be further optimized to improve overall performance.

Debugging and Simulation of Android Systems

Debugging Android software has some special challenges, so some methods and devices have been developed to assist developers with the debugging procedure. The most common debugging methods include those described in the following sections.

System Simulator

Early system simulators were realized with instruction set emulators, that is, the technology of simulating a system architecture using software. In other words, software is used to interpret machine codes to simulate a certain processor. Modern system simulators include analog peripherals except CPU simulation. The analog peripherals are used to achieve system simulation results. Some books call the simulator a virtual machine or emulator.

Instruction set emulation includes homogenous emulation and heterogeneous emulation. Homogenous emulation means using software on one processor to emulate a virtualized machine that has the same architecture. At present, the common Microsoft Virtual PC or VMware† emulates the execution of processors based on Intel architecture, making it a type of homogenous emulation. Heterogeneous emulation means emulating the execution of another processor on one processor. Most of the instruction set emulators are types of heterogeneous emulation. For example, Device Emulator emulates the execution of ARM processors on Intel architecture processors. Some common system simulators are shown in Table 3-2.

Table 3-2. Common System Simulators

Name of Emulator	Simulated Target Platform	Remarks
Microsoft Virtual PC/ Virtual Server	Intel® architecture	
VMware	Intel architecture	Compatible with Windows, Mac†, Linux
Bochs	Intel architecture	Open source projects
Device Emulator	ARM	Simulation of SMDK2410 development board
SkyEye	ARM	Made in China
VirtualBox Advance	ARM	Simulating Nintendo GBA gamer
Oracle VM Virtualbox	X86 and AMD64/Intel64 Virtualization	GPL license, and freely available

When debugging programs on Android systems, the host machine (usually the PC) runs the system simulator and the software of the target machine is run in the system simulator, so no extra hardware is required. The host machine and the target machine are realized on the same machine, which is known as "two uses on one machine." Now remember the cross-development environment mentioned previously? We said the target machine is not necessarily a real device because it might be a software-based emulator. The emulator replaces the actual target machine during cross-development. Emulators not only save overhead on hardware but make debugging more convenient.

Android development tools bundles Android Virtual Device, a manager that is used to create ARM and x86 emulators. Emulators mimic the hardware and software configuration of a target device. Figure 3-5 shows a screenshot of an AVD running in Windows.

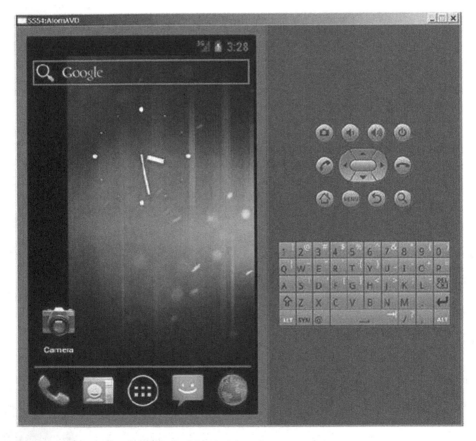

Figure 3-5. *AVD (Android Virtual Device) interface*

The Android emulator is also called *goldfish*. Each AVD simulates a set of mobile devices that run the Android platform, which includes the kernel, system image, and data partitioning as well as the SD card, user data, and the display. Android emulators are based on Qemu, which is a popular open source virtualizer project. The source code for Android emulators is under the external/qemu directory.

AVD simulates the common components of the target machine such as the CPU, screen, keyboard, audio output, camera, and also sensors such as GPS, touch, and gravity acceleration. For example, AVDs with Intel architecture include Intel x86 system images corresponding to each API level. Of course compared to the real device, an AVD has certain shortcomings, which include:

- Inability to place or accept actual calls; but it can simulate phone calls (incoming and outgoing) via control station

- No USB connection

- Inability to capture digital photos or videos

- Inability to capture audio input, but does support output (replay)

- Lack of support for extended earphones

- Inability to determine the battery level or charging status of AC power

- Inability to determine whether an SD card has been inserted or removed

- Lack of support for Bluetooth†

In addition, AVD can simulate USB and network connections between the host machine and the target machine. AVD uses the host machine as the default gateway and NAT (address translator) to connect to the network. In other words, if you can access the Internet on the host machine, you can also do so on the AVD-simulated target machine.

Other Debugging Tools

Android systems have other debugging tools besides system emulators. Although these tools are not used in Android, you should have a basic understanding of them to get a complete picture.

Cross-Debugging

When the OS supports cross-debugging Android applications, you should try to use this method. Cross-debugging is similar to cross-compilation: the program being debugged runs on the target machine while the display, monitor, and control of debugging are done on the host machine.

Cross-debugging can only be performed in the online mode. The host machine needs to be connected to the target machine by USB cable, network, or JTAG-ICE. A debugging server is usually run on the target machine and is called a *stub* in the GNU tool chain. The front end running the debugging procedure on the host machine is actually the client. The front end interacts with the developer who makes requests to debugging server. The debugging server receives the commands from the front end, controls application execution, and sends the results to the front end for display, as illustrated in Figure 3-6.

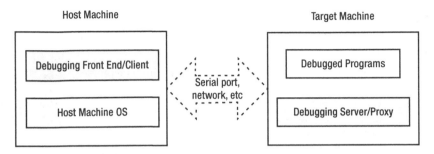

Figure 3-6. *Software environment for cross-debugging*

For example, if you set a breakpoint at the front end to observe the values of a variable, the debugging server receives the breakpoint setup request and inserts an interruption at corresponding place in the program. When the application reaches the breakpoint, the debugging server takes over control, suspends the application, and sends back the values of the corresponding variable to the front end, which then displays the value.

Many development tools support cross-debugging, such as, for example, GNU debugger. Android Debug Bridge (adb), a common debugging tool, also supports cross-debugging. The adb debugger is based on the client/server model. It works on the principle that the local working platform serves as the debugging client while the machine on which remote applications are installed serves the role of the debugging server. When using adb, the debugging process of the remote applications (on the target machine) may be different from local debugging. Adb manages the device, emulates status, and carries out the following operations:

- Fast code updating in the device and emulators, such as applications or Android system updates

- Running shell commands on the device

- Managing predetermined ports of the devices or emulators

- Copying or pasting files on the devices or emulators

Some common operations of adb include the following:

adb shell

This command allows you to enter the Linux shell environment of the device or emulator where you can execute many Linux commands. If you want to execute just one shell command, you can enter:

adb shell[command]

For [command], enter the particular command you want to execute, for example: adb shell dmesg, which outputs the debugging information of the kernel. Note: the Linux shell for Android adb has been simplified, so it is not compatible with many of the common Linux commands. We're going to discuss the command line in the subsequent sections.

Adb can be run independently in command line form or integrated as a plug-in into your favorite IDE (integrated development environment) such as Eclipse†. Figure 3-7 shows a screenshot of debugging an Android application in Eclipse. Adb provides many common debugging tools such as breakpoint setup, observing variables, single-step execution, and checking debugging output. The debugging process is the same as the debugging process for local applications. Many developers cannot even tell that the application is running on the target machine and not the host machine.

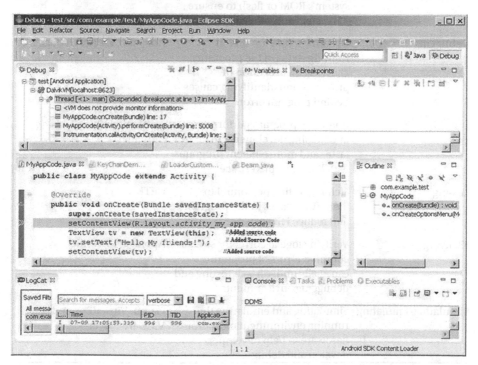

Figure 3-7. Android application debugging in Eclipse

In the next sections we're going to show examples of using adb commands and Eclipse debugging.

Typical Development Tool Chains

All stages of Android software development have corresponding tools to help developer complete tasks. Groups of development tools are called *tool chains*, or *toolsets*. The typical tool chains are listed in Table 3-3.

Table 3-3. *Typical Tool Chains for Android Software Development*

Development Stage	Function Description	Typical Examples
Editing	Writing and editing source code	vi, Emacs, Windows Notepad
Compiling and linking	Compiling and linking source programs into executable binary files	gcc, icc (Intel Compiler)
Flashing	Burning executable binary programs into the Android system's ROM or flash to ensure the system automatically starts up	J-fFlash, Sjflash
Debugging	Dynamic follow-up on the running status of the programs; checking on execution of programs and identifying causes behind program errors	Gdb, adb, Kernel Debugger
Optimizing	Analyzing program performance and helping developers create faster and more efficient programs with little occupied space	gprof, Intel Vtune™ Amplifier
Testing	Helping testing personnel to identify mistakes in the programs and reduce HR costs	CETK
Verifying	Verifying logical correctness and common errors of programs, especially under harsh testing and debugging environments	Application Verifier
Simulating/Emulating	Simulating and emulating the running environment of Android hardware to help developers develop and debug	Qemu, VirtualBox and VMware Player

Many toolsets are available, provided by different companies and organizations, each with its own characteristics. Icc, the Vtune Amplifier, and idb are provided by Intel, while gcc, gdb, and gproof by the free software organization GNU; and CETK, Application Verifier, Device Emulator are provided by Microsoft. Some of these tools are free like the GNU toolsets. Others, such as the Microsoft toolsets, must be purchased. These tools run on different platforms. For example, Jflash runs on the Linux platform while most of the Microsoft tools are based on Windows (including desktop Windows OS and Android OS-Windows CE/Mobile). And some are even cross-platform tools; for example, GNU toolsets can run on multiple platforms such as Linux, Windows, and Mac operating systems.

The way in which these toolsets are used falls into two categories: one is command line and the other is integrated development environment (IDE). Command line toolsets are executed by single commands entered in their command lines. In the case of IDEs, all functions are integrated into one tool, including editing, compiling, linking, deploying, and debugging, so that the full development process can be performed in one application. Most of the GNU tools run on command lines. Probably the most widely used IDE is Microsoft Visual Studio†. Anjuta DevStudio is a Linux-based IDE. The Android development tool, Eclipse, is an IDE that can run on multiple operating systems including Windows and Linux. In this book, we're going to use the Windows version.

GNU toolsets can run on multiple platforms; their openness, large usage scope, and compatibility with other tools have made them a common choice for Android application development.

■ **Tip   GNU, GPL, and LGPL** GNU is by far the largest, most famous, and influential free software organization. It was created by Richard Stallman in 1985 who founded the Free Software Foundation (FSF) to break away from commercial software. You must comply with GNU software license before using GNU software.

GPL, short for GNU General Public License, is one of the GNU software licenses. GPL allows the public to enjoy the freedom of running, copying, and sharing software, obtaining source code, and improving the software and sharing it with the public. GPL also stipulates that as long as one part or the entirety of the altered content comes from the programs complied by GPL, then the sharing of the altered software must comply with GPL requirements, which means that you need to publish the changed source code and refrain from adding restrictions on the sharing of the improved software. GPL was the catalyst for developing and publishing the Linux OS and related software.

LGPL, which means Lesser GPL, is also one of the GNU software licenses. It is a variant of GPL. What's different is that users enjoy private usage on LGPL-authorized free software. And the new software developed can be proprietary instead of free. Before using the free software, users must obtain LGPL or other variants of GPL. LGPL was initially used for some GNU program libraries (software libraries). So it was called Library GPL. Mozilla and OpenOffice.org are examples of software developed under LGPL.

GNU development tools are free. Anyone who agrees to GPL license can download them. GNU has also provided complete tool chains for software development on Android systems and Intel architecture systems. Such tools include compiler, assembly, linker, and debugging tools. They can be run independently from command lines or integrated into an IDE such as Eclipse. The GNU tool chains are listed in Table 3-4.

Table 3-4. *GNU Tool Chains*

Function	Component	Description
Editing	vi, Emacs, ed	Text editor used for editing source code
Compiling & linking	gcc	A set of multi-programming language compilers
Debugging	gdb	Debugger
Optimizing	gproof	Optimization tool for analyzing program performance and helping developers to create faster-running programs
Project Management	make	Auto management tool for software compilation
System Building	autotools	All materials and files required for build projects

The components are further explained below.

Editor

Any text editing tool can be used to write and edit source code. The Linux platform has two categories of editors: one includes line editors such as ed and ex; the other includes full-screen editors such as vi, Emacs, and gedit. Line editors can only operate on one line, while full-screen editors can edit an entire screen of code and the edited files are displayed, thus overcoming the shortcomings of line editing and making it easier to use. Full-screen editors have a larger feature set than line editors.

In an IDE, editors are integrated into the tool and need not be used separately to write source code.

Compiler and Linker

The editing process involves grammar, semantic, and lexical analyses, generation and optimization of intermediate codes, symbol table management and error management. The GNU editor is gcc. Gcc is considered the standard compiler of Linux.

Gcc was initially the C language editor of GNU. Now it supports C, C++, Object-C, FORTRAN, Java, and ADA. To some degree, gcc is the combination of all GNU editors. Gcc compiles source code and does the linking process. Users can choose the command parameters to compile, link, and generate executable files.

Intel Compiler also optimized code paths to improve application performance on Intel platforms. Intel Compiler is bundled with the tools offering from Intel called Intel Integrated Native Developer Experience.

Debugger

A debugger makes it easier for programmers to debug programs. But it is not necessarily a tool required for code execution. During the compilation process, the time spent on debugging is more than the time on encoding. Therefore a full-featured debugger that's easy to use is necessary.

The GNU debugger is gdb (abbreviation of GNU Debugger). It is also open source code and is a command line–based debugger. All debugging commands are realized through the commands of the control station.

Build Manager

GNU provides one build manager called make, a tool for controlling compilation of multiple software files. It is similar to Visual C++† project in Windows. In addition, it can automatically manage the contents, means, and timing of software compilation to help programmers so they can focus on coding instead of organizing compiling sequences.

Make can call gcc to compile and link source codes into executable files for the target machine according to the makefile defined by the developer.

Makefile Auto Generation Tool

Makefile can help make to perform the target file generation task. But encoding a makefile is not an easy job, especially for big projects. GNU provides a series of autotools to make makefiles. Such tools are aware of system configuration issues to help developers deal with migration issues. Autotools include aclocal, autoscan, autoconf, autoheader, automake, and libtool.

Several methods are used for generating target files from source code as shown in Figure 3-8.

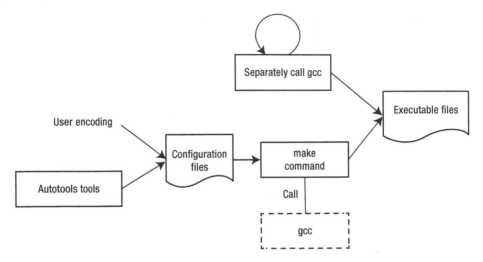

Figure 3-8. *Methods for generating target files using GNU tool chain*

- Method 1: Use gcc (or Intel compiler ICC) to compile and link all source code files to generate executable target files

- Method 2: Use an IDE, such as Eclipse, to compile a makefile and other configuration files and then use make to generate executable target files

- Method 3: Use system build tools-autotools to make makefile and other configurations, and then use make to generate executable target files

Optimizing Tools -- gprof

To help developers optimize their programs, GNU provides a performance analyzer, gproof, one of the GNU binutils tools.

Gproof can measure the performance of programs and record the called times of each function and corresponding execution time so that the optimization effort can be centered on the most time-consuming portions. In addition, gproof can also generate function call relations during programming execution, including number of called times, to help programmers analyze how programs are executing. By relying on the function call relations, developers do not need to go through all the details of a program's execution, improving their work efficiency. And this function is also helpful for maintaining old code or analyzing open source projects. With the calling diagram, you can get a basic understanding of the running framework and "skeleton" of the programs. Then analyzing them is less difficult, especially for code and open source projects you may not be familiar with.

Overview, Installation, and Configuration of Android Application Development Tool Chains on Intel® Architecture

Android provides a complete set of tool chains (or toolsets) for application development. Originally, Android ran only on ARM architecture hardware platforms. But now, to support Android tool chains on the Intel Atom hardware platform, Intel has added important plug-ins, libraries, and other auxiliary components. In addition, to give better play to the performance advantages of Intel hardware, Intel has added special development tools such as compilers and optimizers.

This chapter introduces the general processes and methods for Android application development on the Intel Atom platform. In the subsequent sections, we're going to discuss the methods for using special Intel tools to achieve optimized performance and low energy consumption.

The Android and GNU development tool chains and the functions corresponding to Android cross development stages are shown in Table 3-5.

Table 3-5. *Comparison between GNU and Android Tool Chains*

Stages of Cross Development	GNU Tool Chains	Android Development Tool Chains for Intel® Architecture	Remarks
Editing	vi, Emacs, ed	Eclipse, Android SDK	Android development tools and Intel related plug-ins
Compiling and linking	Gcc		
Project management	Make		
Auto generation tool-makefile	Autotools		
Deployment	\		
Debugging	gdb		
Simulation/emulation	\	Android Virtual Device (AVD)	
Optimization	gprof	Vtune™ analyzer	Intel series of tools

65

In addition to the differences with GNU tools shown above, Intel also provides some special performance libraries, including Intel® Integrated Performance Primitives (Intel® IPP), Intel® Math Kernel (Intel® MKL), and Intel® Threading Building Blocks (Intel® TBB). Some of the libraries have already provided special services such as the C++ template based threading services API in Intel TBB. Some of them use the Intel architecture instruction potential to achieve optimized performance, such as, for example, the Fast Fourier Transform (FFT) in Intel IPP. Some of the libraries still do not have direct Java interfaces. We're going to discuss them in subsequent sections.

Table 3-5 shows that the Android development tool chain for Intel architecture basically includes two parts: one part is the Android development tools. The Intel tools here include an Intel architecture emulator, development library, and other plug-ins. The other part is the independent Intel tools. While the Android development tools support most of the steps of application development such as editing, building, packaging, deployment, and debugging, the Intel tools involve mainly optimization.

Android development tools mean the software environment consisting of JDK (Java SE Development Kit), Android SDK (Software Development Kit), and an IDE (Integrated Development Environment)—Eclipse. Android development tools can run on Linux, OS X, and Windows systems. In this book, we're going to discuss the Windows scenario.

The Android development tools can be run in command-line format or an IDE. The general development process of the Android command line tool in the Android SDK is shown in Figure 3-9. Eclipse, a graphic user interface tool, is typically the tool used for IDE mode, integrating the functions of editing, compiling, linking, deployment, and debugging. We're going to discuss the method based on the IDE.

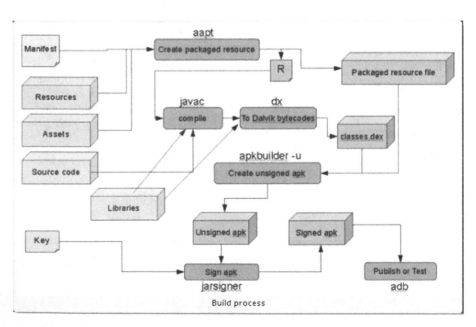

Figure 3-9. *Development process of the Android SDK command line*

The directory structure of the Android SDK is shown below. It can be obtained by running the tree command from the command line.

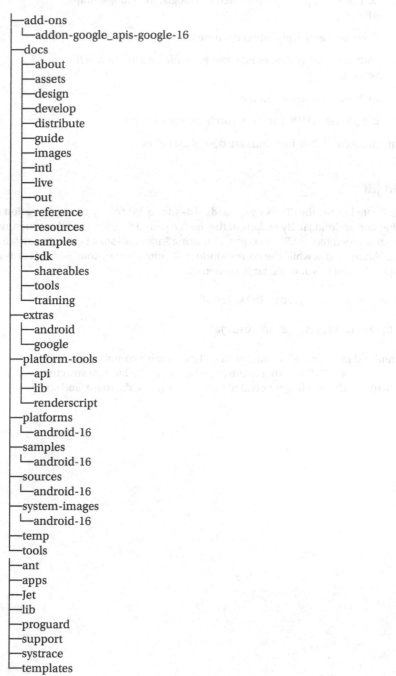

```
├─add-ons
│ └─addon-google_apis-google-16
├─docs
│ ├─about
│ ├─assets
│ ├─design
│ ├─develop
│ ├─distribute
│ ├─guide
│ ├─images
│ ├─intl
│ ├─live
│ ├─out
│ ├─reference
│ ├─resources
│ ├─samples
│ ├─sdk
│ ├─shareables
│ ├─tools
│ └─training
├─extras
│ ├─android
│ └─google
├─platform-tools
│ ├─api
│ ├─lib
│ └─renderscript
├─platforms
│ └─android-16
├─samples
│ └─android-16
├─sources
│ └─android-16
├─system-images
│ └─android-16
├─temp
│ └─tools
├─ant
├─apps
├─Jet
├─lib
├─proguard
├─support
├─systrace
└─templates
```

The main files you should notice are:

- add-ons: API packages provided by Google, like Google Maps APIs

- docs: help and explanation documents

- platforms: API packages nd some example files for each SDK version

- tools: some general tool files

- usb_driver: AMD64 and Intel architecture driver files

The main files and their functions are described below.

android.jar

This file is located under the directory of %android-sdk%\platforms, and each version of Android has one android.jar. By looking at the .jar file you can understand the structure and organization of internal API packages. The string %android-sdk% here is the install directory of Android SDK while the corresponding directory for version 16 is android-16. For example, the author's android.jar is located in:

```
C:\Documents and Settings>dir D:\Android\
......
2012-07-08 20:02 18,325,478 android.jar
```

The android.jar is a standard zip package that contains compiled zipped files and all APIs. You can use WinRAR, or other archiving tool, to view its internal structure as shown in Figure 3-10. Its API kit is further divided into app, content, database, and so on.

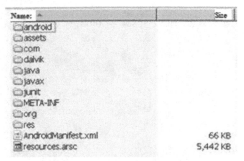

1. Root Directory Structure

2. Internal Structure of app

Figure 3-10. *Content structure of android.jar*

ddms.bat

The debugging monitor service ddms.bat, shown in Figure 3-11, is integrated in Dalvik (the virtual device of the Android platform) and used for managing the processes of emulators or devices and assisting debugging work. It can eliminate some processes and choose one certain program for debugging, generate follow-up data, check threading data, or take snapshots of emulators or devices.

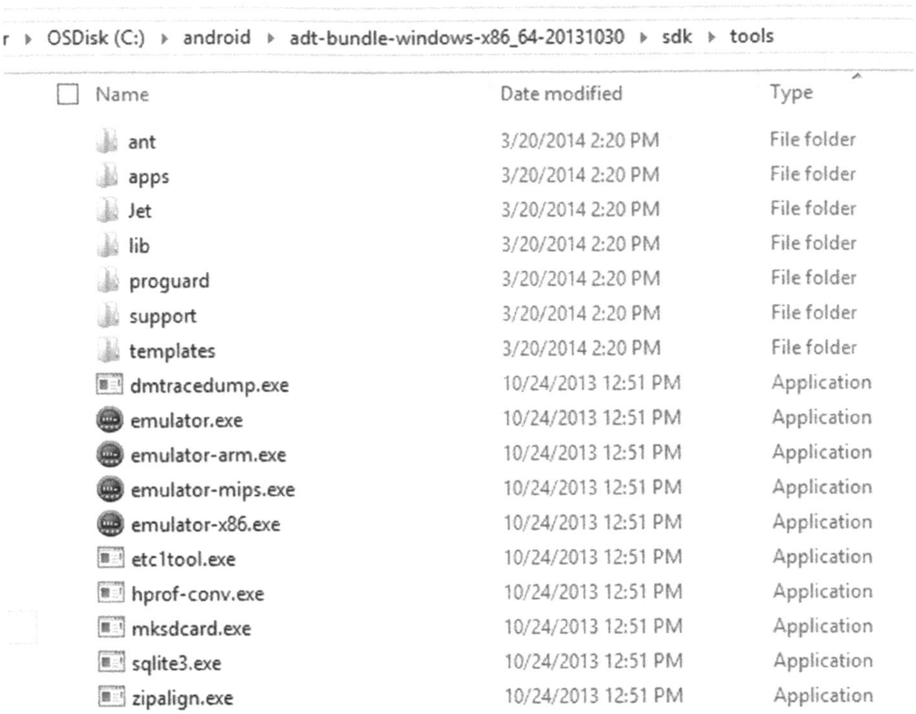

r ▸ OSDisk (C:) ▸ android ▸ adt-bundle-windows-x86_64-20131030 ▸ sdk ▸ tools

Name	Date modified	Type
ant	3/20/2014 2:20 PM	File folder
apps	3/20/2014 2:20 PM	File folder
Jet	3/20/2014 2:20 PM	File folder
lib	3/20/2014 2:20 PM	File folder
proguard	3/20/2014 2:20 PM	File folder
support	3/20/2014 2:20 PM	File folder
templates	3/20/2014 2:20 PM	File folder
dmtracedump.exe	10/24/2013 12:51 PM	Application
emulator.exe	10/24/2013 12:51 PM	Application
emulator-arm.exe	10/24/2013 12:51 PM	Application
emulator-mips.exe	10/24/2013 12:51 PM	Application
emulator-x86.exe	10/24/2013 12:51 PM	Application
etc1tool.exe	10/24/2013 12:51 PM	Application
hprof-conv.exe	10/24/2013 12:51 PM	Application
mksdcard.exe	10/24/2013 12:51 PM	Application
sqlite3.exe	10/24/2013 12:51 PM	Application
zipalign.exe	10/24/2013 12:51 PM	Application

Figure 3-11. *The debugging monitor service ddms.bat*

adb.exe

Android Debug Bridge (adb) is a multipurpose tool that can help you manage the state of devices or emulators. As mentioned before, this file is located under %android-sdk%\platform-tools. For example, the author's adb.exe is located in the C:\ android\adt-bundle-windows-x86_64-20131030\sdk\platform-tools directory, as shown in Figure 3-12.

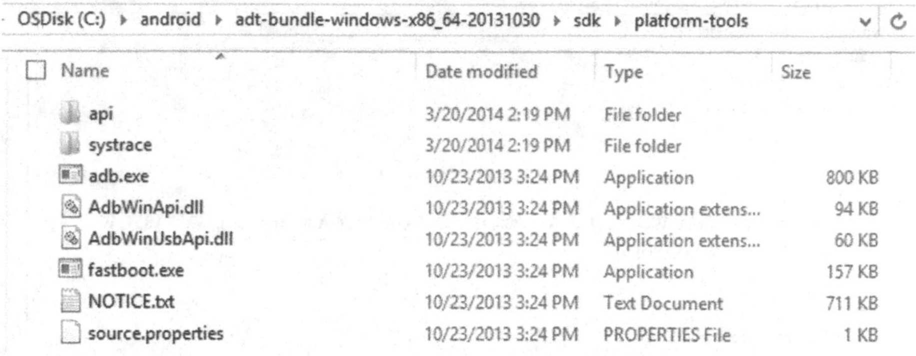

OSDisk (C:) ▸ android ▸ adt-bundle-windows-x86_64-20131030 ▸ sdk ▸ platform-tools			∨ ⟳

☐ Name	Date modified	Type	Size
📙 api	3/20/2014 2:19 PM	File folder	
📙 systrace	3/20/2014 2:19 PM	File folder	
▣ adb.exe	10/23/2013 3:24 PM	Application	800 KB
🗞 AdbWinApi.dll	10/23/2013 3:24 PM	Application extens...	94 KB
🗞 AdbWinUsbApi.dll	10/23/2013 3:24 PM	Application extens...	60 KB
▣ fastboot.exe	10/23/2013 3:24 PM	Application	157 KB
📄 NOTICE.txt	10/23/2013 3:24 PM	Text Document	711 KB
📄 source.properties	10/23/2013 3:24 PM	PROPERTIES File	1 KB

Figure 3-12. *File location of the adb.exe tool*

aapt.exe

With the Android resource packaging tool (aapt.exe), you can create .apk files that contain binary files and resource files for Android applications. The file location is the same as adb.exe.

aidl.exe

The Android interface description language (aidl.exe) is used for generating inter-process interface codes. The file location is the same as adb.exe.

sqlite3.exe

Android can create and use SQLite3 database files. Developers and users can easily access such SQLite data files. The file location is the same as ddms.bat.

dx.bat

Rewrite class byte code as Android byte code (saved in a dex file). The file location is the same with that of adb.exe.

android.bat

The android.bat file is under the same directory as ddms.bat. This command is used for displaying and creating the AVD.

```
D:\Android\android-sdk\tools>android list targets
Available Android targets:
----------
id: 1 or "android-16"
        Name: Android 4.1
        Type: Platform
        API level: 16
        Revision: 1
        Skins: HVGA, QVGA, WQVGA400, WQVGA432, WSVGA, WVGA800 (default), WVGA854, W
XGA720, WXGA800, WXGA800-7in
            ABIs : armeabi-v7a
----------
id: 2 or "Google Inc.:Google APIs:16"
        Name: Google APIs
        Type: Add-On
        Vendor: Google Inc.
        Revision: 1
        Description: Android + Google APIs
        Based on Android 4.1 (API level 16)
        Libraries:
          * com.google.android.media.effects (effects.jar)
              Collection of video effects
          * com.android.future.usb.accessory (usb.jar)
              API for USB Accessories
```

```
          * com.google.android.maps (maps.jar)
              API for Google Maps
        Skins: WVGA854, WQVGA400, WSVGA, WXGA800-7in, WXGA720, HVGA, WQVGA432, WVGA
800 (default), QVGA, WXGA800
            ABIs : armeabi-v7a
```

Figure 3-13. *The command shows that two target machine development libraries are installed on the machine*

Intel Environment Setup for Android (OS X Host)

The Environment Setup for Android (OS X Host) Integrates common Intel and third-party tools into your preferred IDE for productivity-oriented designing, coding, and debugging. Supported IDEs include Eclipse and Android Studio. This beta release, formerly known as Beacon Mountain beta, will be part of the Intel® Integrated Native Developer Experience (Intel® INDE) for OS X hosts and can be downloaded at https://software.intel.com/en-us/inde/environment-setup-osx. Table 3-6 provides a list of what is included in the Environment Setup for Android (OS-X Host).

Table 3-6. *Environment Setup for Android (OS-X Host)*

Product Installs	• Android Studio beta
	• Intel® Integrated Native Developer Experience
	  (Intel® INDE) native project template for Android Studio
	• Android SDK
	• Android NDK
	• Intel® Hardware Accelerated Execution Manager
	  (Intel® HAXM)
	• Apache Ant
	• Intel® INDE plugins for Eclipse

IDEs	• Eclipse • Android Studio beta
Host Support	• OS X
Target Support	• Android* 4.3 and up (based on ARM and Intel® architecture)

Android Development on Linux-based Host Machines

The following Android development tools for Linux-based host machines are available for download at:

- Intel® Graphics Performance Analyzers
  (https://software.intel.com/en-us/vcsource/tools/intel-gpa)

- Intel® Hardware Accelerated Execution Manager (Intel® HAXM)
  (https://software.intel.com/en-us/android/articles/
  intel-hardware-accelerated-execution-manager/)

- Intel® Threading Building Blocks (Intel® TBB)
  (https://software.intel.com/en-us/intel-tbb)

- Intel® C++ Compiler for Android
  (https://software.intel.com/en-us/c-compiler-android/)

- Intel® Integrated Performance Primitives (Intel® IPP)
  (https://software.intel.com/en-us/intel-ipp)

Intel® Integrated Native Developer Experience beta

The Intel Integrated Native Developer Experience (Intel INDE) is a beta release of Intel's cross-platform development suite designed to quickly and easily create applications targeting Android and Windows devices with native performance, outstanding battery-life, and exposure to unique platform capabilities. INDE provides a complete and consistent set of C++/Java tools, libraries, and samples for environment setup, code creation, compilation, debugging, and analysis on Intel architecture-based devices and select capabilities on ARM-based Android devices.

As a native cross-platform development suite, Intel INDE includes C++/Java native tools and samples for Android and Microsoft Windows, integration of tools into popular IDEs, and automatic updates to the latest tools and technology.

Tools and Libraries

Media: easily add visually compelling native video and audio extensions that work across the latest popular Android phones and tablets. The Intel INDE Media Pack for Android provides source code and samples to enhance apps with:

- Camera and screen capture

- Video editing

- Video streaming

- Audio fingerprinting

- Support for Intel architecture and ARM-based Android devices running 4.3 and up.

Threading: efficiently implement higher-level, task-based parallelism using the Intel Threading Building Blocks (Intel TBB). Intel TBB is an award-winning C++ template library for the development of higher-performance, scalable applications. Apps created using the parallelism tool can run on Intel architecture and ARM processor-based Android 4.3 and up devices, as well as Microsoft Windows 7-8.1 client.

Compiling: bring a heritage of industry-leading performance to your Android apps with performance-oriented compiling with the Intel® C++ Compiler for Android. The compiler is source-code compatible with GCC, enabling easy usage. The GNU C++ Compiler is also provided through the Android NDK, which is a customization option in the Environment Setup component of Intel INDE. Apps created using the Intel C++ Compiler can run on Intel architecture-based devices running Android 4.3 and up.

Compute Code Builder: maximize performance with programmable graphics - develop code that executes on computing devices beyond the CPU using the Compute Code Builder. This tool assists with creating, compiling, debugging and analyzing compute APIs like Google Renderscript† and OpenCL†. The compute code builder can be used in standalone mode or integrated with Microsoft Visual Studio or Eclipse. Apps created can run on Intel architecture-based Android 4.4 devices, as well as Microsoft Windows 7-8.1 client. Visit Intel's Getting Started Guide for more information.

- Analyzing and Debugging: Use Analysis and optimization tools suite includes the Intel Graphics Performance Analyzer (Intel GPA) System Analyzer, Intel GPA Platform Analyzer, Intel GPA Frame Analyzer, and Intel Frame Debugger. You can use them to do the following:

- Real-time trace analysis of code execution, CPU/GPU usage and task data, and more

- Frame-capture analysis and debugging

- Platform-wide and application-specific GPU metric analysis and graphics pipeline overrides

Apps created using the analysis and debugging tools can run on Intel architecture-based devices running Microsoft Windows 7–8.1 or Android 4.4.

Setup

Setting up an environment for Intel INDE is easy. You can build your custom environment in minutes instead of hours:

- Selectively choose tools to install, allowing for a customized environment.

- Choose from the Google Android SDK (including Eclipse), vs-Android plug-in for Microsoft Visual Studio, Android NDK, Android Design, Apache Ant, and Intel HAXM.

Apps created using the environment setup can run on Intel architecture and ARM-based targets running Android 4.3 and up.

Intel INDE Installation

The following sections describe the Intel INDE installation process.

Downloading Intel INDE

Go to `https://software.intel.com/en-us/intel-inde`, click the Download link, and accept the license agreements. You will receive an e-mail with a download link, as shown in Figure 3-14.

Figure 3-14. Download screen for INDE

Installing Intel INDE

Run the downloaded file: IntelHubSetup.exe. An Intel INDE window displays license terms and conditions, as shown in Figure 3-15.

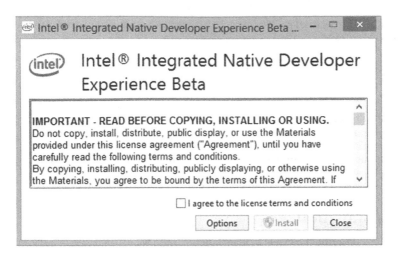

Figure 3-15. INDE install window

Check the box to agree to the license terms and conditions, and click Install. The setup process starts, and several command-line windows flash. An Intel INDE icon and an NDK.cmd icon are created on your desktop. When the process is complete, you are ready to launch, as shown in Figure 3-16.

Figure 3-16. INDE setup complete

Launching Intel INDE

Click the Launch icon, and the main Intel INDE window will start as shown in Figure 3-17.

Figure 3-17. *Main window for INDE*

Follow each tool and application to download the necessary software. You're ready to begin cross-platform development.

Configure Eclipse

1. Start Eclipse and select the Window menu, then Preferences, as shown in Figure 3-18.

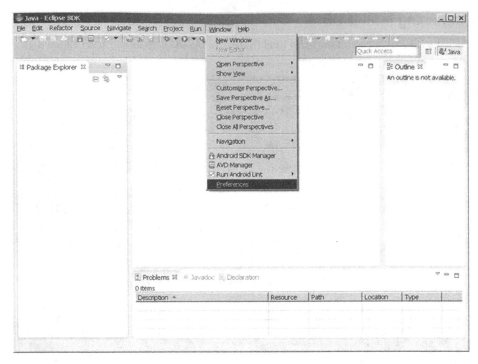

Figure 3-18. *Startup page for configuring Eclipse*

2. A Preferences dialog box will pop up. Select the Android branch and then type the correct path in the SDK Location box (usually this is auto-populated), as shown in Figure 3-19. Note: After clicking the Android branch, a dialog box will pop up. Click Proceed to continue.

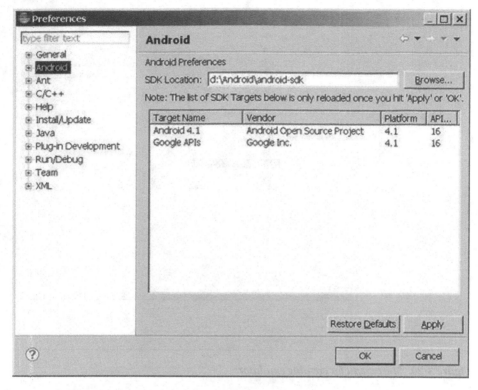

Figure 3-19. *Directory Location Setting of Android SDK*

Create AVD (Emulator)

1. On the menu bar, select Window, then AVD Manager, as shown in Figure 3-20.

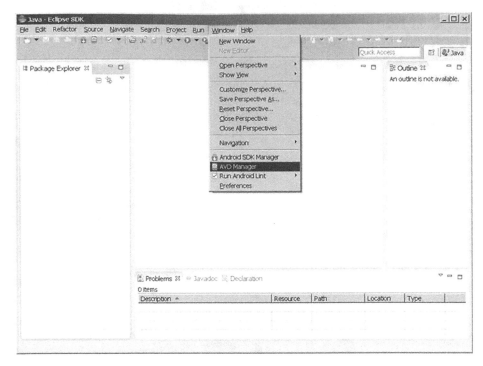

Figure 3-20. *Start menu for creating emulator*

2. The Android Virtual Device Manager dialog box will pop up, as shown in Figure 3-21. Click the New button.

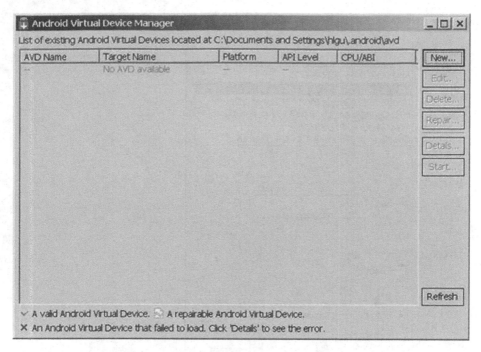

Figure 3-21. Initial page of emulator list

3. When the Create new Android Virtual Device (AVD) dialog box displays, as shown in Figure 3-22, type an appropriate name and, for Target, select the version of Android you wish to use. The CPU/ABI box will automatically display Intel Atom(x86). The size field for the SD card is the amount of space allocated for it on the hard disk (in this example, 1024 MB). If your target device has a larger SD card, enter the correct size. When the settings are correct, click Create AVD to close the dialog box.

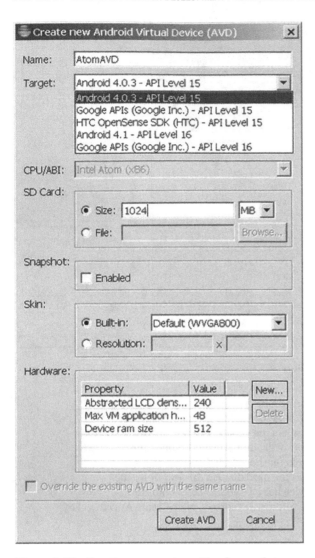

Figure 3-22. Creation parameter setting for emulator

4. The Android Virtual Device Manager will then display, as shown in Figure 3-23, and you can see the newly added item in the list. Click the close button (the x) to close the dialog box.

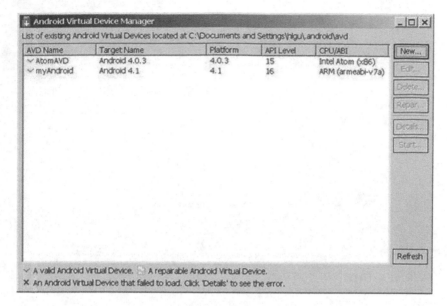

Figure 3-23. *Display of created list of emulator*

Summary

So far, you have finished installing the development environment tools for an emulator target machine. The next chapter discusses how, if your target machine is a real device (for example, a smartphone or tablet), you need to install and configure the development environment for developing and testing apps on that device.

■ ■ ■

## CHAPTER 4

Real Device Environment Installation

So far, you have completed installing the development environment for an emulator target machine. But if your target machine is a real device (for example, a mobile phone or a tablet with the Intel Inside logo), you need to install and configure the development environment for it. This chapter discusses how to build an application development with a real Android device, including how to install drivers and connect the device to your development host machine. Later, you see how to create an application and test it on both an emulator and a real device.

Mobile Phone Setting

There are many ways to set up a real device to support the Android SDK adb connection, and the settings vary from device to device. For example, in the case of the Lenovo K900 smartphone, you open the debugging function of the Android device by selecting Settings ➤ Applications ➤ Development and clicking USB Debugging. For some other devices, the USB Debugging option is not available because the developer option by default is not enabled. One example is the Dell Venue 8 Android tablet. To enable the developer option on a Dell Venue Android tablet, you need to go to Settings ➤ About ➤ Build Number; tap Build Number seven times to enable the Dell Venue Developer Option, which will then appear under System Category.

Installing the USB Driver on the Host Machine

This chapter uses the Lenovo K900 smartphone as an example of how to install a mobile phone USB driver on the host machine:

1. Connect the mobile phone to the development PC via USB cable.

2. The mobile phone is named Unknown Device in Device Manager (see Figure 4-1).

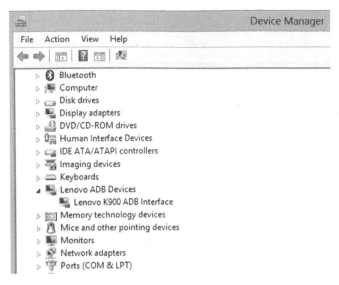

Figure 4-1. *Lenovo K900 ADB device in Device Manager (a yellow ? appears on top of the icon if Device Manager is unable to recognize the mobile phone when a USB driver is not installed)*

3. Install the driver. The driver can be found from the phone manufacturer or sometimes, as for the K900, from the emulated CD-ROM device when the phone USB connection is set to Driver Installation mode.

When you connect a Lenovo phone using a USB cable to your Windows laptop, a CD-ROM is mounted to the directory as shown in Figure 4-2. The file structure of the USB memory stick of the Lenovo Intel phone is

```
E: \Lenovo Kxxx Mobile phone driver>dir

2011-09-21 09:08        30 Autorun.inf
2012-03-23 17:10        2,366,976 bootstrap.exe
2012-03-23 17:15        69 bootstrap.ini
2012-03-23 10:57        10,993,152 LeDrivers.msi
```

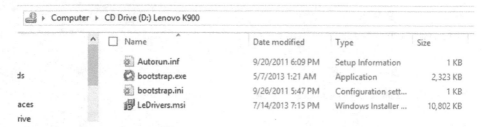

Name	Date modified	Type	Size
Autorun.inf	9/20/2011 6:09 PM	Setup Information	1 KB
bootstrap.exe	5/7/2013 1:21 AM	Application	2,323 KB
bootstrap.ini	9/26/2011 5:47 PM	Configuration sett...	1 KB
LeDrivers.msi	7/14/2013 7:15 PM	Windows Installer ...	10,802 KB

Figure 4-2. Directory display on the Windows host machine

4. Double-click LeDrivers.msi, and start installing the USB driver (see Figure 4-3).

Figure 4-3. Lenovo K900 Device Drivers Setup dialog

5. Restart the host machine after installation.

You can see that the ADB interface has been installed. In the software list, the Lenovo Racer-A Device Drivers have been successfully installed (see Figure 4-4).

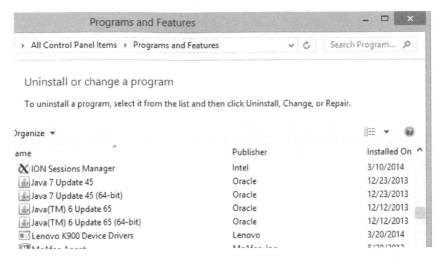

Figure 4-4. Software list for the Lenovo K900 after installation

Interaction between the Host Machine and the Target Machine

With the environment configured, the host and target machines can now use the Android development environment to provide auxiliary tools for more interaction in addition to the deployment operation during application development. You have more control over the target machine, including an emulator-type target machine. The use of these tools is introduced in the following sections.

Developing Android Applications

This section explains how to use Eclipse with the Android SDK to create a project, edit it, and run the application using an emulator and a real device.

Creating a Project

To create a project, follow these steps:

1. Start Eclipse, and select File ➤ New ➤ Project. In the New Project dialog box, select Android ➤ Android Application Project, and click Next to continue (see Figure 4-5).

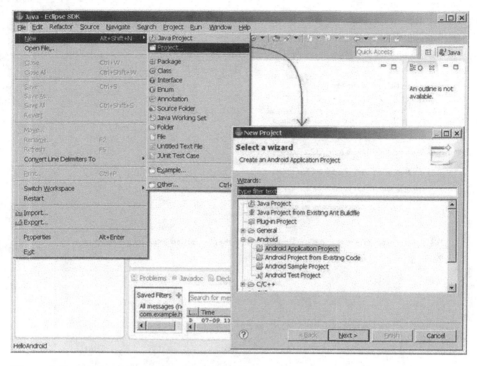

Figure 4-5. Starting a new Android project

2. In the New Android Application dialog box, enter an application name in the Application Name field, as shown in Figure 4-6. The Project Name and Package Name are auto-populated. Note that the set project name is also the application name on the target machine.

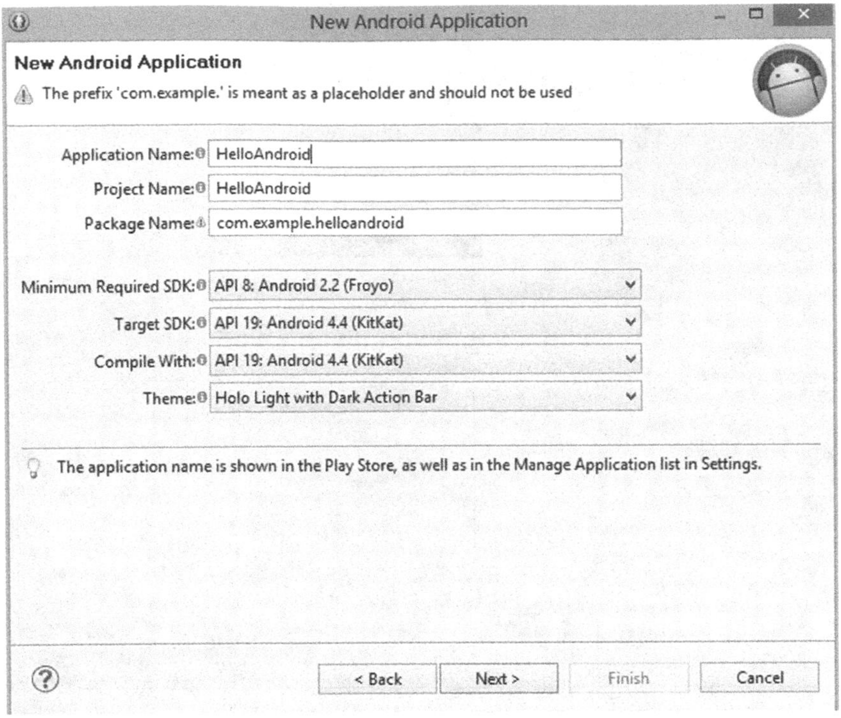

Figure 4-6. *New project (application) name*

3. Use the default configuration, and click Next. The Configure
   Launcher Icon dialog box appears (see Figure 4-7).

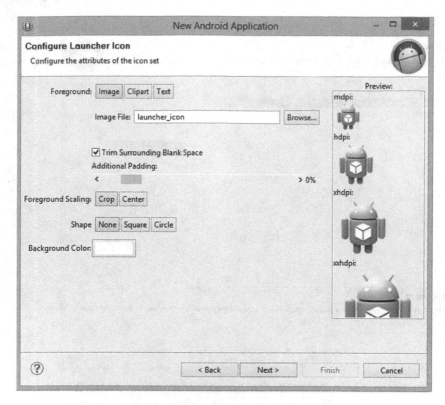

Figure 4-7. *New project—application icon setting*

4. Use the default configuration, and click Next. The Create Activity dialog box appears (see Figure 4-8).

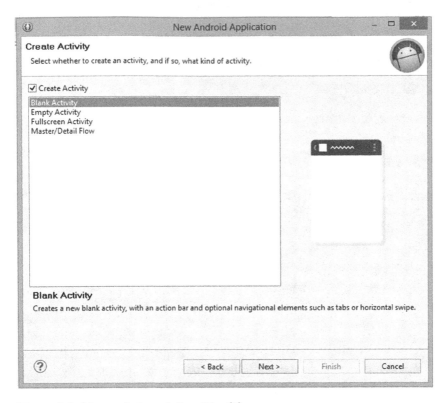

Figure 4-8. *New project—activity setting (1)*

5. Use the default configuration, and click Next. The New Blank
    Activity dialog box appears (see Figure 4-9).

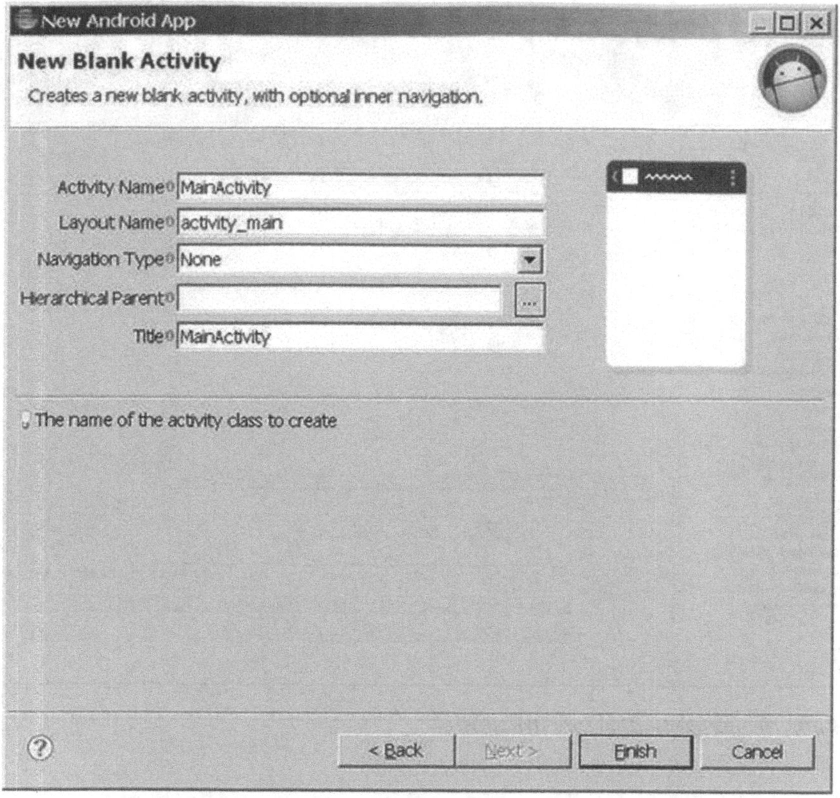

Figure 4-9. *New project—activity setting (2)*

The file structure and content look like Figure 4-10.

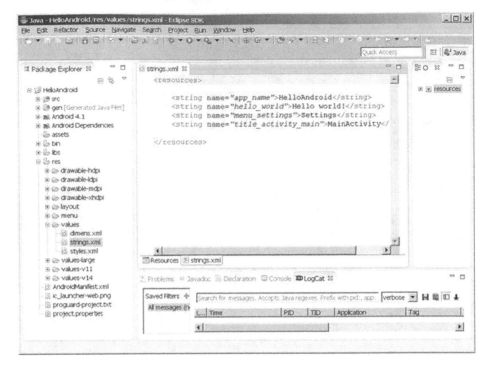

Figure 4-10. *New project—directory structure*

Editing and Running (on the Emulator)

To test run the application using emulator, please do the following steps:Perform the
following steps.

1. Right-click the project name, and select Run As ➤ Run
   Configuration on the shortcut menu. Or, from the menu,
   select Run ➤ Run Configuration.

2. In the dialog box, right-click Android Application (current
   project name), and select New. Left-click the Target tab, and
   click the Automatically Pick Compatible check box. Select the
   Intel Atom-related AVD in the list. Click Apply and then Close
   to close the dialog (see Figure 4-11).

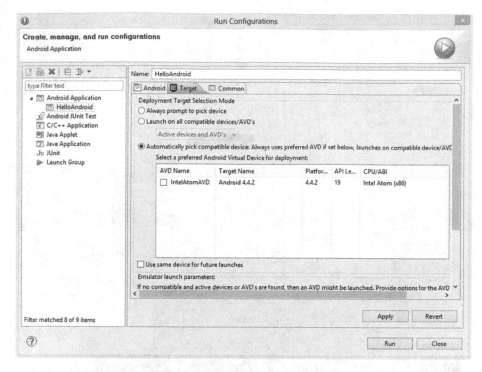

Figure 4-11. Runtime configuration of the emulator target machine

3. Right-click the project name, and select Run As ➤ Android
    Application from the shortcut menu (see Figure 4-12).

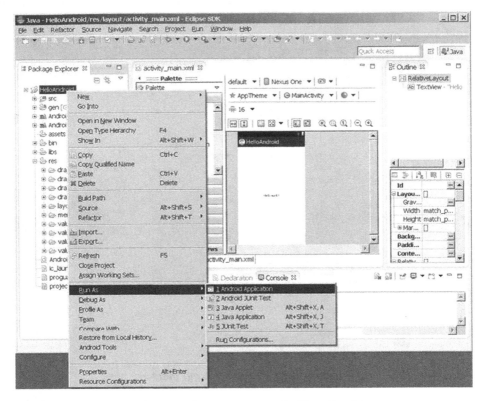

Figure 4-12. *Editing and runtime for starting an Android application*

4. Before running, the message box shown in Figure 4-13 appears. Click OK to continue. The emulator window appears and shows the running results.

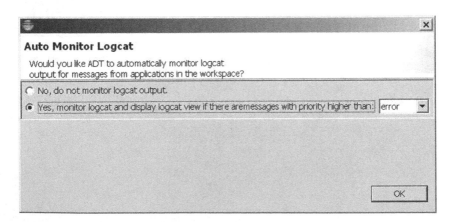

Figure 4-13. *Message prompt before running Android*

On the host machine, the console window of Eclipse shows the progress of editing, deploying, and running, as shown in Figure 4-14.

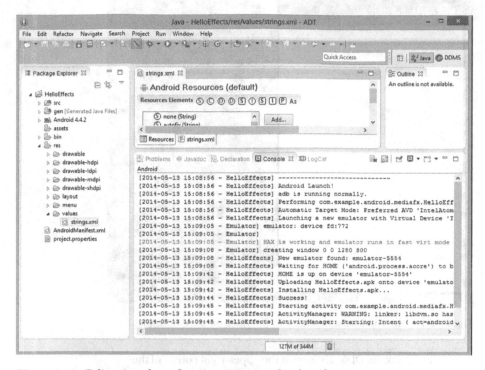

Figure 4-14. Eclipse interface when running an Android application

When the last sentence appears, the emulator screen displays the application window, as shown in Figure 4-15. Note: This process takes about 2 minutes if Intel HAXM is installed and working on your host machine.

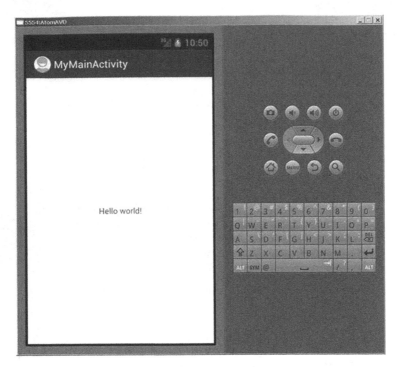

Figure 4-15. *An application running an interface on the emulator*

5. Click the DDMS button in the upper-right corner of the
    Eclipse window to enter the DDMS interface. The pane on
    the left shows the applications currently running on the
    target machine (emulator). In this example, com.example.
    helloandroid and helloandroid are running (see Figure 4-16).

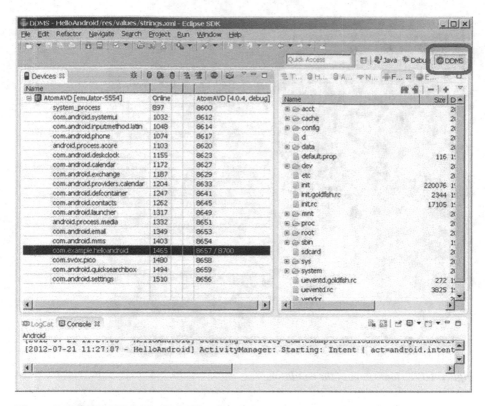

Figure 4-16. *DDMS interface of Eclipse*

6. You can see that the menu changes on the target machine. Click the Home button on the keyboard to see the interface shown in Figure 4-17. Then click the third button from the left at the bottom of the screen.

|<Home>

Figure 4-17. *Home page of the emulator*

In the application list shown in Figure 4-18, you can see the new MainActivity application.

Figure 4-18. The application list on the emulator

7. To stop running the application, click the DDMS button in
    the upper-right corner of Eclipse to enter the DDMS interface.
    Select the debugging software from the progress list on the left
    (usually com.example.[project name]). Click Stop Process (see
    Figure 4-19) to end running the process on the target machine.

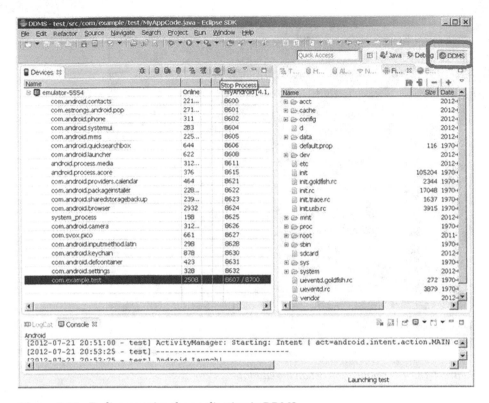

Figure 4-19. *Ending running the application in DDMS*

Then you see the page of the emulator's default application, as shown in Figure 4-20.

Figure 4-20. *Initial page of the emulator*

8. Click Java at upper left in Eclipse. The IDE interface goes back to the original editing status (see Figure 4-21).

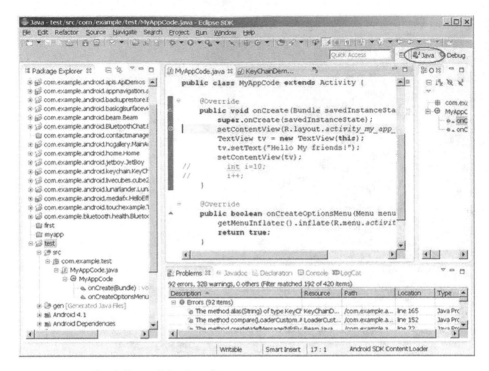

Figure 4-21. *The Eclipse editing interface*

    9.   Close the emulator window.

Running on the Real Device

To run the application on the real device, follows these steps:

    1.   Connect the mobile phone to the PC.

    2.   Enter the Eclipse window, and right-click the project name. In the shortcut menu, select Run As ➤ Run Configuration; or, in the Eclipse menu, select Run ➤ Run Configuration.

    3.   In the dialog box, left-click Android Application, [current project name]. Left-click the Target tab, and click Launch On All Compatible Devices/AVD's, which is set to Active Devices And AVD's. Click Apply and Close to close the dialog (see Figure 4-22).

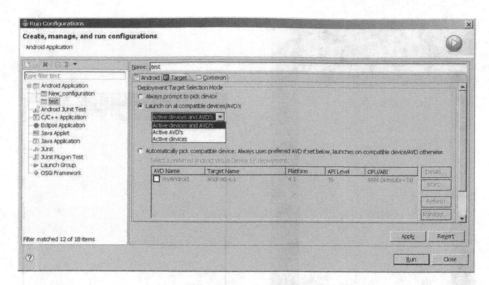

Figure 4-22. *Setup for running an application on the real device*

4. Right-click Project Name, and select Run As ➤ Android
   Application from the shortcut menu.

On the real device, you can see the interface running on the application, as shown in Figure 4-23.

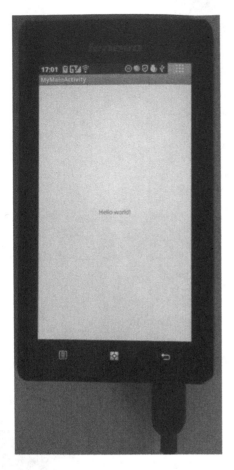 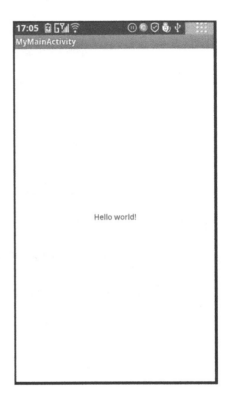

(a) The interface running on the application   (b) Snapshot of DDMS

Figure 4-23. *Application interface on the real device*

The application icon appears on the mobile phone menu. And you can see in Figure 4-24 that MyMainActivity has already been installed on the mobile phone menu.

(a) Snapshot of DDMS (Note: Non-English titles of the apps have been removed for a clear view)

Figure 4-24. *Application list on the real device*

(b) Screenshot of the menu on the real device (Note: Non-English titles of the apps have been removed for a clear view)

Figure 4-24. (*continued*)

What's interesting is that the application process on the real device is much smaller than on the virtual device (see Figure 4-25). It has only one application process.

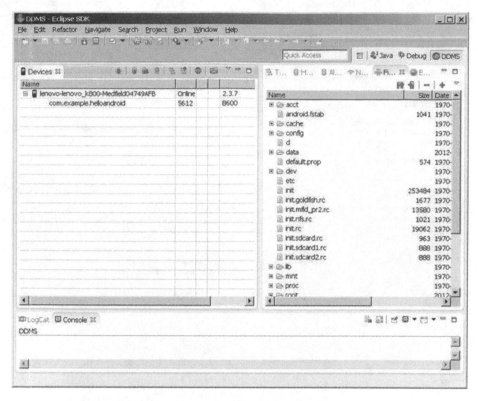

Figure 4-25. *DDMS interface of Eclipse*

In contrast to running your application on the emulator, the Eclipse console pane (see Figure 4-26) does not provide much information about editing and deployment.

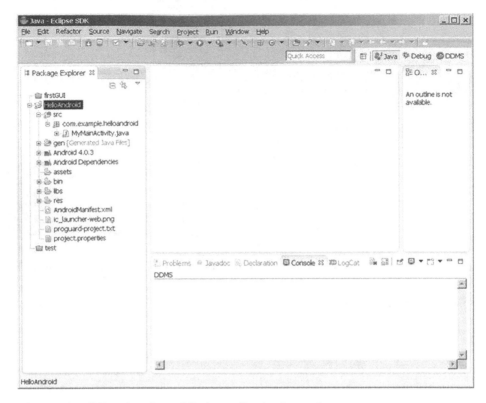

Figure 4-26. *Eclipse interface while the application is running*

5. Stop running the application by following the same steps as for the emulator.

Debugging Android Applications

Debugging is an important step in the application development process. For x86 platform targets, you need an x86-based device or x86 simulator to test and debug the application. With IA phones and tablets like the Lava Xolo and Lenovo K900 and tablets such as Samsung Galaxy Tab 10.1 and Dell Venue 7/8 on the market, you can test and debug apps on real x86-based tablets and phones.

If you don't have x86 devices for testing, the x86 simulator works just fine. You can use Android SDK Manager to install the x86 simulator.

Editinging the Source Code

In the Eclipse project file pane, find the \XXX\src\com.example.XXX***.java file, where XXX is the project name. Double-click the file name, and the source code is displayed on the right. Edit the source code by adding the lines of code shown in Figure 4-27 (shaded lines).

```
package com.example.test;
import android.os.Bundle;
import android.app.Activity;
import android.view.Menu;
import android.view.MenuItem;
import android.support.v4.app.NavUtils;
```

```
import android.widget.TextView;
import android.util.Log;

public class MyAppCode extends Activity {
    @Override
    public void onCreate(Bundle savedInstanceState) {
        super.onCreate(savedInstanceState);
        setContentView(R.layout.activity_my_app_code);
        TextView tv = new TextView(this);
        tv.setText("Hello My friends!");
        setContentView(tv);
        int i;
        i = 0;
        Log.d("ProgTraceInfo","i =" + i);
        i++;
        Log.d("ProgTraceInfo","i =" + i);
    }
    @Override
    public boolean onCreateOptionsMenu(Menu menu) {
        getMenuInflater().inflate(R.menu.activity_my_app_code, menu);
        return true;
    }
}
```

Figure 4-27. Modifying the source code in Eclipse

Setting Breakpoints

With the cursor over the code, right-click Toggle Breakpoint in the shortcut menu, as shown in Figure 4-28.

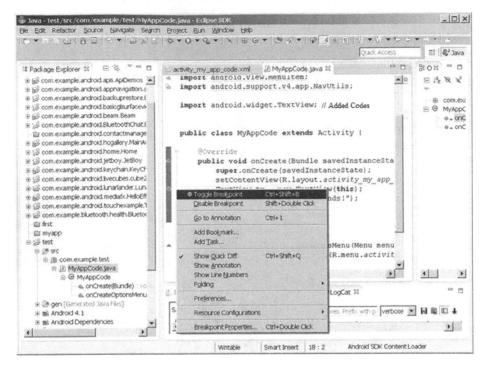

Figure 4-28. *Menu to set a breakpoint*

A green icon is displayed on the left side of the code that has a breakpoint set, as shown in Figure 4-29.

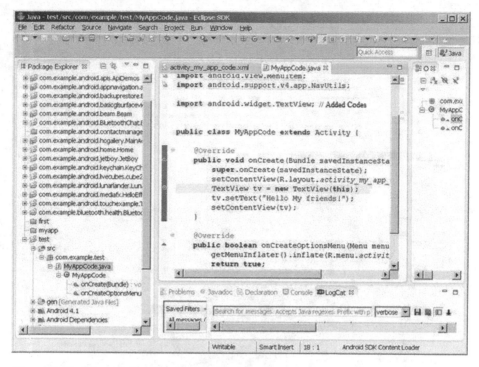

Figure 4-29. Display after a breakpoint is set

Repeat this process to cancel a breakpoint set on a line of code.

Starting Debugging

To start debugging, follow these steps:

1. Right-click the project name. In the pop-up menu, select Debug As ➤ Android Application (see Figure 4-30).

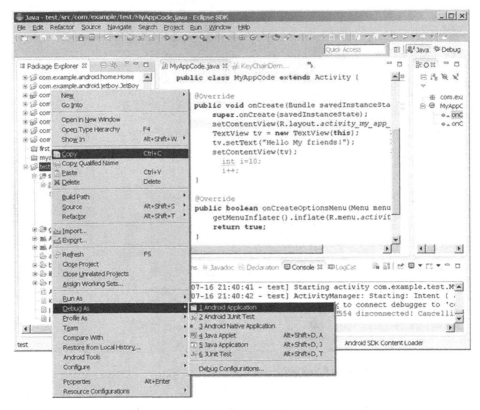

Figure 4-30. *Entering the debugging state*

2. In the warning dialog box (Figure 4-31), click Yes to continue.

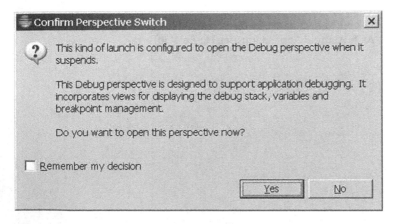

Figure 4-31. *Message box after entering the debugging state*

3. The Eclipse IDE enters the debugging interface, as shown in
   Figure 4-32. Where possible, the initial running interface of
   the target machine (real device or emulator) is as shown
   in Figure 4-33.

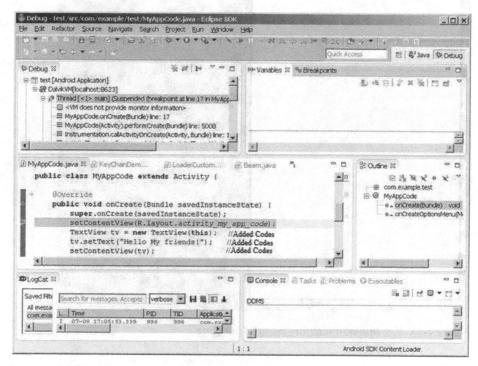

Figure 4-32. Interface of the Eclipse IDE during debugging

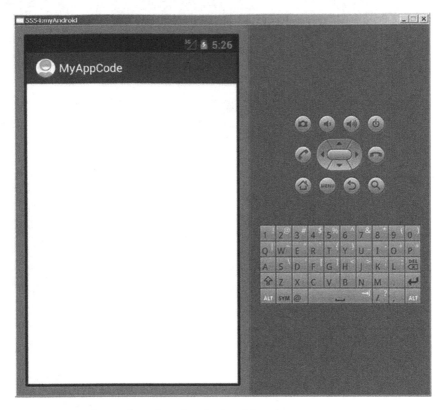

Figure 4-33. *The emulator interface during debugging*

Program Execution Techniques

If you want to carry out single-step execution, click in the code window to make it the active window (see Figure 4-34). You can highlight the code section and right-click to access the menu shown in Figure 4-34. From the menu, select Step Over, Step Into, or Step Return to execute.

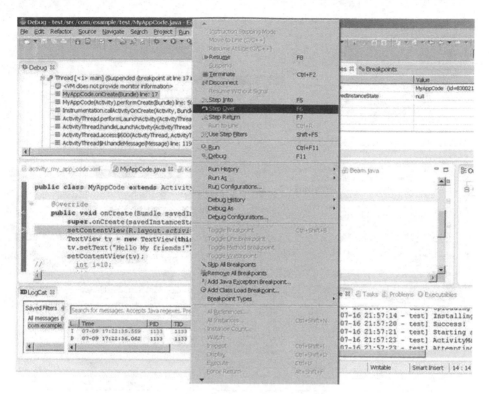

Figure 4-34. *Single-step execution*

Observing the Debugging Output of the Log.X Function

The Log.X function is equivalent to the MFC TRACE function and is used to output information in the Eclipse LogCat window. To observe the debugging output of Log.X, follows these steps:

1. If the LogCat pane is not shown, click Window ➤ Show View ➤ LogCat (see Figure 4-35). The LogCat may not be found depending on the ADT version you are using. If you cannot find LogCat, you can select Other to display more options and add LogCat into your list. LogCat is in the Android category.

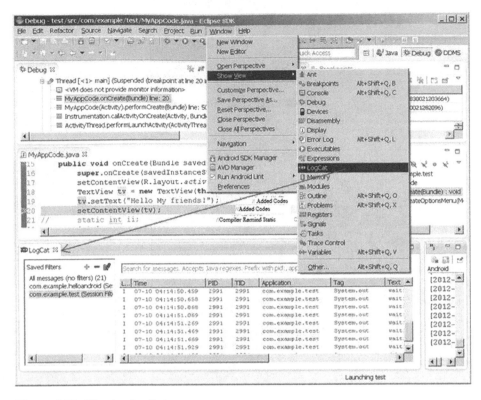

Figure 4-35. *Viewing LogCat*

2. Single-step execute two Log.d sentences:

    a. Click and activate the code window.

    b. Press the F6 key to browse the code. You may need to press F6 multiple times to reach the latest output of these sentences in the LogCat window (see Figure 4-36).

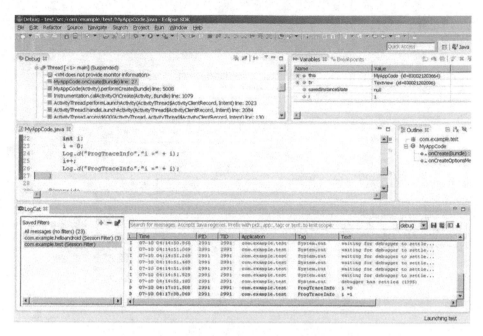

Figure 4-36. *Viewing output in the LogCat window*

3. Create a filter for the debugging output information by clicking the Add A New LogCat Filter button in the upper-right corner of the LogCat window (see Figure 4-37). Enter the Filter Name and By Log Tag in the dialog box. Filter Name can be any name you like, but By Log Tag must be the first parameter (string) of the Log.d() function in the source code. Then click OK to close the window.

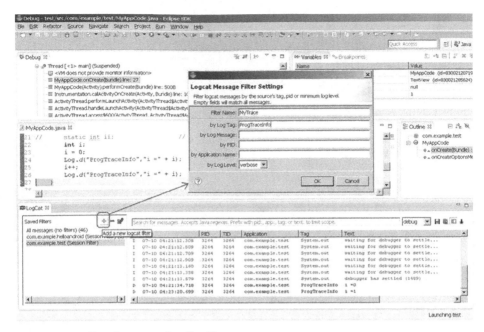

Figure 4-37. *Creating a new LogCat filter*

In Figure 4-38, you can see the the called output information of Log.X dislayed in the LogCat window.

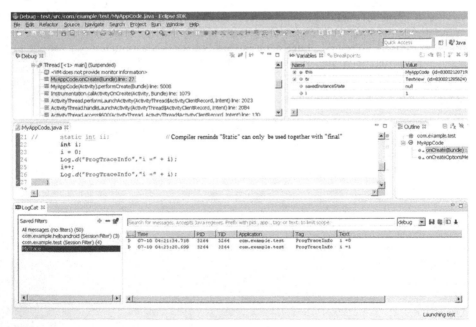

Figure 4-38. *The LogCat window displaying the filtered output*

Observing Variables

To observe variables, select Run ➤ Watch, as shown in Figure 4-39.

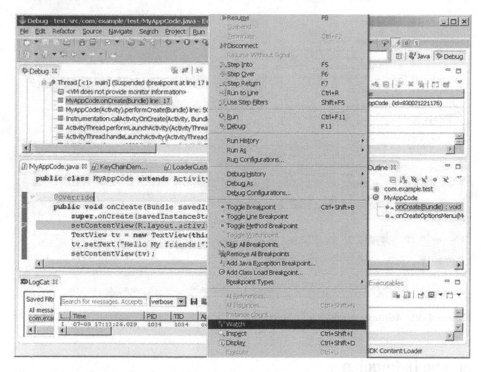

Figure 4-39. *The Watch command*

Right-click the Expression tab to pop up the menu as shown. Click Add New
Expression as shown in Figure 4-40 to add variables for observation.

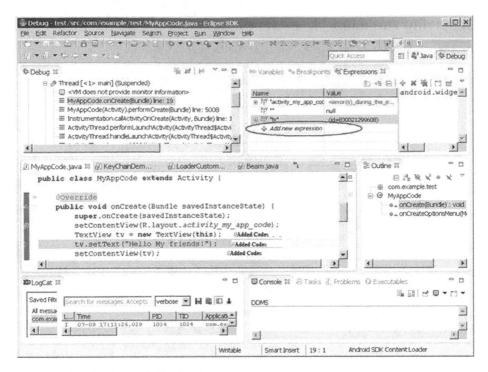

Figure 4-40. Adding variables for observation

Ending Debugging

Click Terminate on the toolbar (Figure 4-41) or select Terminate on the Run menu to end debugging.

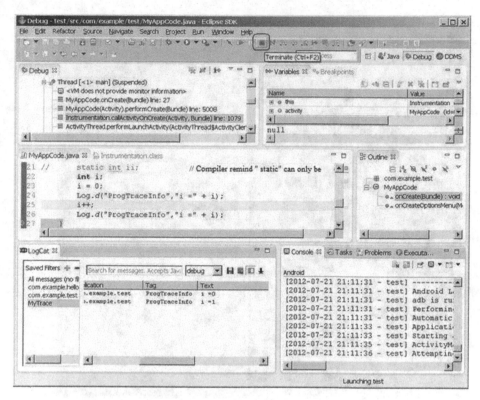

Figure 4-41. *Ending debugging by clicking the Terminate button*

You can see the default application page displayed by the emulator, as shown in Figure 4-42.

Figure 4-42. *The default application page displayed by the emulator*

Go back to the editing home page. Click Java the upper-left corner in Eclipse; the IDE interface goes back to the original editing status.

Intel Auxiliary Tools for Android Application Development

Intel provides a series of tools for software development on Intel Atom processor-based systems. These tools are auxiliary to the Android development tool chains and further support Android application development. In chapter 3, you saw how to get the Beacon Mountain tools for Apple OS X and Linux Host system, which are compatible with Eclipse and support popular Android SDKs including the Android NDK; and the Intel Integrated Native Developer Experience (Intel INDE) for expanded tools, support, and more for creating Android applications using on a Microsoft Windows 7-8.1 host system. The following are introductions to some of those tools.

Intel C++ Compiler (Intel ICC)

Intel C++ Compiler (Intel ICC) is a set of C/C++ encoders that can run on multiple platforms, including Windows, Linux, and OS X. On Linux platforms, it can replace gcc in completing C/C++ code compilation and linking.

The Intel ICC encoder can produce instructions that tap into the potential of Intel processors. Intel ICC-encoded code has relatively better performance on Intel processors. ICC running on IA-32 and Intel 64 can generate automatic vector components for SIMD instructions such as SSE, SSE2, SSE3, and SSE4 and generate variables for Intel Wireless MMX. Intel ICC supports the automatic parallelization of OpenMP and symmetric multiprocessor (SMP). With additional cluster OpenMP, Intel ICC-compiled code can pass interface calls for distributed memory multiprocessing (DM-SMP) to generate messages in OpenMP instructions. This is detailed in the performance optimization section.

Intel ICC and gcc both have editing and linking functions. Intel ICC can be run in command-line format, such as

```
icc [options] [@response_file] file1 [file2...]
```

where

- `options` means zero or multiple encoding potions

- `response_file` is a text file that lists options for encoding file(s) to be compiled and can include C or C++ files (suffixes: .C, .c, .cc, .cpp, .cxx, .c++, .i, .ii) and assembly files (suffixes: .s, .S), target files (suffix: .o), and static libraries (suffix: .a)

The common options of Intel ICC are shown in Table 4-1.

Table 4-1. *Common Intel C++ Compiler Encoding Options*

Options	Description
-fast	An abbreviation for several options: -O3 -ipo -static -xHOST -no-prec-div. Note: The explanation on the xhost label explains on which processor the optimization is based. The processor label might be rewritten during practice.
-g	Produces debugging information versions for debugging gdd and idb debuggers.
-help [CODE]	Displays help information on the command line. CODE explains the type and options of the help group.
-m32	Tells the encoder to produce IA-32 code.
-m64	Tells the encoder to produce IA-64 code.
-O0	Tells the encoder to not perform optimization.
-O1	Tells the encoder to optimize code sizes.
-O2	Optimizes on running speed and starting optimizations
-O3	Starts all optimizations including O2 and intensive cycle optimization.
-prof-gen	Compiles programs into the running mode of the code profiler.
-prof-use	Compiles and processes the code profiler information during each step. This option can be applied only to programs to which prof_gen encoding has been applied.
-x0	Initiates SSE3, SSE2, and SSE instruction set optimization for non-Intel CPUs.
-xS	Generates SSE vector encoders and media acceleration instructions.

The options listed in the table are unique to Intel ICC. Intel ICC's compatibility with gcc means gcc's encoding options can also be used in Intel ICC. For example, the -o option can be used to name the target file; -S is used for explaining thecompiled assembly codes ; -c only compiles the files and does not link into executable files (namely resisting links).

Intel Graphics Performance Analyzers for Android OS

The Intel Graphics Performance Analyzers (Intel GPA) suite is a set of powerful graphics and gaming analysis tools that are designed to work the way game developers do, saving valuable optimization time by quickly providing actionable data to help you find performance opportunities from the system level down to the individual draw call.

Intel GPA now supports Intel Atom-based phones and tablets running the Google Android OS. This version of the toolset enables you to optimize OpenGL ES workloads using your choice of development systems: Windows, OS X, or Ubuntu OS. With this capability, as an Android developer you can do the following:

- Get a real-time view of over two dozen critical system metrics covering the CPU, GPU, and OpenGL ES API

- Conduct a number of graphics pipeline experiments to isolate graphics bottlenecks

- When using a tablet based on an Intel Atom processor, run Intel GPA Frame Analyzer to perform detailed frame analysis and optimization

- When using an Android device based on Intel Atom processor with PowerVR Graphics, run Intel GPA Platform Analyzer to perform detailed platform analysis

To download a free copy of Intel GPA, browse to the Intel GPA Home Page (https://software.intel.com/en-us/vcsource/tools/intel-gpa), and click the Download button for the appropriate version of the product. For developing games or applications for the Android OS platform, select a version of Intel GPA depending on your development system.

Intel System Studio

Intel System Studio is a comprehensive and integrated tool suite that provides advanced system tools and technologies to help accelerate the delivery of the next generation of power-efficient, high-performance, and reliable embedded and mobile devices.

Intel System Studio 2014 now allows you to develop for embedded and mobile Android and Tizen IVI systems, adds cross-development from Windows hosts, and provides expanded JTAG debug support for all IA platforms. The new agent-based UEFI debug helps you accelerate time-to-market and strengthen reliability of these increasingly complex embedded and mobile systems. Eclipse integration and cross-build capabilities allow for faster system development with Intel System Studio 2014.

Intel System Studio includes the components listed in Table 4-2.

Table 4-2. *Intel System Studio Components*

Component	Description
Intel VTune Amplifier for Systems	Advanced CPU and system-on-chip (SoC) performance profiling and tuning.
Intel Energy Profiler	Advanced GPGPU and SoC power profiling and tuning.
Intel System Analyzer	Real-time system-level performance analysis with CPU and GPU metrics for Android targets.
Intel JTAG debugger	System debugger for in-depth SoC platform insights, featuring low-overhead event tracing, logging, source-level debug of EFI/UEFI firmware via JTAG and the EDKII debug agent, bootloader, OS kernel, and drivers.
gdb debugger	Software debugger for fast application-level defect analysis for increased system stability, application-level instruction trace, and data-race detection.
Intel Inspector for Systems	Dynamic and static analyzer that identifies difficult-to-find memory and threading errors to ensure functional reliability.
Intel C++ Compiler	Industry- leading C/C++ compiler including the Intel Cilk Plus parallel model for highly optimized performance. Binary and source compatible with gcc compilers and cross-compilers.
Intel Integrated Performance Primitives	Extensive library of high-performance software building blocks for signal, data, and multimedia processing.
Intel Math Kernel Library	Highly optimized linear algebra, Fast Fourier Transform (FFT), vector math, and statistics functions.
System Visible Event Nexus (SVEN) 1.0 technology	Ultra-low-overhead event tracing.

Intel System Studio development tools combined with Intel Quark, Intel Atom, Intel Core, and Intel Xeon processor platforms provides added value and competitive edge in delivering robust embedded and mobile platform solutions across a wide range of markets.

Intel Project Anarchy: a Free Mobile Game Engine by Havok

Project Anarchy is a free mobile game engine for iOS, Android (including X-86), and Tizen. It includes Havok's Vision Engine along with Havok Physics, Havok Animation Studio, and Havok AI. It has an extensible C++ architecture, optimized mobile rendering, a flexible asset-management system, and Lua scripting and debugging. Complete game samples are included with the SDK along with extensive courseware on the Project Anarchy site that game developers can use to quickly get up to speed with the engine and bring their game ideas to life:

- Extensible C++ plug-in–based architecture

- Comprehensive game samples with full source art and source code

- Focus on community with forums for support, Q&A, feedback, and hands-on training

- No commercial restrictions on company size or revenue

- Upgrades for additional platforms and products, source, and support available

- Includes FMOD, the industry's leading audio tool

Intel Performance Libraries

Special performance libraries include Intel Integrated Performance Primitives (Intel IPP), Intel Math Kernel (Intel MKL), and Intel Threading Building Blocks (Intel TBB).

Intel IPP 8.1 is an extensive library of software functions for multimedia processing, data processing, and communications applications for Windows, Linux, Android, and OS X environments. It includes a broad range of functions, including communication and image processing, computer vision, voice recognition, data compression, encryption and decryption, string operation, voice processing, video formatting, photorealistic rendering, and 3D data processing. It also includes sophisticated primitives for building audio, video, and voice encoders/decoders such as MP3, MPEG-4, H.264, H.263, JPEG, JPEG2000, GSM-AMR, and G723.

By supporting all data types and function layout, the number of data structure types is minimized. During application design and optimization, the Intel IPP library provides a variety of option sets. All kinds of data types and layouts are supported by each function. The minimized data structure of Intel IPP software provides maximum flexibility in generating optimized applications and higher-level software modules and library functions. The Linux version of Intel IPP provides independent software packages that support IA-32, Intel64, IA-64, and Intel Atom processors.

Intel TBB is a widely used, award-winning C and C++ library for creating high-performance, scalable, parallel applications. It enhances productivity and reliability with a rich set of components to efficiently implement higher-level, task-based parallelism. You gain performance advantages by building future-proof applications to tap multicore and many-core power. The advanced threading library is compatible with multiple compilers and portable to various operating systems.

Intel IPP and TBB provide convenience and help optimize program runtime performance. You can reduce the amount of code you have to write by calling the functions in the libraries. Intel performance libraries can provide the same or similar services and functions as third-party libraries. They fully use the instruction capacity of Intel and compatible processors; therefore the same or similar services perform better than third-party libraries or ones provided by the OS. This topic is discussed at length in the code-optimization sections in Chapters 8 and 9.

Summary

In this chapter, you discussed how you setup and configure the Application development on host system, install USB driver for Android real device so that the connection can be built between the devices and host systems to allow you to test and debug the application. You also discussed how to use Intel emulator, and all the steps required to accelerate the emulator and how to work with it. In next chapter, you will discuss Android Operation System, and understand the principles of Android OS on Intel Architecture.

CHAPTER 5

■ ■ ■

The Android OS

At the heart of all compute devices is the operating system, or OS. Development and execution of application software are based on the OS and the software platform as a whole. In this chapter, you learn about the Android OS—the recommended software platform for Intel Atom-based machines—to build your competence for subsequent development of embedded applications.

Android Overview

Android is a comprehensive operating environment based on the Linux kernel (in 2014, Kernel version 3.10.x has been used by major OEMs). Initially, the deployment target for Android was the mobile phone category, including smartphones and lower-cost flip-phone devices. However, Android's full range of computing services and rich functional support have the full potential to extend beyond the mobile phone market for use on other platforms and applications, such as tablets.

In addition to the kernel, the Android OS for x86 requires some drivers and technologies, including those commonly found on mobile devices:

- USB driver for host and client

- Video driver for video encode as well as decode

- Display and graphics: 2D and 3D rendering; planes, pipes, ports

- Flash memory driver

- Camera driver: usually a Linux-based v41 (video for) driver

- Audio driver: usually an Advanced Linux Sound Architecture (ALSA) based advanced Linux (sound system) driver

- Near field communication (NFC)

- Wi-Fi Driver: IEEE 802.11-based driver

- Keyboard driver

- Security (DRM, trusted boot, and so on)

- Bluetooth driver

- Binder IPC: a special driver of Android, with separate device nodes to provide inter-process communications (IPC) functions

- Power management: drivers for three different CPU Standby states: Active Stand-by (S0i1), Always On Always Connected (AOAC) Stand-by (S0i2), and Deep Sleep Stand-by (S0i3)

With Android's breadth of capabilities, it would be easy to confuse it with a desktop OS; Android is a layered environment and includes rich functions.

Android applications are generally written in the Java programming language and can include many different kinds of resource files (in the res directory). An APK package is generated after the Java program and other related resources are compiled. Google also provides support for multiple APK files. This is a feature of Google Play that allows developers to publish different APKs for the application that are each targeted to different device configurations. Android offers many core applications including Home, Contact, Phone, and Browser. In addition, you can use the APIs in the application framework layer to develop your own applications.

The Android UI subsystem includes

- Windows

- Views

- Widgets for displaying common elements such as edit boxes, lists, and drop-down lists

It also includes an embeddable browser built on WebKit, the same open source browser engine powering the Apple iPhone's Mobile Safari browser.

Android boasts a healthy array of connectivity options, including Wi-Fi, Bluetooth, and wireless data over a cellular connection (for example, GPRS, EDGE, 3G, and 4G/LTE). A popular technique in Android applications is to link to Google Maps to display an address directly within an application. Support for location-based services (such as GPS) and accelerometers is also available in the Android software stack, although not all Android devices are equipped with the required hardware. There is also camera support. Historically, two areas where mobile applications have struggled to keep pace with their desktop counterparts are graphics/media and data-storage methods. Android addresses the graphics challenge with built-in support for 2D and 3D graphics, including the OpenGL ES library. The data-storage burden is eased with the popular open source SQLite database included on the Android platform.

Android Architecture

A simplified block diagram of the Android software architecture is shown in Figure 5-1.

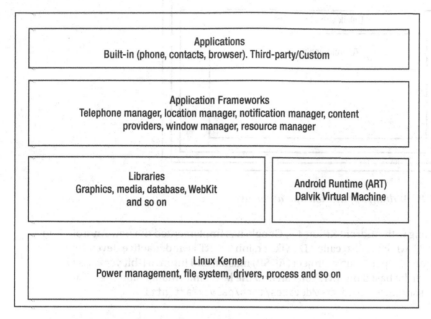

Figure 5-1. Android software architecture

As mentioned, Android runs on top of a Linux kernel. Java-based applications are run within a virtual machine (VM). It's important to note that the VM is not a JVM, as you might expect, but is the Dalvik virtual machine (DVM), an open source technology. Each Android application runs within an instance of the DVM, which in turn resides within a Linux kernel–managed process, as shown in Figure 5-2.

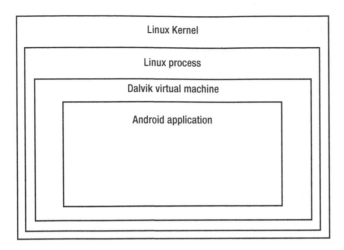

Figure 5-2. *Android application operation layer*

Starting with Android KitKat 4.4, Google has implemented the new Android Run Time (ART), which is also called Dalvik version 2. ART is under active development in the Android Open Source Project (AOSP) master, and future 64-bit versions of Android will be based on ART. You can find the latest information about ART at https://source.android.com/devices/tech/dalvik/art.html.

Basic Android Functionality from a Programming Perspective

Android is a version of Linux. This section recaps some basic Linux commands and common practices for Android developers with two scenarios: one based on the Android emulator provided in the Android SDK and the other for developers who own a real Android smartphone or tablet with Intel inside it (in the examples, the Lenovo K900 smartphone). If you are an experienced Android/Linux developer, you can safely skip the rest of this chapter and move to the next chapter.

Android System Interface

The Android mobile system interface is a key aspect in which major manufacturers differ. Personalized system interfaces are not only a selling point, but also a platform for mobile phone users to communicate with their friends. This section uses the Lenovo K900 smartphone as an example to discuss Android system UI design. The four-leaf clover design used by Lenovo K900 is shown in Figure 5-3.

Figure 5-3. *Lenovo K900 main interface*

The Lenovo phone adopts the conventional "slide up to unlock" mode, which is simple and convenient. The shortcuts in the main interface can be changed by long-pressing a leaf, as shown in Figure 5-4. It's worth noting that during the main interface operation, the shortcut-setting option does not appear if you click the menu key, as on some other Android phones. In addition, you cannot add or delete the home screen (the shortcuts in leaves can be changed).

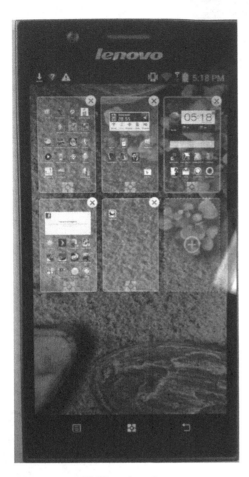

Figure 5-4. *All Menu interface*

The Lenovo phone's drop-down menu is personalized and includes four options: Notification, Switch, Call, and Message. In the Switch interface, you can make quick settings for the mobile phone or long-press an option to enter the option's detailed settings interface.

Some Android phones allow you to add widgets and shortcuts when you long-press any blank space on the interface, but the Lenovo phone doesn't have this function. You can use the menu key to add tools and shortcut keys (except the)home screen. When you press the screen with two fingers, the multiscreen interface appears where you can perform a quick search, as shown in Figure 5-5.

(a) Initial multiscreen interface. (b) Click the thumbnail with a "+" sign, the second row on the right, –allow you to add additional screen to hold more applications.

Figure 5-5. *Multiscreen interface of the Lenovo phone*

The menu interface in 20-rectangle-grid design is fashionable and elegant, but some icons are blurred.

The main hardware and OS configuration information of the Lenovo K900 phone are shown in Figure 5-6.

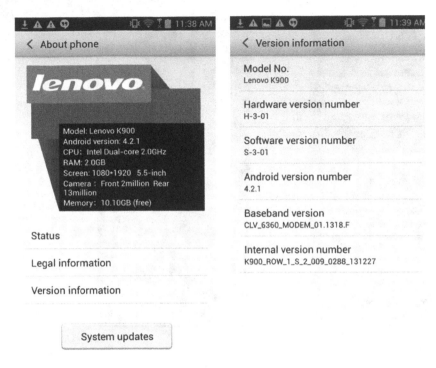

(a) Device information. (b) System information.

Figure 5-6. *Parameters of the Lenovo K900 phone*

Terminating an Application in Android

Android offers three different methods to terminate an application, as described in the following sections.

Method 1 (for Real Devices)

1. Select the following options in the mobile device menu:
    Settings ➤ Applications ➤ Running Services ➤ Running
    Applications. The applications that are executing are shown.
    This list may vary on different devices. For example, on the
    Samsung Galaxy Note, Applications is replaced with Application
    Manager, and on the Dell Venue (Android KitKat 4.4), it is
    replaced with Apps.

2. Click the application to delete from the list, and the Force Quit
    and Uninstall buttons pop up on the screen. Click Force
    Quit to terminate the process.

138

Method 2

Press Return when the application occupies the current top-level window screen (that is, the application is running).

Method 3

Terminate the process in the Dalvik Debug Monitor Server (DDMS) on a host system. This can be achieved when the Android device is connect to a host system that has an IDE with an Android SDK that supports DDMS, such as Eclipse.

Using the Web Browser in the Android Emulator

If you have a smartphone, there is no doubt that you can connect to the Internet easily. If you are running Android on an emulator, you can follow these steps to use the web browser:

1. Click the Home ● button on the keyboard, and the interface shown in Figure 5-7 appears. Click the bottom-right button.

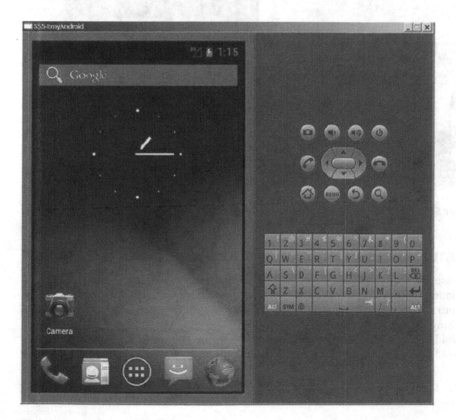

Figure 5-7. *Web browser startup interface*

2. The web browser window pops up. Click the address bar to bring up the keyboard on the emulated device, as shown in Figure 5-8. Input the address on the emulated keyboard, and then click Go.

Figure 5-8. *Web browser initial interface*

Common Linux Commands and Operations

Because Android is based on Linux, Android supports most Linux commands. The following sections present some common Linux commands that are supported on an Ubuntu system–based host machine and an Android system–based target machine. If you are using a Windows host system to develop applications for Android, you can use the Android Debug Bridge (adb) command provided by the Android SDK to connect to an Android device or emulator to run these commands.

Check Users

The following command checks the current logged-in user's name:

```
$ who am i
```

or

```
$echo $USER
```

The following command displays username information:

```
$ id
```

```
uid=1000(cereal) gid=1000(cereal)
groups=4(adm), 20(dialout), 24(cdrom), 46(plugdev), 106(lpadmin),
121(admin), 122(sambashare), 1000(cereal)
```

The output data shows the current user is cereal, the user ID is 1000, the user belongs to the cereal group, the group ID is 1000, and so on.

Changing a Password

The following command changes the current user's password:

```
$ passwd
```

Here is the output:

```
Changing password for cereal.
(current) UNIX password:
Enter New UNIX password:
Retype New UNIX password:
Password changed
```

The passwd command can also be used to change the Rootpassword. For example, if you log in with the username cereal, you can use the following command to set the password of the root user:

```
$ sudo passwd root
```

In desktop Linux, a login window usually appears as the system starts, requiring you to enter the username and password. But Android doesn't have this process. Android automatically logs in using the default username and password, which are invisible to the user; the system resources are used under the user's identity.

If the password of the root user is uncertain after Android installation, you can set it as shown earlier using the passwd root command. sudo means the command is executed under the root identity, but execution of the command only requires confirmation by inputting the password of an ordinary user.

Clearing the Screen

You can use the clear command to clear the screen:

```
$ clear
```

Superuser Root Operation

Linux has a unique superuser *root* (different from multiple superusers for Windows), which can access all files and directories and operate all applications in the system. Use the su command to enter the root user account:

```
$ su
```

Then, enter the root user's password. After you enter the root user account, the command-line prompt changes from $ to #. If the su command is not followed by any parameter, the default is to switch to the root user but not the root user's home directory—that is, the root login environment is not changed after the switch. It is still the default login environment. When a parameter is entered, the root user as well as the environment of the root user are changed:

```
$ su -
```

Use the exit command to exit the root user account and return to the ordinary user identity:

```
#exit
```

After exiting, the command line prompt changes from # to $.

When you enter the root user account with the su command, subsequent operations are made under the root identity. To execute the current command under the root user identity and return to the ordinary user identity after the execution of the command, add the prefix sudo before the command, as shown earlier. As sudo is executed, the system asks you to enter the password of the current user (not the root user) to confirm the identity.

Theoretically, an ordinary user doesn't necessarily have sudo permissions; the permissions are specified in the document /etc/sudoers. In desktop Linux, this should always be edited or set via commands such as visudo. But in Android, the default is that the installer has sudo permissions.

Displaying Files and Directories

You use the ls command to display directory and file information. The common format of ls is as follows:

```
ls [-l] [<directory name>]
```

Here, ls -l shows file or directory, size, modified date and time, file or folder name and owner of file and it's permission. By default, the information of the current directory is displayed. For example (the current directory is /home/cereal):

Changing and Displaying the (Current) Directory

Use the cd command to change the current directory. For example, to change the current directory to \embedded\pkgs, input the following command (note that the root directory and directory are separated by / in Linux):

```
$ cd /home/cereal/Document
```

This path, beginning with / to indicate the directory, is called an *absolute path*. If the current directory is /home/cereal, the relative path can be used:

```
$ cd Documents
```

If no parameters are entered, the cd command changes to the home directory of the current user:

```
$ cd
```

.. means the parent directory, accessed with the following command:

```
$ cd ..
```

Use the pwd command to display the absolute path name of the current directory:

```
$ pwd
/home/cereal
```

There are also symbols to represent special directories in Linux. For example, ~ indicates the user's home directory, so you can use the following command to go to the home directory:

```
$ cd ~
```

Searching for Files

Use the find command to search for files. The format of the command is

```
find directory name -name file name
```

You can search for specified files in the specified directory and all child directories. For example, input the following command to search for ifconfig files in the entire file system:

```
# find / -name ifconfig
```

This command starts at the root directory and searches for ifconfig files under all subdirectories. The command accesses all directories, many of which are not accessible to an ordinary user, so it's recommended that you execute this command under the root identity.

File Operation

Android has file-operation commands similar to those in Windows. The commands are listed in Table 5-1.

Table 5-1. *Android File-Operation Commands*

Command	Function	Format	Format description
cat	Show file contents	cat [-n] <file list>	n: Show the line number.
ln	Establish a hard/soft link	ln [-sf] <original file><destination file>	s: Soft link; the default is hard link. f: The destination file, if it exists, will be replaced
mkdir	Make a directory	mkdir <directory name>	Create a directory with given name
rmdir	Delete an empty directory	rmdir <directory name>	The directory to be deleted must be empty. To delete a non-empty directory, use the following command: rm –rf <directory name>

(continued)

Table 5-1. (*continued*)

Command	Function	Format	Format description
cp	Copy a file	cp [option] [<source path>]<source file> <destination path>[<destination file>]	Copy SOURCE to DEST, or multiple SOURCE(s) to DIRECTORY
mv	Move and rename a file	mv <source file> <destination file>	Rename SOURCE to DEST, or move SOURCE(s) to DIRECTORY.
rm	Delete a file	rm [option] <file name>	-i: Ask whether to delete. -f: Don't ask whether to delete. -r: Recursively delete the entire directory, like rmdir.
cmp	Compare files	cmp <file 1> <file 2>	Compares two files of any type and writes the results to the standard output.

For example, you can use the following command to display the contents of the /etc/passwd file:

$ cat /etc/passwd

Use the following command to copy the /etc/passwd file to the current directory:

$ cp /etc/passwd .

The . in this command indicates the current directory.

Modifying File/Directory Permissions

As mentioned, every file or directory has its own permission. Only users with the corresponding permission can perform operations. The permission must be modified if it doesn't match. Table 5-2 lists the Linux commands to modify file permissions.

Table 5-2. *File/Directory Permission-Modification Commands*

Command	Function	Format
chmod	Change the file/directory access permission (only the file owner and root user can do this)	chmod <octal digit>/<+/- w/r/x> <file name>
chgrp	Change the file group	chgrp <group name> <file name>
chown	Change the file owner (only the root user can do this)	chown <new owner> <file name>

For example, this command adds write permission for other users of the report.doc file:

chmod o+w report.doc

In Linux, the owner, users in the same group, and other users are represented by u, g, and o, respectively. The previous command adds write permission for other users (o).

The next example sets the group permission of report.doc tp rw (deletes x permission):

chmod g=rw report.doc

Permissions can also be represented by digits: the values for read, write, and execute are 4, 2, and 1, respectively. The digit of the allocated permissions is the sum of the three. For example, the following command sets the user permission of report.doc to rw (4 + 2 + 0 = 6), sets the group permission to r (4 + 0 + 0 = 4), and gives no permission for other users (0 + 0 + 0 = 0):

chmod 640 report.doc

This command allocates report.doc to the managers groups:

chgrp managers report.doc

To set the owner of report.doc to cereal and set its group to managers, you can use this command:

chown cereal.managers report.doc

This command changes the owner of all files under the current directory to cereal:

chown cereal *

Generally, only root users can use chown to change the owner of a file or directory.

In Windows, executability of a file is based on its suffix (such as .exe), but Linux doesn't have any requirement for the name of an executable file and determines whether the file is executable by the file attributes In Android, to make a file executable or non-executable, you usually use the chmod command to add or delete permission to execute.

Many command functions, such as file operations and permission operations, are usually performed in a file explorer, text editor, or other graphical user interface application. But with command-line operations, you have a new way to perform commands quickly. Android doesn't provide GUI applications such as a file explorer, so in most cases, you have to use the command line to complete those functions.

Working with the Executable File Path

If a path is not specified for an executable file, Linux can find the file with the path it saved in the system variable PATH, also called the *default path* or *path*. By default, Windows finds executable files in the current directory, but Linux only finds executable files in their default paths. So, you can use the following command to execute the executable file under the current directory:

```
./directory name of executable file
```

The following command shows the current path:

```
$ echo $PATH
```

You can also use the which command to find out whether the directory of an executable file has been included in the default path. For example, the following command finds out whether the gcc directory has been included in the default path:

```
$which gcc
```

If it is present in the default path, this command outputs the directory of the executable file: for example, /usr/bin/gcc. Otherwise, the command outputs nothing.

To add a directory in the default path, you can use the following command:

```
$ PATH=$PATH:/tools/bin
$ export PATH
```

or

```
$ export PATH=$PATH:/tools/bin
```

Add a /tools/bin path under PATH with : as the separator. Changing the PATH value or any environment variable must be exported through export; otherwise, the new PATH value will not take effect. This works only for the current user.

The export command can be added to shell files such as .bash_profile, .profile, and .bashrc so the command is executed before the command line starts each time.

A simple way of executing executable files without modifying the default path is to specify the absolute path before the executable file name.

Piping and Screening

The Linux pipe operation symbol | takes the output of one command as the input of the second one. Its function is the same as in Windows. For example, you can use the following command to show file content screen by screen:

```
$ cat /etc/passwd | more
```

The more command shows files screen by screen, suspending execution after each page of output; you tell it to continue by pressing any key. In the previous command, cat/etc/passwd means to output the content of the passwd file, and the output is used as the input (using the pipe command) of the more command.

The grep command can search and display certain lines in a file. For example:

```
$ grep cereal /etc/passwd
```

This command finds and displays lines containing "cereal" in the passwd file. The output is like this:

```
cereal:x:1000:1000:cereal,,,:/home/cereal:/bin/bash
```

The string to search can be enclosed with single quotes (' ') or double quotes (""). The text in ' ' is taken literally, whereas some special characters in "" are given special meaning by the shell. The previous command can also be written in these forms:

```
$ grep 'cereal' /etc/passwd
```

and

```
$ grep "cereal" /etc/passwd
```

In most cases, you use the pipe and grep commands to show screens of command output. For example:

```
$ ls -l /home/cereal/Document | grep qt
```

This command shows the corresponding line of the file/directory containing the qt field in the /home/cereal/Document directory.

Another command you have used is

```
$ ps -e | grep ssh
```

which lists all active processes containing the text "ssh" in the process name.

Running Commands in the Background

The execution of commands usually occupies the input/output of the console or the command-line window, which means you cannot input a command before the one that is executing ends. In contrast, if an application runs in the background, the console's input/output is not occupied. To run a command in the background, simply add & to the end of the command.

Interrupting the Execution of Commands in the Foreground

Press Ctrl+C to interrupt commands executing in the foreground. For example, the Linux ping command will endlessly ping a host, but you can end its execution as follows:

```
$ ping 127.0.0.1

PING 127.0.0.1 (127.0.0.1) 56(84) bytes of data.
64 bytes from 127.0.0.1: icmp_seq=1 ttl=64 time=0.027 ms
64 bytes from 127.0.0.1: icmp_seq=2 ttl=64 time=0.028 ms
64 bytes from 127.0.0.1: icmp_seq=3 ttl=64 time=0.029 ms
64 bytes from 127.0.0.1: icmp_seq=4 ttl=64 time=0.030 ms
64 bytes from 127.0.0.1: icmp_seq=5 ttl=64 time=0.031 ms
^C
--- 127.0.0.1 ping statistics ---
5 packets transmitted, 5 received, 0% packet loss, time 4462ms rtt min/avg/
max/mdev = 0.027/0.029/0.031/0.001 ms
$
```

After the fifth ping output item, the command was interrupted by pressing Ctrl+C, and the screen shows ^C.

Checking Hardware Information (Such as OS Version and CPU)

The uname command displays system information, including information related to the computer and OS. The syntax of the command is

```
uname [-amnrsv][--help][--version]
```

The parameters are as follows:

-a (all): Show all information

-m (machine): Show computer type

-n (nodename): Show the host name on the network

-r (release): Show the issue number of the OS

-s (sysname): Show the OS name

-v (version): Show the OS version

--help: Show help

--version: Show version information

For example, the following command shows the type of OS on the machine:

```
$ uname
Linux
```

The machine's OS is Linux.
This command shows the issue number of the Linux kernel:

```
$ uname -r
2.6.31-14-generic
```

The issue number is 2.6.31-14.
Linux puts the processor information in the cpuinfo file in the /proc directory, allowing you to check this through the file. You can check the processor model with the following command:

```
$ cat /proc/cpuinfo | grep "model name"
```

The output on an Asus Eee PC 1000HC netbook is

```
model name : Intel(R) Atom(TM) CPU N270 @ 1.60GHz
model name : Intel(R) Atom(TM) CPU N270 @ 1.60GHz
```

The machine has an Intel Atom processor N270.
Now check the number of logical CPUs:

```
$ cat /proc/cpuinfo | grep "processor"
```

The output on an Asus Eee PC 1000HC netbook is

```
processor : 0
processor : 1
```

The processor has two logical CPUs.
The following command will displays the ID of each logical CPU:

```
$ cat /proc/cpuinfo | grep "core id"
```

The output on an Asus Eee PC 1000HC netbook is

```
core id : 0
core id : 0
```

The two logical CPUs have the same core ID, which means the hyperthreading of the processor is open—that is, the hyperthreading technology simulates two CPUs.

Using the Android Development and Auxiliary Tools

The following sections describe how to use emulator, help file, DDMS, (adb), and common Android and telnet commands.

Using the Emulator

Android Virtual Device (AVD), the Android emulator, is a good tool to run to debug mobile applications. Using AVD was briefly introduced earlier in the book, and this section provides a more in-depth discussion.

The emulator can be started using one of three methods.

Method 1

Start the emulator in Eclipse by following these steps:

1. Start Eclipse, select Run ➤ Run Configuration, as shown in Figure 5-9.

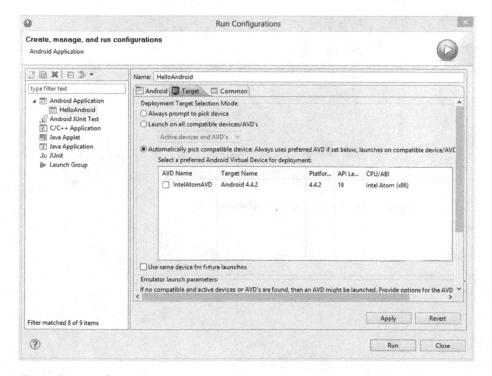

Figure 5-9. Emulator startup menu

2. In the Debug Configuration box, select \Android
    Application\XXX in the left column, and then click Target ➤
    "Automatically pick compatible device: Always uses preferred
    AVD ...". Click the Start button on the right after checking the
    specified emulator.

3. A Launch Options information box pops up (see Figure 5-10).
    Click Launch, and the emulator window opens (see Figure 5-11).

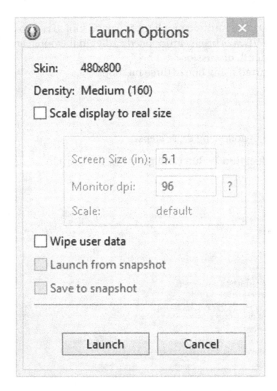

Figure 5-10. *Launch Options information box*

Figure 5-11. *Initial interface of the emulator when started separately*

Method 2

To start the emulator while running the application in Eclipse, on the menu bar, select Window ➤ Android Virtual Device Manager (see Figure 5-12).

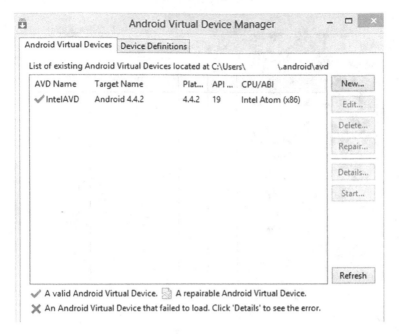

Figure 5-12. *The Android Virtual Device Manager*

Sometimes, when this method is used, the interface locks up. That is to say, after running the project (application) in Eclipse, the emulator sometimes shows an interface like the one in Figure 5-13. The application's interface is not visible, indicating the emulator is locked up.

Figure 5-13. *Interface when the emulator locks up at startup*

The solution is to click the menu button. If a window pops up, click Wait To Continue, and the application's interface will appear, as shown in Figure 5-14.

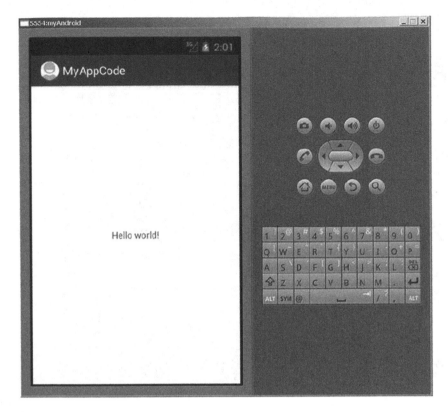

Figure 5-14. Interface after unlock

Method 3

AVD configurations can also be created and managed from command line using "android" tool as discussed here: http://developer.android.com/guide/developing/devices/managing-avds-cmdline.html

Example Creation of AVD from command line for Intel Architecture: avd create avd –n HC –t android-13 –s WXGA

Accept "yes" for custom hw and choose x86 for hw.cpu.arch propertyUsing the Help File

The Android development help file provides descriptions, explanations, and use examples for class and method prototypes involved in application development. You can read the help file either online, or offline as local files. The online reading function is more powerful because it supports auto-complete and search of class names. However, depending on the network speed, online reading may not be as responsive as offline reading. The two methods are explained next.

When you use Android SDK Manager (by selecting Window from the top menu in Eclipse) to download the Android packages, you see Documentation for Android SDK in each package. After you select and install it, all documents are copied into the docs folder, which is the subdirectory of the android-sdk installation directory in your system. The local help file is accessed through the index.html file in the docs. To use local help files, follow these steps:

1. Open the index.html file under the docs subdirectory of the android-sdk installation directory (in this case, D:\Android\ android-sdk\docs\index.html). In the browser window, an information bar asking to run ActiveX may pop up. Click to run the control.

2. Click Reference below the top of the page, as shown in figure 5-15.

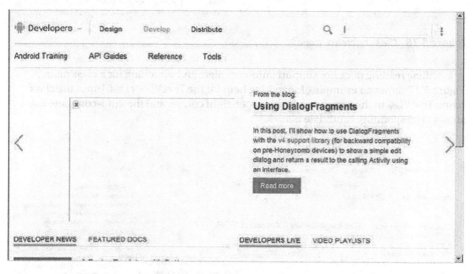

Figure 5-15. *Entry page for class references*

The help interface appears, as shown in Figure 5-16.

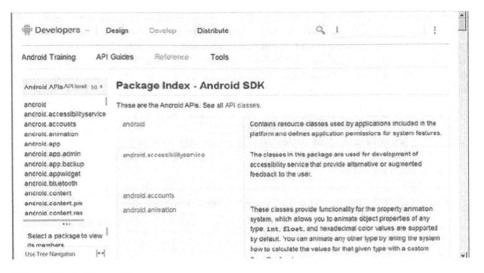

Figure 5-16. *Class reference page*

Offline reading does not support auto-complete and searching for a class name. Figure 5-17 shows an example of searching help for the TextView class. Input the class name TextView in the search bar in the upper-right corner, and the auto-complete list shows corresponding candidate names.

Figure 5-17. *Input interface for auto-complete and search of pages in offline reading mode*

When selecting a candidate in the list (in this example, the first one, android.widget.TextView, is selected), a network connection error will appear if no connection is available. The help file will not show corresponding information.

The online reading function is more powerful, and the steps are as follows:

1. Enter the URL http://android.com in the address bar of the web browser, and a screen like the one in Figure 5-18 appears.

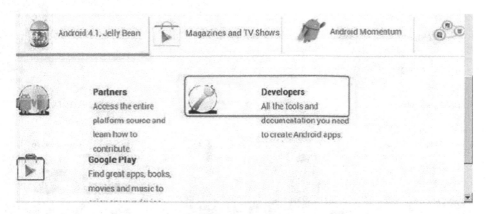

Figure 5-18. *Initial page of online reading*

2. Click Get The SDK on the bottom of the page, as shown in Figure 5-19.

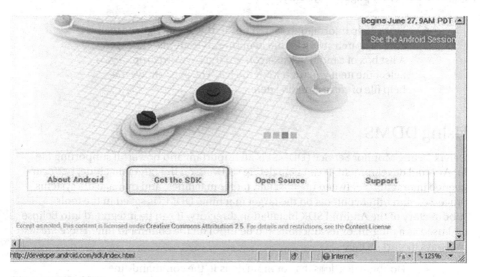

Figure 5-19. *SDK entry page*

3. Click Reference on the new page, as shown in Figure 5-20.

Figure 5-20. Entry page for references

4. In the help information search box in the upper-right corner, enter a search string for the item (in this example, "Log"). A list box of candidates that contain the keyword drops down. Select the item you want from the list. The page shows the help file of corresponding item.

Using DDMS

Dalvik Debug Monitor Service (DDMS) is an important and powerful supporting file for Android development. It can help debug software on the target machine, perform needed interactions between the host and target machines, and manage file systems, processes, and other contents on the target machine. DDMS is saved in the tools subdirectory of the Android SDK installation directory. It can be integrated into Eclipse and used as a plug-in, or its functions can be input on the command line. There are also two ways to start DDMS:

- Double-click ddms.bat or input ddms in the command-line window to run it.

- Start DDMS during program debugging in Eclipse.

DDMS can perform its functions on both the emulator and connected devices. If the system detects that both of them are running, DDMS is directed to the emulator by default.

DDMS sets up the link between the IDE and the target machine, which listen for debugging information through their respective ports, while DDMS can monitor the connection of the test terminal in real time. When a new test terminal is connected, DDMS captures the ID of target machine and sets up the debugger through adb, thus enabling instructions to be sent to the test terminal.

The following instructions show how to use DDMS integrated in Eclipse.

Showing the DDMS Button

In Eclipse, the DDMS interface is on the same level as the development editing and debug interfaces. Click the DDMS button to enter the DDMS interface. By default, Eclipse doesn't show the button, so you need to follow these steps:

1. Click Open Perspective in the toolbar.

2. Select DDMS in the pop-up box. The DDMS button is displayed in the upper-left corner of Eclipse, as shown in Figure 5-21.

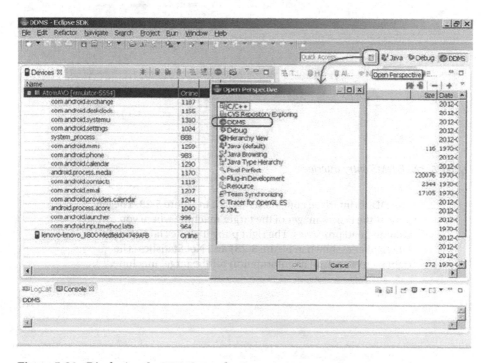

Figure 5-21. Displaying the DDMS start button

Starting DDMS

With the DDMS button now visible, you can perform the following steps to use the interface:

1. Start Eclipse, connect the phone or start the AVD emulator, and click DDMS in the upper-right corner of the window, as shown in Figure 5-22.

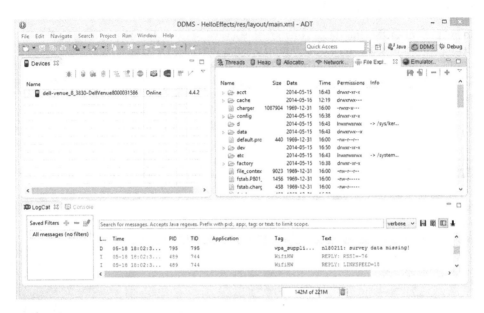

Figure 5-22. *DDMS entry interface*

2. The DDMS interface appears, as shown in Figure 5-23. The left pane is the task manager of the target machine where you can view and end processes. The right pane includes tabs such as File Explorer (shown in Figure 5-23) and Net Statistics. The right pane also displays information for the target machine.

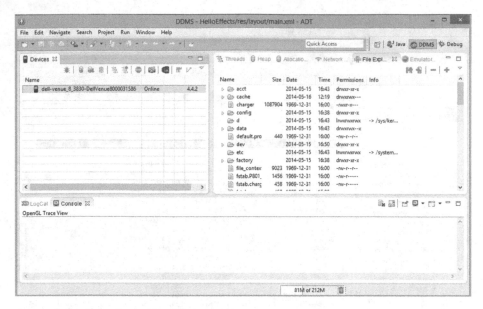

Figure 5-23. *DDMS initial interface*

File Transfer between Host and Target Machines, and File Management

DDMS can also perform file transfers (mutual copy) between the host and target machines (real device or emulator) and manage files on the target machine, as described next.

Copying a File from the Host Machine to the Target Machine

Follow these steps:

1. Click File Explorer in the right pane of DDMS interface. You see the buttons Pull A File From The Device, Push A File Onto The Device, and Delete The Selection In The Toolbar, as shown in Figure 5-24.

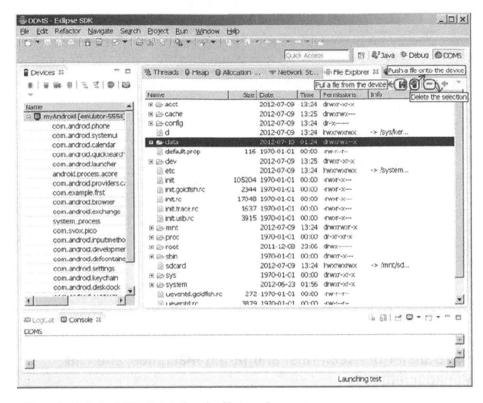

Figure 5-24. *Initial DDMS interface for file transfers*

2. In the right pane, you can see the entire file system of the target machine (the emulator is running in this example). Click to select the folder (the data folder in this example), click the Push A File Onto The Device button on the toolbar, and select a file (on the host machine) in the pop-up box, as shown in Figure 5-25.

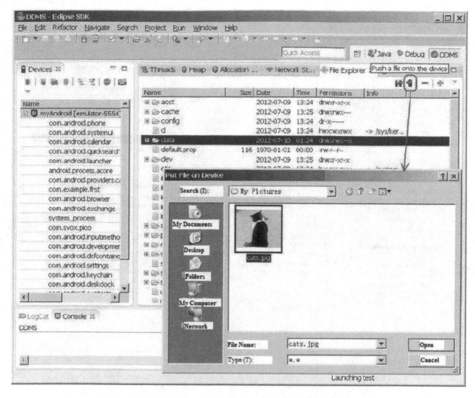

Figure 5-25. *Selecting a file to copy from the host machine to the target machine*

You can see the copied file (`cats.jpg` in this example) on the target machine, as shown in Figure 5-26.

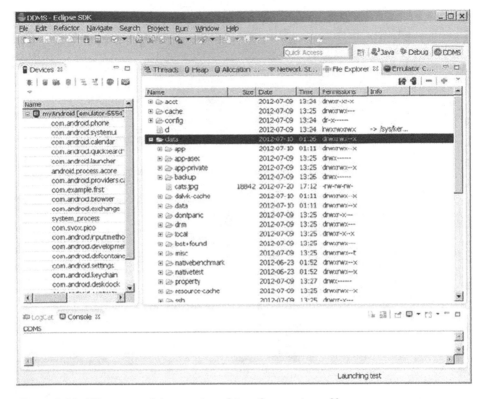

Figure 5-26. *File system of the target machine after copying a file*

Note that some folders on the target machine are not allowed to be uploaded due to the restriction on user authority. For example, if you select the root folder to upload files, an error will appear in the bottom message box, as shown in Figure 5-27.

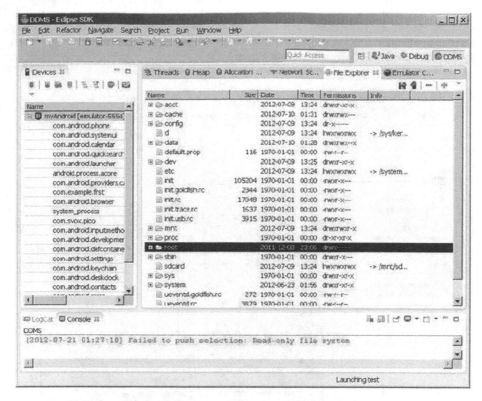

Figure 5-27. *Uploading a file under the root directory on the target machine*

Copying a File from the Target Machine to the Host Machine

Follow the same steps as in the previous section, but this time click the button Pull A File From The Device.

Deleting a File

Follow the same steps as in the section "Copying a File from the Host Machine to the Target Machine," but click the Delete The Selection button.

Process Management on the Target Machine

In DDMS, you can view the processes running on the target machine and perform some management tasks, such as Stop Process. Following is an introduction.

Starting Process Management for the Target Machine

Start an application (the test project in this example whose source code file is
MyAppCode.java) in Eclipse, as shown in Figure 5-28.

Figure 5-28. *Applications that have started before process view*

The application's interface running on the emulator is shown in Figure 5-29.

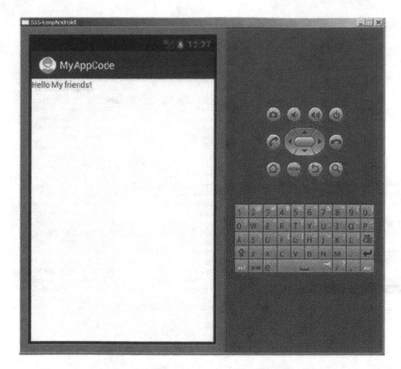

Figure 5-29. Application's interface started before process view

Start the DDMS interface by clicking the DDMS button at the upper-right corner in the Eclipse window of the host machine. You see the list of processes running on the target machine in the left pane. Find the process (com.example.test in this example) corresponding to the application in the list, as shown in Figure 5-30.

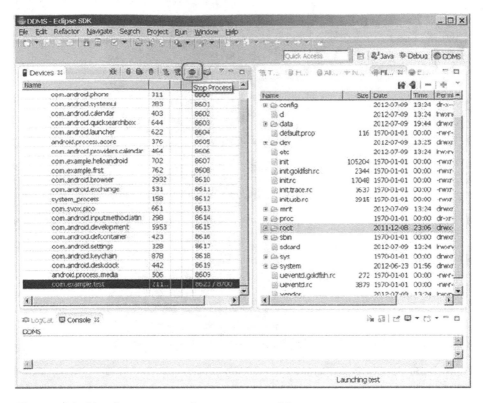

Figure 5-30. *List of processes running on target machine*

As you can see in the figure, DDMS monitors the first process `com.android.phone` (process ID: 311) on port 8600. If there are more target machines or more application processes, the monitoring port will increment in ascending order: The second process monitoring port will be assigned as 8601, the third process monitoring port will be assigned as 8602, and so on. DDMS receives all terminal commands via port 8700, which is called the *base port*.

In the upper-right corner is a row of very important buttons: Debug The Selected Process, Update Threads, Update Heap, Stop Process, and Screen Capture, which complete the corresponding operations. The following sections illustrate the use of these buttons, using Stop Process as the example.

Stopping a Designated Process

To stop an application, select the application process and then click the Stop Process button in the upper toolbar. You can see the application on the simulator has been terminated, as shown in Figure 5-31; the original process (`com.example.test`) is no longer shown in the DDMS process list in Eclipse.

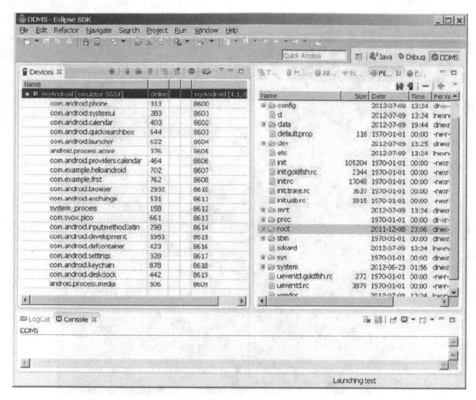

Figure 5-31. DDMS interface on the host machine after process termination

Taking a Target Machine Screen Capture

DDMS can also be used to capture a shot of the target machine's screen. The screenshot can be saved as a file on the host machine. The steps are as follows:

1. Start the target machine application, as shown in Figure 5-32.

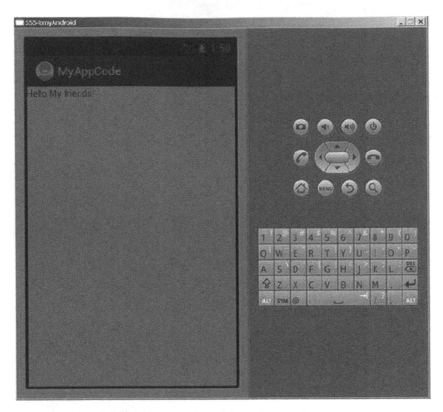

Figure 5-32. *Interface of the target machine before screen capture*

2. In the Eclipse environment of the host machine, click the Screen Capture button on the upper toolbar of the left pane, click the Save button in the pop-up box, and then click the Done button to close the dialog box, as shown in Figure 5-33.

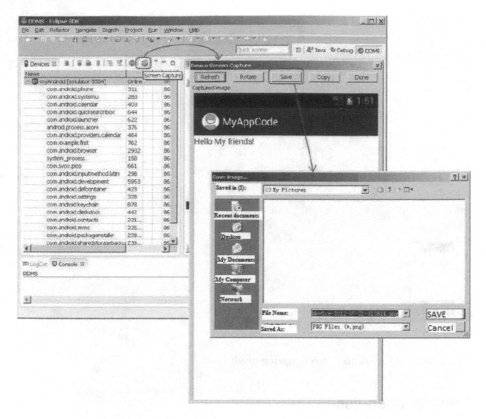

Figure 5-33. *Performing a screen capture on the target machine*

You can see the screenshot in the folder on the host machine, as shown in Figure 5-34.

Figure 5-34. *Host machine screen capture result*

Emulator Operation

If the target machine is an emulator, you can see the emulator operation interface by clicking the Emulator Control tab in the right pane of DDMS, as shown in Figure 5-35.

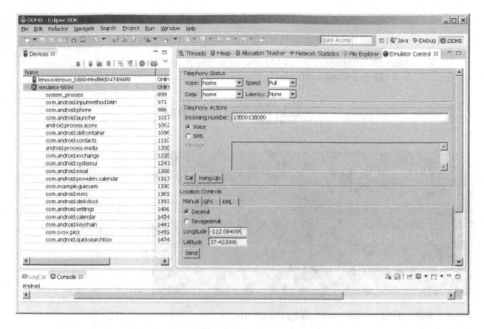

Figure 5-35. *Emulator control interface of DDMS*

Functions on this panel allow the test device to easily simulate some interactive functions of real phones, such as answering phone calls, simulating various network conditions according to options, and simulating the receiving of SMS and sending of virtual address coordinates to test GPS functions. Here are several function descriptions.

- *Telephony status*: Simulate voice quality and signal connection mode by using options

- *Telephony actions*: Simulate telephone answering and sending SMS to the test device

- *Location control:* Simulate geographical coordinates, or simulate the dynamic change of route coordinates and display the default geographical indications in the following three ways:

    - *Manual*: Send two-dimensional latitude and longitude coordinates to the test device manually

    - *GPX*: Import a sequence of dynamically changing geographical coordinates via a GPX file to simulate the changing GPS value during the movement

    - *KML*: Import unique geographical indications via a KML file and show them on the test device dynamically according to the changing geographical coordinates

Following you see how to use these functions, using as an example sending SMS:

1. Complete the Emulator Control\Telephony Actions box.

2. After clicking Send, open Messaging in the Android emulator. You see the SMS, as shown in Figure 5-36.

Figure 5-36. *Title of SMS received by the emulator*

3. Click the new SMS to view its details, as shown in Figure 5-37.

Figure 5-37. *Content of the SMS received by the emulator*

176

Using adb at Command Prompt

Android Debug Bridge (adb) is a general-purpose debugging tool provided by Android. With this tool, you can manage the status of the device or phone simulator and perform the following operations:

- Quickly update the code on the device or phone emulator, such as the application or Android system

- Run shell commands on the device

- Manage the reserved ports on the device or the phone emulator

- Copy and paste files on the device or the phone emulator

adb's functions are generally integrated into the Eclipse development environment. This section introduces other functions of adb, which generally are entered on the command line. Table 5-4 lists the three frequently used commands.

Table 5-4. *Common Commands for Viewing Information on the Target Machine*

Command	Description
adb devices	View the information of the target machine
adb get-product	View the product model of the target machine
adb get-serialno	View the serial number of the target machine

Using adb at Command Prompt is very helpful when the emulator isn't started or a phone isn't connected, the output result is empty after you type this command in the host machine's Windows command line:

```
C:\Documents and Settings>adb devices
List of devices attached
```

If the adb service has not been started, the above command will prompt information for start-up:

```
C:\Documents and Settings>adb devices
* daemon not running. starting it now on port 5037 *
* daemon started successfully *
List of devices attached
```

After starting the emulator, run the command, and the emulator device information is displayed:

```
C:\Documents and Settings>adb devices
List of devices attached emulator-5554 device
```

After starting the emulator and connecting to the phone, the command displays the following

```
C:\Documents and Settings>adb devices
List of devices attached emulator-5554 device Medfield04749AFB device
```

where emulator-5554 refers to the target machine corresponding to the emulator, and Medfield04749AFB refers to the target machine corresponding to the Lenovo phone.

When only the phone is connected, the adb get-serialno command only outputs the serial number of the effective target machine:

```
C:\Documents and Settings>adb get-serialno
Medfield04749AFB
```

Running Commands on the Target Machine

You know that Android is based on Linux, and you have been introduced to the Linux commands supported by Android. However, most mobile devices running Android have no physical keyboard for command input. Even then, the Linux commands are useful. You can make use of some auxiliary tools, such as adb, to achieve remote input of Android commands. By using adb shell commands, you can enter commands on the host machine and make the target machine execute them. In other words, the keyboard and screen of the host machine simulate a terminal on the target machine. The target machine here can be either a real device or an emulator. Follow these steps:

1. Enter the adb shell command on the host machine's Windows command line:

    ```
    C:\Documents and Settings> adb shell
    ```

2. Input the Android command of the target machine. For example:

```
# pwd
pwd
/
# ls -l
ls -l
drwxr-xr-x root     root     2012-07-09 13:24 acct
drwxrwx--- system   cache    2012-07-09 13:25 cache
dr-x------ root     root     2012-07-09 13:24 config
lrwxrwxrwx root     root     2012-07-09 13:24 d -> /sys/kernel/debug
drwxrwx--x system   system   2012-07-09 19:44 data
-rw-r--r-- root     root     116 1970-01-01 00:00 default.prop
drwxr-xr-x root     root     2012-07-09 13:25 dev
lrwxrwxrwx root     root     2012-07-09 13:24 etc -> /system/etc
-rwxr-x--- root     root     105204 1970-01-01 00:00 init
-rwxr-x--- root     root     2344 1970-01-01 00:00 init.goldfish.rc
```

```
-rwxr-x--- root      root      17048 1970-01-01 00:00 init.rc
-rwxr-x--- root      root      1637 1970-01-01 00:00 init.trace.rc
-rwxr-x--- root      root      3915 1970-01-01 00:00 init.usb.rc
drwxrwxr-x root      system    2012-07-09 13:24 mnt
dr-xr-xr-x root      root      1970-01-01 00:00 proc
drwx------ root      root      2011-12-08 23:06 root
drwxr-x--- root      root      1970-01-01 00:00 sbin
lrwxrwxrwx root      root      2012-07-09 13:24 sdcard -> /mnt/sdcard
drwxr-xr-x root      root      1970-01-01 00:00 sys
drwxr-xr-x root      root      2012-06-23 01:56 system
-rw-r--r-root         root      272 1970-01-01 00:00 ueventd.goldfish.rc
-rw-r--r-- root      root      3879 1970-01-01 00:00 ueventd.rc
lrwxrwxrwx root      root      2012-07-09 13:24 vendor -> /system/vendor
# cd
cd
cd: HOME not set
# echo $PATH
echo $PATH
/sbin:/vendor/bin:/system/sbin:/system/bin:/system/xbin
# ifconfig eth0
ifconfig eth0
eth0: ip 10.0.2.15 mask 255.255.255.0 flags [up broadcast running multicast]
```

3. Use the exit command to stop execution on the target
    machine and return to the command-line interface on the
    host machine:

    ```
    # exit
    exit
    C:\Documents and Settings>
    ```

■ **Note**   The Linux shell in Android has been simplified a lot. As a result, many common Linux commands are not supported.

Installing Application Packages on the Target Machine

You can use the adb install command to install or uninstall application packages on the target machine. The format of the software installation command is

```
adb install XXX.apk
```

where XXX.apk is a file in the current directory of the host machine. For example, to install file browser software, follow these steps:

1. The original application on the target machine (emulator) is shown in Figure 5-38.

Figure 5-38. *Application executing on the virtual machine before software installation*

2. Run the following commands at the command line on the host machine:

```
E:\temp\temp>adb install file_browser.apk
92 KB/s (2617375 bytes in 27.546s)
pkg: /data/local/tmp/file_browser.apk
Success
```

The installation file, file_browser.apk, is located under the current directory (E:\temp\temp in this example) of the host machine.

You can see that the target machine has the new application ES File Explorer installed, as shown in Figure 5-39.

Figure 5-39. *Virtual machine application after software installation*

You can start the new app by clicking its icon, as shown in Figure 5-40.

Figure 5-40. *Operation interface of the newly installed software*

The software can be installed on a real phone in the same way.

Uninstalling Software on the Target Machine

You can use the adb shell command rm to uninstall software on the target machine. For example:

```
E:\temp\temp>adb shell rm /data/app/*.apk
```

The software (*.apk) is installed via adb and located in the /data/app/ directory; therefore, it is not necessary to designate a path during installation. It is only required that you execute the rm command during uninstallation. However, the rm command is very powerful and can cause irreversible loss of data if not used properly. The safe and recommended method to uninstall an app is

```
adb uninstall packagename
```

Transferring Files between the Host and Target Machines

The command adb push can be used to copy files from the host machine to the target machine, and the command adb pull can be used to copy files from the target machine to the host machine.

Enabling and Disabling the adb Service

You can disable the adb service using the adb kill-server command and enable it with the adb start-server command.

Other Functions

The following is a list of some other useful adb functions:

Port forwarding (forwards the default port TCP5555 to port 1234)

adb forward adb forward tcp:5555 tcp:1234

Access the database sqlite3

adb shell sqlite3

Wait for running devices

adb wait-for-devices

View the bug report

adb bugreport

Record the radio communication log

adb shell logcat -b ratio

Generally speaking, there are many radio communication logs, and it is unnecessary to get the record during operation, but you can get the record by command.

Using Android Commands

Android commands are provided by the batch file android.bat, located under the tools subdirectory in the android-sdk installation directory. These commands can manage the emulator and the APIs, mostly through Eclipse. Of course, management can also be achieved by entering Android commands on the command line. The following sections introduce these commands.

Viewing the Installed Emulator

You can view the installed emulator by running the android list avd command. For example:

```
C:\Documents and Settings>android list avd
Available Android Virtual Devices:
Name: AtomAVD
Path: C:\Documents and Settings\hlgu\.android\avd\AtomAVD.avd
Target machine: Android 4.0.3 (API level 15)
ABI: x86
Skin: WVGA800
Sdcard: 1024M
---------
Name: myAndroid
Path: C:\Documents and Settings\hlgu\.android\avd\myAndroid.avd
Target machine: Android 4.1 (API level 16)
ABI: armeabi-v7a
Skin: WVGA800
Sdcard: 1024M
Snapshot: true
```

The output shows that the system has two emulators installed: AtomAVD emulator (name line) with CPU of x86 (ABI line) and myAndroid emulator with CPU of armeabi-v7a.

Viewing the Version Information of the Currently Supported APIs

You can view the version information of the currently supported APIs by running the android list target command. For example:

```
C:\Documents and Settings>android list target
Available Android targets:
----------
id: 1 or "android-15"
Name: Android 4.0.3
Type: Platform
API level: 15
Revision: 3
Skins: HVGA, QVGA, WQVGA400, WQVGA432, WSVGA, WVGA800 (default), WVGA854,
WXGA720, WXGA800
ABIs : x86
----------
id: 2 or "Google Inc.:Google APIs:15"
Name: Google APIs
Type: Add-On
Vendor: Google Inc.
```

Revision: 2
Description: Android + Google APIs
Based on Android 4.0.3 (API level 15)
Libraries:
* com.google.android.media.effects (effects.jar)
Collection of video effects
* com.android.future.usb.accessory (usb.jar)
API for USB Accessories
* com.google.android.maps (maps.jar)
API for Google Maps
Skins: WVGA854, WQVGA400, WSVGA, WXGA720, HVGA, WQVGA432, WVGA800 (default),
QVGA, WXGA800
ABIs : armeabi-v7a
----
id: 3 or "HTC:HTC OpenSense SDK:15"
Name: HTC OpenSense SDK
Type: Add-On
Vendor: HTC
Revision: 2
Based on Android 4.0.3 (API level 15)
Libraries:
* htc-extension (HTCSDK.jar)
HTC generic extension library
Skins: WVGA854, WQVGA400, WSVGA, WXGA720, HVGA, WQVGA432, WVGA800 (default),
QVGA, WXGA800
ABIs : no ABIs.
----
id: 4 or "android-16"
Name: Android 4.1
Type: Platform
API level: 16
Revision: 1
Skins: HVGA, QVGA, WQVGA400, WQVGA432, WSVGA, WVGA800 (default), WVGA854,
WXGA720, WXGA800, WXGA800-7in
ABIs : armeabi-v7a
----
id: 5 or "Google Inc.:Google APIs:16"
Name: Google APIs
Type: Add-On

Vendor: Google Inc.
Revision: 2
Description: Android + Google APIs
Based on Android 4.1 (API level 16)

```
Libraries:
* com.google.android.media.effects (effects.jar)
Collection of video effects
* com.android.future.usb.accessory (usb.jar)
API for USB Accessories
* com.google.android.maps (maps.jar)
API for Google Maps
Skins: WVGA854, WQVGA400, WSVGA, WXGA800-7in, WXGA720, HVGA, WQVGA432,
WVGA 800 (default), QVGA, WXGA800
ABIs : armeabi-v7a
```

The output shows that the current development environment has several APIs installed including android-15, Google Inc.: Google APIs:15, HTC:HTC OpenSense SDK:15, android-16, and Google Inc.:Google APIs:16.

Creating an Emulator

The Android create avd -n command can be used to create an emulator, but you generally create it in Eclipse.

Starting the Emulator

Most of the time, you start the emulator in Eclipse using the emulator command. For example:

```
C:\Documents and Settings>emulator -avd myAndroid
```

myAndroid is the name of emulator listed by the android list avd command. This command will start the myAndroid emulator.

Using Telnet for Emulator Commands

You can use Telnet to enter commands on the target machine (emulator) from the host machine and make the target machine (emulator) execute the commands. In this way, the host machine (Windows, Linux, and Mac systems) becomes a console terminal of the emulator. The format of Telnet commands is

```
telnet localhost <console-port>
```

For example:

```
telnet localhost 5554
```

In general, the serial number of the Android emulator is 5554. When running Telnet, you need to change the console-port to the serial number of the emulator you intend to connect to: for example, 5554, 5556, or 5558. After connecting to the emulator using telnet localhost 5554, enter the help command.

After logging in to the Android emulator terminal mode, the available commands include event, geo, gsm, kill, network, power, redir, sms, vm, and window; they are used to control the Android emulator. Many of these commands can be replaced by the DDMS emulator graphical operation introduced previously. The following sections introduce these commands.

event Command

The format is

```
event text testmessage
```

This command can send four events—send, types, codes, and text—to the emulator. For example, after event text testmessage sends a literal string "test message" to the emulator, you immediately see this message on the screen of the Android emulator.

geo Command

The format is

```
geo <fix|nmea>
```

For example:

```
geo fix 121.5 25.4 10
geo nmea $GPRMC,071236,A,3751.65,S,14527.36,E,000.0,073.0,130309,011.3,E*62
```

The geo command can send the GPS location to the emulator. geo fix sends a set of fixed GPS locations represented by longitude, latitude, and height, which can be obtained from the map on some web sites, such as longitude 121.5, latitude 25.4, and height 10 meters. When the Android device is connected to an external GPS device via USB, you can use the geo nmea command to send locations to the external GPS device.

The National Electrical Manufacturers Association (NEMA) developed the NEMA 0183 protocol for GPS devices. The format of gps nema command is complicated and composed of 12 fields, but thanks to this complexity, the command provides more accurate positioning than the geo fix command. The format of the gps nema command is as follows:

```
$GPRMC,<1>,<2>,<3>,<4>,<5>,<6>,<7>,<8>,<9>,<10>,<11>,<12>*hh
$GPRMC,hhmmss.ss,A,IIII.II,a,yyyyy.yy,a,x.x,x.x,ddmmyy,x.x,a*hh
$GPRMC (Recommended minimum specific GPS/Transit data)
```

187

The fields are as follows:

- UTC, in the format of hhmmss (hour, minute, and second). For example: 071236.

- Positioning state: A = Available positioning, V = Void positioning.

- Latitude, in the format of ddmm.mm (d refers to degrees, m refers to minutes). For example: 3751.65 = 37 degrees 51.65 minutes.

- Latitude hemisphere N (northern hemisphere) or S (southern hemisphere).

- Longitude, in the format of dddmm.mm. For example: 14527.36 = 145 degrees 27.36 minutes.

- Longitude hemisphere E (east longitude) or W (west longitude).

- Ground speed (000.0 to 999.9 knots; 0 will also be transmitted). For example: stationary 000.0.

- Ground direction (000.0-359.9 degrees; 0 will also be transmitted). For example: 073.0.

- UTC date, in the format of ddmmyy (date, month, and year). For example: 130309.

- Magnetic declination (000.0-180.0 degrees; 0 will also be transmitted). For example: 011.3.

- Direction of magnetic declination: E (East) or W (West).

- Mode indicator (in NEMA 0183 protocol, A = autonomous positioning, D = difference, E = estimate, N = null information). *hh is the checksum. For example: *62 gsm call 5556688.

gsm Command

The gsm command can simulate the calling state of a GSM phone and has parameters including call, busy, hold, accept, cancel, data, voice, and status. Simply by adding any phone number behind a parameter, you can simulate calling a GSM phone in the Android emulator.

kill Command

The kill command immediately closes the emulator window in the terminal mode of the Android emulator.

network Command

The network command is a network-management and -operation command. It has various parameters to complete different network functions. For example:

```
network status
```

This command is used to view the network-transmission status of the Android emulator.

Here are some additional examples:

```
network speed full
network speed umts
```

Network speed can change the phone's network-transmission modes, including gsm (GSM/CSD), gprs (GPRS), edge (EDGE/EGPRS), umts (UMTS/3G), hsdpa (HSDPA/3.5G), and full-speed transmission, which are selected randomly. This is the default network setting of the Android system.

power Command

This command displays whether the current power status of the phone is AC power connected, as well as the battery's remaining power:

```
power display
```

redir Command

Similar to the adb forward command, the redir command can display and manage the emulator's TCP or UDP communication port. For example:

```
redir add tcp: 5000:6000
```

You can use this command to direct the messages received by TCP port 5000 of the hosting system to TCP port 6000 of the Android emulator.

This command lists the TCP or UDP communication port that has been directed:

```
redir list
```

The redir del command can delete the communication port that has been directed:

```
redir del tcp: 5000
```

sms Command

You can use the `sms` command to send SMS:

```
sms send <phone number> <SMS>
```

For example:

```
sms send 5556688 this is a test sms
```

This sends the SMS text "this is a test" to the phone number 5556688, and the Android emulator will immediately receive it.

Window scale? Command

The `window scale` command can change the emulator's window size. For example:

```
window scale factor (factor: 0.1-3.0)
window scale 1.2
```

The first command sets the screen scale factor to between 0.1 and 3.0. The second command scales the window size of the Android emulator 1.2 times.

Summary

For application developers, it is critical that the applications you build can be run on all the devices made by different OEMs and on different platforms. However, OEMs have been tailoring and customizing the Android OS of their devices to meet the unique needs of the set of the software and hardware they use. As a result, understanding Android OS customization is helpful for you to better design applications. The next chapter discusses customization of the Android OS, including the installation and reflash of the Android image, which is the fastest way for you to update your test platform to the latest Android version directly from the device manufacturer.

## CHAPTER 6

Customization and Installation of Android

Due to the characteristics of any embedded systems, such as resource constraints, tailoring and customization are important features for an embedded OS, and Android is no exception. This chapter provides a general discussion of customization in an embedded OS and then explains the customization of Android, specifically.

Tailoring and Customization of an Embedded OS

Not all functions and services provided by the embedded OS are included in a special embedded application, for two reasons. First, the embedded system is always resource constrained, especially with regard to storage space; thus it is impossible to include all redundant functions in the system at release. Second, many commercial embedded OSs collect a licensing fee based on the components chosen by the user. So, users should tailor the embedded OS according to their individual needs. The principle of OS customization is shown in Figure 6-1.

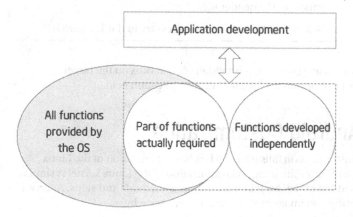

Figure 6-1. Principle of OS customization

For example, Windows XP Embedded OS offers tens of thousands of components—more than the functions of desktop Windows XP. But for a subway baffle-gate system based on Windows XP Embedded, for example, components such as Windows Media Player, the Internet Explorer browser, the DirectX settings panel, and Explorer task manager are not required. Eliminating such components reduces the hardware resources required by the system, thus reducing the cost; and this makes the system operate faster, thereby improving efficiency.

A majority of embedded OSs provide means for customization and tailoring. However, there are many different tailoring modes: some start with compiling source code, which requires the user to configure the option of conditional compilation; some start by linking the target files, linking to different library files according to the user's configuration; and the remaining modes extract precompiled files from the existing binary file library according to the user's choice. Table 6-1 lists the customization modes provided by frequently used embedded OSs.

Table 6-1. *Customization Modes of Different Embedded Operating Systems*

Embedded OS	Customization Modes
Windows CE	Provide Platform Builder IDE and graphical component options. Link different library files according to the selected components.
Embedded Linux	For the kernel, generate config files via make config before; then compile according to the configuration files.
Windows XP Embedded	Provide Target Designer IDE and graphical component options. Extract required binary files according to the selected components; no compilation is necessary for the linking process.
mC/OS-II	Selectively and conditionally compile some part of the code according to the value defined by the C language macro in the header file.
VxWorks	Select which modules are necessary in the Tornado IDE.

After system customization, you get an embedded OS that runs on the target hardware device and has been optimized for the special application field.

Overview of Android Customization

Theoretically, Android customization falls into two levels: customization of the Linux kernel and customization of the entire image. Customization of the Linux kernel is similar to customization of embedded Linux: both involve the same methods and steps. Android customization mainly focuses on image customization. Let's see why.

ROM Package/Image

The Android image is commonly known as a read-only memory (ROM) package, which is the system package of an Android phone. The reason for this naming convention is that mobile phones prior to Android phones, including smartphones (such as Nokia and WM) and non-smart phones (such as Sony Ericsson, Moto P2K platform, and MTK), all have a separate ROM chip storage system file. So, the system file is referred to as ROM package or ROM image.

The image is a cross-compiled binary Linux file that can be installed and run on some embedded device, becoming the OS of the device. To better understand this concept, let's review the typical development process, shown in Figure 6-2.

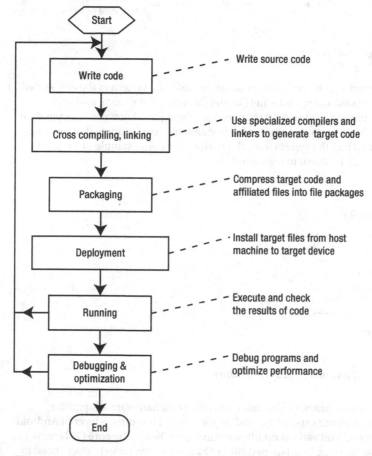

Figure 6-2. Development process for Android software

For embedded software, generally speaking, developing Android software requires the same steps as general-purpose software: designing, encoding, compiling, linking, packaging, deploying, debugging, and optimizing. For some Android systems, testing and verification steps are also required. The OS deployed on the embedded logic device also goes through such phases. For example, for a Linux system, you get its kernel source code, cross-compile, and generate code that can be executed on the embedded target machine; then you compress and package this code to form the image file (see Figure 6-3). The last step is deployment. Unlike the deployment of an application file, the deployment of an OS image file is referred to as *installation* due to the particularity of its operation.

Figure 6-3. *Image use process*

The image file (package) of a complete executable software system in the embedded system consists of the bootloader, OS kernel (kernel for short), file system, and user applications. The actual image file usually adopts a partition (also known as independent layer) structure to store all parts that are located in different areas (modules) of the image, and all parts are loaded into the system from the bottom layer. An example of a typical embedded system image is shown in Figure 6-4.

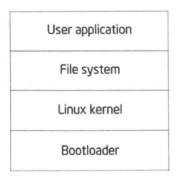

Figure 6-4. *Example of an embedded system image*

The Android image includes a bootloader, the core OS, a hardware adaptation module, a file system, the user experience, and applications. The core OS layer of Android includes the Linux kernel and various middleware modules. Below the core OS layer is the hardware adaptation layer. To adapt to different hardware, diversified drivers need to be installed for the OS. Without these drivers, the OS cannot use the hardware to operate as usual. Therefore, the image consists of the drivers and any applications developed by the user.

The Android image usually exists in the form of a compressed file (.zip, tar.gz, or a similar file format), which usually contains the file and folders shown in Table 6-2. The file structure can be seen after the compressed file is decompressed.

Table 6-2. *File Structure of an Android Image File*

Name	Property r	Remarks
META-IN	Directory	Optional; may be unavailable in some images
system	Directory	
boot.img	File	

The function and structure of the files and folders are as follows:

boot.img *file:* The system image, including the Linux kernel, bootloader, and ramdisk launched by the system. A ramdisk is a small file system that holds the core files needed to initialize the system. The boot.img file is created using an open source tool called mkbootimg.

META-INF *directory:* The system-update script, with the path META-INF\com\google\android\updater-script.

system\app *directory:* All system-provided applications such as calendar, contacts, Gmail, and so on. You can put your application's .apk file in this directory so it can be directly installed when the ROM is reflashed.

system\bin *directory:* System commands such as top, which can be executed after logging in through the adb shell.

system\etc *directory:* Configuration files.

system\font *directory:* All kinds of fonts.

system\framework *directory:* Java core files, such as .jar files. Under the Dalvik virtual machine (DVM), it supports the framework developed by the user via Java.

system\lib *directory:* Android local shared libraries that consist of .so files, which are shared objects in the form of ELF binaries, compiled by assembler, C, or C++.

system\media *directory:* Media files such as bootanimation.zip, which consists of .png pictures used for boot animation and for changing the boot image. Under the audio directory are some audio files that are used as ringtones and for notifications.

Overview of Android Image Customization

Android image customization, commonly known as *creating Android ROM* (*creating ROM* for short), is an academic term. The Android core OS layer has multiple components, and the applications vary in different systems; image customization decides which components and applications are written into the image file of the target system. The process makes a personal customized system file into a flashable ROM image. This is also known as a *system firmware update*.

The ready-made Android image can be installed onto an Intel Atom processor-based system (that is, a mobile phone, tablet, or the like) via USB flash and SD card. Then the system with the Android image will have the capability to enter the Android operating environment at self-start.The MicroSD card, originally called the TransFlash Card, was launched by SanDisk. It is 15 × 11 × 1 mm, about the size of a fingernail. It can be used in an SD card slot via an SD adapter card and is widely used in mobile phones.

You can create Android ROM in the following ways:

- Compile the Android source code, which is a little complex.

- Create or customize your own ROM based on the existing ROM.

The process of Android image customization is shown in Figure 6-5.

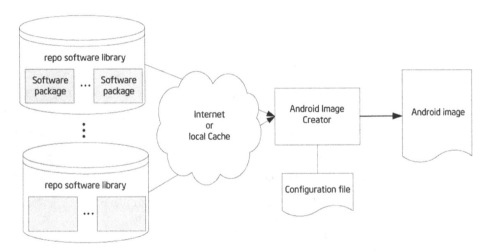

Figure 6-5. *Process of Android image customization*

Example of Android Image Customization

The following example illustrates the second way to customize Android: by creating ROM using the cloned ROM image released by device manufacturer for targeted hardware. In this way, the Android customization includes structure parsing for Android system folder, application software updates, and the customization of the ROM signature package. The steps are as follows:

1. Download the compiled ROM package from Android's official website, your mobile phone manufacturer's official website (for example, the website for the Lenovo K900 mobile phone), or websites providing an Android image. For example, the ROM provided by the Lenovo K900 mobile phone's website (www.lenovocare.com.cn/ProductDetail.aspx?id=719) is shown in Table 6-3. Be noted that since the Lenovo K800 and K900 phones are sold in China market, the software dates are only provided by Lenovo's official site in Chinese language.

Table 6-3. *Information in the ROM Package on the Lenovo K900 Website*

ROM Name	Description	Android Version	Date of Release
K900_1_S_2_162_0074	Official update	4.0.4	Aug. 8, 2012
K900_1_S_2_162_0086	Official update	4.0.4	Aug. 15, 2012
K900_1_S_2_019_0113_130903	Official update	4.2.0	Sep. 3, 2013
K900_source	Official update	4.4	May 23, 2014

2. Compress all the ROM files into one folder (named NewsROM" in this example).

3. Delete and add files in the ROM folder (NewsROM in this example) to tailor and customize Android.

   Some customization examples are as follows:

   • Go to the data\app directory to check whether the preinstalled applications are what you need. At this point you can remove unnecessary apps. You can also add the default installed applications you need.

   • Go to the system\app directory and customize the system applications for your device. You can delete unwanted system applications or add your special-built or customized applications (as customized .apk files). Be careful: some system applications are dependent on others, so best practice is to test before the customization to fix dependencies and other issues prior to implementing the changes to the Android system image.

   • Go to the system\media directory to make modifications such as changing the boot image or adding a customized ringtone.

   • Go to the system\bin directory to add commands and so forth.

If you're worried about deleting some files accidently and thus causing failure at startup, you should adopt a conservative approach: execute delete or add operations only for files in the data/app and system/app folders.

4. Compress the modified ROM folder as a .zip file. Ensure that the contents, including META-INF, system, boot.img, and data (optional), are displayed when you double-click the compressed file.

5. Install and configure the Java environment. The Java environment is required in the following steps to support the operation of the auto-sign tool, so you need to install and set up Java operation. Download the latest JDK (jdk1.7.0 in this example), and install it; then follow these steps:

   a. Set the Java environment variable as follows: right-click My Computer and select [Properties] ➤ [Advanced] ➤ [Environment Variables] ➤ [System Variables] ➤ [New] in the pop-up shortcut menu.

   b. In the dialog box, set [Variable Name] to "JAVA_HOME variable value: JAVA installation directory". Find [path] in the same place, double-click it, and add "C:\JDK1.7.0;.;C:\JDK1.7.0\bin" after the variable value.

   c. Reboot the system.

   d. Test. Enter Java commands in the command-line window. The configuration is successful if no error message appears.

6. Use the sign tool to sign the .zip packages. The steps are as follows:

   a. Download the auto-sign tool and unpack it under a directory (myautosign in this example). The tool can be downloaded at http://androidforums.com/developer-101/8665-how-signing-roms.html.

   b. Rename the .zip file package to update.zip, and copy it to the directory where you unpacked auto-sign (the myautosign directory).

   c. Run the sign.bat file under the directory where you unpacked auto-sign.

   d. After the customization build, the directory contains an update_signed.zip file, which is the signed ROM package and the customized ROM package you need.

Installation/Reflash of the Android Image

Image installation is required to use the customized image on the target machine. In other words, the process of image customization and use must go through two stages: image generation (production) and image installation, as shown in Figure 6-6.

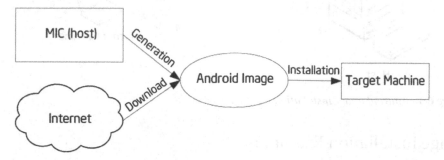

Figure 6-6. *Image generation and installation*

Image installation means installing the Android image on the target device or emulator. This process is commonly known as *reflashing*. Reflashing an Android phone is equivalent to reinstalling the system for the phone, which is similar to computer system reinstallation. Generally speaking, when a computer needs system reinstallation, you use a system disk or an image file. When an Android phone needs to be reflashed, you burn an official or third-party ROM image file into the ROM via a tool and install a new system for the phone.

The official Android website often releases the latest Android image systems for users, so you can download image files directly to skip image-generation stage. For users, the customization and installation process can be very simple: download the image, and reflash.

Android installation also involves *recovery* and *wiping*:

> *Recovery* is a mode of the mobile device. Through recovery, users can install the system (that is, reflash ROM), empty various data from the phone, partition a memory card, back up and restore data, and so on. Recovery is similar to the Ghost one-key recovery function on a computer.

> *Wipe* means to erase and remove. Wiping is an option in recovery mode; it removes various data from the phone, similar to restoring factory defaults. Wipe is most commonly used before the reflash. Users may see the Wipe prompt, which suggests the need to clear data before the reflash.

As mentioned, Android installation is essentially an issue of deployment in the process of software cross-development, but generally you adopt offline programming instead of online programming. In the installation process, the media you use are SD cards and other portable external storage devices. This process is shown in Figure 6-7. The installation is divided into two steps: first, place the image from the host on the portable SD card external storage device; second, start the machine from the portable external storage device and install Android on the target machine.

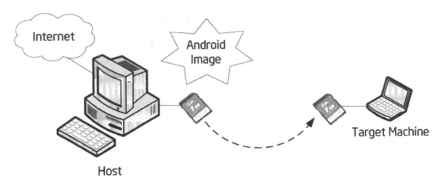

Figure 6-7. *Android image installation*

Image Installation Example

Following is an example of image installation. The path/directory may be different from different OEMs or from different Android versions (this example is based on a Lenovo phone):

1. Empty the phone's SD card. This step is optional and can be done either on the host or on the phone. It is very simple to complete the step on the host: unplug the SD card from the phone, insert it in the SD card reader of the host, and delete all files from the removable disk at the host (for example, in Windows).

   Empty the SD card on the phone by following these steps:

   a. Connect the phone to the host.

   b. Execute the following commands successively in the command-line window at the host:

   ```
   adb devices
   adb remount
   adb shell
   su
   rm -r /system/sd/*
   ```

   (Note: sdcard is usually mounted under /storage/sdcard0 or /sdcard, However, the location may be different if you're using a device from a different OEM or on another Android version.)

2. Copy the customized ROM file (update_signed.zip in the example) to the SD card, and rename it update.zip.

3. Make sure the SD card has been inserted in the phone. Restart the phone, and enter Recovery mode. Follow these steps:

   a. Shut down the phone normally.

   b. Press the power button and the <volume+> button of the device at the same time: the phone starts while vibrating and enters BKB Provisioning OS mode. Double-click the <volume+> button quickly to make the system enter Test mode.

   c. Press <volume+> and <volume-> to move to the sixth option (SD Update), and click Enter in the lower-left corner. Automatic reflash begins.

4. Reboot.

The entire reflash process takes a few minutes. The phone restarts automatically after vibrating twice; the first reboot takes longer, and then the familiar four-leaf clover interface appears.

After reboot, choose Settings ➤ System Information to check the phone, network, battery, and version information; IMEI code; and internal version number to confirm whether the upgrade has been successful.

Automating the Procedure with flash_device.sh

There is a script that will perform all the previously described procedures for you. This script is located here:

```
<Path-to-your-project>/vendor/intel/support/flash_device.sh
```

You can add this script to your bin folder and run it from a terminal window. You should be able to find the section on this topic in the user manual from the OEM.

Intel Build Tools Suite

Intel has developed an Android Build Tools Suite (see Figure 6-8) to help developers easily and quickly do the Android system build and customization. The suite provides the following features:

- Device customization

- Ability to generate a customized firmware module and Android OS image

- Final customization and localization

- Ability to compile a single image and load the image into a supported device

- Ability to verify configuration readiness

- Troubleshooting and calibration

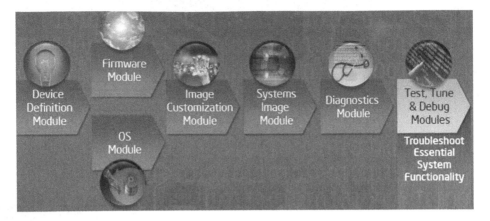

Figure 6-8. Intel Build Tools Suite

Summary

This chapter completed the discussion of system-level topics for Android. Starting in the next chapter, you begin to learn application development for Android on x86, and you see how to develop user interfaces suitable for the UX and interaction characteristics of mobile devices on Android. You start by learning about Android graphic user interface (GUI) design, because it's an indispensable part of human-computer interaction (HCI). Because resources are limited for a mobile phone or tablet, GUI design of Android systems is more challenging than for desktops. In addition, users have more rigorous demands and expectations for a user-friendly experience. Interface design has become one of the important factors determining the success of applications for Android on the market.

■ ■ ■

## CHAPTER 7

GUI Design for Android Apps, Part 1: General Overview

Since its emergence in the 1980s, the concept of the *graphical user interface* (GUI) has become an indispensable part of *human-computer interaction* (HCI). As embedded systems have evolved, they have gradually adopted this concept as well. The Android embedded OS running on the Intel Atom hardware platform is at the forefront of this movement.

Because resources are limited, the GUI design of Android systems is more challenging than that of desktop systems. In addition, users have more rigorous demands and expectations for a high-quality user experience. Interface design has become one of the important factors in determining the success of systems and applications on the market. This chapter introduces how to develop user interfaces suitable for typical user interaction on Android embedded systems.

Overview of GUIs for Embedded Applications

These days, the user interface (UI) and user experience (UX) of software are increasingly important factors in determining whether software will be accepted by users and achieve market success. UX designs are based on the types of input/output or interaction devices and must comply with their characteristics. Compared to desktop computer systems, Android systems have different interaction devices and modalities. If a desktop's UI designs are copied indiscriminately, an Android device will present a terrible UI and unbearable UX, unacceptable to users. In addition, with greater expectations for compelling user experiences, developers must be more meticulous and careful in designing system UIs and UXs, making them comply with the characteristics of embedded applications.

This chapter first introduces the general GUI design method for desktop systems and then shows how designing UIs for embedded systems is different. The aim is to help you quickly master general methods and principles of GUI design for Android applications.

Characteristics of Interaction Modalities of Android Devices

A general-purpose desktop computer has powerful input/output (or interaction) devices such as a large, high-resolution screen, a full keyboard and mouse, and diverse interaction modalities. Typical desktop computer screens are at least 17 inches, with resolutions of at least 1,280 × 960 pixels. The keyboard is generally a full keyboard or an enhanced keyboard. On full keyboards, letters, numbers, and other characters are located on corresponding keys—that is, full keyboards provide keys corresponding to all characters. Enhanced keyboards have additional keys. The distance between keys on a full keyboard is about 19 mm, which is convenient for users to make selections.

The GUI interactive mode of desktop computers based on screen, keyboard, and mouse is referred to as WIMP (windows, icons, menus, and pointers), which is a style of GUI using these elements as well as interactive elements including buttons, toolbars, and dialog boxes. WIMP depends on screen, keyboard, and mouse devices to complete the interaction. For example, a mouse (or a device similar to a mouse, such as a light pen) is used for pointing, a keyboard is used to input characters, and a screen shows the output.

In addition to screens, keyboards, mice, and other standard interaction hardware, desktop computers can be equipped with joysticks, helmets, data gloves, and other multimedia interactive devices to achieve multimedia computing functions. By installing cameras, microphones, speakers, and other devices, and by virtue of their powerful computing capabilities, users can interact with desktop computers in the form of voice, gestures, facial expressions, and other modalities.

Desktop computers are also generally equipped with CD-ROM/DVDs and other large-capacity portable external storage devices. With these external storage devices, desktop computers can release software and verify ownership and certificates through CD/DVD.

As a result of the embeddability and limited resources of embedded systems, as well as user demand for portability and mobility, Android systems have interaction modalities, methods, and capabilities that are distinct from those of desktop systems. Due to these characteristics and conditions, interaction on Android systems is more demanding and more difficult to achieve than it is on desktop systems.

The main differences between Android devices and desktop computers are described next.

Screens of Various Sizes, Densities, and Specifications

Instead of large, high-resolution screens like those on desktop computers, Android device screens are smaller and have various dimensions and densities measured in dots per inch (DPI). For example, the K900 smartphone's screen is 5.5 inches with a resolution of 1920 ×1080 pixels, and some smartphone screens are only 3.2 inches.

The aspect ratio of Android device screens is not the conventional aspect ration of 16:9 or 4:3 used by desktop computers. If Android devices adopted the interaction mode of desktop computers, many problems would result, such as a blurry display and errors in selecting targets.

Keypads and Special Keys

Desktop computers have full keyboards, where a key corresponds to every character and the generous distance between keys makes typing convenient. If an Android device has a keyboard, it's usually a keypad instead of the full keyboard. Keypads have fewer keys than full keyboards; several characters generally share one key. A keypad's keys are smaller and more tightly spaced than on full keyboards, making it harder to select and type characters. As a result, keypads are less convenient to use than full keyboards. In addition, some keypads provide special keys that are not found on standard full keyboards, so users must adjust their input on the Android device.

Generally speaking, on Android devices, keys and buttons are a unified concept. Whether you press a button or a key, the action is processed as a keyboard event with a uniform numbering scheme. Keyboard events in Android have corresponding android.view.KeyEvent classes. Figure 7-1's button/key callouts correspond to the event information listed in Table 7-1.

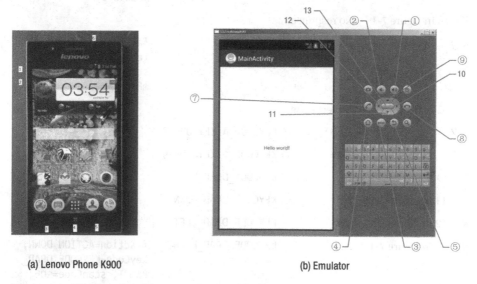

(a) Lenovo Phone K900　　　　　　　　(b) Emulator

Figure 7-1. *Keyboard and buttons of an Android phone*

See help documents like that for android.view.KeyEvent for details. Table 7-1's contents are excerpts.

Table 7-1. *Android Event Information Corresponding to Key and Button Events*

Key/Button	Key Code	Another Name	Key Event
Key ① in Figure 7-1	24	KEYCODE_VOLUME_UP	{action=0 code=24 repeat=0 meta=0 scancode=115 mFlags=8}
Key ② in Figure 7-1	25	KEYCODE_VOLUME_DOWN	{action=0 code=25 repeat=0 meta=0 scancode=114 mFlags=8}
Key ③ in Figure 7-1	82	KEYCODE_MENU	{action=0 code=82 repeat=0 meta=0 scancode=139 mFlags=8}
Key ④ in Figure 7-1	No response		
Key ⑤ in Figure 7-1	4	KEYCODE_BACK	{action=0 code=4 repeat=0 meta=0 scancode=158 mFlags=8}
Key ⑥ in Figure 7-1	No response		
A–Z	29–54	KEYCODE_A–KEYCODE_Z	
0–9	7–16	KEYCODE_0–KEYCODE_9	
Key ⑨ in Figure 7-1	19	KEYCODE_DPAD_UP	
Key 11 in Figure 7-1	20	KEYCODE_DPAD_DOWN	
Key 12 in Figure 7-1	21	KEYCODE_DPAD_LEFT	
Key 10 in Figure 7-1	22	KEYCODE_DPAD_RIGHT	{ action=ACTION_DOWN, keyCode=KEYCODE_DPAD_RIGHT, scanCode=106, metaState=0, flags=0x8, repeatCount=0, eventTime=254791, downTime=254791, deviceId=0, source=0x301 }

(continued)

Table 7-1. (*continued*)

Key/Button	Key Code	Another Name	Key Event
Key 13 in Figure 7-1	23	KEYCODE_DPAD_CENTER	{ action=ACTION_DOWN, keyCode=KEYCODE_DPAD_CENTER, scanCode=232, metaState=0, flags=0x8, repeatCount=0, eventTime=321157, downTime=321157, deviceId=0, source=0x301 }
Key ⑦ in Figure 7-1	5	KEYCODE_CALL	{ action=ACTION_DOWN, keyCode=KEYCODE_CALL, scanCode=231, metaState=0, flags=0x8, repeatCount=0, eventTime=331714, downTime=331714, deviceId=0, source=0x301 }
Key ⑧ in Figure 7-1	6	KEYCODE_ENDCALL	

Touch Screens and Styluses, in Place of Mice

A *touch screen* is an input device covering a display device to record touch positions. By using the touch screen, users can have a more intuitive reaction to the information displayed. Touch screens are widely applied to Android devices and replace a mouse for user input. The most common types of touch screens are resistive touch screens, capacitive touch screens, surface acoustic wave touch screens, and infrared touch screens, with resistive and capacitive touch screens being most often applied to Android devices. Users can directly click videos and images on the screen to watch them.

A stylus can be used to perform functions similar to touch. Some styluses are auxiliary tools for touch screens and replace fingers, helping users complete elaborate pointing, selecting, line drawing, and other operations, especially when the touch screen is small. Other styluses implement touch and input functions along with other system components. With the first type of auxiliary tool styluses, users can touch and input characters with fingers. But the second type of stylus is an indispensable input tool and is used instead of fingers.

Touch and styluses can perform most functions that mice typically do, such as click and drag, but can't achieve all the functions of mice, such as right-click and left-click/right-click at the same time. When designing embedded applications, you should control the interaction mode within the range of functions that touch screens or styluses can provide and avoid operations that are not available.

Onscreen Keyboards

Onscreen keyboards, also known as *virtual keyboards* or *soft keyboards*, are displayed on the screen via software. Users tap the virtual keys like they would tap the keys on physical keyboards.

Few Multimodal Interactions

Multimodal interaction refers to human-computer interaction with the modes involving the five human senses. It allows the user to interact through input modalities such as speech, handwriting, and hand gesture. Because computing capability is limited, Android devices generally do not adopt multimodal interaction.

Few Large-Capacity Portable External Storage Devices

Most Android devices do not have the CD-ROM/DVD drives, hard disks, or other large-capacity portable storage peripherals such as solid-state drives (SSDs) that are usually configured on desktop computers. These devices cannot be used on Android devices to install software or verify ownership and certificates. However, Android devices usually support microSD cards, which now have capacities of up to 128 GB; and more and more cloud-based storage solutions such as Dropbox, One Drive, and Google Drive are being developed for Android devices, with Android-compatible client apps available for download from Google Play Store.

UI Design Principles for Embedded Systems

This section introduces interactive design issues and corrective measures to take when transforming traditional desktop applications to embedded applications.

Considerations of Screen Size

Compared to desktop computer systems, Android systems have smaller screens with different display densities and aspect ratios. Such screen differences result in many problems when migrating applications from desktop systems to Android systems. If developers reduce desktop system screens proportionally, the graphic elements become too small to be seen clearly. In particular, it is often difficult to see the text and icons, select and click some buttons, and place some application pictures on the screen appropriately. If developers migrate application graphic elements to Android systems without changing their sizes, the screen space is limited and can only accommodate a few of the graphic elements.

Size of Text and Icons

Another problem is the size of text and icons. When an application is reduced from a typical 15-inch desktop screen to a typical 5- or 7-inch phone or tablet screen, its text is too small to be seen clearly. In addition to the size of the text font, the text window (such as a chat window) also becomes too small to read the text. Trying to reduce the font size to suit smaller windows makes the text hard to recognize.

Therefore, the design of embedded systems should use as few text prompt messages as possible; for example, replace the text with graphic or sound information. In addition, where text is necessary, the text size should be adjustable. On Android, some predefined fonts and icons are available in the res directory, such as `drawable-hdpi`, `drawable-mdpi`, and `drawable-xhdpi`.

Clickability of Buttons and Other Graphical Elements

Similar to the problem of small text, buttons and other graphical elements also bring interaction problems when migrating applications. On desktop systems, the size of buttons is designed for mouse clicks, whereas on Android systems, the button size should be suitable for fingers (on touch screens) or styluses. Therefore, when porting a Windows-based app to support Android devices, the application UI needs to be redesigned; and predefined drawables provided by the Android SDK should be selected in order to suit fingers or styluses.

Developers should use bigger and clearer buttons or graphic elements to avoid such problems and leave enough gap between graphic elements to avoid errors, which are common when a small touch screen is used for selecting by fingers or styluses. In addition, if an application has text labels near buttons, the labels should be part of the clickable area connected with the buttons, so the buttons are easier to click.

Size of Application Windows

Many applications, such as games, use windows with fixed sizes instead of windows that automatically adjust to fill any size screen. When these applications are migrated to Android systems, because the screen's aspect ratio does not match its resolution, part of the picture may not be seen, or part of the area may not be reachable.

These problems may be more complicated on smartphones and tablets because their screens have various densities such as small (426 dp × 320 dp), normal (470 dp × 320 dp), large (640 dp × 480 dp), and extra large (960 dp × 720 dp). Their aspect ratios are diverse and different from those commonly adopted by desktop systems.

One good way to solve such problems is to place the entire application window proportionally on the smartphone or tablet screen, such as the large and extra-large screens, which are typically 640 × 480 pixels and 960 × 720 pixels; or rearrange the UI to make full use of the entire widescreen area; or make the entire app window a scrollable view. In addition, you can allow users to use multiple touch fingers touch to zoom in, zoom out, or move the application window on the screen.

Considerations Arising from Touch Screens and Styluses

As mentioned earlier, touch screens and styluses are used on many Android systems to perform some traditional mouse functions. Such input devices are called *tap-only touch screens*. However, tap-only touch screens cannot provide all mouse functions. There is no right button, and the current finger/stylus location cannot be captured when the screen is not touched. So, desktop applications that allow functions such as cursor moves without clicking, different operations for left-clicks and right-clicks, and so on, cannot be realized on Android systems using touch screens and styluses.

The following sections talk about several problems often seen when migrating applications from desktop systems to Android systems using tap-only touch screens.

Correctly Interpreting the Movement and Input of the Cursor (Mouse) on Tap-Only Touch Screens

Many applications need mouse movement information when no mouse key is pressed. This operation is called *moving the cursor without clicking*. For example, a lot of PC shooting games[1] simulate the user's field of vision such that moving the mouse without clicking is interpreted as moving the game player's vision field; but the cursor should always stay in the middle of the new vision field. However, an embedded device with a tap-only touch screen does not support the operation of moving the cursor without clicking. Once the user's finger touches the screen, a tap event is triggered. When the user moves a finger on the screen, a series of tap events at different positions is triggered; these events are interpreted by the existing game code as additional interaction events (that is, moving the aiming position of the game player's gun).

The original interaction mode needs to be modified when migrating this type of application to Android systems. For example, this problem can be modified into a click operation: once the user touches the screen, the game screen should immediately switch to the vision field, in which the cursor is located at the screen center. This way, the cursor is always displayed at the screen center and not at the position the user actually touched. One advantage you benefit from on mobile platforms is that most smartphones and tablets on the market are equipped with sensors such as accelerometers, gyroscopes, GPS sensors, and compasses, and they allow applications to read data from the sensors. As a result, developers have more options than just touch input.

More generally, if an application needs to track the cursor's movement from point A to point B, the tap-only touch screen can define this input by the user clicking first point A and then point B, without the need to track the movement between point A and point B.

Setting Screen Mapping Correctly

Many applications run in full-screen mode. If such applications do not perfectly fill the entire tap-only touch screen (that is, they are smaller or bigger than the screen), input mapping errors result: there is a deviation between the display position and the click position.

---

[1]A typical example is the game Counter-Strike (CS).

One situation that often occurs in migrating a full-screen application to a tap-only touch screen with a low aspect ratio is the application window being centered on the screen with blank space showing on both sides. For example, when a desktop application window with a resolution of 640 × 480 (or 800 × 600) pixels is migrated to a tap-only touch screen with a resolution of 960 × 720 (or 1280 × 800, a WXGA on Dell Venue 8) pixels, it appears on the screen as shown in Figure 7-2. The resulting mapping errors cause the app to incorrectly respond to user interaction. When the user taps the position of the yellow arrow (the target), the position identified by the application is the point where the red explosion icon is located. These kinds of errors also occur when the user taps a button.

Figure 7-2. *Screen-mapping errors due to a low aspect ratio*

You should consider the position-mapping logic and take this blank space into consideration, even if the blank space is not part of the migrating application's window. By making these changes, the tap-only touch screen can map the touch position correctly.

Another situation occurs when the desktop full-screen window is migrated to a tap-only touch screen with a higher aspect ratio. The height of the original application window does not fit on the tap-only touch screen, and mapping errors occur in the vertical direction instead of the horizontal direction.

Figure 7-3 shows the original application window filling the screen horizontally but not vertically on a tap-only touch screen with a higher aspect ratio. Here, when the user taps the position of the yellow arrow (the target), the position identified by the application is the point where the red explosion icon is located. These errors are caused by the difference in shape between the physical display and the application window.

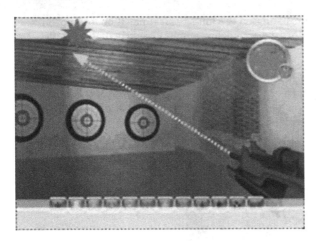

Figure 7-3. *Screen-mapping errors due to a high aspect ratio*

One solution is to ensure that the OS accurately maps the tap-only touch screen to the entire visible area of the screen. The OS provides special services to complete the screen stretching and mouse position mapping. Another solution is to consider, at the beginning of application development, allowing configuration options to support preconfigured display densities and aspect ratios provided by the Android SDK, such as screens with a resolution of 640 × 480, 960 × 720, or 1,080 × 800 pixels. This way, if the final dimension deformation is acceptable, the application may automatically stretch the window to cover the whole screen.

How to Solve Hover-Over Problems

Many applications allow hover-over operations: that is, users can place the mouse over a certain object or locate the mouse over an application icon to trigger an animated item or display a tooltip. This operation is commonly used to provide instructions for new players in games; but it is not compatible with the characteristics of tap-only touch screens, because they do not support the mouse hover-over operation.

You should consider selecting an alternative event to trigger animations or tips. For example, when the user touches the operation of applications, relevant animated themes and tips are triggered automatically. Another method is to design an interface interaction mode that temporarily interprets tap events as mouse hover-over events. For example, the action of pressing a certain button and moving the cursor would not be interpreted as a tap operation.

Providing Right-Click Functionality

As mentioned before, tap-only touch screens generally do not support right-click operations on mice. A commonly used alternative is a delayed touch (much longer than the tap time) to represent a right-click. This could result in the wrong operation occurring if the user accidentally releases their finger too soon. In addition, this method cannot perform simultaneous left-click and right-click (also known as *double-click*).

You should provide a user-interaction interface that can replace the right-click function: for example, using double-click or installing a clickable control on the screen to replace the right-click.

Keyboard Input Problems

As mentioned earlier, desktop computers use full keyboards, whereas Android systems usually have much simpler keypads, button panels, user-programmable buttons, and a limited number of other input devices. These limitations cause some problems when designing embedded applications that are not seen in desktop systems.

Restricting the Input of Various Commands

The keyboard limitations on Android systems make it difficult for users to type a large number of characters. Therefore, applications that require users to input many characters, especially those depending on command input, need appropriate adjustments when migrating to an Android system.

One solution is to provide an input mode that restricts the number of characters by reducing the number of commands or selectively using convenient tools like menu item shortcut keys. A more flexible solution is to create command buttons on the screen, especially context-sensitive buttons (that is, buttons that appear only when needed).

Meeting Keyboard Demand

Applications need keyboard input, such as naming a file, creating personal data, saving progress, and supporting online chat. Most applications tend to use the screen keyboard to input characters, but the screen keyboard does not always run or show at the front of the application interface, making character-input problems hard to solve.

One solution is to either design a mode without explicit conflict with the onscreen keyboard application (for example, not using the full-screen default operation mode) for applications, or provide an onscreen keyboard in the UI that appears only when needed. Another simple way of minimizing keyboard input is to provide default text string values, such as default names of personal data and default names of saved files, and allow users to select by touching. To obtain other information required by the text string (for example, prefix and suffix of file names), you can add a selection button that provides a list of character strings you've established, from which the user can select. The name of a saved file can also be uniquely obtained by combining various user information items extracted from the screen or even using the date-time stamp. Some text input services (such as a chat service) should be disabled if they are not the core functions of an application. This will not cause any negative impact on the user experience.

Software Distribution and Copyright Protection Problems

Desktop computers are generally equipped with CD-ROM/DVD drives, and their software is generally distributed via CD/DVD. In addition, for anti-piracy purposes, CD/DVD installation usually requires users to verify the ownership of the disk or load contents dynamically from the CD/DVD, especially video files. However, Android systems (smartphones and tablets, for instance) generally do not have CD-ROM/DVD drives; Android does support an external microSD card, but directly installing an application from it is still not supported.

A good solution is to allow users to download or install applications via the Internet instead of installing from CD/DVD. Consumers buy and install applications directly from application stores such as the Apple App store, Google Play, and Amazon Appstore. This popular software release model allows mobile developers to use certificates, online accounts, or other software-based ways to verify ownership, instead of physical CD/DVDs. Similarly, you should consider providing the option of placing content on an online cloud service instead of requiring users to download videos and other content from a CD/DVD.

Android Application Overview

The following sections describe the application file framework and component structure of Android applications.

Application File Framework

Figure 7-4 shows the file structure after the generation of the HelloAndroid app (this is an Eclipse screen shot).

Figure 7-4. *Example file structure of an Android project*

Even if you are not using Eclipse, you can directly access the project folder and see the same file structure, as listed next:

```
E:\Android Dev\workspace\HelloAndroid>TREE /F
E:.
    .classpath
    .project
    AndroidManifest.xml
    ic_launcher-web.png
    proguard-project.txt
    project.properties
```

```
├─.settings
│      org.eclipse.jdt.core.prefs
│
├─assets
├─bin
│      AndroidManifest.xml
│      classes.dex
│      HelloAndroid.apk
│      resources.ap_
│
│   ├─classes
│   └─com
│       └─example
│           └─helloandroid
│                   BuildConfig.class
│                   MainActivity.class
│                   R$attr.class
│                   R$dimen.class
│                   R$drawable.class
│                   R$id.class
│                   R$layout.class
│                   R$menu.class
│                   R$string.class
│                   R$style.class
│                   R.class
│
│   └─res
│       ├─drawable-hdpi
│       │      ic_action_search.png
│       │      ic_launcher.png
│       │
│       ├─drawable-ldpi
│       │      ic_launcher.png
│       │
│       ├─drawable-mdpi
│       │      ic_action_search.png
│       │      ic_launcher.png
│       │
│       └─drawable-xhdpi
│              ic_action_search.png
│              ic_launcher.png
│
├─gen
│   └─com
│       └─example
│           └─helloandroid
│                   BuildConfig.java
│                   R.java
```

216

```
─libs
       android-support-v4.jar

─res
  ├─drawable-hdpi
  │     ic_action_search.png
  │     ic_launcher.png
  │
  ├─drawable-ldpi
  │     ic_launcher.png
  │
  ├─drawable-mdpi
  │     ic_action_search.png
  │     ic_launcher.png
  │
  ├─drawable-xhdpi
  │     ic_action_search.png
  │     ic_launcher.png
  │
  ├─layout
  │     activity_main.xml
  │
  ├─menu
  │     activity_main.xml
  │
  ├─values
  │     dimens.xml
  │     strings.xml
  │     styles.xml
  │
  ├─values-large
  │     dimens.xml
  │
  ├─values-v11
  │     styles.xml
  │
  └─values-v14
        styles.xml

─src
  └─com
     └─example
        └─helloandroid
                MainActivity.java
```

Let's explain the features of this Android project file structure:

- `src` *directory*: Contains all source files.

- `R.java` *file*: Is automatically generated by the Android SDK integrated in Eclipse. You do not need to modify its contents.

- *Android library*: A set of Java libraries used by Android applications.

- `assets` *directory*: Stores mostly multimedia files and other files.

- `res` *directory*: Stores preconfigured resource files such as drawable layouts used by applications.

- `values` *directory*: Stores mostly `strings.xml`, `colors.xml`, and `arrays.xml`.

- `AndroidManifest.xml`: Equivalent to an application configuration file. Contains the application's name, activity, services, providers, receivers, permissions, and so on.

- `drawable` *directory*: Stores mostly image resources used by applications.

- `layout` *directory*: Stores mostly layout files used by applications. These layout files are XML files.

Similar to general Java projects, a `src` folder contains all the `.java` files for a project; and a `res` folder contains all the project resources, such as application icons (drawable), layout files, and constant values.

The next sections introduce the `AndroidManifest.xml` file, a must-have of every Android project, and the `R.java` file in the gen folder, which is included in other Java projects.

AndroidManifest.xml

The `AndroidManifest.xml` file contains information about your app essential to the Android system, which the system must have before it can run any of the app's code. This information includes activities, services, permissions, providers, and receivers used in the project. An example is shown in Figure 7-5.

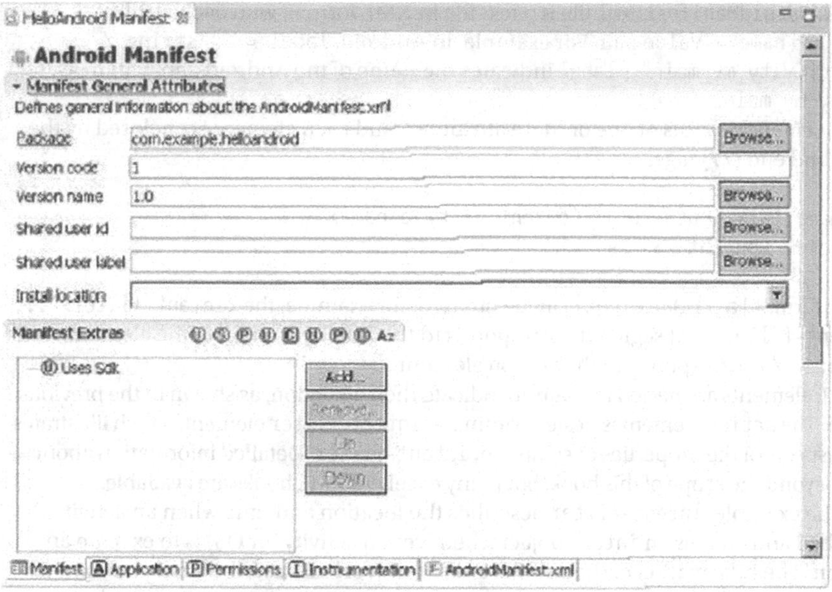

Figure 7-5. The content of AndroidManifest.xml displayed in Eclipse

The file's code is as follows:

```xml
<manifest xmlns:android="http://schemas.android.com/apk/res/android"
    package="com.example.helloandroid"
    android:versionCode="1"
    android:versionName="1.0" >
    <uses-sdk
        android:minSdkVersion="8"
        android:targetSdkVersion="15" />
    <application
        android:icon="@drawable/ic_launcher"
        android:label="@string/app_name"
        android:theme="@style/AppTheme" >
        <activity
            android:name=".MyMainActivity"
            android:label="@string/title_activity_my_main" >
            <intent-filter>
                <action android:name="android.intent.action.MAIN" />
                <category android:name="android.intent.category.LAUNCHER" />
            </intent-filter>
        </activity>
    </application>
</manifest>
```

The AndroidManifest.xml file is a text file in XML format, with each attribute defined by a name = value pair. For example, in Android, label = "@ string / title_activity_my_main", label indicates the name of the Android application as activity_my_main.

An element consists of one or more attributes, and each element is enclosed by the start (<) and end (/>) tags:

```
<Type Name [attribute set]> Content </ type name>
<Type Name  Content />
```

The format [attribute set] can be omitted; for example, the <intent-filter> ... </ intent-filter> text segment corresponds to the activity content of the element, and <action... /> corresponds to the action element.

XML elements are nested in layers to indicate their affiliation, as shown in the previous example. The action element is nested within the intent-filter element, which illustrates certain aspects of the properties or settings of intent-filter. Detailed information about XML is beyond the scope of this book, but many excellent XML books are available.

In the example, intent-filter describes the location and time when an activity is launched and creates an intent object whenever an activity (or OS) is to execute an operation. The information carried by the intent object can describe what you want to do, which data and type of data you want to process, and other information. Android compares the intent-filter data exposed by each application and finds the most suitable activity to handle the data and operations specified by the caller.

Descriptions for the main attribute entries in the AndroidManifest.xml file are listed in Table 7-2.

Table 7-2. *The Main Attribute Entries in the AndroidManifest.xml File*

Parameter	Description
Manifest	Root node that contains all contents in the package.
xmlns:android	Contains the manifest of the namespace.
	xmlns:android=http://schemas.android.com/apk/res/android. Makes various standard properties usable in the file and provides data to most elements.
package	Package of manifest application.
Application	Contains the root node of the application-level component manifest in the package. This element can also contain some global and default properties for the application, such as label, icon, theme, and necessary permissions. One manifest may contain zero or one (no more than one) element.
android:icon	Icon of the application.
android:label	Name of the application.

(continued)

Table 7-2. (*continued*)

Parameter	Description
Activity	Name of the initial page to load when users start the application. It is an important tool for user interaction. Most other pages are displayed when other activities are performed or manifested by other activity flags.
	Note: Each activity must have a corresponding <activity> flag whether it is used externally or in its own package. If an activity has no corresponding flag, you cannot operate it. In addition, to support a searching activity, an activity can contain one or several <intent-filter> elements to describe the operations it supports.
android:name	Default activity launched by the application.
intent-filter	Is formed by manifesting the intent value supported by a designated component. In addition to specifying different types of values, intent-filter can specify properties for describing a unique label, icon, or other information required by an operation.
Action	Intent action supported by a component.
Category	Intent category supported by a component. The default activity launched by the application is designated here.
uses-sdk	Related to the SDK version used by the application.

R.java

The R.java file is generated automatically when a project is created. It is a read-only file and cannot be modified. R.java is an index file defining all resources of the project. For example:

```
/* AUTO-GENERATED FILE.  DO NOT MODIFY.
   ... ...
 */
package com.example.helloandroid;
public final class R {
    public static final class attr {
    }
    public static final class dimen {
        public static final int padding_large=0x7f040002;
        public static final int padding_medium=0x7f040001;
        public static final int padding_small=0x7f040000;
    }
```

```java
    public static final class drawable {
        public static final int ic_action_search=0x7f020000;
        public static final int ic_launcher=0x7f020001;
    }
    public static final class id {
        public static final int menu_settings=0x7f080000;
    }
    public static final class layout {
        public static final int activity_my_main=0x7f030000;
    }
    public static final class menu {
        public static final int activity_my_main=0x7f070000;
    }
    public static final class string {
        public static final int app_name=0x7f050000;
        public static final int hello_world=0x7f050001;
        public static final int menu_settings=0x7f050002;
        public static final int title_activity_my_main=0x7f050003;
    }
    public static final class style {
        public static final int AppTheme=0x7f060000;
    }
}
```

You can see that many constants are defined in this code. The names of these constants are the same as the file names in the res folder, which proves that the R.java file stores the index of all resources of the project. With this file, it is more convenient to use resources in applications and identify the resources required. Because this file does not allow manual editing, you only need to refresh the project when adding new resources to it. The R.java file automatically generates the index of all resources.

Definition File of Constants

The values subdirectory of the project contains a definition file for the strings, colors, and array constants; the string constant definitions are in the strings.xml file. These constants are used by other files in the Android project.

Eclipse provides two graphic view tabs, Resources and strings.xml, for the strings.xml file. The Resources tab provides a structured view of the name-value, and the strings.xml tab directly displays the contents of a text file format. The strings.xml file of the HelloAndroid example is shown in Figure 7-6.

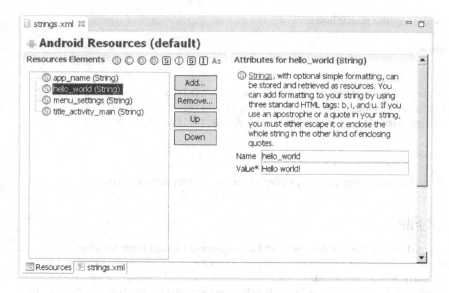

(a) Resource View

(b) XML view

Figure 7-6. *IDE graphic view of the* `strings.xml` *file of HelloAndroid*

The file content is as follows:

```
<resources>

    <string name="app_name">HelloAndroid</string>
    <string name="hello_world">Hello world!</string>
    <string name="menu_settings">Settings</string>
    <string name="title_activity_main">MainActivity</string>

</resources>
```

The code is very simple; it only defines four string constants (resources).

Layout Files

Layout files describe the size, location, and arrangement of each screen *widget* (combination of *window* and *gadget*). A layout file is the "face" of the application. Layout files are text files in XML format.

Widgets are visual UI elements, such as buttons and text boxes. They are equivalent to controls and containers in the Windows system terminology. Buttons, text boxes, scroll bars, and so forth are widgets. In the Android OS, widgets generally belong to the View class and its descendant classes and are stored in the android.widget package.

An application has a main layout file corresponding to the application's screen display at startup. For example, the layout file and the main interface of the HelloAndroid example are shown in Figure 7-7. When an application is created, Eclipse automatically generates a layout file for the application's main screen display. The file is located in the project folder's res\layout directory. The file name in the generated application projects is specified in the next section: in this case, the source code file name corresponds to the [Layout Name] key, so the file is named activity_main.xml.

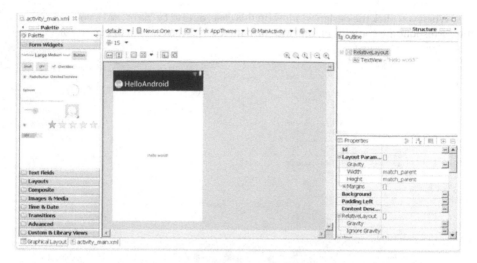

(a) The main graphic ayout file in Eclipse

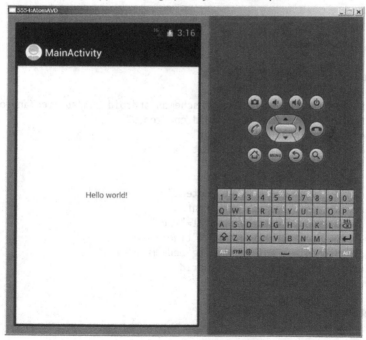

(b) The user interface

Figure 7-7. *The main graphic layout and user interface*

When you click the design window (in this case, `activity_main.xml`), you can see the corresponding contents of the XML-formatted text file, as shown in Figure 7-8.

Figure 7-8. *The main layout file of the HelloAndroid example*

The contents of the file are as follows:

```xml
<RelativeLayout xmlns:android="http://schemas.android.com/apk/res/android"
    xmlns:tools="http://schemas.android.com/tools"
    android:layout_width="match_parent"
    android:layout_height="match_parent" >

    <TextView
        android:layout_width="wrap_content"
        android:layout_height="wrap_content"
        android:layout_centerHorizontal="true"
        android:layout_centerVertical="true"
        android:padding="@dimen/padding_medium"
        android:text="@string/hello_world"
        tools:context=".MainActivity" />

</RelativeLayout>
```

In this code, there are several layout parameters:

- <RelativeLayout>: The layout configuration for the relative position.

- android:layout_width: Customizes the screen width of the current view; match_parent represents the parent container (in this case, the activity) match; fill_parent fills the entire screen; wrap_content, expressed as text fields, changes depending on the width or height of this view.

- android:layout_height: Customizes the screen height occupied by the current view.

Two other common parameters, not shown in this layout file, are as follows:

- android:orientation: Here means the layout is arranged horizontally.

- android:layout_weight: Give a value for the importance assigned to multiple views of a linear layout. All views are given a layout_weight value; the default is zero.

Although the layout file is an XML file, you do not have to understand its format or directly edit it, because the Android Development Tools and Eclipse provide a visual design interface. You simply drag and drop widgets and set the corresponding properties in Eclipse, and your actions are automatically recorded in the layout file. You can see how this works when you walk though the application development example in following sections.

Source Code File

When a project is built, Eclipse generates a default .java source code file that contains the application basic runtime code for the project. It is located in the project folder under the src\com\example\XXX directory (where XXX is the project name). The file name of the generated application projects in this case is the source code file name that corresponds to the [Activity Name] key, so the file is named MainActivity.java.

The content of MainActivity.java is as follows:

```
package com.example.flashlight;

import android.os.Bundle;
import android.app.Activity;
import android.view.Menu;
import android.view.MenuItem;
import android.support.v4.app.NavUtils;

public class MyMainActivity extends Activity {
    @Override
    public void onCreate(Bundle savedInstanceState) {
        super.onCreate(savedInstanceState);
        setContentView(R.layout.activity_my_main);
    }
```

```
    @Override
    public boolean onCreateOptionsMenu(Menu menu) {
        getMenuInflater().inflate(R.menu.activity_my_main, menu);
        return true;
    }
}
```

Component Structure of Applications

The Android application framework provides APIs for developers. Because the application is built in Java, the first level of the program contains the UI needs of the various controls. For example, views (View components) contain lists, grids, text boxes, buttons, and even an embedded web browser.

An Android application usually consists of five components:

- Activity

- Intent receiver

- Service

- Content provider

- Intent and intent filters

The following sections discuss each components a bit more.

Activity

Applications with visual UIs are implemented using activities. When a user selects an application from the main screen or an application launcher, it starts an action or an activity. Each activity program typically takes the form of a separate interface (screen). Each activity is a separate class that extends and implements the activity's base class. This class is shown as the UI, consisting of View components responding to events.

Most programs have multiple activities (in other words, an Android application is composed of one or more activities). Switching to another interface loads a new activity. In some cases, a previous activity may give a return value. For example, an activity that lets the user select a photo returns the photo to the caller.

When a user opens a new interface, the old interface is suspended and placed in the history stack (interface-switching history stack). The user can go back to an activity that has been opened in the history stack interface. A stack that has no historical value can be removed from the history stack interface. Android retains all generated interfaces in the history stack for running the application, from the first interface to the last one.

An activity is a container, which itself is not displayed in the UI. You can roughly imagine an activity as a window in the Windows OS, but the view window is not only for displaying but also for completing a task.

Intent and Intent Filters

Android achieves interface switching through a special class called intent. An intent describes what the program does. The two most important parts of the data structure are the action and the data processed in accordance with established rules (data). Typical operations are MAIN (activity entrance), VIEW, PICK, and EDIT. Data to be used in the operation is presented using a Universal Resource Identifier (URI). For example, to view a person's contact information, you need to create an intent using the VIEW operation, and the data is a pointer to the person's URI.

A class associated with an intent is called an IntentFilter. An intent encapsulates a request as an object; IntentFilter then describes what intentions an activity (or, say, an intent receiver, explained in a moment) can process. In the previous example, the activity that shows a person's contact information uses an IntentFilter, and it knows how to handle the data VIEW operation applied to this person. The activity in the AndroidManifest.xml file using IntentFilter is usually accomplished by parsing the intent activity switch. First, it uses the startActivity (myIntent) function to start the new activity, next it systematically checks the IntentFilter of all installed programs, and then it finds the activity that is the best match with the myIntent corresponding to IntentFilter. This new activity receives the message from intent and then starts. The intent-resolution process occurs in real time in the startActivity called. This process has two advantages:

- The activity emits only one intent request and can reuse the function of other components.

- The activity can always be replaced by an equivalent new activity of the IntentFilter.

Service

A *service* is a resident system program that has no UI. You should use a service for any application that needs to run continuously, such as a network monitor or checking for application updates.

The two ways of using a service are *start-stop mode* and *bind-unbind mode*. The process flow chart and functions are shown in Table 7-3.

Table 7-3. *The Usage Model of a Service*

Mode	Start	End	Visit	Notes
Start/ stop	Context.start Service()	Context.stop Service()		Even if the process of the startService call is ended, the service is still there until the process calls stopService() or the service causes its own demise (stopSelf() is called).
Bind/ unbind	Context.bind Service()	Context.unbind Service()	Context.Service Connection()	When calling bindService(), the process is dead; then the service it binds to must be ended.

When two modes are in mixed use—for example, one mode calls startService() and other modes call bindService()—then only when both the stopService call and the unbindService call occur will the service be terminated.

A service process has its own life cycle, and Android tries to keep a service process that has been started or bound. The service process is described as follows:

- If the service is the implementation process of the method onCreate(), onStart, or onDestroy(), then the main process becomes a foreground process to ensure that this code is not stopped.

- If the service has started, the value of its importance is lower than that of the visible process but above all invisible processes. Because only a few processes are visible to the user, as long as the memory is not particularly low, the service does not stop.

- If multiple clients have bound to the service, as long as any one of the clients is visible to the user, that service is visible.

Broadcast Intent Receiver

When you want to execute some code associated with external events, such as have a task performed in the middle of the night or respond to a phone ringing, use IntentReceiver. Intent receivers have no UI and use NotificationManager to inform users that their event has happened. An intent receiver is declared in the AndroidManifest.xml file but can also be declared using Context.registerReceiver(). The program does not have to run continuously to wait for IntentReceiver to be called. When an intent receiver is triggered, the system starts your program. Programs can also use Context.broadcastIntent() to send their intent broadcast to other programs.

Android applications can be used to handle a data element or to respond to an event (such as receiving text messages). Android applications are deployed to the device together with an AndroidManifest.xml file. AndroidManifest.xml contains the necessary configuration information, so the application is properly installed on the device. AndroidManifest.xml also includes the necessary class names and the types of events that can be handled by the application, as well as the necessary permissions to run the application. For example, if an application needs to access the network—to, say, download a file—the manifest file must be explicitly listed in the license. Many applications may enable this particular license. This declarative security can help reduce the possibility of damage to equipment from malicious applications.

Content Provider

You can think of content providers as database servers. A content provider's task is to manage persistent data access, such as a SQLite database. If the application is very simple, you might not need to create a content-provider application. If you want to build a larger application or need to build applications to provide data for multiple activities or applications, you can use the content provider for data access.

If you want other programs to use their own programs' data, a content provider is very useful. The content-provider class implements a series of standard methods that allows other programs to store and read data that can be processed by the content provider.

Android Emulator

Android does not use the ordinary Java virtual machine (JVM); it uses the Dalvik virtual machine (DVM) instead. The DVM and JVM are fundamentally different. The DVM takes up less memory, is specifically optimized for mobile devices, and is more suitable for mobile phones used in embedded environments. Other differences are as follows:

- The general JVM is based on the stack-based virtual machine, but the DVM is a register-based virtual machine. The latter is better because applications can achieve maximum optimization based on the hardware, which is more in line with the characteristics of mobile devices.

- The DVM can run multiple virtual machine instances simultaneously in limited memory, so that each DVM application executes as a separate Linux process. In the general JVM, all applications run in a shared JVM, and therefore individual applications are not running as separate processes. With each application running as a separate process, the DVM can be prevented from closing all programs in the event of the collapse of the virtual machine.

- The DVM provides a less restrictive license platform than the general JVM. The DVM and JVM support different generic code. The DVM does not run standard Java bytecode, but rather Dalvik executable format (.dex). Java code compilation of Android applications actually consists of two processes. The first step is to compile the Java source code into normal JVM executable code, which uses the file-name suffix .class. The second step is to compile the bytecode into Dalvik execution code, which uses the file-name suffix .dex. The first step compiles the source code files under the src subdirectory in the project directory into .class files in the bin\class directory; and the second step moves the files from the bin\class subdirectory to classes.dex files in the bin directory. The compilation process is integrated into the Eclipse build process; however, you can also use the command line to compile manually.

Introducing Android Runtime (ART)

ART is an Android runtime that first became available in Google Android KitKat (4.4) as a preview feature. It is also called Dalvik version 2 and is under active development in the Android Open Source Project (AOSP). All smartphones and tablets with Android KitKat keep Dalvik as the default runtime. This is because some OEMs still do not support ART in Android implementations, and most third-party applications are still built based on Dalvik and have not yet added support for the new ART.

As described by Google on the Android developer site, most existing apps should work when running with ART. However, some techniques that work on Dalvik do not work on ART. The differences between Dalvik and ART are shown in Table 7-4.

Table 7-4. *Dalvik vs. ART Summary*

	Dalvik	ART
Application	APK package with DEX class file	Same as Dalvik
Compile Type	Dynamic compilation (JIT)	Ahead-of-time compilation (AOT)
Functionality	Stable and went through extensive QA	Basic functionality and stability
Installation Time	Faster	Slower due to compilation
App Launch Time	Mostly slower due to JIT compilation and interpretation	Mostly faster due to AOT compilation
Storage Footprint	Smaller	Larger, with precompiled binary
Memory Footprint	Larger due to JIT code cache	Smaller

ART offers some new features to help with application development, performance optimization, and debugging, such as support for the sampling profiler and debugging features like monitoring and garbage collection. Transitioning from Dalvik to ART is likely to take some time, and Dalvik and ART will both be provided in Android to allow smartphone and tablet users to select and switch. However, future 64-bit Android will be based on ART.

Summary

This chapter introduced the general GUI design method for desktop systems and then showed how designing the UI and UX for embedded systems is different. You should now understand the general methods and principles of GUI design for Android applications and be ready to learn about the Android-specific GUI. The next chapter describes the state transition of activities, the Context class, intent, and the relationship between applications and activities.

■ ■ ■

## CHAPTER 8

GUI Design for Android Apps, Part 2: The Android-Specific GUI

This chapter describes the state transitions of activities and discusses the Context class, intent, and the relationship between applications and activities.

State Transitions of Activities

As mentioned in Chapter 7, the activity is the most important component. Activities have their own state and transition rules, and they are the basis of what you need to understand to write Android applications.

Activity States

When activities are created or destroyed, they enter or exit the activity stack. And as they do, they transition among four possible states:

> *Active*: An activity in the active state is visible when it is on the top of the stack. Typically, it is the foreground activity that is responding to user input. Android will ensure that it executes at all costs. If required, Android will destroy stack activities further down to ensure required resources for the active activity. When another activity becomes active, this activity is paused.

> *Paused*: In some cases, an activity is visible but does not have focus. At this moment, it is suspended. When the active activity is fully transparent or is the non-full screen activity, the activity below reaches this state. Paused activities are considered active but do not accept user input events. In extreme cases, Android will kill a paused activity to restore resources to the active activity. When an activity is completely invisible, it becomes stopped.

Stopped: When an activity is not visible, it is stopped. This activity remains in memory to save all state and member information. But when the system needs memory, this activity is "taken out and shot." When an activity stops, it is very important to save the data and the current UI state. Once the activity exits or is closed, it becomes inactive.

Inactive: When an activity is killed, it becomes inactive. Inactive activities are removed from the activity stack. When you need to use or display the activity, it needs to be started again.

The activity state transition diagram is shown in Figure 8-1.

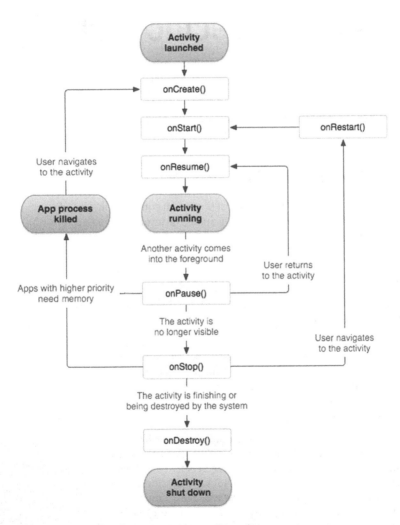

Figure 8-1. *Android activity state transition diagram*

State change is not artificial and is controlled entirely by the Android memory manager. Android first closes applications that contain inactive activities, followed by those with stopped activities. In extreme cases, it removes paused activities.

To ensure a flawless user experience, transition of these states is invisible to users. When an activity returns to active status from the paused, stopped, or inactive state, the UI must be nondiscriminatory. So, when an activity is stopped, it is very important to save the UI state and data. Once an activity becomes active, it needs to recover the saved values.

Important Functions of Activities

The activity state transition triggers the function of the corresponding `activity` class (that is, the Java method). Android calls these functions; developers do not have to explicitly call them. They are called *state-transition functions*. You can override the state-transition functions so they can complete their work at the specified time. There are also some functions that are used to control the state of the activity. These functions constitute the basis of activity programming. Let's learn about those functions.

onCreate State-Transition Function

The `onCreate` function prototype is as follows:

```
void  onCreate(Bundle savedInstanceState);
```

This function is run when the activity is first loaded. When you start a new program, its main activity's `onCreate` event is executed. If the activity is destroyed (`OnDestroy`, explained later) and then reloaded into the task, its `onCreate` event participants are re-executed.

An activity is likely to be forced to switch to the background. (An activity switched to the background is no longer visible to the user, but it still exists in the middle of a task, such as when a new activity is started to "cover" the current activity; or the user presses the Home button to return to the home screen; or other events occur in the new activity on top of the current activity, such as an incoming caller interface.) If the user does not view the activity again after a period of time, the activity may be automatically destroyed by the system along with the task and process. If you check the activity again, the `onCreate` event initialization activity will have to be rerun.

And sometimes you may want users to continue from the last open operating state of the activity, rather than starting from scratch. For example, when the user receives a sudden incoming call while editing a text message, the user may have to do other things immediately after the call, such as saving the incoming phone number to a contact. If the user does not immediately return to the text-editing interface, the text-editing interface is destroyed. As a result, when the user returns to the SMS program, that user may want to continue from the last edit. In this case, you can override the activity's void `onSaveInstanceState (Bundle outState)` events by writing the data you want to be saved before the destruction of the state of activity or information through `outState`, so that when the activity executes the `onCreate` event again, it transmits information previously saved through the `savedInstanceState`. At this point, you can selectively use the information to initialize the activity, instead of starting it from scratch.

onStart State-Transition Function

The onStart function prototype is as follows:

```
void onStart();
```

The onStart function executes after the onCreate event or when the current activity is switched to the background. When the user switches back to this activity by selecting it from switch panel, if it has not been destroyed, and only the onStop event has been performed, the activity will skip onCreate event activities and directly execute onStart events.

onResume State-Transition Function

The onResume function prototype is as follows:

```
void onResume()
```

The onResume function is executed after the OnStart event or after the current activity is switched to the background. When the user views this activity again, if it has not been destroyed, and if onStop events have not been performed (activities continue to exist in the task), the activity will skip onCreate and onStart event activities and directly execute onResume events.

onPause State-Transition Function

The onPause function prototype is as follows:

```
void onPause()
```

The onPause function is executed when the current activity is switched to the background.

onStop State-Transition Function

The onStop function prototype is as follows:

```
void onStop()
```

The onStop function is executed after the onPause event. If the user does not view the activity again for some time, the onStop event of the activity is executed. The onStop events are also executed if the user presses the Back key, and the activity is removed from the current task list.

onRestart State-Transition Function

The onRestart function prototype is as follows:

```
void onRestart()
```

After the onStop event is executed, if the activity and the process it resides in have not been systematically destroyed, or if the user views the activity again, the onRestart event(s) of the activity are executed. The onRestart event skips the onCreate event activities and directly executes the onStart events.

onDestroy State-Transition Function

The onDestroy function prototype is as follows:

```
void onDestroy()
```

After an onStop event of the activity, if the user does not view the activity again, it is destroyed.

The finish Function

The finish function prototype is as follows:

```
void finish()
```

The finish function closes the activity and removes it from the stack, which leads to a call to the onDestroy() state-transition function. One way to resolve this is for the user to navigate to the previous activity using the Back button.

In addition to the activity switch, the finish function triggers the activity's state-transition function, and the startActivity and startActivityForResult methods of the context class (described in the next sections) also activate it. Functions such as Context. startActivity also cause the construction of activity objects (that is, create new ones).

Typical causes of the triggers and corresponding functions are listed in Table 8-1.

Table 8-1. *Triggers and Their Functions*

Typical Trigger Cause	Corresponding Method of Activity Executed	Explanations
Context. startActivity[ForResult]() Note: As long as the activity is displayed and viewable on the screen, this method will be called.	new Activity() onCreate()	Completes the constructor function, Saves the activity object to the application object, and initializes the various controls (such as View).
	onStart()	Similar to View.onDraw().
Activity.finish()	onDestroy()	Completes the constructor function, such as removing the activity object from the application.

Functions such as Context.startActivity in Table 8-1 trigger three actions: constructing new Activity objects, onCreate, and onStart. When an activity that is moved from off screen places to the top of the screen display (that is, displayed in front of the user), it generally only includes functions being called by onStart.

The Context Class

The Context class is an important Android concept to know. The class is inherited from the Object function, whose inheritance is as follows:

```
java.lang.Object
   ↳ android.content.Context
```

The literal meaning of *context* is the text in the adjacent area, which is located in the android.content.Context of the framework package. The Context class is a LONG type, similar to the Handle handler in Win32. Context provides the global information interface about the application environment. It is an abstract class, and its execution is provided by the Android system. It allows access to resources and characterized types of applications. At the same time, it can start application-level operations, such as starting activities and broadcasting and receiving intents.

Many methods require the caller to be identified through a context instance. For example, the first parameter of Toast is Context; and usually you use this to replace the activity, which indicates that the caller's instance is an activity. But other methods, such as a button's onClick (View view), cause errors if you use this. In this case, you may use ActivityName.this to solve the problem, because the class implements the context of several major Android-specific models like activities, services, and broadcast receivers.

If the parameter—especially the constructor parameter of the class (such as Dialog)—is the Context type, the actual parameters are typically activity objects, generally [this]. For example, the Dialog constructor prototype is

```
Dialog.Dialog(Context context)
```

Here's an example:

```
public class MyActivity extends Activity{
    Dialog d = new Dialog(this);
```

Context is the ancestor of most classes of Android, such as broadcasting, intents, and so on, and it provides the interface of the global information application environment. Table 8-2 lists the important subclasses of Context. You can find a detailed description in the help documentation for the Android Context class.

Table 8-2. Important Subclasses of `Context`

Subclass	Explanation
`Activity`	User-friendly interface class
`Application`	Base class that provides global application state maintenance
`IntentService`	Base class used to handle asynchronous requests for the service (expressed in an `Intent` way)
`Service`	A component of the application that represents either a time-consuming operation that has no interaction with the user or a task that provides functionality for other application tasks

Classes are called *offspring classes* because they are direct or indirect subclasses of `Context` and have an inheritance relationship like activities:

```
java.lang.Object
  ↳ android.content.Context
    ↳ android.content.ContextWrapper
      ↳ android.view.ContextThemeWrapper
        ↳ android.app.Activity
```

`Context` can be used for many operations in Android, but it main function is to load and access resources. There are two commonly used contexts: the application context and the activity context. The activity context is usually passed between a variety of classes and methods, similar to the code of `onCreate` for an activity, as follows:

```
protected void onCreate(Bundle state) {
    super.onCreate(state);
    TextView label = new TextView(this); // Pass context to view control
    setContentView(label);
}
```

When the activity context is passed to the view, it means that view has a reference pointed to an activity and references resources taken by the activity: view hierarchy, resource, and so on.

You can also use the application context, which always accompanies the application's life but has nothing to do with the activity life cycle. The application context can be acquired with the `Context.getApplicationContext` or `Activity.getApplication` method.

Java usually uses a static variable (singleton and the like) to synchronize states between activities (between classes inside a program). Android's more reliable approach is to use the application context to associate these states.

Each activity has a context, which contains the runtime state. Similarly, an application has a context that Android uses to ensure that it is the only instance of that context.

If you need to make a custom application context, first you must define a custom class that inherits from `android.app.Application`; then describe the class in the application's `AndroidManifest.xml` file. Android automatically creates an instance of this class. By using the Context.getApplicationContext() method, you can get the application context inside each activity. The following example code gets the application context in the activity:

```
class MyApp extends Application {
// MyApp is a custom class inherited from android.app.Application
   public String aCertainFunc () {
        ......
    }
}

class Blah extends Activity {
       public void onCreate(Bundle b){
       ... ...
       MyApp appState = ((MyApp)getApplicationContext());
// Get Application Context
       appState.aCertainFunc();
//Use properties and methods of the application
       ... ...
    }
}
```

You can get global information about the application environment using the get function of Context. The main functions are shown in Table 8-3 and are either ContextWrapper or direct context methods.

Table 8-3. *Commonly Used Methods for Obtaining Context*

Function Prototype	Function
abstract Context ContextWrapper.getApplicationContext ()	Returns the current process corresponding to the global context of a single application.
abstract ApplicationInfo ContextWrapper.getApplicationInfo ()	Returns the context package corresponding to the information of the entire application.
abstract ContentResolver ContextWrapper.getContentResolver ()	Returns the content-resolver instance of the corresponding application package.
abstract PackageManager ContextWrapper.getPackageManager ()	Returns the package-manager instance for finding all package information.
abstract String ContextWrapper.getPackageName ()	Returns the current package name.

(continued)

Table 8-3. (*continued*)

Function Prototype	Function
`abstract Resources ContextWrapper.getResources ()`	Returns the resource instance of the (user) application package.
`abstract SharedPreferences ContextWrapper.getSharedPreferences (String name, int mode)`	Finds and holds the contents of the preference file whose name is specified by the parameter name. Returns the value of the shared preferences (`SharedPreferences`) that you can find and modify. When using a proper name, only one instance of `SharedPreferences` is returned to the caller, which means once the changes are complete, the results are shared with each other.
`public final String Context.getString (int resId)`	Returns a localized string from the application package's default string table.
`abstract Object ContextWrapper.getSystemService (String name)`	Returns processing system-level services according to the name specified by the variable name. The returned object classes vary based on the name of the request.

Introduction to Intent

Intent can be used as a message-passing mechanism to allow you to declare intent to take an action, usually with specific data. You can use intent to implement interaction between components of any application on Android devices. Intent turns a group of independent components into systems with one-to-one interactions.

It can also be used to broadcast messages. Any application can register a broadcast receiver to listen and respond to these intent broadcasts. Intent can be used to create internal, system, or third-party event-driven applications.

Intent is responsible for the description of an operation and the action data of the application. Android is responsible for finding the corresponding component described under the sub-intent, passing intent to the component being called, and completing the component calls. Intent plays the decoupling role between the caller and the one who is called.

Intent is a mechanism of runtime binding; it can connect two different components in the process of running the program. Through intent, the program can request or express willingness to Android; Android selects the appropriate components to handle the request based on the contents of the intent. For example, suppose an activity wants to open a web browser to view the content of a page; this activity only needs to issue a

WEB_SEARCH_ACTION request to Android. Based on the content request, Android will check the intent filter declared in the component registration statement and find an activity for a web browser.

When an intent is issued, Android finds one or more exact matches for the activity, service, or broadcastReceiver as a response. Therefore, different types of intent messages do not overlap and are not simultaneously sent to an activity or service, because startActivity() messages can be sent only to an activity and startService() intents can only be sent to a service.

The Main Roles of Intent

The main roles of intent are as follows.

Triggering a New Activity or Letting an Existing Activity Implement the New Operation

In Android, intent directly interacts with the activity. The most common use of intent is to bind application components. Intent is used to start, stop, and transfer application activities. In other words, intent can activate a new activity or make an existing activity perform a new operation. This can be accomplished by calling the Context.startActivity() or Context.startActivityForResult() method.

To open a different interface (corresponding to an activity) in an application, you call the Context.startActivity() function to pass an intent. Intent can either explicitly specify a specific class to open or include an action required to achieve the goals. In the latter case, the runtime will choose which activity to open, using a well-known process of intent resolution in which the Context.startActivity() finds and starts a single activity that best matches the intent.

Triggering a New Service or Sending New Requests to Existing Services

Opening a service or sending a request to an existing service is also completed by the intent class.

Trigger BroadcastReceiver

You can send BroadcastIntent using three different methods: Context.sendBroadcast(), Context.sendOrderedBroadcast(), and Context.sendStickyBroadcast().

Intent Resolution

The intent transfer process has two ways to match target consumers (such as another activity, IntentReceiver, or service) with the respondents of the intent.

The first is *explicit matching*, also known as *direct intent*. When constructing an intent object, you must specify the recipient as one of the intent's component properties (by calling setComponent (ComponentName) or setClass (Context, Class)). By specifying a component class, the application notification starts the corresponding components. This method is similar to an ordinary function call but varies in the reuse of the granularity.

The second is *implicit matching*, also known as *indirect intent*. The sender of the intent does not know or care who the recipient is when constructing an intent object. The attribute is not specified in the component intent. This intent needs to contain sufficient information so that the system can determine which components to use out of all those available to meet this intent. This method differs significantly from function calls and helps to reduce coupling between the sender and receiver. Implicit matching resolves to a single activity. If there are multiple activities that can implement a given action based on particular data, Android selects the best one to start.

For direct intent, Android does not need to do parsing because the target component is very clear. However, Android needs to resolve indirect intent. Through analysis, it maps the indirect intent to the activity, IntentReceiver, or service that processes the intent.

The mechanism of intent resolution mainly consists of the following:

- Looking for all <intent-filter>s and the intent defined by those filters, which are registered in AndroidManifest.xml

- Finding and handling the component of the intent through PackageManager (PackageManager can get information about the application package installed on the current device)

Intent filters are very important. A non-declared <intent-filter> component can only respond to explicit intent requests that the component name matches, but it cannot respond to implicit intent requests. A declared <intent-filter> component can respond to either explicit intent or implicit intent requests. When resolving implicit intent requests, Android uses three attributes of the intent—action, type, and category—to make the resolution. The specific resolution methods are described next.

Action Test

A <intent-filter> element should contain at least one <action>, or no intent requests can be matched to the <intent-filter>. If the action requested by an intent has at least one match of an <action> in <intent-filter>, then the intent passed the action test of this <intent-filter>.

If there is no description of a specific action type in the intent request or <intent-filter>, then one of the two following tests applies:

- If <intent-filter> does not contain any action type, regardless of what the intent requests are, there is no match to this <intent-filter>.

- If the intent request has no set action type, as long as the <intent-filter> contains an action type, this intent request will successfully pass the action test of <intent-filter>.

Category Test

For an intent to pass the category test, every category in the Intent must match a category in the filter. When every category of intent requests have exact matches with the `<category>` of one `<intent-filter>` of the components the intent request pass the test. The excess `<category>` declaration of `<intent-filter>` does not cause the match failure. Any `<intent-filter>` that does not specify a category test only matches intent requests that the configuration is not set for.

Data Test

The `<data>` element specifies a data URI and data type of the intent request that you want to receive. A URI is divided into three parts that match: scheme, authority, and path. The URI data type and scheme of the Internet request set by `setData()` must be the same as specified in `<intent-filter>`. If `<intent-filter>` also specifies authority or path, they have to match to pass the test.

This decision process can be expressed as follows:

- If the intent specifies the action, then the action list of the `<intent-filter>` of the target component must contain this action. Otherwise, it is not considered matched.

- If the intent does not provide a type, the system gets the data types from the data. And for some action methods, the target component's data-type list must contain the data type of the intent. Otherwise it cannot be matched.

- If the data for the intent is not the URI of the content, and the category and intent also do not specify its type, the matching is based on the data scheme of the intent (for instance, `http:` or `mailto:`), and the intent's scheme must appear in the scheme list of the target component.

- If the intent specifies one or more categories, these categories must all appear in the category list of the component. For instance, if the intent contains two categories, `LAUNCHER_CATEGORY` and `ALTERNATIVE_CATEGORY`, the target component obtained by the parsing must contain at least these two categories.

The Relationship between Applications and Activities

Beginners tend to get confused between applications and activities—in particular, the main activities (those that occur when the application starts). In fact, they are two completely different objects. The behaviors, attributes, and so forth are not the same. Following is a list of differences between applications and activities:

- No matter how many times an application starts, as long as it is not shut down, its value (that is, the object) is constant. It has only one instance.

- No matter where an application starts, as long as it is not closed, its value (that is, the object) is constant. It has only one instance.

- When an activity is not finished, its value (that is, the object) is constant. Each time onStart() is called, the activity displays on the screen front.

- The objects that startActivity starts are different each time. You can say that startActivity actually contains new objects.

  - Although you cannot get a new activity object after startActivity, the Android framework can send parameter values (similar to the actual parameter of the function call) when startActivity starts its corresponding activity objects.

  - Even more surprising is that Android can have an activity coexist in multiple objects. When an activity is closed, Android returns the results to the main activity started through startActivity. As a result, it automatically calls the onActivityResult() method that starts its activity object, and random distribution can be avoided.

- An application can have multiple objects of an activity.

The Basic Android Application Interface

In this section, you use an example to learn about Android development using the Android SDK integrated in the Eclipse IDE. You create an application named GuiExam using the Android SDK and learn about the Android interface design by following the steps of the process.

GuiExam Application Code Analysis

This section provides analysis of the GuiExam sample application. First, let's create the GuiExam application using the Android SDK in Eclipse. For the application name, type GuiExam. For the Build SDK, choose API 19, which includes the x86 instructions. As shown in Figure 8-2, select the system default configurations for all other entries.

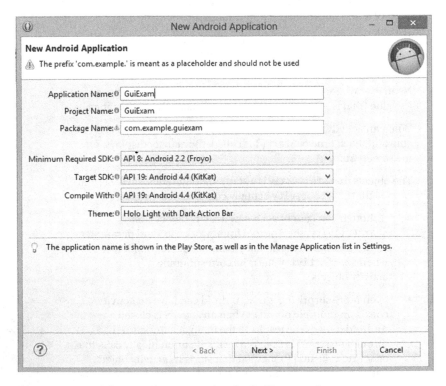

Figure 8-2. *Initial setup when generating the GuiExam project*

The file structure of the project is shown in Figure 8-3, and the user interface is shown in Figure 8-4.

Figure 8-3. *File structure of the GuiExam application*

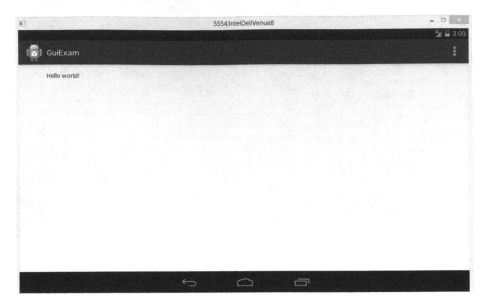

Figure 8-4. *The application interface of GuiExam*

The source code of the application's only Java file (`MainActivity.java`) is shown in Figure 8-5:

```
 MainActivity.java ☒    fragment_main.xml
 1  package com.example.guiexam;
 2
 3⊖ import android.support.v7.app.ActionBarActivity;
 4  import android.support.v7.app.ActionBar;
 5  import android.support.v4.app.Fragment;
 6  import android.os.Bundle;
 7  import android.view.LayoutInflater;
 8  import android.view.Menu;
 9  import android.view.MenuItem;
10  import android.view.View;
11  import android.view.ViewGroup;
12  import android.os.Build;
13
14  public class MainActivity extends ActionBarActivity {
15
16⊖     @Override
17      protected void onCreate(Bundle savedInstanceState) {
18          super.onCreate(savedInstanceState);
19          setContentView(R.layout.activity_main);
20
21          if (savedInstanceState == null) {
22              getSupportFragmentManager().beginTransaction()
23                      .add(R.id.container, new PlaceholderFragment())
24                      .commit();
25          }
26      }
27
28
29⊖     @Override
30      public boolean onCreateOptionsMenu(Menu menu) {
31
32          // Inflate the menu; this adds items to the action bar if it is present.
33          getMenuInflater().inflate(R.menu.main, menu);
34          return true;
35      }
36
```

Figure 8-5. *The typical source codes in Java file MainActivity.java*

You know the MainActivity.OnCreate() function is called when the event is created. The source code of the function is very simple. The superclass function is called in line 12, and the setContentView function is called in line 13. This function sets the UI display of the activity. In the Android project, most of the UI is realized by the view and view subclasses. View represents a region that can handle the event and can also render this region.

The code in line 13 indicates that the view is R.layout.activity_main. The auto-generated R.Java file under the gen directory of the project includes code such as this (excerpted):

```
Line #    Source Code
......
8 package com.example.guiexam;
9
10 public final class R {
    ......
```

```
26     public static final class layout {
27          public static final int activity_main=0x7f030000;
28     }
29     public static final class id {
30          public static final int menu_settings=0x7f080000;
31     }
32     public static final class string {
33          public static final int app_name=0x7f050000;
34          public static final int hello_world=0x7f050001;
35          public static final int menu_settings=0x7f050002;
36          public static final int title_activity_main=0x7f050003;
37     }
       . . . . . .
41     }
```

You can see that R.layout.activity_main is the resource ID of the main layout file activity_main.xml. This file reads as follows:

```
Line#     Source Code
1 <RelativeLayout xmlns:android="http://schemas.android.com/apk/res/android"
2      xmlns:tools="http://schemas.android.com/tools"
3      android:layout_width="match_parent"
4      android:layout_height="match_parent" >
5
6      <TextView
7          android:layout_width="wrap_content"
8          android:layout_height="wrap_content"
9          android:layout_centerHorizontal="true"
10          android:layout_centerVertical="true"
11          android:padding="@dimen/padding_medium"
12          android:text="@string/hello_world"
13          tools:context=".MainActivity" />14
15 </RelativeLayout>
```

The first line of this code indicates that the content is a RelativeLayout class. By checking the Android help documentation, you can see that the inheritance relationship of RelativeLayout is

```
java.lang.Object
    ↳ android.view.View
        ↳ android.view.ViewGroup
            ↳ android.widget.RelativeLayout
```

This class is indeed seen as a view class. This layout contains a TextView class, which is also the offspring class of the view. Line 12 indicates that its text property is @string/hello_world and its display text is the contents of the variable hello_world in strings.xml: "Hello world!"

As a superclass of the layout, ViewGroup is a special view that can contain other view objects or even ViewGroup itself. In other words, the ViewGroup object treats the objects of other views or ViewGroups as member variables (called *properties* in Java). The internal view objects contained in ViewGroup objects are called *widgets*. Because of the particularity of the ViewGroup, Android makes it possible for a variety of complex interfaces for applications to be automatically set.

Using Layouts as Interfaces

You can modify or design layouts as part of the application interface design. For example, you can modify the activity_main.xml file as follows:

1. Change TextView's Text property to "Type Here".

2. Pick a button widget from the Form Widgets column, and drop it into the activity_main screen. Set its Text property to "Click Me", as shown in Figure 8-6.

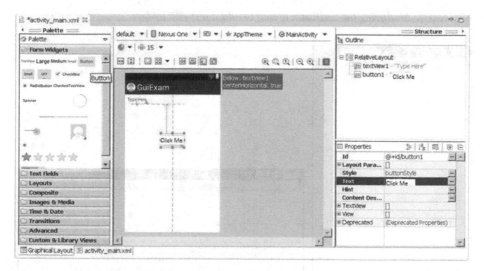

Figure 8-6. *Modifying the GuiExam layout to add a button*

3. Drag a plain text widget from the Text Fields section of the left column and drop it into the activity_main screen. Change the Width property under the layout parameters branch to fill_parent, and then drag plain text until it fills the entire layout, as shown in Figure 8-7.

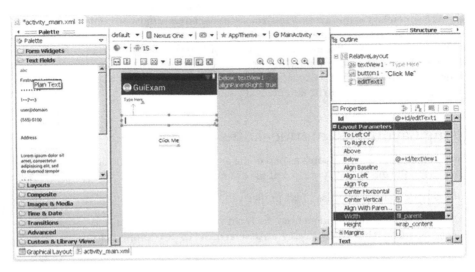

Figure 8-7. *Modifying the GuiExam layout to add a text-edit widget*

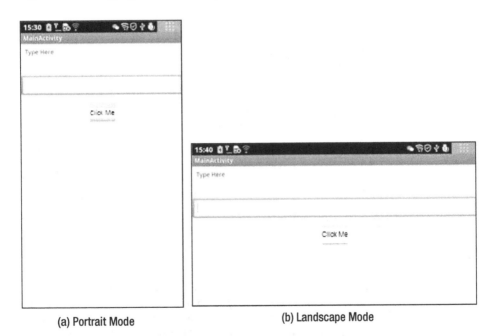

(a) Portrait Mode   (b) Landscape Mode

Figure 8-8. *The user interface of GuiExam after the layout has been modified*

From these examples, you can see the general structure of the interface. The activity set through setContentView (layout file resource ID) is: the activity contains a layout, and the layout contains various widgets, as shown in Figure 8-9.

254

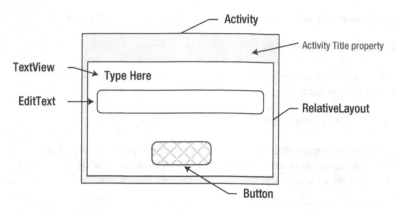

Figure 8-9. *Interface structure of the activity*

You may be wondering why Android introduced this layout concept. In fact, this is a developer-favored feature of Android, compared to the programming interface of Windows Microsoft Foundation Class (MFC). The layout isolates differences in screen size, orientation, and other details on the device, which makes the interface screen adaptive to a variety of devices. So, applications running on different device platforms can automatically adjust the size and position of the widget without the need for user intervention or code modification.

For example, the application you created can run on different Android phones, tablets, and television device platforms without your needing to change any code. The location and size of the widget are automatically adjusted. Even when you rotate a phone 90 degrees, the interface for portrait or landscape mode is automatically resized and maintained in its relative position. The layout also allows widgets to be arranged according to local national habits (most countries arrange them from left to right, but some countries arrange them from right to left). The details that need to be considered for the interface design are all completed by the layout. You can imagine what would happen if there were no layout classes—you would have to write code for each Android interface layout for each device. The complexity of this level of work is unthinkable.

Using the View Directly as an Interface

Earlier you saw an interface structure and code framework for activities. You also saw that most of the UI is implemented by the view and view subclasses. So, you can use the setContentView function to specify a view object, instead of a layout. The prototype of the setContentView function of the activity class includes the following.

This function sets a layout resource as the interface of the activity:

```
void setContentView(int layoutResID)
```

The first type of the function sets an explicit view as the interface of the activity:

```
void setContentView(View view)
```

The 2nd type f the function sets an explicit view as the interface of the activity, according to the specified format:

```
setContentView(View view, ViewGroup.LayoutParams params)
```

Here you work through an application example that uses the view directly as an activity interface, using the second function setContentView()You can modify the code of the MainActivity.java file as follows:

```
......
import android.widget.TextView;

public class MainActivity extends Activity {
    @Override
    public void onCreate(Bundle savedInstanceState) {
        super.onCreate(savedInstanceState);
        TextView tv = new TextView(this);  // Create a TextView Object that
        belongs to current Activity
        tv.setText("Hello My friends!");    // Set Display text of TextView
        setContentView(tv);                 // Set View as the main display
        of the Activity
}
```

The application interface is shown in Figure 8-10.

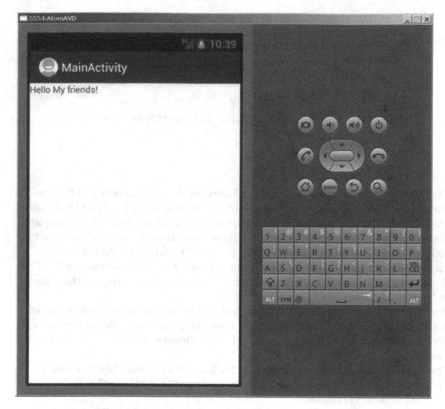

Figure 8-10. GuiExam sets the view directly as the interface

In this case you have TextView widgets, which are direct descendant classes of the view, as the application interface; they are set directly in the setContentView function. This way, the text displayed by the TextView becomes the output of the application interface. To use the TextView class, you use an import android.widget.TextView statement at the beginning of the file to import the package of the class.

Component ID

Now let's go back and look at the application layout shown in Figure 8-6. The ID attribute of the added text-edit widget in the layout is @ + id/editText1, and the button's ID property is @ + id/button1 (as shown in Figure 8-5). What does that mean?

Let's look at the R.java file (excerpted):

```
Line #    Source Code
   ......
8 package com.example.guiexam;
9
10 public final class R {
   ......
```

```
22      public static final class id {
23          public static final int button1=0x7f080001;
24          public static final int editText1=0x7f080002;
25          public static final int menu_settings=0x7f080003;
26          public static final int textView1=0x7f080000;
27      }
28      public static final class layout {
29          public static final int activity_main=0x7f030000;
30      }
        ......
43 }
```

Compared with the R.java file in the "GuiExam Application" section, you can see that lines 23 and 24 are new; they are the resource ID number of the newly added button and text-edit box. The type is int, which corresponds to the ID attribute values of these widgets. From the R.java file, you can find the ID of these widgets—the static constant R.id.button1 is the resource ID of the widgets (buttons) for which the ID attribute value is @ + id/button1, and the static constant R.id.editText1 is the resource ID of the widgets (text edit) for which the ID attribute value is @ + id/editText1. What's the reason for this? Let's see.

Android components (including widgets and activities) need to use a value of type int as a tag This value is the ID attribute value of the component tag. The ID attribute can only accept a value of resources type. That is, the value must start with @, ; for example, @ id/abc, @+id/xyz, and so on.

The @ symbol is used to prompt the parser for XML files to parse the name behind the @. For example, for @string/button1, the parser reads the button1 value of this variable from values/string.xml.

If the + symbol is used right after the @, it means that when you modify and save a layout file, the system will automatically generate the corresponding type int variables in R.java. The variable name is the value after the / symbol; for example, @+id/xyz generates int xyz = value in R.java, where the value is a hexadecimal number. If the same variable name xyz already exists in R.java, the system does not generate a new variable; instead, the component uses this existing variable.

In other words, if you use the @+id/name format and a variable named name exists in R.java, the component will use the value of the variable as an identifier. If the variable does not exist, the system adds a new variable, and the corresponding value for the variable is assigned (not repeated).

Because the component's ID attribute can be a resource ID, you can set any existing resource ID value: for example, @drawable/icon, @string/ok, or @+string/. Of course, you can also set a resource ID that already exists in the Android system, such as @id/android:list, in which the android: modifier in the ID indicates the package where the R class of the system is located (in the R.java file). You can enter android.R.id in the Java code-editing zone, which lists the corresponding resource ID. For example, you can set the ID property value this way.

For the reason just described, you generally set the ID attributes of Android components (including widgets, activities, and so on) to the @+id/XXX format. And you use R.id.XXX to represent the component's resource ID number in the program.

Buttons and Events

In the example in the section "Using Layouts as Interfaces," you created an application that includes Button, EditText, and other widgets, but nothing happens when the button is clicked. This is because you did not assign a response to the click event. This section first introduces Android events and the basics of the listener functions. You review and further explore more advanced knowledge about events in future chapters covering Android's multithreaded design.

In Android, each application maintains an event loop. When an application starts, it completes the appropriate initialization and then enters the event loop state, where it waits for a user action such as clicking the touch screen, pressing a key (a button), or some other input operation. User action triggers the program to generate a response to the *event*; the system generates and distributes the corresponding event class to handle it according to the event location, such as Activity or View. The callback methods are integrated into an interface called the *event listener*. You can achieve the specified event response by overriding the abstraction functions of the interface.

The scope of the event received by different classes is different for each class. For example, the Activity class can receive keypress events but not touch events, whereas the View class can receive both touch and keypress events. In addition, the event attribute details received by different classes also vary. For example, the touch event received by the View class consists of a number of touch points, coordinate values, and other information. It is subdivided into pressing down, bouncing, and moving events. But the Button class, which is a descendent of the View class, only detects a pressing action, and the event does not provide the coordinates of touch points or other information. In other words, Button processes the original event of the view and integrates all touch events into one event that records whether it is *clicked* or not.

Most of the incident-response interfaces of the View class use Listener as a suffix, so it is easy to remember their association with the event-listener interface. Table 8-4 shows examples of a number of classes and their incident-response functions.

Table 8-4. Examples of Classes and Their Incident-Response Functions

Class	Event	Listener Interface and Function
Button	Click	onClick() function of the onClickListener Interface
RadioGroup	Click	onCheckChange() function of the onCheckChangeListener Interface
View	Drop-down list	onTouch() function of the TouchListener interface
	Input focus changes	onFocusChange() function of the onFocusChangeListener interface
	Button	onKey() function of the onKeyListener interface

The process to respond to events is as follows. First, define the implementation class of your listener interface and override the abstract function. Second, call functions such as set ... Listener(). Then set the implementation class of the custom monitor interface to the event listener of the corresponding objects.

For example, you can modify the application source to execute an incident response. There are many coding styles to implement a Java interface. The next section discusses several ways in which the results of the code running these styles is the same.

Inner Class Listener

Modify the MainActivity.java code as follows (the bold text is added or modified):

```
Line #     Source Code
1 package com.example.guiexam;
2 import android.os.Bundle;
3 import android.app.Activity;
4 import android.view.Menu;
5 import android.view.MenuItem;
6 import android.support.v4.app.NavUtils;
7 import android.widget.TextView;

8 import android.widget.Button;                    // Use Button class
9
10 import android.view.View;                         // Use View class
11 import android.view.View.OnClickListener;    // Use View.OnClickListener
   class
12 import android.util.Log;
13 // Use Log.d debugging function
   public class MainActivity extends Activity {
14     private int iClkTime = 1;
15
16 // Count of Button Click
17
   @Override
18     public void onCreate(Bundle savedInstanceState) {
19         super.onCreate(savedInstanceState);
20         setContentView(R.layout.activity_main);
21
22         Button btn = (Button) findViewById(R.id.button1);
23 // Obtain Button object based on the resource ID number
24         final String prefixPrompt ="This is No. ";
25 // Define and set the value of the variable passed
26         final String suffixPrompt ="time(s) that Button is clicked";

27 // Define and set the value of the variable passed
28         btn.setOnClickListener(new /*View.*/OnClickListener(){
29 // Set the event response class of Button's click
30
```

260

```
31          public void onClick(View v) {
32              Log.d("ProgTraceInfo",prefixPrompt + (iClkTime++) +
                suffixPrompt);

        }
    });
}

@Override
public boolean onCreateOptionsMenu(Menu menu) {
    getMenuInflater().inflate(R.menu.activity_main, menu);
    return true;
}
}
```

On lines 18-22, you get the corresponding objects based on the resource ID of EditText and TextView, respectively. To use OnClickListener as an internal class, you add the final modifier in front of the variable. In lines 23 and 24, as the response code of the Button clicks, you first get the contents of EditText using EditText.getText(). Because the function returns a value of type Editable, you convert the type Editable to the type String via the CharSequence.toString() function (CharSequence is a superclass of Editable). Then you call the TextView.setText (CharSequence text) function to refresh the TextView display.

In Android, the accessor functions of a class attribute usually start with set/get, such as the read/write functions of the EditText contents:

```
Editable  getText()
void  setText(CharSequence text, TextView.BufferType type)
```

The interface of this application is shown in Figure 8-11; (a) is the start screen, (b) is the screen after text is entered in the edit text box, and (c) shows the application screen after the button is clicked.

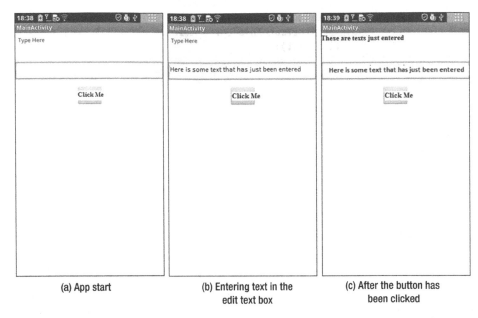

| (a) App start | (b) Entering text in the edit text box | (c) After the button has been clicked |

Figure 8-11. *The interface of the application with a* TextView, *a* Button, *and an* EditText

Using ImageView

Previous sections discussed typical uses of widgets and showed the basic concepts of widget programming. The image is the foundation of multimedia applications and is thus a major part of Android applications. This section introduces the use of the image/picture display widget, ImageView. Through the examples in this section, you learn how to use ImageView and add files to the project's resources.

The following example was originally developed in the section when you created the GuiExam application. Follow these steps to add a picture file to the project:

1. Copy the image file (in this case, morphing.png) into the corresponding /res/drawable-XXX project directory (the directory in which to store project files of different resolution images), as shown in Figure 8-12.

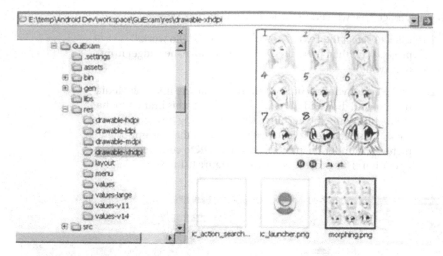

Figure 8-12. *Copy the image file into the project's* `res` *directory*

2. Open the project in Eclipse, and press the F5 key to refresh the project. You can see the file added to the project in Package Explorer (in this case, `morphing.png`), as shown in Figure 8-13.

Figure 8-13. *The Package Explorer window after the image is added*

To place ImageView widgets in the layout, follow these steps:

1. Click to select the TextView widget of the "Hello world!" project, and then press the Del key to remove the widget from the layout.

2. In the editor window of layout.xml, locate the Image & Media branch, and drag and drop the ImageView of this branch to the layout file. When the Resource Chooser dialog box pops up, click and select the Project Resource, select the just-imported picture file under the project, and click OK to complete the operation. This process is shown in Figure 8-14.

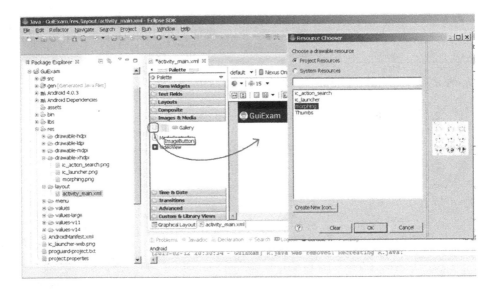

Figure 8-14. *Place the ImageView widget in the layout*

3. Adjust the size and position of the ImageView, and set its properties. This step can use the default values shown in Figure 8-15.

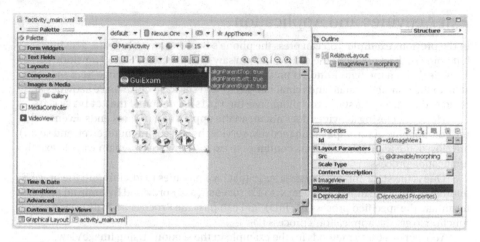

Figure 8-15. The property settings of the ImageView

4.   Save the layout file.

Normally, at this point, you would have to compile the Java code. However, in this example, compiling is not necessary. Figure 8-16 shows the application's interface.

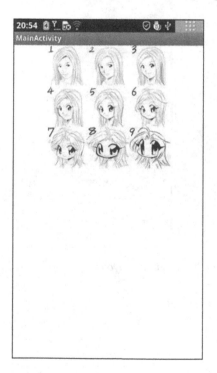

Figure 8-16. Application interface of the ImageView

Exit Activities and Application

In the previous example, you can press the phone's Back button to hide the activity, but doing so does not close the activity. As you saw in the section "State Transitions of Activities," when the Back button is pressed, started activities only change from the active state to the non-active state and remain in the system stack. To close these activities and remove them from the stack, you should use the finish function of the Activity class.

However, closing activities does not mean the application process ends. Even if all the components of the application (activity, service, broadcast intent receiver, and so on) are closed, the application process continues to exist. There are two main ways to exit the application process.

One is the static function System.exit that Java provides to forcibly end the process; another is the static function Process.killProcess (pid) provided by Android to terminate the specified process ID (PID). You can pass the Process.myPid() static function to get the application's process ID.

You can use these methods for the example in the section "Using ImageView." The specific steps are as follows:

1. Add two buttons to the layout file with the Text property "Close Activity" and "Exit Application" respectively and ID attributes @+id/closeActivity and @+id/exitApplication respectively. Adjust the buttons' size and position, as shown in Figure 8-17.

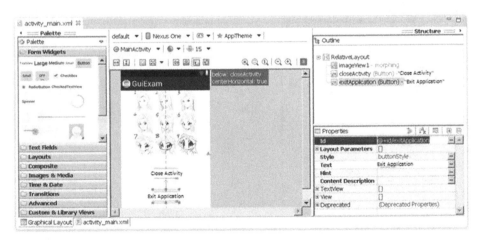

Figure 8-17. *Add Close Activity and Exit Application buttons in the layout*

2. Modify the source code of the MainActivity.java file as
    follows (the bold code is either added or modified, and the
    lines with strikethrough indicate deleted code):

```
Line #     Source Code
1 package com.example.guiexam;
2 import android.os.Bundle;
3 import android.app.Activity;
4 import android.view.Menu;
5 //import android.view.MenuItem;
6 //import android.support.v4.app.NavUtils;
7 import android.widget.Button;                    // Use Button class
8 import android.view.View;                        // Use View class
9 import android.view.View.OnClickListener;        // Use View.
  OnClickListenerClass
10 import android.os.Process;                       // Use killProcess method

11 public class MainActivity extends Activity {
12      @Override
13      public void onCreate(Bundle savedInstanceState) {
14          super.onCreate(savedInstanceState);
15          setContentView(R.layout.activity_main);
16          Button btn = (Button) findViewById(R.id.closeActivity);
17 // Get Button object of <Closed activity>
18          btn.setOnClickListener(new /*View.*/OnClickListener(){
19 // Set response code for Clicking
20              public void onClick(View v) {
21                  finish();                        // Close main activity
22              }
23          });
24          btn = (Button) findViewById(R.id.exitApplication);
25 // Get Button object of <Exit Application>
26 // Set the response code to Clicking
27              public void onClick(View v) {
28                  finish();                        // close main activity
29                  Process.killProcess(Process.myPid()); // Exit application
                     process

30              }
31
32
33
34
35          });
   }
```

```
    @Override
    public boolean onCreateOptionsMenu(Menu menu) {
        getMenuInflater().inflate(R.menu.activity_main, menu);
        return true;
    }
}
```

In lines 5 and 6, you remove the unused import statements. You set the response code for the Close Activity button in lines 16-21 and set the response code for the Exit Application button in lines 22-28. The only difference is that the latter adds the application-exit code Process.killProcess (Process.myPid ()). Both buttons use the same finish() function of the Activity class to close the activity. The code in lines 7-10 imports related classes.

The application interface is shown in Figure 8-18.

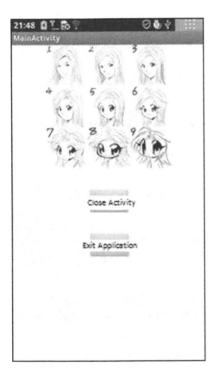

Figure 8-18. *The Close Activity and Exit Application interface of the application*

When you click the Close Activity or Exit Application button, the main interface of the application is turned off. The difference is that the application process (com.example.guiexam) does not quit for Close Activity; but for Exit Application, the process closes. This is clearly shown in the Devices pane of the DDMS view in Eclipse, in which you can see a list of processes on the target machine, as shown in Figure 8-19.

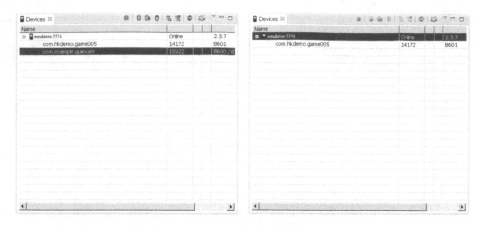

(a) Processes after clicking Close Activity

(b) Processes after clicking Exit Application

Figure 8-19. *The process in DDMS when the Close Activity and Exit Application application is running*

Summary

This chapter introduced Android interface design by having you create a simple application called GuiExam. You learned about the state transitions of activities, the Context class, intent, and the relationship between applications and activities. You also saw how to use the layout as an interface by changing the layout file activity_main.xml, and you saw how the button, event, and inner event listeners work. The next chapter describes how to create an application with multiple activities using the activity-intent mechanism and shows the changes needed in the AndroidManifest.xml file.

CHAPTER 9

■ ■ ■

GUI Design for Android Apps, Part 3: Designing Complex Applications

In the previous chapter, you learned about Android interface design by creating a simple application called GuiExam. The chapter also covered the state transition of activities, the Context class, and an introduction to intents and the relationship between applications and activities. You learned how to use a layout as an interface, and how button, event, and inner event listeners work. In this chapter, you learn how to create an application with multiple activities; examples introduce the explicit and implicit trigger mechanisms of activities. You see an example of an application with parameters triggered by an activity in a different application, which will help you understand the exchange mechanism for the activity's parameters.

Applications with Multiple Activities

The application in the previous example has only one activity: the main activity, which is displayed when the application starts. This chapter demonstrates an application with multiple activities, using the activity-intent mechanism, and shows the changes needed in the AndroidManifest.xml file.

As previously described, an activity is triggered by an intent. There are two kinds of intent-resolution methods: *explicit match* (also known as *direct intent*) and *implicit match* (also known as *indirect intent*). A triggering activity can also have parameters and return values. Additionally, Android comes with a number of built-in activities, and therefore a triggered activity can come from Android itself, or it can be customized. Based on these situations, this chapter uses four examples to illustrate different activities. For the explicit match, you see an application with or without parameters and return values. For the implicit match, you see an application that uses activities that come from the Android system or are user defined.

Triggering an Explicit Match of Activities with No Parameters

Using explicit match without parameters is the simplest trigger mechanism of the activity intent. This section first uses an example to introduce this mechanism and later covers more complex mechanisms.

The code framework of the activity-intent triggering mechanism for explicit matching includes two parts: the activities of the callee (being triggered) and those of the caller (trigger). The trigger is not limited to activities; it can also be a service, such as a broadcast intent receiver. But because you have only seen the use of activities so far, the triggers for all the examples in this section are activities.

1. The source code framework for the activity of the callee does the following:

   a. Defines a class that inherits from the activity.

   b. If there are parameters that need to be passed, then the source code framework of the activity calls the `Activity.getIntent()` function in the onCreate function to obtain the `Intent` object that triggers this activity, and then gets the parameters being passed through functions like `Intent.getData ()`, `Intent.getXXXExtra ()`, `Intent.getExtras ()`, and so on.

   c. Writes code for the normal activity patterns.

   d. If the trigger returns values, does the following before exiting the activity:

      i. Defines an `Intent` object

      ii. Sets data values for the intent with functions like `Intent.putExtras()`

      iii. Sets the return code of the activity by calling the `Activity.setResult()` function

   e. Adds the code for the activity of the callee in the `AndroidManifest.xml` file.

2. The code framework for the activity of the callee does the following:

   a. Defines the `Intent` object, and specifies the trigger's context and the `class` attribute of the triggered activity.

   b. If parameters need to be passed to the activity, sets the parameters for the `Intent` object by calling functions of the intent like `setData()`, `putExtras()`, and so on.

c. Calls `Activity.startActivity(Intent intent)` function to trigger an activity without parameters, or call `Activity.startActivityForResult(Intent intent, int requestCode)` to trigger an activity with parameters.

d. If the activity needs to be triggered by the return value, then the code framework rewrites the `onActivityResult()` function of the `Activity` class, which takes different actions depending on the request code (`requestCode`), result code (`resultCode`), and intentions (`Intent`) values.

In step 2a, the class attribute of the triggered activity is used, which involves a Java mechanism called *reflection*. This mechanism can create and return an object of the class according to the class name. The object of the triggered activity is not constructed before the triggering; therefore triggering the activity also means creating an object of that class so that subsequent operations can continue. That is, triggering the activity includes the operation of the newly created class objects.

The following two examples illustrate the code framework in detail. This section describes the first one. In this example, the triggered activity belongs to the same application as the activity of the trigger, and the triggered activity does not require any parameters and does not return any values. The new activity is triggered via a button, and its activity interface is similar to the interface of the example in the section "Exit Activities and Application." in Chapter 8, Figure 8-16. The entire application interface is shown in Figure 9-1.

(a) Interface when the app starts

(b) Interface when Change To The New Interface Without Parameters is clicked

(c) Interface when Close Activity is clicked

Figure 9-1. *The application interface with multiple activities in the same application without parameters*

After the application starts, the application's main activity is displayed, as shown in Figure 9-1(a). When the Change To The New Interface Without Parameters button is clicked, the app displays the new activity, as shown in Figure 9-1(b). Clicking the Close Activity button causes the interface to return to the application's main activity, as shown in Figure 9-1(c).

Create this example by modifying and rewriting the example in the GuiExam section in Chapter 8, as follows:

1. Generate the corresponding layout file for the triggered activity:

    a. Right-click the shortcut menu in the res\layout subdirectory of the application, and select New ➤ Other Items. A New dialog box pops up. Select the \XML\XML File subdirectory, and click Next to continue. In the New XML File dialog box, enter the file name (in this case noparam_otheract.xml), and click Finish. The entire process is shown in Figure 9-2.

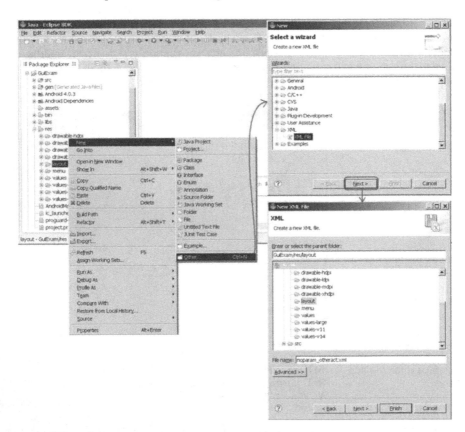

Figure 9-2. *The layout file for the triggered activity*

■ **Note** The file name is the name of the layout file. You must use only lowercase letters for compilation to be successful; otherwise you will get the error "Invalid file name: must contain only a–z0-9_.."

You can see the newly added xxx.xml file (in this case, noparam_otheract.xml) in the project's Package Explorer, as shown in Figure 9-3.

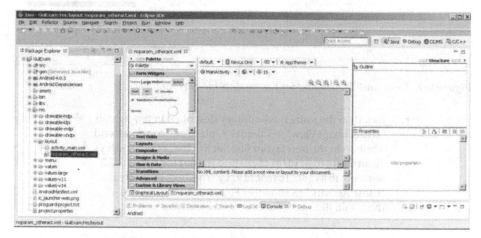

Figure 9-3. *Initial interface of the application's newly added layout file*

■ **Note** The layout editor window on the right is still empty, and there is no visible interface so far.

    b.   Select the Layouts subdirectory in the left palette, and drag the layout control (in this case, RelativeLayout) onto the window in the right pane. You immediately see a visible (phone-screen shaped) interface, as shown in Figure 9-4.

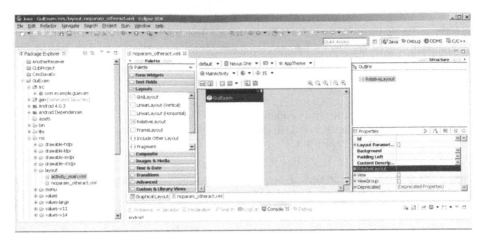

Figure 9-4. *Drag-and-drop layout for the newly added layout file*

    c.   Based on the same methodology described in the section "Using ImageView" in Chapter 8, place an ImageView and a button in the new layout file. Set the ImageView widget's ID attribute to @+id/picture and the Button widget's ID attribute to @+id/closeActivity. The Text property is "Close Activity," as shown in Figure 9-5. Finally, save the layout file.

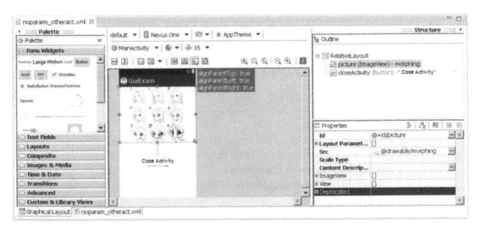

Figure 9-5. *Final configuration of the newly added layout file*

2. Add the corresponding Activity class for the layout file (Java source files). To do so, right-click \src\com.example.XXX under the project directory, and select New ➤ Class on the shortcut menu. In the New Java Class dialog box, for Name, enter the Activity class name corresponding to the new layout file (in this case, TheNoParameterOtherActivity). Click Finish to close the dialog box. The whole process is shown in Figure 9-6.

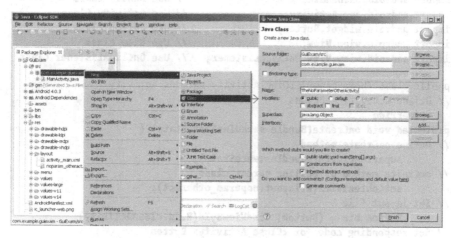

Figure 9-6. *Corresponding class for the newly added layout file*

You can see the newly added Java files (in this case, TheNoParameterOtherActivity.java) and the initial code, as shown in Figure 9-7.

Figure 9-7. *Corresponding class and initial source code of the newly added layout*

277

3. Edit the newly added .java file
(TheNoParameterOtherActivity.java). This class executes
the activity of the triggered activity (callee). Its source code is
as follows (bold text is added or modified):

```
Line #          Source Code
1  package com.example.guiexam;
2  import android.os.Bundle;                   // Use Bundle class
3  import android.app.Activity;                // Use Activity Class
4  import android.widget.Button;               // Use Button class
5  import android.view.View;                   // Use View class
6  import android.view.View.OnClickListener;   // Use OnClickListener Class

7  public class TheNoParameterOtherActivity extends Activity {
8  // Define Activity subclass
9      @Override
10 protected void onCreate(Bundle savedInstanceState) {
11 // Define onCreate method
12         super.onCreate(savedInstanceState);
13 // onCreate method of calling parent class
14         setContentView(R.layout.noparam_otheract);
15 // Set layout file
16         Button btn = (Button) findViewById(R.id.closeActivity);
17 // Set responding code for <Close Activity> Button
18         btn.setOnClickListener(new /*View.*/OnClickListener(){
19             public void onClick(View v) {
                   finish();
// Close this activity
               }
           });
       }
}
```

In line 7, you add the superclass Activity for the newly
created class. The code in lines 8 through 18 is similar to the
application's main activity. Note that in line 14, the code calls
the setContentView() function to set the layout for Activity,
where the parameter is the prefix name of the new layout XML
file created in the first step.

4. Edit the code for the trigger (caller) activity. The trigger
activity is the main activity of the application. The source code
is MainActivity.java, and the layout file is activity_main.xml.
The steps for editing are as follows:

   a. Edit the layout file, delete the original TextView widgets,
   and add a button. Set its ID property to
   @+id/goTONoParamNewAct and its Text property to
   "Change to interface without Parameter," as shown in
   Figure 9-8.

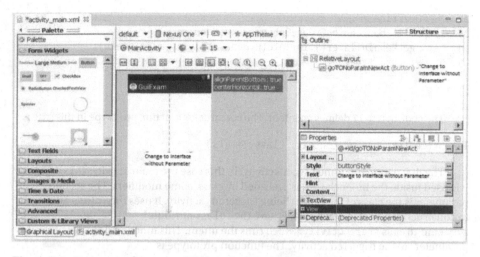

***Figure 9-8.** Layout configuration for the trigger activity*

b. Edit the source code file of the trigger activity (in this case, MainActivity.java) as follows (bold text is either added or modified):

```
Line #        Source Code
1  package com.example.guiexam;
2  import android.os.Bundle;
3  import android.app.Activity;
4  import android.view.Menu;
5  import android.content.Intent;              // Use Intent class
6  import android.widget.Button;               // Use Button class
7  import android.view.View.OnClickListener;
8  import android.view.View;

9  public class MainActivity extends Activity {
10    @Override
11    public void onCreate(Bundle savedInstanceState) {
12      super.onCreate(savedInstanceState);
13      setContentView(R.layout.activity_main);
14      Button btn = (Button) findViewById(R.id.goTONoParamNewAct);
15      btn.setOnClickListener(new /*View.*/OnClickListener(){
16        public void onClick(View v) {
17          Intent intent = new Intent(MainActivity.this,
           TheNoParameterOtherActivity.class);
18          startActivity(intent);
19        }
20      });
21    }
```

```
22      @Override
23      public boolean onCreateOptionsMenu(Menu menu) {
24        getMenuInflater().inflate(R.menu.activity_main, menu);
25        return true;
26      }
27 }
```

The code in line 17 defines an intent. The constructor function prototype in this case is

```
Intent(Context packageContext, Class<?> cls)
```

The first parameter is the trigger activity, in this case the main activity; this, because it is used inside the inner classes, is preceded by class-name modifiers. The second parameter is the class of the callee (being triggered) activity. It uses the .class attribute to construct its object (all Java classes have the .class attribute).

Line 18 calls startActivity, which runs the intent. This function does not pass any parameters to the triggered activity. The function prototype is

```
void Activity.startActivity(Intent intent)
```

     5.   Edit the AndroidManifest.xml file. Add descriptive information for the callee activity (bold text is added) to register the new Activity class:

```
Line #          Source Code
1 <manifest xmlns:android="http://schemas.android.com/apk/res/android"
2      package="com.example.guiexam"
3      android:versionCode="1"
4      android:versionName="1.0" >
...    ... ...
10     <application
11         android:icon="@drawable/ic_launcher"
12         android:label="@string/app_name"
13         android:theme="@style/AppTheme" >
14         <activity
15             android:name=".MainActivity"
16             android:label="@string/title_activity_main" >
17             <intent-filter>
18                 <action android:name="android.intent.action.MAIN" />
19
20                 <category android:name="android.intent.category.LAUNCHER" />
21             </intent-filter>
22         </activity>
23         <activity android:name=".TheNoParameterOtherActivity"
                              android:label="the other Activity"/>
24     </application>
25
26 </manifest>
```

You can also replace this XML code with the following methods:

- Method 1:

```
<activity android:name="TheNoParameterOtherActivity"
android:label=" the other Activity"> </activity>
```

- Method 2:

```
<activity android:name=".TheNoParameterOtherActivity " />
```

- Method 3:

```
<activity android:name=".TheNoParameterOtherActivity">
</activity>
```

The content of the android: name text field is the class name of the callee's activity:
TheNoParameterOtherActivity.

Note that if a period (.) is added before the name of the Activity class android:
name, the compiler will give you the following warning at this line in the XML file
(only a warning, not a compile error):

```
Exported activity does not require permission
```

Triggering Explicit Matching of an Activity with Parameters of Different Applications

The previous sections introduced triggering another activity without parameters in the
same application. The activity of the trigger is that the callee allows the exchange of
parameters: the trigger can specify certain parameters to the callee, and the callee can
return those parameter values to the trigger on exit. Additionally, the callee and the
trigger can be in completely different applications. This section shows an example of
an application with parameters triggered by an activity in a different application. This
example will help you understand the exchange mechanism for the activity's parameters.

Use the same GuiExam application from Chapter 8. The interface is shown in
Figure 9-9.

(a) Interface when the GuiExam application starts

(b) Interface after clicking Enter New Interface To Modify the Weather

(c) Entering a new value in the Set New Weather text box

(d) Interface after clicking Confirm Change

(e) Interface after clicking Enter New Interface To Modify The Weather and entering a new value in the Set New Weather text box

(f) Interface after clicking Cancel Change

Figure 9-9. *The interface of multiple activities in different applications*

As shown in Figure 9-9, the trigger activity is in the GuiExam application, where there is a variable to accept the weather condition entry. The interface in Figure 9-9(a) displays when the GuiExam application is opened. Click the Enter New Interface To Modify The Weather box to trigger the activity in HelloAndroid. When this activity starts, it displays the new weather condition passed in the Set New Weather text box, as shown in Figure 9-9(b). Now enter a new weather condition value in the Set New Weather, and click OK Change to close the trigger's activity. The new value returned from Set New Weather refreshes the Weather variable in the trigger's activity, as shown in Figure 9-9(d). If you click Cancel Change, it does the same thing and closes the activity, but the value Weather does not change, as shown in Figure 9-9(f).

The process list for the executing application is shown in Figure 9-10 (displayed in the DDMS window of the host machine in Eclipse).

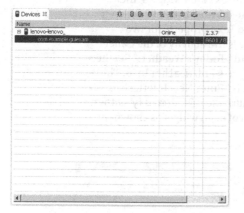

(a) When the GuiExam application starts

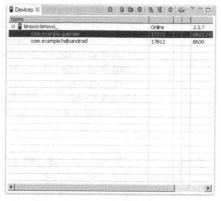
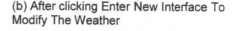

(b) After clicking Enter New Interface To Modify The Weather

(c) After clicking Confirm Change or Cancel Change

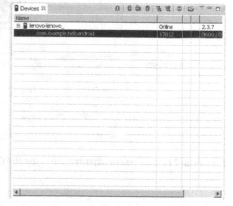

(d) After the GuiExam application exits

Figure 9-10. *Process list in DDMS for the multiple-activity application*

Figure 9-10 shows that when the application starts, only the process for the trigger, GuiExam, is running. But when you click Enter New Interface To Modify The Weather, the new activity is triggered and the process for the new activity HelloAndroid runs, as shown in Figure 9-10(b). When you click Confirm Change or Cancel Change, the triggered activity turns off, but the HelloAndroid process does not quit, as shown in Figure 9-10(c). Interestingly, even though the GuiExam trigger process exits, the HelloAndroid process to which the triggered activity belongs is still in the running state.

The build steps are as follows:

1. Modify the GuiExam code of the trigger application:

    a. Edit the main layout file (`activity_main.xml` in this case) by deleting the original TextView widgets; then add three new TextView widgets and a button. Set their properties as follows: set the Text property for two TextViews to "This interface is the activity of the Caller in GuiExam application" and "Today's Weather:". Set the third TextView's ID property to @+id/weatherInfo. The Text property of the button is "Enter New Interface to Change Weather", and its ID attribute is @+id/modifyWeather. Adjust the size and position of each widget as shown in Figure 9-11.

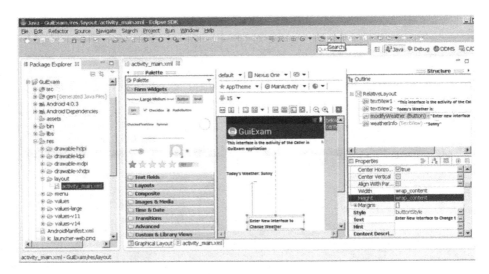

Figure 9-11. *The main layout design for the GuiExam trigger application*

b.   Modify the content of MainActivity.java as shown here:

```
Line #          Source Code
1  package com.example.guiexam;
2  import android.os.Bundle;
3  import android.app.Activity;
4  import android.view.Menu;
5  import android.widget.Button;            // Use Button class
6  import android.view.View;                // Use View class
7  import android.view.View.OnClickListener; // Use View.OnClickListener class
8  import android.widget.TextView;          // Use TextView class
9  import android.content.Intent;           // Use Intentclass
10 public class MainActivity extends Activity {
11     public static final String INITWEATHER = "Sunny; // /Initial Weather
12     public static final int MYREQUESTCODE =100;
13 // Request Code of triggered Activity
14     private TextView tv_weather;
15 // The TextView Widget that displays Weather info
16     @Override
17     public void onCreate(Bundle savedInstanceState) {
18         super.onCreate(savedInstanceState);
19         setContentView(R.layout.activity_main);
20         tv_weather = (TextView)findViewById(R.id.weatherInfo);
21         tv_weather.setText(INITWEATHER);
22         Button btn = (Button) findViewById(R.id.modifyWeather);
23 // Get Button object according to resource ID #
24         btn.setOnClickListener(new /*View.*/OnClickListener(){
25 // Set responding code click event
26             public void onClick(View v) {
27                 Intent intent = new Intent();
28                 intent.setClassName("com.example.helloandroid",
29 // the package ( application) that the triggered Activity is located
30                     "com.example.helloandroid.
                       TheWithParameterOtherActivity");
31 // triggered class ( full name)
32                 String wthr = tv_weather.getText().toString();
33 // Acquire the value of weather TextView
33                 intent.putExtra("weather",wthr); // Set parameter being
                                                     passed to Activity
34                 startActivityForResult(intent, MYREQUESTCODE);
35 // Trigger Activity
36             }
37         });
38     }
39
```

```
40      @Override
41      protected void onActivityResult(int requestCode, int resultCode,
                                        Intent data) {
42 // Triggered Activity finish return
43          super.onActivityResult(requestCode, resultCode, data);
44          if (requestCode == MYREQUESTCODE) {
45 // Determine whether the specified Activity end of the run
                if (resultCode == RESULT_CANCELED)
46                      {        }
47 // Select "Cancel" to exit the code, this case is empty
48                  else if (resultCode == RESULT_OK) {
49 // Select <OK> to exit code
50                      String wthr = null;
51                      wthr = data.getStringExtra("weather");
    // Get return value
                        if (wthr != null)
                            tv_weather.setText(wthr);
    // Update TextView display of weather content
                    }
                }
            }

        @Override
        public boolean onCreateOptionsMenu(Menu menu) {
            getMenuInflater().inflate(R.menu.activity_main, menu);
            return true;
        }
    }
```

The code in lines 23–28 triggers the activity with parameters in other applications. Lines 23–25 establish the trigger intent, which uses the Intent.setClassName() function. The prototype is

```
Intent Intent.setClassName(String packageName, String className);
```

The first parameter is the name of the package where the triggered activity is located, and the second parameter is the class name (required to use the full name) of the triggered activity. By using the startActivity ... function to trigger the activity, the system can accurately locate the application and activity classes.

Line 28 attaches the parameter as additional data to the intent. Intent has a series of putExtra functions to attach additional data and another series of getXXXExtra functions to extract data from the intent. Additional data can also be assembled by the Bundle class. Intent provides a putExtras function to add data and a getExtras function to get the data. putExtra uses a *property-value* data pairing or *variable name-value* data pairing to add and retrieve data. In this example, Intent.putExtra("weather", "XXX") saves the data pair consisting of the name of the weather variable and the value "XXX" as additional data for the intent.

The code line with `Intent.getStringExtra("weather")` gets the value of the weather variable from the attached intent data and returns the string type.

More details about these functions and the `Bundle` class can be found in the documentation on the Android web site. They are not discussed any further here.

In lines 33–46, you rewrite the `onActivityResult` function of the `Activity` class. This function is called when the triggered activity is closed. In line 36, you first determine which activity is closed and returned according to the request code. Then you judge whether it is returned by an OK or a Cancel click, based on the result code and the request code. Lines 40–50 get the negotiated variable values from the returned intent. Line 42 updates the interface based on the return value of the variable. In this function, if the user clicks Cancel to return, you do nothing.

2. Modify the code of the callee application `HelloAndroid` as shown in Figure 9-12:

   a. Using the method described in the section "Triggering Explicit Matching of an Activity with Parameters of Different Applications earlier in this chapter, add a layout file (in this case named `param_otheract.xml`), and drag and drop a `RelativeLayout` layout into the file.

   b. Edit this layout file by adding two `TextView` widgets, an `EditText`, and two `Button` widgets. Set their properties as follows:

      • Text property for the two `TextView` widgets: "This interface is the activity of the caller in HelloAndroid application" and "Set new weather as:"

      • ID property for the `EditText`: `@+id/editText_NewWeather`

      • Text property for the two Buttons: "Confirm Changes" and "Cancel Changes"

      • ID attribute for the two Buttons: `@+id/button_Modify` and `@+id/button_Cancel`

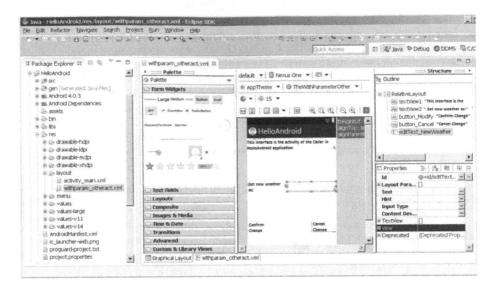

Figure 9-12. *New layout design of the triggered (callee) application* HelloAndroid

Then adjust their size and position.

    c.   As described in the section "Triggering Explicit Matching of an Activity with Parameters of Different Applications," add the corresponding class (in this case, TheWithParameterOtherActivity) for the new layout file, as shown in Figure 9-13.

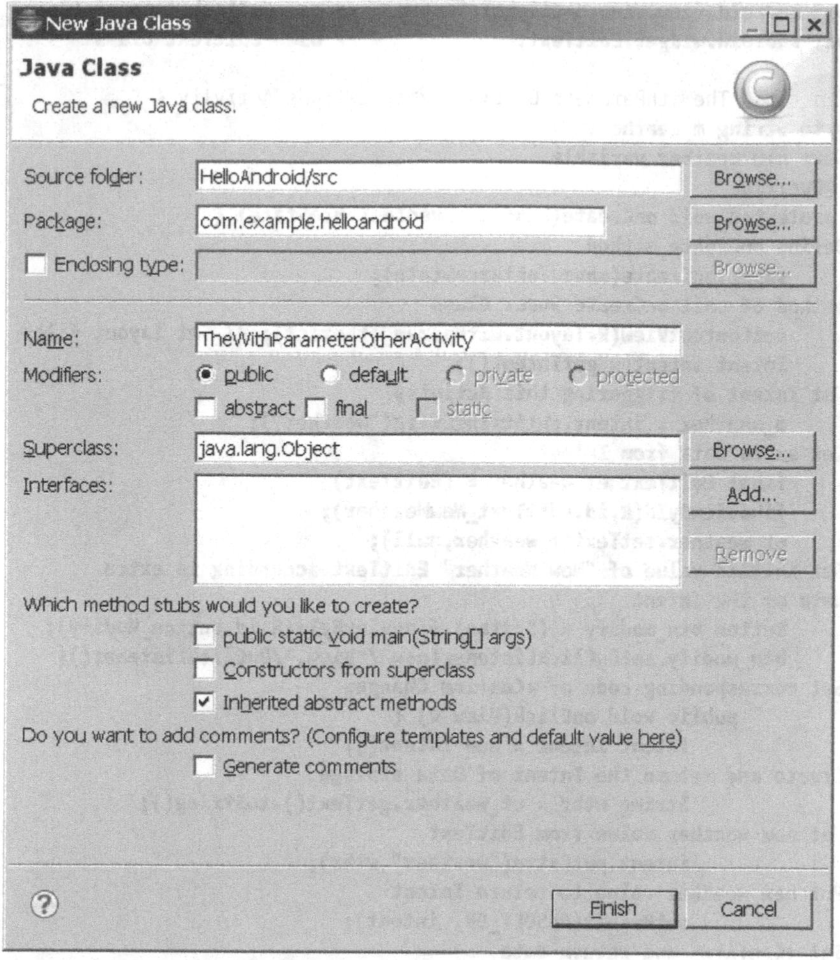

Figure 9-13. Add the corresponding class for the newly added layout file in the HelloAndroid project

        d.   Edit the class file for the newly added layout file (in this
                example, TheWithParameterOtherActivity.java). The
                content is as follows:

```
Line #          Source Code
1   package com.example.helloandroid;
2   import android.os.Bundle;              // Use Bundle Class
3   import android.app.Activity;           // Use Activity Class
4   import android.content.Intent;         // Use Intent Class
5   import android.widget.Button;          // Use Button Class
6   import android.view.View;              // Use View Class
```

```
7  import android.view.View.OnClickListener;   // Use OnClickListener Class
8  import android.widget.EditText;             // Use  EditText Class

9  public class TheWithParameterOtherActivity extends Activity {
10 private String m_weather;
11 // Save new weather variable
12    @Override
13    protected void onCreate(Bundle savedInstanceState) {
14 // Define onCreate method
15        super.onCreate(savedInstanceState);
16 // method of call onCreate Super Class
17        setContentView(R.layout.withparam_otheract); // Set layout file
18        Intent intent = getIntent();
19 // Get Intent of triggering this Activity
20        m_weather = intent.getStringExtra("weather");
21 // Get extra data from Intent
22        final EditText et_weather = (EditText)
           findViewById(R.id.editText_NewWeather);
23        et_weather.setText(m_weather,null);
24 // Set initial value of "New Weather" EditText according to extra
   data of the Intent
25        Button btn_modify = (Button) findViewById(R.id.button_Modify);
26        btn_modify.setOnClickListener(new /*View.*/OnClickListener(){
27 // Set corresponding code of <Confirm Change>
28            public void onClick(View v) {
29                Intent intent = new Intent();
30 // Create and return the Intent of Data storage
31                String wthr = et_weather.getText().toString();
32 // Get new weather value from EditText
33                intent.putExtra("weather",wthr);
34 // Put new weather value to return Intent
35                setResult(RESULT_OK, intent);
36 // Set <Confirm> and return data
37                finish();        // Close Activity
            }
        });
        Button btn_cancel = (Button) findViewById(R.id.button_Cancel);
        btn_cancel.setOnClickListener(new /*View.*/OnClickListener(){
   //Set corresponding code for <Cancel Change>
            public void onClick(View v) {
                setResult(RESULT_CANCELED, null);
   // Set return value for <Cancel>
                finish();     // Close this Activity
            }
        });
    }
}
```

This code follows the framework of an activity. It sets the activity layout in line 11 such that the layout name is the same as the layout file name created in step 1 (no extension). In lines 19-22, it first constructs an intent for the return and then adds extra data to the Intent object as the return data. In line 21, it sets the return value of the activity and the intent as a return data carrier. The prototype of the setResult function is

```
final void Activity.setResult(int resultCode, Intent data);
```

If resultCode is RESULT_OK, the user has clicked OK to return; and if it is RESULT_CANCELLED, the user has clicked Cancel to return. In this condition, the return data carrier intent can be null, which is set in line 27.

3. Modify AndroidManifest.xml, which is triggered by the application, with the following code:

```
Line #          Source Code
1 <manifest xmlns:android="http://schemas.android.com/apk/res/android"
2     package="com.example.helloandroid"
3     android:versionCode="1"
4     android:versionName="1.0" >
5
6     <uses-sdk
7         android:minSdkVersion="8"
8         android:targetSdkVersion="15" />
9
10    <application
11        android:icon="@drawable/ic_launcher"
12        android:label="@string/app_name"
13        android:theme="@style/AppTheme" >
14        <activity
15            android:name=".MainActivity"
16            android:label="@string/title_activity_main" >
17            <intent-filter>
18                <action android:name="android.intent.action.MAIN" />
19
20                <category android:name="android.intent.category.LAUNCHER" />
21            </intent-filter>
22        </activity>
23        <activity
24            android:name="TheWithParameterOtherActivity">
25            <intent-filter>
26                <action android:name="android.intent.action.DEFAULT" />
27            </intent-filter>
28        </activity>
29    </application>
30
31 </manifest>
```

4. Lines 24–29 are new. As in previous sections, you add an additional activity description and specify its class name, which is the class name of the triggered activity generated in the second step. See the section "Triggering an Explicit Match of Activities with No Parameters" for information about modifying the `AndroidManifest.xml` file. Unlike in that section, you add not only an activity and the documentation of its `name` attribute, but also the intent-filter instructions and state to accept the default actions described in the `Action` element and trigger this `Activity` class. The activity cannot be activated in the absence of the intent-filter description of the activity.

5. Run the callee application to register components of the activity. The modifications to `AndroidManifest.xml` file are not registered to the Android system until the callee application, `HelloAndroid`, is executed once. Thus this is an essential step to complete the registration of its included activity.

Implicit Matching of Built-In Activities

In the examples in the previous two sections, before you trigger the activity of the same application or different applications through the `Activity.startActivity()` function or the `Activity.startActivityForResult()` function, the constructor of the `Intent` objects explicitly specifies the class, either through the `.class` attribute or through the class name in a string. This way, the system can find the class to be triggered. This approach is called *explicit intent matching*. The next example shows how to trigger a class that is not specified. Instead, the system figures it out using an approach called *implicit intent matching*.

In addition, Android has a number of activities that have already been implemented, such as dialing, sending text messages, and so on. Examples in this section explain how you use can implicit matching to trigger these built-in activities. The application interface is shown in Figure 9-14.

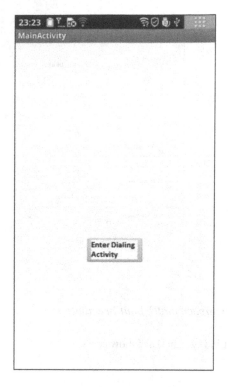 

(a) Application's start interface

(b) Interface after clicking Enter Dialing Activity

Figure 9-14. *The application interface when using implicit intent to trigger a built-in activity*

The user start the GuiExam application and clicks the Enter Dialing Activity button on the screen. It triggers dial-up activities that come with the system.

In this case, you modify the GuiExam project and use this application as a trigger. The implicit match triggered activity is the dial-up activity. The steps to build this example are as follows.

1. In the layout file (activity_main.xml) of the GuiExam application, delete the original TextView widgets, add a button, and set its ID attribute to @+id/goTODialAct and its Text property to "Enter Dialing Activity". Adjust its size and position as shown in Figure 9-15.

Figure 9-15. *Layout file of the application for the implicit match built-in activity*

2. Modify the source code file (MainActivity.java) as follows:

```
Line #       Source Code
1  package com.example.guiexam;
2  import android.os.Bundle;
3  import android.app.Activity;
4  import android.view.Menu;
5  import android.widget.Button;              // Use Button Class
6  import android.view.View;                  // Use View Class
7  import android.view.View.OnClickListener;  // Use View.OnClickListener Class
8  import android.content.Intent;             // Use Intent Class
9  import android.net.Uri;                    // Use URI Class

10 public class MainActivity extends Activity {
11     @Override
12     public void onCreate(Bundle savedInstanceState) {
13       super.onCreate(savedInstanceState);
14       setContentView(R.layout.activity_main);
15       Button btn = (Button) findViewById(R.id.goTODialAct);
16       btn.setOnClickListener(new /*View.*/OnClickListener(){
17 // Set corresponding Code for Click Activity
18          public void onClick(View v) {
19            Intent intent = new Intent(Intent.ACTION_DIAL,
                 Uri.parse("tel:13800138000"));
```

```
20          startActivity(intent); // Trigger corresponding Activity
21        }
22      });
      }
23
24      @Override
25      public boolean onCreateOptionsMenu(Menu menu) {
26        getMenuInflater().inflate(R.menu.activity_main, menu);
27        return true;
28      }
    }
```

The code in line 16 defines an *indirect intent* (that is, intent of implicit match. It is called an indirect intent because the class that needs to be triggered is not specified in the constructor of the object; the constructor only describes the function of the class that needs to be triggered to complete dialing. The constructor functions for the indirect intent are as follows:

```
Intent(String action)
Intent(String action, Uri uri)
```

These functions require the classes (activities) that can complete the specified action when they are called . The only difference between the two is that the second function also comes with data.

This example uses the second constructor, which requires the activity that can complete the dialing and extra data as a string of phone numbers. Because the application does not specify the trigger type, Android finds the class to handle this action (for example, `Activity`) from the registered class list and triggers the start of the event.

If multiple classes can handle the specified action, Android pops up a selection menu, and users can select which one to run.

The parameter `action` can use the system-predefined string. In the previous example, `Intent.ACTION_DIAL` is the string constant of `ACTION_DIAL`, which is defined by the `Intent` class. Some system-predefined `ACTION` examples are shown in Table 9-1.

Table 9-1. *Some System-Predefined* ACTION *Constants*

ACTION Constant Name	Value	Description
ACTION_MAIN	android.intent. action.MAIN	Start up as the initial activity of a task with no data input and no returned output.
ACTION_VIEW	android.intent. action.VIEW	Display the data in the intent URI.
ACTION_EDIT	android.intent. action.EDIT	Request an activity to edit data.
ACTION_DIAL	android.intent. action.DIAL	Start a phone dialer, and use preset numbers in the data to dial.
ACTION_CALL	android.intent. action.CALL	Initiate a phone call, and immediately use the number in the data URI to initiate a call.
ACTION_SEND	android.intent. action.SEND	Start an activity to send specific data (the recipient is selected by activity resolution).
ACTION_SENDTO	android.intent. action.SENDTO	Generally, start an activity to send a message to a contact designated in the URI.
ACTION_ANSWER	android.intent. action.ANSWER	Open an activity to process an incoming call. Currently it is handled by a local phone-dialing tool.
ACTION_INSERT	android.intent. action.INSERT	Open an activity that can insert a new project at the addition cursor in a specific data field. When it is called as the child activity, it must return the URI of the newly inserted project.
ACTION_DELETE	android.intent. action.DELETE	Start an activity to delete a data port at the URI position.
ACTION_WEB_SEARCH	android.intent. action.WEB_SEARCH	Open an activity, and run a web page search based on the text in the URI data.

The ACTION constant name is the first parameter used in the constructor of the implicit-match intent. The value of the ACTION constant, used in the AndroidManifest.xml statement of the activity that receives this action, is not used in this section, but is used in the next section. You can find more information about predefined ACTION values in the android.content.Intent help documentation.

Implicit Match that Uses a Custom Activity

The previous example used implicit matching to trigger activities that come with the Android system. In this section, you see an example of how to use an implicit match to trigger a custom activity.

The configuration of this example application is similar to the one in the section "Triggering Explicit Matching of an Activity with Parameters of Different Applications." The triggering application is hosted in the GuiExam project, and the custom activity triggered by implicit match is in the HelloAndroid application. The interface is shown in Figure 9-16.

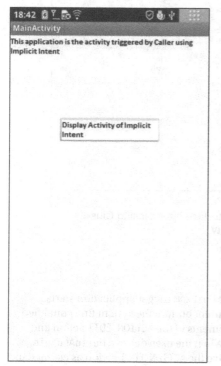

(a) Application's start interface

(b) Interface after clicking Display Activity Of Implicit Intent

Figure 9-16. The interface of implicit match that uses a custom activity

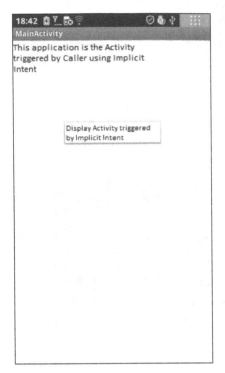 

c) Interface after selecting HelloAndroid   (d) Interface after clicking Close
Activity

Figure 9-16. *(continued)*

Figure 9-16(a) shows the interface when the GuiExam trigger application starts. When you click the Display Activity Of Implicit Intent button, the system finds qualified candidates for activities according to the requirements of the ACTION_EDIT action and displays a list of events of these candidates (b). When the user-defined HelloAndroid application is selected, the activity that can receive the ACTION_EDIT action as claimed in the intent-filter in HelloAndroid application is displayed (c). When you click the Close Activity button, the application returns to the original GuiExam activity interface (d).

Like the previous ones, this example is based on modifying the GuiExam project. The steps are as follows:

1. Edit the main layout file (activity_main.xml). Delete the original TextView widgets, and then add a TextView and a button. Set the TextView's Text property to "This application is the Activity triggered by Caller using Implicit Intent". Set the button's Text property to "Display Activity triggered by Implicit Intent" and its ID attribute to @+id/goToIndirectAct, as shown in Figure 9-17.

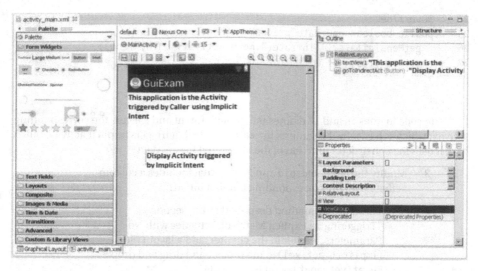

Figure 9-17. *The main layout design for the GuiExam trigger application*

2. Edit MainActivity.java as follows:

```
Line #          Source Code
1  package com.example.guiexam;
2  import android.os.Bundle;
3  import android.app.Activity;
4  import android.view.Menu;
5  import android.widget.Button;              // Use Button Class
6  import android.view.View;                  // Use View class
7  import android.view.View.OnClickListener;  // Use View.OnClickListener class
8  import android.content.Intent;             // Use Intent Class

9  public class MainActivity extends Activity {
10     @Override
11     public void onCreate(Bundle savedInstanceState) {
12         super.onCreate(savedInstanceState);
13         setContentView(R.layout.activity_main);
14         Button btn = (Button) findViewById(R.id.goToIndirectAct);
15         btn.setOnClickListener(new /*View.*/OnClickListener(){
16 // Set respond Code for Button Click event
17         public void onClick(View v) {
18             Intent intent = new Intent(Intent.ACTION_EDIT);
19 // Construct implicit Inent
20             startActivity(intent);         // Trigger Activity
21         }
        });
22     }
23
```

```
24    @Override
25    public boolean onCreateOptionsMenu(Menu menu) {
26      getMenuInflater().inflate(R.menu.activity_main, menu);
27      return true;
    }
  }
```

The code in lines 16 and 17 defines the implicit intent and triggers the corresponding activity, which is basically the same as the earlier code that triggers implicit activity, but here it uses the constructor function of the intent that has no data.

3. Modify the HelloAndroid application that includes a custom activity with the corresponding implicit intent:

    a. Based on the method described in the section "Triggering an Explicit Match of Activities with No Parameters," earlier in the chapter, add a layout file (implicit_act.xml) to the project and drag and drop a RelativeLayout layout into the file.

    b. Edit the layout file, and add TextView, ImageView, and Button widgets. Set the attributes as follows:

        • Text property of the TextView: "This interface is an Activity of the HelloAndroid, which is responsible for action triggered by the ACTION_EDIT".

        • ImageView: Set up exactly as in the section "Using ImageView" in Chapter 8.

        • Text property of the Button: "Close Activity".

        • ID property of the Button: @+id/closeActivity.

Then adjust their respective size and position, as shown in Figure 9-18.

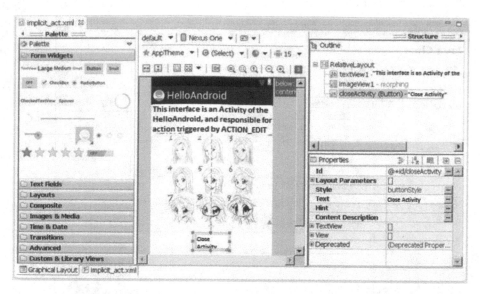

Figure 9-18. *Layout file for the custom activity of the corresponding implicit intent*

4. Similar to the process described in the section "Triggering an Explicit Match of Activities with No Parameters," add the corresponding class to the project for the new layout file (TheActivityToImplicitIntent), as shown in Figure 9-19.

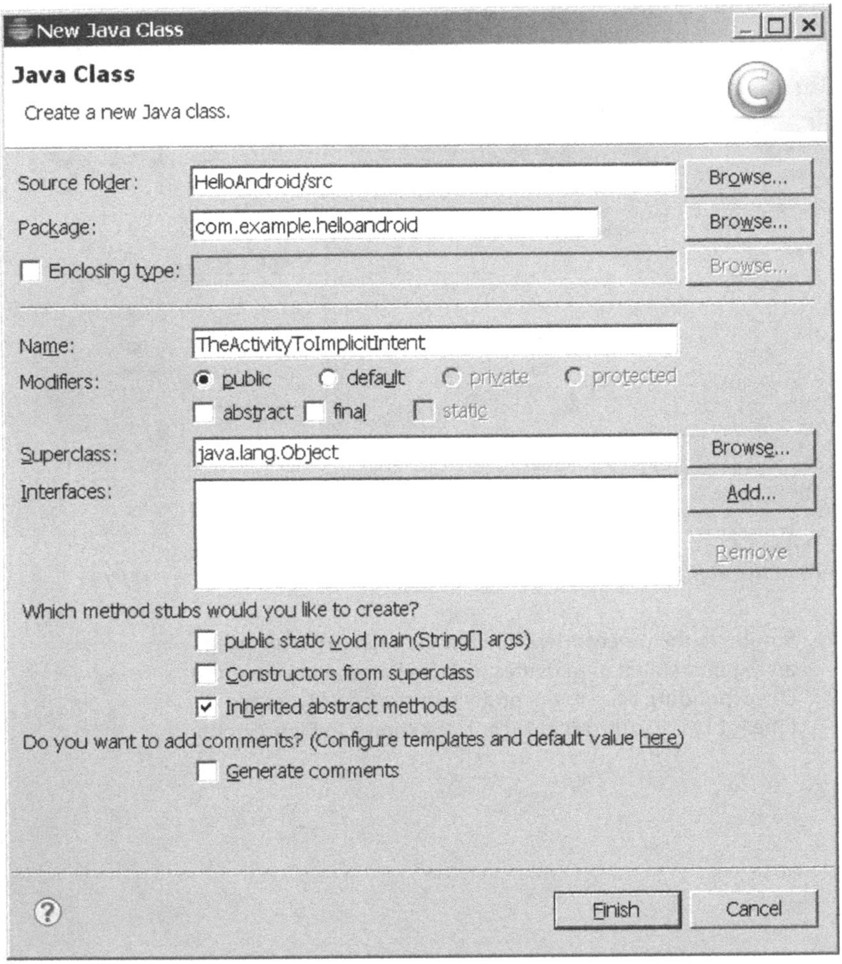

Figure 9-19. New class for the custom activity of the corresponding implicit intent

5. Edit the class file for the newly added layout file
(TheActivityToImplicitIntent.java), which reads
as follows:

```
Line #        Source Code
1 package com.example.helloandroid;
2 import android.os.Bundle;
3 import android.app.Activity;
4 import android.widget.Button;            // Use Button Class
5 import android.view.View;                // Use View class
6 import android.view.View.OnClickListener; // Use View.OnClickListener class
```

```
7 public class TheActivityToImplicitIntent extends Activity {
8     @Override
9     public void onCreate(Bundle savedInstanceState) {
10        super.onCreate(savedInstanceState);
11        setContentView(R.layout.implicit_act);
12    Button btn = (Button) findViewById(R.id.closeActivity);
13    btn.setOnClickListener(new /*View.*/OnClickListener(){
14 // Set response code for <Close Activity> Click
15        public void onClick(View v) {
16        finish();
17        }
18    });
19    }
   }
```

6. Modify the AndroidManifest.xml file of the HelloAndroid
    custom application containing the corresponding implicit
    intent, as follows:

```
Line #          Source Code
1 <manifest xmlns:android="http://schemas.android.com/apk/res/android"
2
3     package="com.example.helloandroid"
4
5     android:versionCode="1"
6
7     android:versionName="1.0" >
8
9     <uses-sdk
10        android:minSdkVersion="8"
11        android:targetSdkVersion="15" />
12
13    <application
14        android:icon="@drawable/ic_launcher"
15        android:label="@string/app_name"
16        android:theme="@style/AppTheme" >
17        <activity
18            android:name=".MainActivity"
19            android:label="@string/title_activity_main" >
20            <intent-filter>
21                <action android:name="android.intent.action.MAIN" />
22
23                <category android:name="android.intent.category.LAUNCHER" />
24            </intent-filter>
25        </activity>
```

```
26          <activity
27              android:name="TheActivityToImplicitIntent">
28              <intent-filter>
29                  <action android:name="android.intent.action.DEFAULT" />
30                  <action android:name="android.intent.action.EDIT" />
31                  <category android:name="android.intent.category.DEFAULT" />
32              </intent-filter>
33          </activity>
        </application>
    </manifest>
```

The code in lines 24–32 (in bold) gives the activity information for receiving the implicit intent. Line 26 specifies that you can receive an `android.intent.action.EDIT` action. This value corresponds to the constant value of the `ACTION` parameter `Intent.ACTION_EDIT` of the trigger's intent constructor function (the `MainActivity` class of `GuiExam`). This is a predetermined contact signal between the trigger and the callee. Line 27 further specifies that the default data type can also be received.

7. Run the application `HelloAndroid`, which now contains a custom activity for the corresponding implicit intent and registers its `AndroidManifest.xml` file in the system.

Summary

So far, three chapters have covered Android interface design. The simple `GuiExam` application has demonstrated the state transition of an activity, the `Context` class, intents, and the relationship between applications and activities. You also learned how to use a layout as an interface and how the button, event, and inner event listener work. Examples with multiple activities introduced the explicit and implicit trigger mechanisms for activities. You saw an example of an application with parameters triggered by an activity in a different application, and you now understand the exchange mechanism for the activity's parameters.

The application interface discussed so far is basically similar to a dialog interface. The drawback of this mode is that it is difficult to obtain accurate touchscreen input, making it difficult to display accurate images based on the input interface. The next chapter, which covers the last part of Android interface design, introduces the view-based interaction style interface. In this interface, you can enter information with accurate touchscreen input and display detailed images, as required by many game applications.

■ ■ ■

## CHAPTER 10

GUI Design for Android Apps, Part 4: Graphic Interface and Touchscreen Input

So far, three chapters have been devoted to Android interface design. The application interface discussed so far is similar to a dialog interface. The drawback is that it is difficult to obtain accurate touchscreen input information, so it is hard to display accurate images based on the input interface. This chapter introduces the view-based interaction style interface. In this mode, you can enter information with accurate touchscreen input and display detailed images, which happen to be requirements for lots of game applications.

Display Output Framework

Unlike the dialog box–style interface, which consists of TextView, EditText, Button, and other window components, an interactive UI display directly uses a View class. This section introduces the basic framework of drawing in the view (that is, displaying images or graphics).

To display images and graphics in a view, you need to put drawing code into its onDraw function. The onDraw function is called whenever images need to be redrawn in a view, such as when the view is displayed when the application starts, when the front cover object (such as a view, an event, or a dialog box) on top of the graphic view is moved away, when the view from the bottom layer is moved into the top layer with the activity, or in similar circumstances. You're advised to put the drawing code in the View.onDraw function, so you can ensure when the view needs to be displayed to the user. The view window can also immediately be displayed in its total output; otherwise, certain graphic view areas may not be refreshed or repainted.

Android drawing functions such as draw rectangle, draw oval, draw straight line, and display text are usually integrated into the Canvas class. When the View.onDraw callback executes, it brings with it a Canvas parameter that is used to get the Canvas object.

Android uses the Paint class to draw a variety of graphics. Paint contains a variety of brush attributes, such as color, fill style, font, and font size.

As described earlier in the book, the interface configuration style of the application code generated in Eclipse is as follows: an activity includes layouts, and a layout contains two layers of widget structures. For this reason, you set parameters for the setContentView function in the onCreate function of the activity as the layout to achieve this effect. To use the view-based interface, you need to change the default parameter layout of the setContentView function to a custom view class.

Here is an example that illustrates the process. Modify the GuiExam example project by using the following steps:

1. Using the same steps as in the section "Triggering an Explicit Match of Activities with No Parameters" in Chapter 9, create a new class (MyView), as shown in Figure 10-1.

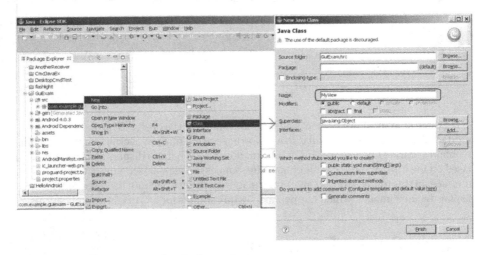

Figure 10-1. *Create a new class in the project*

2. Edit the source code of the newly added class (MyView.java). The content is shown next.

```
Line#     Source Code
1  package com.example.guiexam;
2
3  import android.view.View;
4  import android.graphics.Canvas;
5  import android.graphics.Paint;
6  import android.content.Context;

7  import android.graphics.Color;
8  import android.graphics.Paint.Style;
9  import android.graphics.Rect;
```

```
10 import android.graphics.Bitmap;
11 import android.graphics.BitmapFactory;
12 import android.graphics.Typeface;

13 public class MyView extends View {
14     MyView(Context context) {
15         super(context);
16     }

17     @Override
18     public void onDraw(Canvas canvas) {
19         Paint paint = new Paint();
20         paint.setAntiAlias(true);          // Sett anti-aliasing
21 // paint.setColor(Color.BLACK);            // Set Color Black
22 // paint.setStyle(Style.FILL);             // Set Fill Style
23         canvas.drawCircle(250, 250, 120, paint);   // Draw Circle

24         paint.setColor(Color.RED);          // Set color red
25         paint.setStyle(Style.STROKE);       // Set style-Stroke ( no fill)
26         canvas.drawRect(new Rect(10, 10, 120, 100), paint); // draw rect

27         paint.setColor(0xff0000ff /*Color.BLUE*/ );
28         String str = "Hello!";
29         canvas.drawText(str, 150, 20, paint);  // display text

30         paint.setTextSize(50);                 // Set Text Size
31         paint.setTypeface(Typeface.SERIF);     // Set Typeface: Serif
32         paint.setUnderlineText(true);          // Set Underline Text
33         canvas.drawText(str, 150, 70, paint);  // Display text

        Bitmap bitmap = BitmapFactory.decodeResource(getResources(),
        R.drawable.ic_launcher);
        canvas.drawBitmap(bitmap, 0, 250, paint); // Display image
    }
}
```

307

The code in line 13 adds extends View, which makes a custom class; in this case, MyView inherits from the View category. Lines 13-16 create a custom class constructor function that calls the superclass. This constructor function is essential to prevent the following compilation error:

```
Implicit super constructor View() is undefined. Must explicitly invoke
another constructor
```

Lines 17-34 override the View.onDraw function to program various pieces of drawing code. You construct a brush—that is, a Paint object—for drawing in line 16, and you set it to eliminate jagged edges in line 17. Line 23 draws a circle (x = 250, y = 250); line 24 sets the brush color to red, and so forth.

The prototype of the setColor function is

```
void Paint.setColor(int color);
```

In Android, a four-byte integer is used to represent a color, based on α, red, green, and blue. This integer data format looks like this:

αα	rr	gg	bb

From left to right, the first four bytes represent α, red, green, and blue values. For example, blue is 0xff0000ff, as is also reflected in line 27. In addition, the Android Color class also defines a constant for some colors, such as BLACK, RED, GREEN, BLUE, and so on, as reflected in line 24.

The setStyle function sets the fill mode of the brush. The function prototype is

```
void  Paint.setStyle(Paint.Style style)
```

The parameter style can take Paint.Style.STROKE (hollow fill), Paint.Style.FILL (filled), or Paint.Style.FILL_AND_STROKE (solid and filled). These values are constants defined in the Paint.Style class; their corresponding display styles are shown in Table 10-1.

Table 10-1. *Fill Mode Parameters and Examples*

Image Displayed	Graphic Function Parameter Setting
	Color=BLACK, Style=FILL
	Color=BLACK, Style=STROKE
	Color=BLACK,Style=FILL_AND_STROKE

3. Modify the main Activity class (MainActivity.java) as follows:

```
Line#    Source Code
1   package com.example.guiexam;
2   import android.os.Bundle;
3   import android.app.Activity;
4   import android.view.Menu;
5   public class MainActivity extends Activity {
6       @Override
7       public void onCreate(Bundle savedInstanceState) {
8           super.onCreate(savedInstanceState);
9   // setContentView(R.layout.activity_main);
10          setContentView(new MyView(this));
11  }
12      ......
```

The system automatically overrides the code in line 7 with the code in line 8. This allows a custom view class instead of the default layout as the interface of the activity.

The application interface is as shown in Figure 10-2; (a) shows the entire interface, and (b) is the enlarged section of the graphical display.

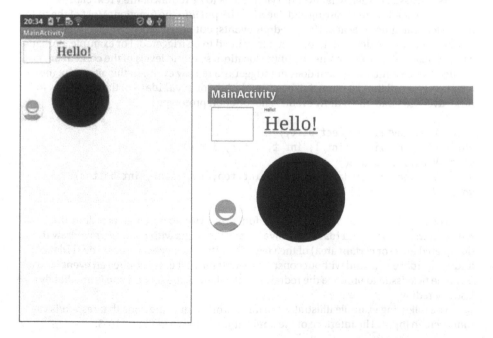

(a) Application's full UI   (b) Enlarged section of the application UI

Figure 10-2. *The interface of the display output framework of the GuiExam application*

Drawing Framework for Responding to Touchscreen Input

The previous example application only displays images/graphics and cannot respond to touchscreen input. In this section, you see how to respond to touchscreen input and control the view display.

View has an onTouchEvent function with the following function prototype:

```
boolean View.onTouchEvent(MotionEvent event);
```

When a user clicks, releases, moves, or does other interactive actions on the touchscreen, a touch input event is generated. This touch input event triggers the call to View.onTouchEvent. To allow users to process touchscreen input, you need to rewrite this function. The response code needs to be written in the function's body.

View.onTouchEvent has a parameter of type MotionEvent that defines the coordinate position of the touch point, event type, and so on of the MotionEvent class. The event types can be MotionEvent.ACTION_DOWN, MotionEvent.ACTION_MOVE, MotionEvent.ACTION_UP, or equivalent, as defined constants in the MotionEvent class. The constants represent interactive actions such as a touchscreen press, touchscreen move, touchscreen pop-up, and so on.

As discussed earlier, whenever the view needs to be redrawn, the View.onDraw function is called, so the drawing code needs to be put into the function. Most of the time, the system can automatically trigger redraw events; but because users design their own redraws, the system does not know when they need to be triggered. For example, perhaps a user updates the display content, but the location, size, and levels of the content are not changed; as a result, the system does not trigger the redraw event. In this situation, the user needs to call the class function postInvalidate or invalidate of the View class to proactively generate the redraw events. The function prototype is

```
void   View.invalidate(Rect dirty)
void   View.invalidate(int l, int t, int r, int b)
void   View.invalidate()
void   View.postInvalidate(int left, int top, int right, int bottom)
void   View.postInvalidate()
```

The postInvalidate and invalidate functions with no parameters redraw the entire view; the postInvalidate and invalidate functions with parameters redraw the designated area (or certain area) of the view. The difference between postInvalidate and invalidate with and without constants is that the first case requires an event loop until the next issue to produce the redraw event, whereas the second one immediately issues a redraw.

The following example illustrates the framework of drawing code that responds to touchscreen input. The interface of the application is shown in Figure 10-3.

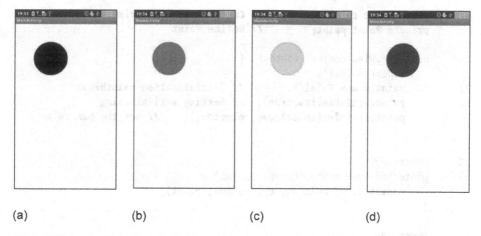

(a)   (b)   (c)   (d)

Figure 10-3. *The interface of a GuiExam input graphics framework that responds to the touchscreen*

The application starts in Figure 10-3(a). When the user clicks inside a circle (touches the screen within the circle area), the color of the circle changes: it cycles through black, red, green, and blue, as shown in Figure 10-3(a)–(d). If you click outside the circle, the circle does not change colors.

Using the same example as in the earlier section, modify the custom view class MyView.java as follows:

```
Line#    Source Code
1   package com.example.guiexam;
2
3   import android.view.View;
4   import android.graphics.Canvas;
5   import android.graphics.Paint;
6   import android.content.Context;
7
8   import android.graphics.Color;
9   import android.view.MotionEvent;
10      import java.lang.Math;

11 public class MyView extends View {
12     private float cx = 250;    // Default X Coordinate of Circle
13     private float cy = 250;    // Default Y Coordinate of Circle
14     private int radius = 120;  // Radius
15     private int colorArray[] = {Color.BLACK, Color.RED, Color.GREEN,
                                    Color.BLUE };
16 // Defines an array of colors
```

```
17      private int colorIdx = 0;    // Custom color subscript
        private Paint paint;         // Define Paint
18
19      public MyView(Context context) {
20          super(context);
21          paint = new Paint();         // Initialization paintbrush
22          paint.setAntiAlias(true);   // Setting anti-aliasing
23          paint.setColor(colorArray[colorIdx]);    // Set the pen color
        }
24
25      @Override
26      protected void onDraw(Canvas canvas) {
27          canvas.drawCircle(cx, cy, radius, paint);
        }
28
29      @Override
30      public boolean onTouchEvent(MotionEvent event) {
31          float px = event.getX();
32 // defined the touch point in the X, Y coordinates
33          float py = event.getY();
34          switch (event.getAction()) {
35          case MotionEvent.ACTION_DOWN:
36 // Touch  screen pressed
37              if (Math.abs(px-cx) < radius && Math.abs(py-cy) < radius){
38 // Touch location inside the circle
39                  colorIdx = (colorIdx + 1) % colorArray.length;
40                  paint.setColor(colorArray[colorIdx]);
41 // Set paintbrush color
42                  }
43              postInvalidate();            // Repaint
44              break;
45          case MotionEvent.ACTION_MOVE:  // Screen touch and move
46              break;
47          case MotionEvent.ACTION_UP:    // Screen touch unpressed
                break;
            }
            return true;
        }
    }
```

Lines 15 and 16 define an array of colors and color indices, and line 17 defines paintbrush variables. Lines 20–22 of the constructor function complete the initialization of the brush property settings. The reason you do not put the code for the paintbrush property set in View.Ondraw is to avoid repeated calculations for each redraw. The only work for the onDraw function is to display the circle.

In lines 28–46, you create the new touch input event response function onTouchEvent. In lines 30 and 32, you first get the X, Y coordinates of the touch point using the getX and getY functions of the MotionEvent class. Then you obtain the input action type through the getAction function of the MotionEvent class in line 34, followed by a case statement to complete the different input actions. The response to the action of pressing the touchscreen is in lines 37–43. You determine whether the touch point is within the circle in line 37. Then you modify the codes that set the colors and change the pen color in lines 39–40. You call the postInvalidate function notification to redraw in line 43 and provide it with the final finishing touch.

Multi-Touch Code Framework

Most Android devices support multi-touch touchscreens. The good news is that the Android system software also provides multi-touch support. This section covers the multi-touch code framework.

The touch event class MotionEvent has a getPointerCount() function that returns the current number of touch points on the screen. The function prototype is

```
final int MotionEvent.getPointerCount();
```

You can also use the getX and getY functions discussed earlier to obtain the coordinates of the touch point. The prototypes are as follows:

```
final float  MotionEvent.getX(int pointerIndex)
final float  MotionEvent.getX()
final float  MotionEvent.getY(int pointerIndex)
final float  MotionEvent.getY()
```

In the previous section, you got the coordinates of a single touch point using a function with no parameters. The getX/getY functions with parameters are used to get the position of the touch point in the multi-point touch situation, where the parameter pointerIndex is the index number for the touch point. This is an integer number starting at 0.

Here is an example to illustrate the multi-touch programming framework. This example is a two-point touch application that zooms a circle in and out. The application interface is shown in Figure 10-4.

(a) Initial interface after the application starts

(b) Enlarged circle after a two-point touch zoom-in

(c) Downsized circle after two-point touch zoom-out

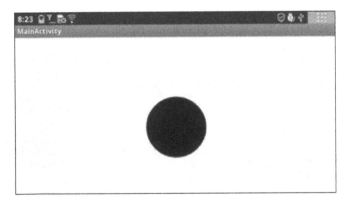

(d) Interface with the screen rotated 90 degrees

Figure 10-4. *The interface of the two-point touch zoom-in/zoom-out GuiExam graphic application*

The application's launch interface is shown in Figure 10-4(a). The circle is always at the center of the view, but the size of the circle (its radius) can be controlled by a two-point touch. The center is the center of the view, not the center of the activity or the center of the screen. The so-called two-point touchscreen means there are two touch points, or two fingers moving on the screen at the same time, either in an expand gesture where the circle becomes larger (b) or in squeeze gesture where the circle becomes smaller (c). The code is as follows:

```
Line#    Source Code
1  package com.example.guiexam;
2
3  import android.view.View;
4  import android.graphics.Canvas;
5  import android.graphics.Paint;
6  import android.content.Context;
7
8  import android.view.MotionEvent;
9  import java.lang.Math;
10 public class MyView extends View {
11     private static final int initRadius = 120; // initial value of the radius
12     private float cx;                    // X coordinate of the circle
13     private float cy;                    // Y coordinate of the circle
14     private int radius = initRadius; // Set initial value of the radius
15     public float graphScale = 1;     // Set Scale factor for one two-point
                                          touch move
16     private float preInterPointDistance;  // Pre-distance of two touch
                                               points
17     private boolean bScreenPress = false;  // The sign of the screen
                                               being pressed down
18     private Paint paint;                 // Define paintbrush
19     public MyView(Context context) {
20         super(context);
21         paint = new Paint();            // Initialize paintbrush
22         paint.setAntiAlias(true);       // Set Anti Alias
23     }
24     @Override
25     protected void onDraw(Canvas canvas) {
26         cx = canvas.getWidth()/2;  // Let circle center positioned at the
                                          screen of the screen
27         cy = canvas.getHeight()/2;
28         canvas.drawCircle(cx, cy, radius*graphScale, paint);
29     }
```

```
30      @Override
31      public boolean onTouchEvent(MotionEvent event) {
32          float px1, py1;  // Define the X,Y coordinates of 1st touch point
33          float px2, py2;  // Define the X,Y coordinates of 2nd touch point
34          float interPointDistance;  // distance between two  touch points
35          switch (event.getAction()) {
36          case MotionEvent.ACTION_DOWN:   // Screen touch pressed
37              break;
38          case MotionEvent.ACTION_MOVE:   // Screen touch move
39              if (event.getPointerCount() == 2 ) {
40                  px1 = event.getX(0);      // Get the X,Y coordinate of the
                                              first touch point
41                  py1 = event.getY(0);
42                  px2 = event.getX(1);       // Get the X,Y coordinate of the
                                              second touch point
43                  py2 = event.getY(1);
44                  interPointDistance = (float) Math.sqrt((px6-px2)*
                    (px6-px2)+(py1 - py2)*(py1 - py2));
45                  if (!bScreenPress){
46                      bScreenPress = true;
47                      preInterPointDistance = interPointDistance;
48                  } else {
49                      graphScale = interPointDistance / preInterPointDistance;
50                      invalidate();        // Redraw graphics
51                  }
52              } else {
53                  bScreenPress = false;
54                  radius = (int)(radius * graphScale);
55 // One downsize/enlarge circle end. Record final scale factor
56              }
57              break;
58          case MotionEvent.ACTION_UP:       // Screen touch lift up
59              bScreenPress = false;
60              radius = (int)(radius * graphScale);
61 // One downsize/enlarge circle end. Record final scale factor
62              break;
63          }
64          return true;
        }
    }
```

This code defines a scaling factor graphScale for a two-point touch in line 15 and a variable preInterPointDistance in line 16 to record the distance between the two touch points. Line 17 defines the flag variable bScreenPress when the screen is pressed.

Lines 26 and 27 call getWidth and getHeight of the Canvas class in the onDraw function to get the view's width and height, and then allocate the center of the circle in the center of the view. The advantage of this step is that, when the screen rotates 90 degrees, the circle remains in the center of the view, as shown in Figure 10-4(d). The difference between these examples and the previous one is that this time the radius of the circle being drawn is equal to the radius of the circle multiplied by the scaling factor graphScale.

Lines 32–61 contain onDraw based on the modified example in the previous section. Lines 38–56 are the response code for a touch-move activity. Line 3 determines whether there are two touch points; if there are, you run code lines 40–51; otherwise, you run lines 53–54. You set the flag bScreenPress to false to indicate when the two touch points are first pressed, and then you record the final radius as equal to the current value of the radius multiplied by the scaling factor graphScale. You get the position coordinates of the two touch points in lines 40–43. Line 44 calculates the distance between the two touch points. Line 45 determines whether it is the first press; if it is, lines 46 and 47 run, and record the distance between the two touch points; otherwise, the code in lines 49–50 runs. Here you calculate the scaling factor based on the current distance between the points and the distance in the previous movement. After this, the graphic is redrawn.

To handle the location of the flag bScreenPress, you execute the response code of the screen touch-up activity in lines 58–60, which is similar to the non-two-point touch code in lines 53 and 54.

Responding to Keyboard Input

Most Android devices have a number of hardware buttons, such as Volume +, Volume -, Power, Home, Menu, Back, Search, and so on. Some Android devices are also equipped with keyboards. Keyboards, including the device's hardware buttons, are important input methods for Android applications. Keyboard input corresponds to keyboard events, named KeyEvent (also known as a *pressing key event*). In this section, you learn about the methods to respond to keyboard input.

In Android, both the Activity and View classes can receive pressed-key events. Key events trigger calls to the onKeyDown function of the Activity or View class. The function prototype is

```
boolean    Activity.onKeyDown(int keyCode, KeyEvent event);
boolean    View.onKeyDown(int keyCode, KeyEvent event);
```

The keyCode parameter is the index code of the key that is pressed. Each key in Android has a unique number, which is the keyCode. Some of the key codes were described in Table 7-1. The key event, KeyEvent, contains properties related to buttons, such as the frequency with which they are pressed. To handle key events, you need to override the onKeyDown function and add your own response-handling code.

Interestingly, although the Activity and View classes can receive key events, the view is often included in the activity. When the button is pressed, the event first sends external activity; that is, the activity receives the event sooner. The following example shows how you respond to the button press by rewriting the activity's onKeyDown function.

This example shows how to use the arrow keys to move the circle in the application. The application interface is shown in Figure 10-5.

(a) Interface when the application starts

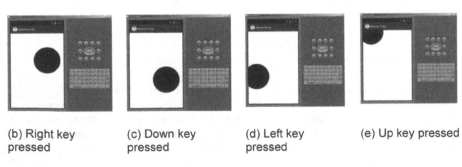

(b) Right key pressed

(c) Down key pressed

(d) Left key pressed

(e) Up key pressed

Figure 10-5. *Using keys to control the movement of the circle in the application interface*

318

The Lenovo phone on which we are testing has no keypad, so we chose to run the application on a virtual machine. The virtual machine has Left, Down, Right, and Up keys to achieve these circle movements. The application startup interface is shown in Figure 10-5(a). Pressing the Left, Down, Right, or Up button makes the circle move in the corresponding direction. The interface examples are shown in Figure 10-5(b) through (e).

This application is based on the example, created at the beginning of this chapter (Figure 10-1) and modified per the following procedure:

4. Modify the source code of MyView.java as follows:

```
Line#     Source Code
1   package com.example.guiexam;
2
3   import android.view.View;
4   import android.graphics.Canvas;
5   import android.graphics.Paint;
6   import android.content.Context;

7   public class MyView extends View {
8       private float cx = 250;              // X coordinate of the circle
9       private float cy = 250;              // Y coordinate of the circle
10      private static final int radius = 120;  // Radius of the circle
11      private Paint paint;                 // define paint brush
12      private static final int MOVESTEP = 10; // the step length for
                                                //    pressing direction key

13      public MyView(Context context) {
14          super(context);
15          paint = new Paint();             // Paint brush initialization
16          paint.setAntiAlias(true);        // Set Anti Alias
17      }

18      @Override
19      protected void onDraw(Canvas canvas) {
20          canvas.drawCircle(cx, cy, radius, paint);
21      }
22      ////// Self-define function:press key to move graphic (circle) //////
23      public void moveCircleByPressKey(int horizon, int vertical){
```

```
24          if (horizon < 0)                    // horizontal move
25              cx -= MOVESTEP;
26          else if (horizon > 0)
27              cx += MOVESTEP;
28          if (vertical < 0)
29              cy += MOVESTEP;                  // vertical move
30          else if (vertical > 0)
31              cy -= MOVESTEP;
32          postInvalidate();                    // note to repaint
33      }
34 }
```

In lines 23–33, you add a function to the view class to move the image (the circle) by pressing the horizon or vertical key. This function takes two arguments: horizon and vertical. If horizon is less than 0, you decrease the X coordinate value of the circle, and as a result, the circle moves to the left. If horizon is greater than 0, you increase the X coordinate value of the circle, which moves the circle to the right. You do a similar operation for the vertical parameters to move the circle up and down. Line 32 updates the graphics routine with new parameters and trigger the view to redraw.

     5.   Modify the source code of the main activity class MainActivity.java as follows:

```
Line#    Source Code
1   package com.example.guiexam;
2   import android.os.Bundle;
3   import android.app.Activity;
4   import android.view.Menu;
5   import android.view.KeyEvent;       // Key press event class

6   public class MainActivity extends Activity {
7       private MyView theView =null;   // View object stored inside the variable

8       @Override
9       public void onCreate(Bundle savedInstanceState) {
10          super.onCreate(savedInstanceState);
11          theView = new MyView(this); // record the View class of the Activity
12          setContentView(theView);
13      }

14      @Override
15      public boolean onCreateOptionsMenu(Menu menu) {
16          getMenuInflater().inflate(R.menu.activity_main, menu);
17          return true;
18      }
```

```
19      @Override                           // Key down response function
20      public boolean onKeyDown(int keyCode, KeyEvent event) {
21          int horizon = 0; int vertical = 0;
22          switch (keyCode)
23          {
24              case KeyEvent.KEYCODE_DPAD_LEFT:
25                  horizon = -1;
26                  break;
27              case KeyEvent.KEYCODE_DPAD_RIGHT:
28                  horizon = 1;
29                  break;
30              case KeyEvent.KEYCODE_DPAD_UP:
31                  vertical = 1;
32                  break;
33              case KeyEvent.KEYCODE_DPAD_DOWN:
34                  vertical = -1;
35                  break;
36              default:
37                  super.onKeyDown(keyCode, event);
38          }
39          if (!(horizon == 0 && vertical == 0))
40              theView.moveCircleByPressKey(horizon,vertical);
41          return true;
42      }
43 }
```

In this code, you want the Activity class to receive and respond to key-down events, so you overwrite the onKeyDown function in lines 19–42 with the button-response code. Although the response function for key buttons is located in the Activity class, the display updates are to be implemented in the view MyView class, so you must make the Activity class aware of its corresponding view object. To do so, you add a record-view object variable theView in line 7. In lines 11 and 12, you let theView record this object when constructing the view object.

In the key-down response function onKeyDown, you use a switchcase statement (lines 22–38) and take different actions according to the different keys. The function's keyCode parameter specifies the key number of the key that is pressed. For example, the code in lines 24–26 is the handling code for the Left key. It sets a horizontal flag to "left" and then calls the self-defined function moveCircleByPressKey of the view class to move the circle in lines 39 and 40. To allow other key-press-down events to be addressed, you call the system's default handler to deal with other keys in lines 36 and 37.

Dialog Boxes in Android

There are three different ways to use dialog boxes in Android, as discussed in this section.

Using an Activity's Dialog Theme

The Dialog class implements a simple floating window that can be created in an activity. By using a basic Dialog class, you can create a new instance and set its title and layout. Dialog themes can be applied to a normal activity to make it look similar to a dialog box.

In addition, the Activity class provides a convenient mechanism to create, save, and restore dialogs, such as onCreateDialog(int), onPrepareDialog(int, Dialog), showDialog(int), dismissDialog(int), and other functions. If you use these functions, the activity can return the Activity object that manages the dialog through the getOwnerActivity() method.

The following are specific instructions for using these functions.

onCreateDialog(int) Function

When you use this callback function, Android sets this activity as the owner of each dialog box, which automatically manages the state of each dialog box and anchors it to the activity. In this way, each dialog inherits the specific attributes of this activity. For example, when a dialog box is opened, the menu button displays the option menu defined for the activity. For example, you can use the volume keys to modify the audio stream that the activity uses.

showDialog(int) Function

When you want to display a dialog box, you call the showDialog(intid) method and pass an integer through this function call that uniquely identifies this dialog. When the dialog box is first requested, Android calls onCreateDialog(intid) from the activity. You should initialize this dialog box. This callback method is passed to the same ID that showDialog(intid) has. When you create the dialog box, the object is returned at the end of the activity.

onPrepareDialog(int, Dialog) Function

Before the dialog box is displayed, Android also calls the optional callback function onPrepareDialog(int id, Dialog). If you want the properties to be changed every time a dialog box is opened, you can define this method. Unlike the onCreateDialog(int) function, which can only be called the first time you open the dialog box, this method is called each time you open the dialog box. If you do not define onPrepareDialog(), then the dialog remains the same as the last time it was opened. The dialog box's ID and the dialog object created in onCreateDialog() can also be passed to the function by this method.

dismissDialog(int) Function

When you are ready to close the dialog box, you can call dismiss() through this dialog box method to eliminate it. If desired, you can also call dismissDialog(int id) method from the activity. If you want to use the onCreateDialog(int id) method to retain the state of your dialog box, then each time the dialog box is eliminated, the status of the object of this dialog box object is kept in the activity. If you decide that you no longer need this object or clear the state, then you should call removeDialog(intid). This removes any internal object references, and even if the dialog box is being displayed, it is eliminated.

Using a Specific Dialog Class

Android provides multiple classes that are expansions of the Dialog class, such as AlertDialog, ProgressDialog, and so on. Each class is designed to provide specific dialog box functions. The screen interface based on the Dialog class is created in all activities that then call the specific class. So it does not need to be registered in the manifest file, and its life cycle is controlled by the activity that calls the class.

Using Toast Reminders

Toasts are special, nonmodular, transient message dialog boxes, usually used in the broadcast receiver and backgroundservices, and used to prompt user events.

Dialog Box Example

Of the dialog box methods discussed, if it is measured by how the implementation of the function is done, the first function is the most powerful, followed by the second and third. In terms of the degree of sophistication of the implementation code, the third method is the simplest, and the first and the second are more complex.

The following example demonstrates the second method. See Android's help documentation and samples (in the samples directory located under the Android SDK installation directory) to learn more about the other implementation methods.

The specific dialog box class that this sample application uses is the Builder inner class of AlertDialog. When you press the Back button, a dialog box pops up, allowing you to decide whether to exit the application. The application interface is shown in Figure 10-6. Using the Android dialog box in this example will help you understand its usage.

 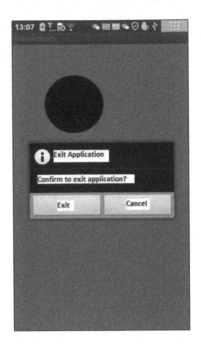

(a) Interface when the application starts, and after Cancel is pressed

(b) Interface after Return key is pressed

Figure 10-6. *The application interface with an Exit dialog box*

The application starts and displays the main activity interface, as shown in Figure 10-6(a). When you press the device's Back button, the Exit dialog box pops up, as shown in Figure 10-6(b). When you click the Exit button, the application exits, and the interface is also closed. When you click the Cancel button, the application returns to the previous screen, similar to Figure 10-6(a).

Modify the source code of the activity class MainActivity.java to read as follows:

```
Line#    Source Code
1   package com.example.guiexam;
2   import android.os.Bundle;
3   import android.app.Activity;
4   import android.view.Menu;
5   import android.view.KeyEvent;          // Key event class
6   import android.app.Dialog;             // Use Dialog class
```

```
7  import android.app.AlertDialog;         // Use AlertDialog class
8  import android.content.DialogInterface;  // Use DialogInterface interface

9  public class MainActivity extends Activity {
10     private MyView theView =null;        // View objects stored inside
                                             the variable
11     private AlertDialog.Builder exitAppChooseDlg = null; // Exit App
                                                            dialog box
12     private Dialog dlgExitApp = null;

13     @Override
14     public void onCreate(Bundle savedInstanceState) {
15         super.onCreate(savedInstanceState);
16         theView = new MyView(this);  // View class of Record My Activity
17         setContentView(theView);

18         exitAppChooseDlg = new AlertDialog.Builder(this);
19 // Define  AlertDialog.Builder object
20         exitAppChooseDlg.setTitle("Exit Selection");
21 // Define the title of the dialog box
           exitAppChooseDlg.setMessage("Confirm to exit application?");
22 // Define the display text of the dialog box
23         exitAppChooseDlg.setIcon(android.R.drawable.ic_dialog_info);
24 // Define the icon of the dialog box
25
26 // Set the leftmost button and click response class
27         exitAppChooseDlg.setPositiveButton("Exit", new
           DialogInterface.OnClickListener() {
28             public void onClick(DialogInterface dialog, int which) {
29                 dialog.dismiss();          // Close Dialog Box
                 /*MainActivity.*/finish(); // Exit (main) Activity
30                 System.exit(0);            // Exit Application
31             }
32         });
33
34 // Set the rightmost button and click response class
35         exitAppChooseDlg.setNegativeButton("Cancel", new
           DialogInterface.OnClickListener() {
36             public void onClick(DialogInterface dialog, int which) {
37                 dialog.cancel();           // Close dialog box
               }
38         });
39         dlgExitApp = exitAppChooseDlg.create();
40 // Create dialog box exit object
41     }
42
```

```
        @Override
43      public boolean onCreateOptionsMenu(Menu menu) {
44          getMenuInflater().inflate(R.menu.activity_main, menu);
45          return true;
46      }
47
48      @Override         // Key down response function
49      public boolean onKeyDown(int keyCode, KeyEvent event) {
50          int horizon = 0; int vertical = 0;
51          switch (keyCode)
52          {
53              case KeyEvent.KEYCODE_DPAD_LEFT:
54                  horizon = -1;
55                  break;
56              case KeyEvent.KEYCODE_DPAD_RIGHT:
57                  horizon = 1;
58                  break;
59              case KeyEvent.KEYCODE_DPAD_UP:
60                  vertical = 1;
61                  break;
62              case KeyEvent.KEYCODE_DPAD_DOWN:
63                  vertical = -1;
64                  break;
65              case KeyEvent.KEYCODE_BACK:
66                  if (event.getRepeatCount() == 0) {
67                      dlgExitApp.show();
68 // Display AlertDialog.Builder dialog box
69                  }
70                  break;
71              default:
72                  super.onKeyDown(keyCode, event);
            }
            if (!(horizon == 0 && vertical == 0))
                theView.moveCircleByPressKey(horizon,vertical);
            return true;
        }
    }
```

Lines 11 and 12 define the AlertDialog.Builder class and its associated variable for the Dialog class in the Activity class. You modify the onCreate function code in lines 18–36 and define the code to prepare the dialog box. In line 18, you construct the AlertDialog.Builder class object; the prototype of this constructor function is

```
AlertDialog.Builder(Context context)
AlertDialog.Builder(Context context, int theme)
```

You use the first prototype in this example to pass the Activity object, which constructs the dialog box as the context of the constructor function. This is followed by setting the title display text, icons, and other attributes of the dialog box in lines 19 and 21.

The AlertDialog.Builder dialog box can take up to three buttons: left, middle, and right. They are set up by the setPositiveButton, setNeutralButton, and setNegativeButton functions, respectively. You can specify how many dialog box buttons you need. This example uses two buttons: left and right.

Lines 23–29 set the left button of the dialog box and click-response code. The prototype of the setPositiveButton function of the AlertDialog.Builder class is

```
AlertDialog.Builder  setPositiveButton(int textId,
DialogInterface.OnClickListener listener)
AlertDialog.Builder  setPositiveButton(CharSequence text,
DialogInterface.OnClickListener listener)
```

You use a second prototype in the example, where the first parameter is text displayed by the button, and the second parameter is the interface object of the click response.

In line 25, you first call the dismissal or cancel function of the DialogInterface class to close the dialog box. DialogInterface is the operating interface of the dialog class (AlertDialog, Dialog, and so on). You use the dismiss function to close the dialog box in line 25 and use a cancel function to close the dialog box in line 33.

Lines 26–27 close the activity and application, as described in the section "Exit Activities and Application." in Chapter 8, Figure 8-16. Interestingly, the internal class DialogInterface.OnClickListener uses a member function of the non-dot external class MainActivity and does not need to add the prefix in front of "class name."

You set the dialog box for the right button and click-response code in lines 36–35. The click-response code is relatively simple, using the cancel function of the DialogInterface class to close the dialog box in line 33.

Finally, line 36 calls the create function of the AlertDialog.Builder class to create the exit dialog box object dlgExitApp. The function returns an AlertDialog object, and its prototype is

```
AlertDialog  create()
```

Because AlertDialog is derived from the Dialog class, the return value can be assigned to the Dialog variable.

You add the Back key response code for the OnKeyDown response function on lines 60-64. The code is relatively simple: you determine whether duplicate keys are pressed on line 61, and then you call the show function of the Dialog class to display a dialog box.

Application Property Settings

In Android device, there are two difference places where you can find out the information about the applications installed. One is the menu list (the interface after you press the setting button), the other is by going to the Settings ➤ Applications ➤ Manage Applications ➤ Downloaded menu item. See Figure 10-7:

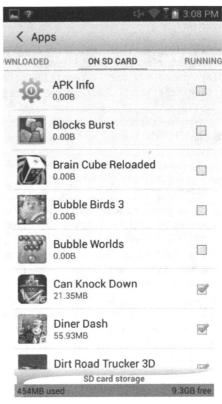

(a) Menu list on the target device

(b) Application settings on the target device

Figure 10-7. The difference of Menulist and Application Setting display on target device

So far, almost all the examples have been based on the code framework of two applications: GuiExam and HelloAndroid. But it is difficult to distinguish between them in the menu on the target device. These applications are indistinguishable in the menu list because you used the default settings instead of applying their own property settings. This section shows you how to apply property settings.

Figure 10-8 shows the applications setting interface before and after applying property settings.

(a) The icon and text of the original application on the menu list of the target device

(b) The icon and text of the application after applying property settings

Figure 10-8. The application on the target device before and after applying property setting

This example uses the GuiExam application to show the steps for changing the application settings:

1. Modify the icon of the application in the menu on the target machine. Based on the ic_launcher.png file size under the application res\drawable-XXX directory (where XXX represents different resolutions—for example, drawable-hdpi represents the directory for high-resolution images), edit your image file, and name it ic_launcher.png.

The common screen resolutions for Android devices and the directories where application icon files are stored are shown in Table 10-2.

Table 10-2. *Common Android Device Screen Resolutions and the Directories Containing Application Icon Sizes*

Directory Name	Size	Description
drawable-ldpi	36 × 36 dpi	Low-resolution screen
drawable-mdpi	48 × 48 dpi	Medium-resolution screen
drawable-hdpi	72 × 72 dpi	High-resolution screen
drawable-xhdpi	96 × 96 dpi	Super-high-resolution screen
drawable-xxhdpi	144 × 144 dpi	Extra-extra-high-resolution screen

2. Put the custom picture file in the corresponding directory res\drawable-XXX, and replace the original file. For example, for the high-resolution screen application, replace the file ic_launcher.png in res\drawable-xhdpi with your own, as shown in Figure 10-9.

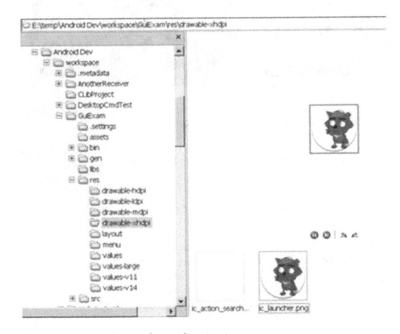

Figure 10-9. *Replacing the application icon*

3. Modify the application's menu text annotation on the target machine.

Open the Package Explorer pane of the \res\values\strings.xml file. The title_activity_my_main string value is set to a custom string (in this case, "GUI examples"), as shown in Figure 10-10.

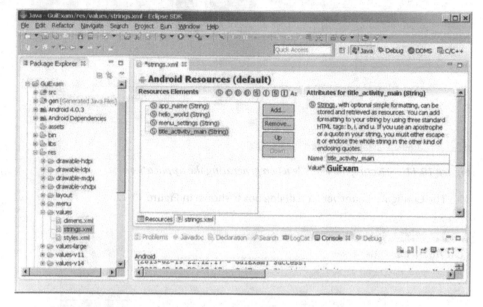

Figure 10-10. Modifying the icon text of the application

After completing these modifications, you can see that the target application's menu item's icon and text label have changed.

Note step 1 can also be implemented by another method that can generate its own set of icons when the application is created. The procedure is as follows:

1. In the Configure Launcher Icon dialog box, click the Image button, and then click the Browse button to the right of Image File.

2. Select the picture file as the application icon (in this case, graywolf.png) in the Open dialog box, as shown in Figure 10-11.

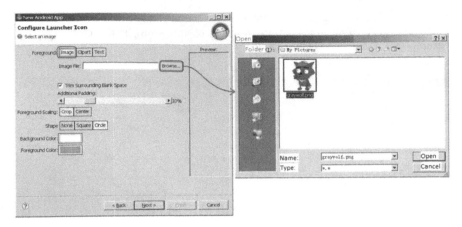

Figure 10-11. *Selecting the icon file when generating the application*

The Configure Launcher Icon dialog box is shown in Figure 10-12.

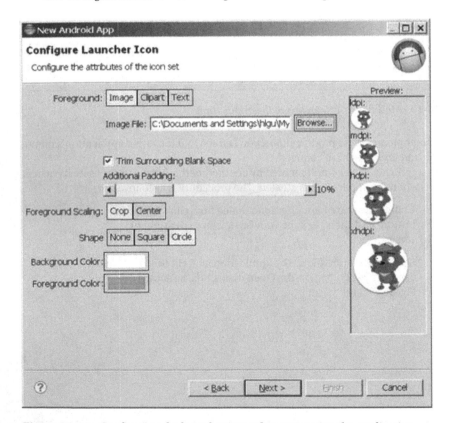

Figure 10-12. *Configuring the launcher icon when generating the application*

In other words, Eclipse can, based on the user-specified image file, automatically generate the various ic_launcher.png files with the appropriate dimensions in the res\drawable-XXX directory. This eliminates the need to manually edit the images.

Summary

In this last chapter covering Android GUI design, you are introduced to the basic framework of drawings in the view, the concept of how the drawing Framework responds to touch screen input, and how to control the display of the view as well as the multi-touch code framework. You use an example that illustrates the multi-touch programming framework and keyboard input response. You learn the methods to respond to keyboard input and hardware buttons that are available on Android devices, such as Volume +, Volume -, Power, Home, Menu, Back, Search, and so on. You are introduced to the three different dialog boxes for Android, which include the activity dialog theme, a specific class dialog, and Toast reminder. At the end of chapter you learn how to change the application property settings. In the next chapter, you will introduce the performance optimization for android application on x86. Android is a resource-limited system, and it therefore requires very strict resource utilization in space and time. Compared with a desktop system, the performance optimization for applications for Android is thus far more critical and urgent. You will first introduce the basic principles of SOC performance optimization, followed by the introduction of principles and methodology of performance optimization for Android-based development on Intel architecture.

CHAPTER 11

■ ■ ■

Performance Optimization for Android Applications on x86

Performance optimization is one of the most important goals every application developer wants to pursue, regardless of whether the application is for a general desktop Windows computer or an Android device. Android is a resource-limited system, and it therefore requires very strict resource utilization. Compared with a desktop system, performance optimization for Android applications is far more critical.

Different applications have different areas of focus regarding optimization. Performance optimization for Android systems generally falls into three categories: application running speed, code size, and power consumption. Generally speaking, storage space and cost for Android on Intel Atom processors is not a bottleneck, so this chapter focuses on performance optimization that makes applications run faster. Chapter 13 covers power-consumption optimization.

The chapter first introduces the basic principles of system on chip (SoC) performance optimization, followed by principles and methodology of performance optimization for Android-based development on Intel architecture. Chapter 12 discusses application development for Android on Intel architecture using the native development kit (NDK).

Principles of Performance Optimization

Optimizing an application's performance really means optimizing the application's *execution speed*. The optimization aims at reducing the time needed to complete a specific task. This is achieved by making structural adjustments to the application based on either hardware or software.

When you're optimizing an application's performance, you need to follow several basic principles:

- *Equal value principle*: There is no change in the result of the application's execution after performance optimization.

- *Efficacy principle*: After performance optimization, the targeted code runs faster.

- *Combined value principle*: Sometimes performance optimization achieves a performance improvement in some areas but degrades performance in others. You must consider combined overall performance in determining whether performance optimization is needed.

One of the most important considerations involves trading time and space. For example, to perform a function calculation, the values of the function can be precalculated and put into a program storage zone (memory) as a table. When a program is running, instead of spending time repeatedly calculating the function, the program can get the value directly from the table and reduce the execution time. Similarly, a search can be done on a large space using the hash method and thereby eliminate the need for a comparison operation.

Performance optimization is based on various techniques. The following sections describe several major ones.

Reducing Instructions and Execution Frequency

The technique that's chosen most frequently to optimize performance involves reducing instructions and execution frequency. For example, from the point of view of data structures and algorithms, the instructions for comparison and exchange in bubbling sequencing need to execute $O(n^2)$ times. However, by using fast sequencing, you can reduce the instruction to $O(n \log n)$ executions.

In loop optimization, code motion can extract irrelevant public code from the loop and reduce the execution time of public code from N to 1, thus dramatically reducing the execution frequency. In addition, you can use inline functions supported by C and C++ to avoid embedding function-call code; you can omit the function-call instructions and the implementation of the return instructions.

Selecting Faster Instructions

You can perform the same function with different instructions. The different instructions take different machine clock cycles, and thus the execution times vary. This gives you the opportunity to choose a faster instruction.

Reducing computational strength is a typical example of performance optimization achieved by selecting a faster instruction set. For example, you can multiply an integer by 4 by shifting the operator two digits to the left. The shift instruction takes many fewer clock cycles and runs much faster than the multiplication or division instruction.

Another example is using special instructions provided by the hardware to replace generic instructions. For example, the Intel Atom processors support the Streaming SIMD Extensions (SSE) instruction set. For vector operations, you should always use SSE instructions: they run much faster thanks to instruction-level parallel processing. The ordinary addition instruction width for Intel Atom is 32 bits, whereas SSE instructions are capable of four times 32-bit data processing. As a result, optimized code using SSE instructions dramatically shortens the time consumed.

Improving the Degree of Parallelism

You can improve the degree of parallelism at multiple levels, including instruction, expression, function, and thread. Many modern embedded processors, including the Intel Atom processor, support instruction-pipeline execution. This lets you use an optimization method called *instruction-level parallelism*. A code chain can be decomposed into several units of code that are not dependent on the chain and can be executed in parallel in the pipeline.

In addition, many embedded system processors, such as the Intel Atom processor, physically support the concurrent execution of threads. Using an appropriate number of concurrent threads rather than a single thread can increase running speed. In order to take advantage of thread-concurrency optimization, you need to consciously adopt multithreading technology; sometimes optimization must be done with compiler support.

Using the Register Cache Effectively

Writing and reading the cache register is much faster than doing the same with memory. The goal of cache optimization is to put data and instructions that are being used and will be used in the cache, to reduce the cache hit rate and reduce cache conflicts. Cache optimization often appears in the optimization process for a nested loop. Register optimization involves the effective use of the register and keeping frequently used data in the register as much as possible.

Cache is based on locality. That is, cache assumes the data to be used is located in the most recent data that is already in use or is in the vicinity of its own register. This is called the *locality principle* or *principle of locality*, which deeply affects hardware, software, and system design and performance. Instructions and data required by the processor are always first read by cache access. If high-speed cache has the needed data, the processor always accesses high-speed cache directly. In this situation, such an access is called a *high-speed cache hit*; if high-speed cache does not contain the needed data, this is referred to as a *failed hit* or *cache miss*.

If this happens, the processor needs to copy data from memory to high-speed cache. If the corresponding location of high-speed cache is occupied by other data, data that is no longer needed in cache is expelled and written back to memory. Failed hits result in a sharp rise in access time; therefore the goal in increasing cache efficiency is to improve the hit rate and lower failure rates. Data exchange between cache and memory is done with a block unit, which is used to block-copy or write back blocks containing needed data as well as write blocks back to memory.

Locality has two meanings:

- *Temporal locality*: Due to temporal locality, the same data object may be reused many times. Once a data object is copied to the cache after a failed hit, there are many follow-up hits on the object. The follow-up hits run faster than the original failed hit.

- *Space locality*: A block usually contains multiple data objects. Due to spatial locality, the cost of a block copy after a failed hit is shared by subsequent references to other objects.

Performance Optimization Methodology

Many methods and techniques area available for performance optimization. You can use one approach or multiple comprehensive optimization principles simultaneously, such as modifying the source code to run faster. Based on the type of criteria, optimization methods can be divided into different categories.

Depending on whether the optimization is associated with hardware, it is either *machine-dependent optimization* and *machine-independent optimization*. In machine-dependent optimization, application and code execution have nothing to do with the machine's characteristics. These techniques are applicable to all machines. For example, moving code out of the loop, eliminating induction variables, and using strength-reduction technology can be applied to any machine or architecture (either x86 or ARM) to obtain the same optimal results.

Machine-dependent optimization can be done only on specific hardware or architecture. For example, switching ordinary vector instruction computing to use SSE instructions depends on many low-level details of the Intel Atom processor and can only be used on Intel processors that support SSE instructions. In general, machine-independent optimization is more complex and difficult to achieve than the machine-dependent optimization.

Performance Optimization Approaches

In an ideal scenario, the compiler should be able to compile any code you write and optimize it into the most efficient machine code. But the reality is that the compiler can automate only some of all possible optimizations, and the optimizations may be blocked by the optimization blocker. Depending on how much of a role human or automated tools play, performance optimization may be performed automatically by the compiler, done manually by the programmer manually, or performed with the assistance of development tools. The following sections present several approaches you can use to achieve performance optimization.

Automatic Optimization by the Compiler

Modern compilers can automatically complete the most common code optimizations, and this is the preferred way to optimize. This is also known as *compiler optimization* or *compiling optimization*. It must be triggered by appropriate extensions or switch variables.

C/C++ code optimization for Android applications can be achieved using the GCC compiler (one of the tools in the GNU toolchain) located in the NDK (the Android local development toolkit) or Intel Compiler (ICC). The next chapter covers this topic in detail.

Performance Optimization Assisted by Development Tools

It is very difficult to achieve overall, comprehensive optimization of a large program. Fortunately, for applications based on Intel architecture, many useful tools are available to help you complete the optimization. For example, Intel VTune Amplifier, Graphics Performance Analyzer (GPA), Power Monitoring Tool, and so on can help you analyze a program and complete the optimization.

GPA is an Intel product-development tool and can be used with Intel processors such as the Intel Atom processor as well as ARM devices. Intel Profiler is a GNU toolchain tool and can be used for all types of processors. You can use Profiler to create a profiling process that shows which areas of a program execute frequently and use more computing resources, and which areas are less frequently implemented. The profiling data provides valuable information you can use to complete the optimization.

A typical example of profile-guided optimization (PGO) is the optimization of the `switch` statement (such as the `switch-case` statement in C#). Based on the profile of the collected sample, after getting the frequency with which each `case` statement occurred, you sort the `case` statement in the `switch` statement by frequency: the most frequent statements are moved to the front (performing this statement required the fewest comparisons), to achieve optimal results with the fewest comparisons.

Intel GPA was originally a tool used for graphics processing unit (GPU) analysis. It has now developed into a comprehensive tool for analyzing CPU speeds, memory analysis, frame rate, and device power consumption. You can use GPA to get information about CPU load, operating frequency, and power consumption. It can guide you as you optimize an application, and it's especially helpful for multithreaded optimization. Intel GPA is not only a speed-optimization tool but also a very handy power-optimization tool. More detailed discussion and use cases are presented later in this chapter and in Chapter 13.

With optimization tools, you will no longer become disoriented or confused when trying to find a starting point for optimizing a large program. You can easily locate the areas that are most in need of optimization: the code segments that are potentially most problematic. Quickly finding the hot spots allows you to achieve optimization with less time and effort. Of course, performance optimization is complicated. The tool only plays a guiding and supporting role—the real optimization must still be completed by the compiler or manually by you.

Using High-Performance Libraries

High-performance libraries are sets of software libraries, usually developed by a hardware OEM or special OEM, that provide commonly used operations and services. The code is carefully optimized based on a combination of processor features and has higher computing speed than ordinary code. Such high-performance databases use the full potential of the processor. For example, the Intel Integrated Performance Primitives (Intel IPP) libraries have been optimized based on SSE instructions for the processor, hyper/multithreaded parallel pipelined execution, and a waterfall process.

For some compute-intensive code and algorithms, using high-performance libraries is a simple, practical optimization method, just like standing on the shoulders of giants. Intel IPP can be used for mathematical calculations, signal processing, multimedia, image and graphics processing, vector calculations, and other fields. It uses a C/C++ programming interface.

Manual Optimization

You should not ignore the human factor during optimization. Some high-level global optimizations, such as optimizing algorithms and data structures, cannot be done by the compiler automatically. You must complete the optimization manually. As a programmer, in order to write efficient code, you should learn algorithms and optimization techniques to help you develop good programming habits and style. Even if the compiler can automatically complete the optimization, programmers still need to write efficient code to assist the compiler optimization at the following levels:

- *Source-code (high-level language) level*: You modify the source code to implement better algorithms or data structures to accomplish the optimization manually.

- *Assembly-language level*: Sometimes the high-level language is not enough to reach optimal results, and you need to modify the code down at the assembly-language level. In some key computing segments, although the process of assembly-level optimization is cumbersome, the performance benefit is totally worth it.

- *Compiling-instruction level*: This optimization is often accomplished through additions and modifications of compiler directives, such as modifying the typical compiler directive pragma and increasing the degree of parallelism in OpenMP.

Program-interactive optimization is a reflection of the art of programming, and the level of accomplishment enters the realm of the unity of human and machine. This is the focus of this chapter. Relatively speaking, optimizations performed at the assembly-language level or the instruction-level compiling phase require you to have comprehensive expertise about processor architecture, hardware, system, and so on. As a result, for Android systems on Intel architecture, we recommend optimizing performance at the source-code level. The following example introduces performance optimization on Android multithreaded design.

Optimization can be achieved in several ways that are related and structurally indivisible, although each has a unique function. The overall process is shown in Figure 11-1.

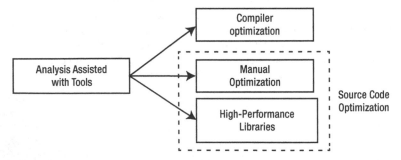

Figure 11-1. Recommended user optimization

As Figure 11-1 shows, manual optimization, compiler optimization, and high-performance library functions are tied together and are the final steps of optimization; you can select one of them to achieve the optimization. Both manual optimization and using high-performance libraries involve modifying the source code. Before you begin those optimizations, analyzing the program using optimization tools is a vital, beneficial step.

Intel Graphics Performance Analyzers (Intel GPA)

Intel GPA is a set of graphical tools for analysis and optimization that Intel launched a few years ago. It has evolved into a comprehensive tool for analyzing processor running state, system power, and other functions.

Introduction to Intel GPA

Intel GPA is only for Intel processors that support Intel Core and Intel Atom processor-based hardware platforms. It provides a GUI for CPU/GPU speed analysis and customization features. It enables you to find performance bottlenecks and optimize applications on devices based on the Intel chipset platform. Intel GPA consists of the System Analyzer, Frame Analyzer, and software development kit (SDK).

The Intel GPA System Analyzer 2014 R2 version supports Android platforms based on the Intel Atom processor. The features it offers include the following:

- Real-time display of dozens of key indicators including CPU, GPU, and OpenGL ES API

- Many graphics pipeline tests to isolate graphics bottlenecks

- A host-development system that can use Microsoft Windows, Mac OS X, or Ubuntu OS

Intel GPA currently only supports real Android devices and does not support the analysis of emulators. It uses a typical hardware deployment model, also called *Android application cross-development*, in which the host system (Windows and Ubuntu) and target device (Android Intel-based devices) are connected via USB to monitor Android applications. Intel GPA uses the Android Debug Bridge (adb) to monitor applications on target devices: the adb server runs on the Android device, and Intel GPA runs on the host system as the adb client application. This structure is shown in Figure 11-2.

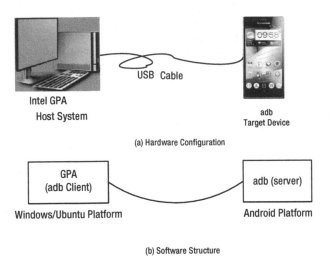

Figure 11-2. Intel GPA configuration for monitoring applications on an Android device

You should be cautious, given that Intel GPA requires adb to work. Both Eclipse and Dalvik Debug Monitor Server (DDMS) also use adb, so Intel GPA may not work properly if GPA, DDMS, and Eclipse are running at the same time, due to the adb conflict. It is best to turn off other Android software-development tools, such as Eclipse and DDMS, when using Intel GPA.

Figure 11-3 shows the Intel GPA graphic interface monitoring an app running on an Android device.

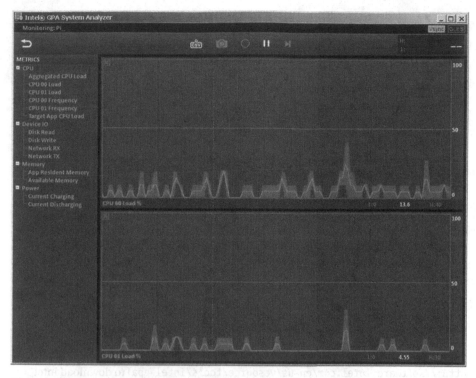

Figure 11-3. *The Intel GPA graphic interface monitoring an app running on an Android device*

As you can see, Intel GPA has two main windows and a toolbar pane. The tree structure in the left pane displays the indicators being monitored:

- Under CPU are Aggregated CPU Load, CPU XX Load, CPU XX Frequency, and Target App CPU Load. CPU XX numbers are determined by how many CPUs are being monitored by Intel GPA. To get CPU information such as numbers of cores, model, and frequency, you can use the `cat /proc/cpuinfo` command in a terminal window. Figure 11-3 is a screenshot for a Lenovo K800 smartphone, which uses a single-core Intel Atom Z2460 processor; it shows two logical processors, because s the processor supports Intel Hyper Threading Technology (Intel HTT). Thus two items are shown in CPU Load and CPU Frequency, indexed 00 and 01. In CPU XX Load, XX is the CPU number: it displays the load status for CPU XX, whereas CPU XX Frequency displays the frequency status for CPU XX. Aggregated CPU Load is the total load of the CPU. Target App CPU Load is the CPU load of the app on the target device.

- Under Device IO are Disk Read, Disk Write, Network RX, and Network TX. These metrics list status and information for disk read, disk write, network packets sent, and network packets received over the network, respectively.

- Under Memory are App Resident Memory and Available Memory.

- Under Power are Current Charging and Current Discharging, which provide the status of charging and discharging.

In the right pane are two real-time status display windows by default. These real-time windows display an oscilloscope-like status for the specified indicators. The horizontal axis is the elapsed time, and the vertical axis is the value of the corresponding indicator. You can drag and drop an index entry from the left pane to one of two windows to display the real-time indicator of that entry. In Figure 11-3, CPU 00 Load has been dragged and dropped to the top display window, and the CPU 01 load is shown in the bottom display window; the vertical axis shows CPU utilization. The maximum is 100%. Above the real-time status display window are tools such as screen capture and pause display. You can use these tools to debug an application.

Installing Intel GPA

GPA for Windows is installed during Beacon Mountain installation (Mac OS X and Ubuntu OS host systems) or Intel INDE installation (Windows host system). For an Ubuntu host, go to the Intel web site (http://intel.com/software/gpa or http://software.intel.com/en-us/vcsource/tools/intel-gpa) to download Intel GPA (this book uses version gpa_12.5_release_187105_windows.exe for the test), as shown in Figure 11-4.

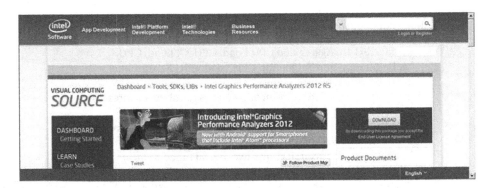

Figure 11-4. *Intel GPA software download site*

Using Intel GPA on Android

The following example demonstrates how to use Intel GPA to monitor applications on an Android device. In this case, the target machine is a Lenovo K800 smartphone running on an Intel Atom processor.

Special requirements must be met to allow Intel GPA to monitor and control applications on Android devices. Only if these set conditions are met can an application can be monitored by Intel GPA. You must follow these two steps: set the Eclipse application parameters and generate and deploy an application, and then use Intel GPA to monitor the application.

The name of the application used as an example here is MoveCircle. The operation interface is shown in Figure 11-5(a).

The application is a simple game. The user interface is very basic: just a circle. When the user touches any point inside the circle and drags around, the black circle follows the touch point and moves. When the user stops touching the spot in the circle, the circle is still. The circle does not move when the user drags outside the circle (that is, the initial touch point within that circle). If the user presses the phone's Back button, the Exit dialog box pops up. Clicking Exit exits the application, as shown in Figure 11-5(b).

(a) Application running

(b) Exit interface

Figure 11-5. The MoveCircle *application*

From the application interface description, the major computing tasks of the application are concentrated in dragging the circle, constantly calculating the circle's new location, and refreshing (redrawing) the display. The application's code framework application is similar to that in section "Dialog Box Example" of Chapter 10 on page 33, and thus the source code is skipped here.

Follow these steps to use Intel GPA to monitor the example application:

1. Build and deploy the application in Eclipse.

2. Use general procedures to create an application project. Name the application MoveCircle:

  a. Write the related code for the project. The document framework is shown in Figure 11-6.

Figure 11-6. *Document framework for the* MoveCircle *application*

  b. Edit the AndroidManifest.xml file, and add the following code:

```
1. <manifest xmlns:android="http://schemas.android.com/apk/res/android"
2.     package="com.example.movecircle"
3.     android:versionCode="1"
4.     android:versionName="1.0" >
5.
6.     <uses-sdk
7.         android:minSdkVersion="8"
8.         android:targetSdkVersion="15" />
9.     <uses-permission android:name="android.permission.INTERNET"/>
10.
```

```
11.      <application
12.          android:icon="@drawable/ic_launcher"
13.          android:debuggable="true"
14.          android:label="@string/app_name"
15.          android:theme="@style/AppTheme" >
16.          <activity
17.              android:name=".MainActivity"
18.              android:label="@string/title_activity_main" >
19.              <intent-filter>
20.                  <action
21.                      android:name="android.intent.action.MAIN" />

22.                  <category android:name="android.intent.category.
                     LAUNCHER" />
23.              </intent-filter>
24.          </activity>
25.      </application>
26.
27. </manifest>
```

In line 9, you add a uses-permission elements, and grant the application Internet write/read access. Line 13 specifies that the application is debuggable.

    c.   Generate the application package, and deploy the application to the real target device.

  3. Start Intel GPA on the host machine to monitor the application.

  4. Connect the Android phone to the PC. Make sure the screen is not locked, or you may get the error "Unsuccessful Phone Connection":

    d.   Make sure you turn off all tools that use adb, such as Eclipse and DDMS. Otherwise, you may get the error "Unsuccessful Phone Connection."

    e.   (This step is optional.) Make sure adb is started and running:

```
C:\Documents and Settings>adb devices
List of devices attached
Medfield04749AFB        device
```

    f.   In Windows, select Start ➤ Program ➤ Intel Graphics Performance Analyzers 2012 RS ➤ Intel GPA System Analyzer to start Intel GPA.

g.   The Intel GPA initial window pops up, suggesting the machine to be monitored, as shown in Figure 11-7. Because the tuning target is a phone in this case, you select the phone (in this case, Medfield04749AFB) by clicking the Connect button.

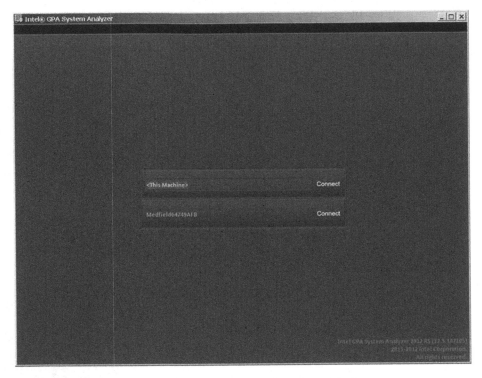

Figure 11-7. Intel GPA interface for connecting to a monitored device

h.   Once connected, Intel GPA does an initial analysis of applications installed on the monitored smartphone, dividing apps into two groups: analyzable application and non-analyzable applications, as shown in Figure 11-8.

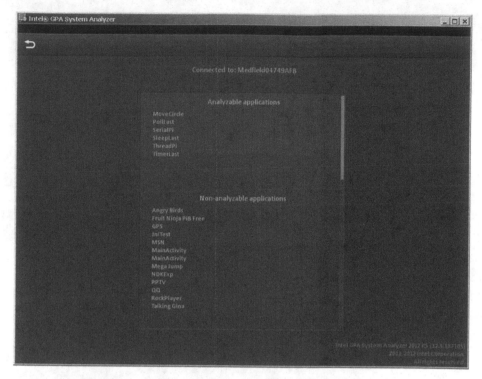

Figure 11-8. *Initial interface (apps list) after Intel GPA is connected to the monitored phone*

In the Analyzable Applications list is the example MoveCircle application. If an application cannot be analyzed by Intel GPA, it is usually because the application's parameters are not set, as described earlier in this section, or because the device is not rooted. As a good exercise, you can skip step 2b, which modifies AndroidManifest.xml; that will cause the application to disappear from the Analyzable Applications list and appear on the list of non-analyzable applications.

      i.   In the Analyzable Applications list, click the name of the application you want Intel GPA to monitor (in this case, MoveCircle). A rolling circle showing ongoing progress appears next to the app. See Figure 11-9.

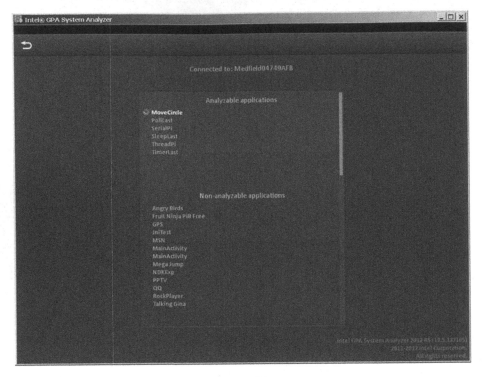

Figure 11-9. App initialization interface in Intel GPA

At the same time, the application startup screen is displayed on the phone. The screen prompts you with the message Waiting For Debugger, as shown in Figure 11-10. Note that you should not click the Force Close button: wait until the message box automatically closes in the interface.

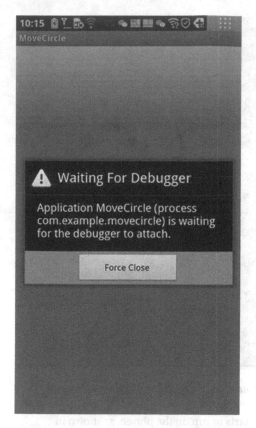

Figure 11-10. *Initial screen on the target phone when Intel GPA starts the application to be monitored*

j.   The Intel GPA monitoring interface appears, as shown in Figure 11-11.

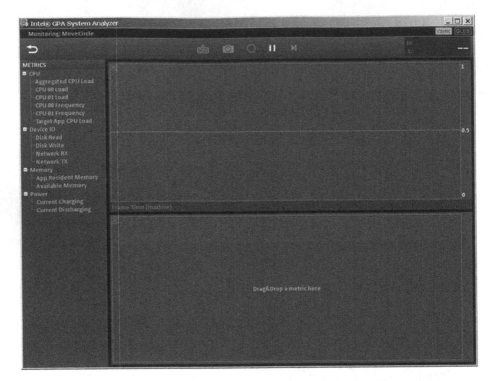

Figure 11-11. *Initial Intel GPA Monitoring interface when the application is started*

At the same time, the MoveCircle app starts to run on the phone, as shown in Figure 11-12.

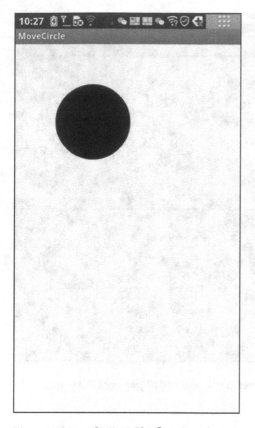

Figure 11-12. The MoveCircle app running on the target phone

k. Drag and drop CPU 00 Load to the top real-time status
    display panel in the display window, and drag and drop
    CPU 01 Load to the bottom real-time status display
    panel. Start to interact with MoveCircle: use your finger
    to click and drag the circle for a few seconds, and then
    stop the interaction for a few seconds. The corresponding
    Intel GPA monitor screen is shown in Figure 11-13.

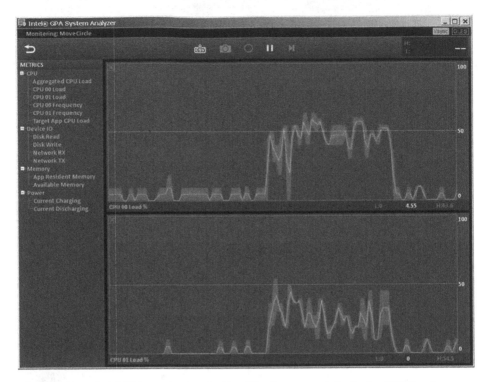

Figure 11-13. *Intel GPA monitoring the* MoveCircle *app and displaying CPU loads in real time*

In Figure 11-13, you can see a rule: when you drag the circle, both CPU loads rise to a certain height; when you do not interact with the app, the two CPU loads immediately drop to near 0%. The application's main computing tasks are concentrated in the circle drag and move, with no or low computing (low or no CPU loads) when the circle is not moved.

1. To end the Intel GPA analysis, exit the app as shown in Figure 11-5(b). Intel GPA returns to the starting interface shown in Figure 11-9.

This example only demonstrates monitoring the load on the CPU. Intel GPA is more useful when you analyze an application that is doing OpenGL rendering; the screenshots here don't show all the GPU and OpenGL metrics. If you are interested, you can try other examples and monitor other metrics. For example, for MoveCircle, we chose the Disk Read metric for the top display window and Disk Write for the bottom. After switching apps to review some photo files and returning to MoveCircle, the action was instantly apparent (see Figure 11-14).

Figure 11-14. Intel GPA monitoring Disk Read and Disk Write for MoveCircle and other apps

Android Multithreaded Design

The Intel Atom processor supports hyperthreading and multi-core configurations. A multithreaded design is a good way to increase the degree of parallelism and improve performance. Intel Atom N-series processors support the parallel execution of multiple threads. Most Intel Atom processors are dual core with HT, and the latest Bay Trail processor has dual core or quad core and physically supports a certain degree of parallel execution.

Note that the word used here is *parallel* rather than *concurrent*. For some tasks, you can follow the classic divide-and-conquer methodology and divide them into two or more basic units. You assign those units to different threads to be executed at the same time. In this way, the performance potential of the processor is fully utilized, and you speed up the software execution. As a result, the software runs faster and more efficiently.

Based on the Java multithreaded programming interface, Android provides a more powerful multithreaded programming interface. With the aid of this programming interface, you can easily implement multithreaded development and design at the Java language level without needing to use the cumbersome underlying OS call interface.

Android Framework of a Thread

The Android threaded programming framework is based on Java. There are two approaches to multithreaded programming in Java: inheriting from the Thread class and overriding the run method; and using the Runnable interface and the run method.

Java Thread Programming Interface

The general code framework for the first method, inheriting from the Thread class, is as follows:

1. Define the Thread class (in this case, MyThread) and its code:

```
class MyThread extends Thread  // Thread inheritance, custom
thread
{
    public MyThread()          // Define a constructor
    {
        super();               // Call the parent class builder
                                  to create objects

    }
    @Override
    public void run()          // To write run code in the run
                                  method of the thread body

    {
        ......                 // The real Run Code of the
                                  thread.

    }
}
```

2. Start the thread code:

```
MyThread myThread = new MyThread();   // create a new thread
myThread.start();                     // start a thread
```

3. Wait for the running thread to end:

```
try {
    myThread.join();                  // Wait for thread process
                                         to end

} catch (InterruptedException e) {

}
```

The second method uses the Runnable interface implementation. Here is the general code framework:

1. Write a custom Runnable interface implementation class:

    ```
    class MyRunnableThread implements Runnable   // implement runnable
                                                               interface
    {
        public void run()
        {
            ......           // actual implementation codes of the
        thread
        }
    }
    ```

2. Start a thread:

    ```
    MyRunnableThread target = new MyRunnableThread();
    // create custom runnable interface implementation object//
    Thread myThread = new Thread(target); // create a Thread class
                                                   object
    myThread.start();                      // Start Thread
    ```

These two methods have the same effects but are used on different occasions. If you are familiar with Java, you know that Java does not have multiple inheritance in C++; it implements interfaces instead. To separately implement a thread, you can use the first method, thread inheritance.

But some classes are inherited from another class. In such cases, if you want the thread to run, you have to use the second method (Runnable interface). In this case, you can declare that the class implements the Runnable interface and then put the code to be run as a thread into the run function. This way, it does not affect its previous inheritance hierarchy and can also run as a thread.

Note the following about Java's threading framework:

- In the Java runtime, the system implements a thread scheduler, which determines the time at which a thread is running on the CPU.

- In Java technology, the thread is usually preemptive, without the need for a time-slice allocation process (assigning each thread process equal CPU time). In the preemptive scheduling model, all threads are in a ready-to-run state (waiting state), but only one thread is running. The thread continues to run until it terminates or returns to a runnable (wait) state or another, higher-priority thread becomes runnable. In the latter case, the low-priority thread terminates to give the right to run to the high-priority thread.

- The Java thread scheduler supports the preemptive approach for threads with different priorities, but it does not support time-slice rotation of threads with the same priority.

- If the operating system where the Java runtime is running supports the rotation of the time slice, then the Java thread scheduler supports time-slice rotation of threads with the same priority.

- Do not overly rely on the system's thread scheduler. For example, the low-priority thread must also get a chance to run.

For more detailed information about Java multithreaded programming methods, you can refer to related Java programming books, including *Learn Java for Android* (www.apress.com/9781430264545), *Pro Android Apps Performance Optimization* (www.apress.com/9781430239994), and *Android Recipes* (www.apress.com/9781430246145).

Android Threaded Programming Extensions and Support

When Android is running, the system (DVM) supports concurrent multiple CPUs. That being said, if the machine has more than one logical processor, the DVM follows certain strategies to automatically assign different threads to run on different CPUs. In this way, Android can physically run different threads in parallel. In addition to the thread-programming interfaces provided by Java, Android also provides important extensions and support. The first is the *looper-message mechanism*.

Android's interface, including a variety of activities, runs in the main thread of the application (also known as the *UI thread*, the *interface thread*, or the *default thread*). The application by default has only one thread, which is the main thread. Thus the application is considered to be single-threaded. Some time-consuming tasks (computing), if run on the main thread by default, cause the main interface to fail to respond for a long time. To prevent this, those time-consuming tasks should be allocated to the independent thread to execute.

The independent thread running behind the scenes (also known as the *assistive thread* or *background thread*) often needs to communicate with the interface of the main thread, such as updating the display. If the behind-the-scenes thread calls a function of an interface object to update the interface, Android gives the execution error message CalledFromWrongThreadException.

For example, in an application (in this case GuiExam), if a worker thread directly calls the setText function of the TextView object in the interface to update the display, the system immediately encounters an error and terminates the running application, as shown in Figure 11-15.

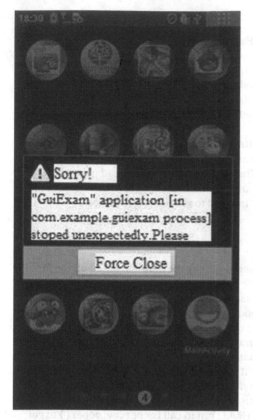

Figure 11-15. *Running error when a worker thread directly calls a function of the UI object*

In order to let the worker thread and the main thread interface communicate, you need to understand the looper-message mechanism. Android has a *message queue* that can combine threads, processing handler and looper components to exchange information.

Message

A *message* is the information exchanged between threads. When a thread behind the scenes needs to update the interface, it sends a message containing the data to the UI thread (the main thread).

Handler

The *handler* is the main processor of the message and is responsible for sending the message and executing and processing the message content. The behind-the-scenes thread, using the processing object passed in, calls the sendMessage(Message) function to send a message. To use a handler, you need a method to implement the class handleMessage(Message), which is responsible for handling the message operation content (such as updating the interface). The handleMessage method usually requires subclassing.

The handler is not used to open a new thread. It is more like the secretary of the main thread, responsible for managing the updated data from the sub thread and then updating the interface in the main thread. The behind-the-scenes thread processes the sendMessage() method to send a message, and the handler calls back (automatically invoked) processing in the HandlerMessage method to process the message.

Message Queue

The *message queue* is used to store the messages sent by the handler, based on the first-in, first-out rule for execution. For each message queue, there is a corresponding handler. The handler uses two methods to send messages to the message queue: SendMessage and post. Messages sent by these two methods are executed in slightly different waya: a message sent by SendMessage is a message queue object and is processed by the HandlerMessage function of the handler; a message sent through the post method is a runnable object and is implemented automatically.

Android has no global message queue. It automatically builds a message queue for the main thread (one of the UI threads), but the message queue is not established in the sub thread; so Looper.getMainLooper() must be called to get the looper of the main thread. The main thread loop does not go to NULL; but to call Looper.myLooper() to get the looper of the current thread loop

Looper

The looper is the housekeeper for each thread's message queue. It is a bridge between the handler and message queues. Program components first pass the message to the looper through the handler, and then the looper puts the message in the queue.

For the main thread of the application's default UI, the system establishes the message queue and looper: there is no need to write the message queue and looper operation code in the source code, and both are transparent to the default main thread. However, the handler is not transparent to the default main thread. In order to send a message to the main thread and handle the message, you must establish your own handler object.

In addition to using the looper-message mechanism to achieve communication between the worker thread and the main GUI thread, you can also use a technique called *asynchronous-tasks (AsyncTask)* mechanism to implement the communication between those threads. The general use of the AsyncTask framework is as follows:

1. AsyncTask.

2. Implement AsyncTask defined by the following one or several methods:

    *   onPreExecute(): Begin preparatory work before execution of the task doInBackground(Params...): Start background execution. You can call the publishProgress function to update real-time task progress.

    *   onProgressUpdate(Progress...): After the publishProgress function is called, the UI thread calls this function to show the progress of the task interface—for example, displaying a progress bar.

    *   onPostExecute(Result): After the operation is complete, send the results to the UI thread.

None of these functions can be called manually. In addition to the doInBackground(Params...)function, the remaining three are UI thread called, so requirements are:

1. The AsyncTask instance must be created in the UI thread;

2. The AsyncTask.execute function must be called in the UI thread.

Keep in mind that the task can be executed only once. Multiple calls are abnormal. You can find a detailed AsyncTask example in the Android help documentation.

Thread Example

This section uses an example to illustrate Android-threaded programming. The running GuiExam application is shown in Figure 11-16.

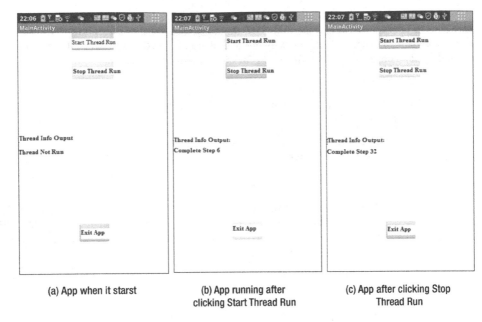

(a) App when it starst

(b) App running after
clicking Start Thread Run

(c) App after clicking Stop
Thread Run

Figure 11-16. *Demo UI of a multithreaded code framework*

As shown in Figure 11-16, the demo app has three main activities buttons: Start Thread Run, Stop Thread Run, and Exit App. The first two control the operation of the auxiliary thread. Click the Start Thread Run button, and the thread starts running, as shown in Figure 11-16(b). Click Stop Thread Run to end the thread run, as shown in Figure 11-16(c). The worker thread refreshes the text display in the TextView every half a section, displaying Complete Step. X in increments from 0 to X. Click Exit App to close the activities and exit the application.

The structure of the demo app and the procedures are as follows:

1. Edit the main activity file (`activity_main.xml`), delete the `originalTextView` window component, and then add three buttons and two TextView window components. The buttons' ID properties are, respectively, `@+id/startTaskThread`, `@+id/stopTaskThread`, and `@+id/exitApp`. The Text property is, respectively, Start Thread Run, Stop Thread Run, and Exit App. The TextView's ID property is `@+id/taskThreadOuputInfo` to display the text output of the worker thread. The entire process is shown in Figure 11-17.

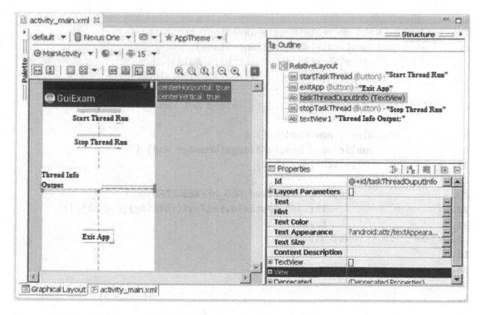

Figure 11-17. Multithreaded code framework in activity_main.xml

> 2. Edit MainActivity.java for the activity_main class as follows:

```
1.  package com.example.guiexam;
2.  import android.os.Bundle;
3.  import android.app.Activity;
4.  import android.view.Menu;
5.  import android.widget.Button;
6.  import android.view.View;
7.  import android.view.View.OnClickListener;
8.  import android.os.Process;
9.  import android.widget.TextView;
10. import android.os.Handler;
11. import android.os.Message;

12. public class MainActivity extends Activity {
13.     private Button btn_StartTaskThread;
14.     private Button btn_StopTaskThread;
15.     private Button btn_ExitApp;
16.     private TextView threadOutputInfo;
17.     private MyTaskThread myThread = null;
18.     private Handler mHandler;;
```

```
19.     @Override
20.     public void onCreate(Bundle savedInstanceState) {
21.         super.onCreate(savedInstanceState);
22.         setContentView(R.layout.activity_main);
23.         threadOutputInfo = (TextView)findViewById(R.
            id.taskThreadOuputInfo);
24.         threadOutputInfo.setText("Thread Not Run");

25.         mHandler = new Handler() {
26.             public void handleMessage(Message msg) {
27.                 switch (msg.what)
28.                 {
29.                 case MyTaskThread.MSG_REFRESHINFO:
30.                     threadOutputInfo.setText((String)(msg.obj));
31.                     break;
32.                 default:
33.                     break;
34.                 }
35.             }
36.         };

37.         btn_ExitApp = (Button) findViewById(R.id.exitApp);
            // Code for <Exit App>Button
38.         btn_ExitApp.setOnClickListener(new /*View.*/OnClickListener(){
39.             public void onClick(View v) {
40.                 finish();
41.                 Process.killProcess(Process.myPid());
42.             }
43.         });

44.         btn_StartTaskThread = (Button) findViewById(R.id.startTaskThread);
45.         // Code for<Start Thread Run>
46.         btn_StartTaskThread.setOnClickListener(new /*View.*/
            OnClickListener(){
47.             public void onClick(View v) {
48.                 myThread = new MyTaskThread(mHandler);  // Create a
                                                               thread

49.                 myThread.start();    // Start Thread
50.                 setButtonAvailable();
51.             }
52.         });

53.         btn_StopTaskThread = (Button) findViewById(R.id.stopTaskThread);
54.         //code for <Stop Thread Run>
55.         btn_StopTaskThread.setOnClickListener(new /*View.*/
            OnClickListener(){
```

```
56.    public void onClick(View v) {
57.        if (myThread!=null && myThread.isAlive())
58.                myThread.stopRun();
59.            try {
60.                if (myThread!=null){
61.                    myThread.join();
62.                    // Wait for Thread Run to end
63.                    myThread =null;
64.                }
65.            } catch (InterruptedException e) {
66.                // Empty statement block, ignored forcibly
                   abort exception
67.            }
68.            setButtonAvailable();
69.        }
70.    });
71.    setButtonAvailable();
72. }

73.    @Override
74.    public boolean onCreateOptionsMenu(Menu menu) {
75.        getMenuInflater().inflate(R.menu.activity_main, menu);
76.        return true;
77.    }

78.    private void setButtonAvailable()    // New function is used to set
                                            the button optional
79.    {
80.        btn_StartTaskThread.setEnabled(myThread==null);
81.        btn_ExitApp.setEnabled(myThread==null);
82.        btn_StopTaskThread.setEnabled(myThread!=null);
83.    }
84. }
```

Lines 17 and 18 define the variable myThread of the defined thread class MyTaskThread, and the default main thread handler object mHandler, respectively. Lines 25–36 define the Handler class. The What attribute field of the message class indicates the type of message. The custom handler class uses a switch-case statement for different handlers depending on the type of message; MSG_REFRESHINFO is the message type of the custom thread class MyTaskThread, which means the worker thread requires an updated interface display message. Lines 29–31 process the message. The code is very simple; it updates the TextView widget display based on the message in the parameter object.

Lines 47–49 are the response code when the Start Thread Run button is clicked. It first creates the custom thread object and then calls the Thread.start function to make the self-defined thread class MyTaskThread run, which runs the execution code in the run function as a single thread. Finally, line 49 calls the custom setButtonAvailable function to set each button's option (grayed and not selectable, or white and selectable).

Lines 55–65 are response code for the Stop Thread Run button. Line 55 first determines whether the thread already exists or is running. Then it stops a thread run in line 56 by calling the defined stop-the-thread prototype function from the custom thread class MyTaskThread and then calling the Thread.join(); it then waits for the thread run to end. Finally, it sets the optional status of the interface buttons.

Lines 75–80 are a custom function that which is used to determine the optional status of each button: white and selectable or gray and selectable.

3. Create a new class MyTaskThread in the application. This class inherits from Thread and is used to implement the worker thread. The source code file MyTaskThread.java of this class is as follows:

```
1. package com.example.guiexam;
2. import android.os.Handler;
3. import android.os.Message;
4.
5. public class MyTaskThread extends Thread {
6.     private static final int stepTime = 500;
7. // Execution timeof each step(unite:ms)
8.     private volatile boolean isEnded;
9. // mark if the thread is running. Used to stop thread run
10.     private Handler mainHandler;
11. // Handler used to send message
12.     public static final int MSG_REFRESHINFO = 1;  // Update message
        on interface
13.
14.     public MyTaskThread(Handler mh)    // Define a constructor
15.     {
16.         super();   // Call the parent class builder to create objects
17.         isEnded = false;
18.         mainHandler = mh;
19.     }
20.
21.     @Override
22.     public void run() // Write run code in thread body run method
23.     {
24.         Message msg ;
25.         for (int i = 0; !isEnded; i++)
26.         {
27.             try {
28.                 Thread.sleep(stepTime); // designate time for every
                                                step of the thread to sleep
29.                 String s = "Complete" + i +"step";
30.                 msg = new Message();
31.                 msg.what = MSG_REFRESHINFO; // Define message type
32.                 msg.obj = s;  // attach data to message
33.                 mainHandler.sendMessage(msg); // send message
```

```
34.              } catch (InterruptedException e) {
35.                  e.printStackTrace();
36.              }
37.          }
38.      }
39.
40.      public void stopRun()  // Stop control function for stop thread run
41.      {
42.          isEnded = true;
43.      }
42. }
```

This document is the implementation code of the custom thread class MyTaskThread, which is the key to this application. The application is using the first approach, thread inheritance, to achieve threading. In line 5, the custom class inherits from Thread; and then, from line 14–39, the threads run code on the rewritten run function. To cope with the work of the thread, lines 6–9 define the relevant variables. The constant stepTime represents the length of every step of the thread-delay time, measured in milliseconds. isEnded controls whether to continue each step in the body of the loop in the run function. Note that the variable is preceded by the volatile modifier: Each time a thread accesses the variable, it reads the final value in memory after the variable has been modified. A write request must be written to memory, too. This avoids the copy in cache or register not matching the value in the memory variable, which would cause an error. The mainHandler variable saves the main thread handler. MSG_REFRESHINFO is a constant that handles custom messages.

Lines 10–15 are a constructor. In this function body, you initialize the value of the thread-running control variable isEnded and then save mainHandler as the main thread-handler object passed as a parameter.

Lines 16–33 are the core thread code that rewrites the run function. The code is composed of a loop to determine whether to continue to use the control variable isEnded. Here one loop is a step. Every step is also simple: when the Thread class static function sleep is called in line 28 after a specified time, a message is generated and assembled in lines 24–27. Finally, in line 28, the message is sent to the specified (message loop) handler.

Lines 34–37 are a custom control function to stop the thread from running. The purpose of the code is very simple: to change the run-loop control variable's value.

Thread Synchronization

A multithreaded process inevitably involves a problem: how to deal with threads' access to shared data, which relates to thread synchronization. Thread data sharing is also known as *critical section*. Access to shared data is also known as *competition* for resource access. In general OS textbooks, thread synchronization includes not only the synchronization of this passive selected access to shared data, but also active-choice synchronization between threads to collaborate to complete a task. In Java, thread synchronization is focused on access to shared data. This section discusses synchronization issues related to shared data access.

In multithreaded programming, if access to shared data does not use certain synchronization mechanisms, data consistency and integrity cannot be guaranteed. There are two ways to perform Java thread synchronization: an internal lock data object, and synchronization. Both approaches are implemented with the synchronized keyword. Statements modified by the synchronized block can guarantee the exclusivity of the operations between threads: they are unique, or *atomic*. In Java, this process is simply called *synchronization*. A synchronized block is also known as *genlock*.

In the first approach to locking data objects, at any time, only one thread may access the object that is locked. The code framework is as follows:

```
Object var;     // Object variable
synchronized(var) {
    ... ...     // Operation of the shared variable
}
```

In this code, var must be the variable that each thread can access, so it becomes a synchronization variable. In practice, the synchronization variable and shared variables can be either the same or different. The Object class in the previous code can be replaced with a subclass of Object, because in addition to the simple classes in Java, any class can be the Object offspring class.

Note that the synchronization variable cannot be a simple type (such as int and float, but not the the String class):

```
int var;
synchronized(var) {     // compiler error:int is not a valid type's argument
                        for the synchronized statement

    ... ...
}
```

When you use the second approach—the synchronization method—at any time, only one thread visits a code segment:

```
class MyClass {
    public synchronized void method1()
    { ... }
}
```

The previous code is the synchronization for the general class (function). In addition, there is also synchronization for the class's static function:

```
class MyClass {
    public synchronized static void method2()
    { ... }
}
```

Using the synchronization method, the object that calls the synchronization method is locked. When an object of MyClass: obj1 implements the synchronization method in a different thread, mutual exclusion achieves the synchronization result. But another object, obj2, generated by the class MyClass, can call this method with the synchronized keyword. As a result, the previous code can be written equivalently as shown next:

- Synchronization (general) method:

```
class MyClass {
    public void method1()
    {
        synchronized (this)
            { .../* function body */ }
    }
}
```

- Static synchronization method:

```
class MyClass {
    public static void method2()
    {
        synchronized (MyClass.class)
            { .../* function body */ }
    }
}
```

In the static method, a class literal is treated as a lock. It generates the same result as the synchronized static function. The timing to get a lock is also special: the lock is acquired when calling the class that this object belongs to, and no longer the specific object that this class generates.

Following are the generalized rules that Java uses to implement a lock via the synchronized function:

Rule 1: When two parallel threads visit the synchronized(this) synchronization code segment of the same object, only one thread can be run at any one time. Other threads must wait until the current thread finishes running this code segment to run the same code segment.

Rule 2: When a thread visits a synchronized(this) synchronization code segment of an object, another thread can still visit a non-synchronized(this) synchronization code segment of an object.

Rule 3: When a thread visits a synchronized(this) synchronization code segment of an object, visits by all other threads to all other synchronized(this) synchronization code segments of the object are blocked.

Rule 4: When a thread visits a `synchronized(this)` synchronization code segment of an object, it acquires the object's object lock. As a result, visits from other threads to all `synchronized(this)` synchronization code segments of an object are temporally locked.

Rule 5: These rules apply to all other object locks.

Although `synchronized` can guarantee granularity of the object or executed block of statements, mutual exclusivity of this granularity degrades thread concurrency; so, the code, which originally could run in parallel, must run in serial execution. Therefore, you need to be cautious when you use the `synchronized` function, and limit it to cases when you need the `synchronized` lock. On the other hand, you should make the lock granularity as small as possible, in order to both ensure the correctness of the program and improve operational efficiency by making the degree of concurrency as great as possible.

Thread Communication

In multithreaded design, with data exchange among threads, setting the signal collaboration to complete a task is a common problem. Most significant are generalized threading issues, such as a typical example of the producer-consumer problem. These are the threads that must cooperate to accomplish a task.

In classic books on the OS, it is generally recommended that you use a semaphore to achieve thread-synchronization primitives. Java does not directly provide the semaphore primitives or programming interface, but achieves the function of the semaphore with class functions such as `wait`, `notify`, `notifyAll`, and so on.

`wait`, `notify`, and `notifyAll` belong to the function of the `Object` class and are not part of the `Thread` class. Every object has a waiting queue (`Wait Set`) in Java. When an object has just been created, its wait queue is empty.

The `wait` function can make the objects in the current thread wait until another thread calls the `notify` or `notifyAll` method of this object. In other words, when a call waits in the object's queue, the thread enters a wait state. Only when the `notify` method is called can you remove the thread from the queue to make it a runnable thread. The `notifyAll` method waits for all threads in the queue inside the object to become runnable threads. `Notify` and `notifyAll` are similar in functionality.

The `wait`, `notify`, and `notifyAll` functions need to be used in conjunction with `synchronized` to establish the synchronization model, which can guarantee the granularity of the former functions. For example, before calling `wait`, you need to get the object's synchronization lock so that this function can be called. Otherwise, the compiler can call the `wait` function, but it will receive an `IllegalMonitorStateException` runtime exception.

Following are several examples of code frameworks for wait, notify, and notifyAll:

- Waiting for a resource code:

```
synchronized(obj) {
    while(!condition)
        try {
            obj.wait();
        } catch (InterruptedException e) {
        }
    ......Use code of obj
}
```

- Providing resources (example: complete use of resources and returning to the system):

```
synchronized(obj) {
    condition = true;
    obj.notify();
}
```

The previous code is the standalone use case of the synchronization object obj. You can also write synchronization code in a class. The framework of this code can be written as follows:

```
class MyClass{
    public synchronized void func1 {
        while (!condition)
            try {
                wait();
            } catch (InterruptedException e) {
            }
        ...... codes for using MyClass resource
    }
    public synchronized void func2 {
        condition = true;
        notifyAll();
    }
}
```

The thread that is waiting for resources can call the myclass.func1 function, and the thread that provides resources calls the myclass.func2 function.

Principles of Multithreaded Optimization for the Intel Atom Processor

Multithreaded software design allows program code in different threads to run at the same time. However, blind use of multithreading or excessive use of multithreaded programming may not lead to performance improvement and may even downgrade software performance. Therefore, you need to understand the principles of multithreaded optimization on Android x86.

First, the start, or scheduling, of a thread requires a certain amount of overhead and occupies a certain amount of processor time. Processors that do not support hyperthreading and multi-core processing cannot physically let these threads run at the same time. To support multithreaded programs, there is significant overhead if you split one physical processor into multiple logical processors with virtualization technologies so that each thread can run on a logical core. Such a multithreading strategy not only makes it difficult to achieve improvement in performance, but may even lead to the multithreaded execution speed being slower than a single-threaded program. Therefore, to achieve multithreaded performance acceleration (a prerequisite to being faster than single-threaded execution speed) using multithreaded design, the processor must support hyperthreading or multi-core.

Second, for processors that support hyperthreading or multi-core, it is not always true that more threads will make software run faster. You must consider the performance/price ratio. The physical basis of multithreaded design for performance tuning is to allow multiple threads to run at the same time in parallel on the physical layer. Therefore, the maximum number of concurrently running threads supported by the processor is the optimum number of threads for multithreaded optimization.

According to Intel's official statement, Intel Hyper-Threading Technology can support two threads running in parallel, with multi-core support for multiple threads running in parallel. For example, for a dual-core Intel processor that supports Intel Hyper-Threading Technology, the maximum number of threads supported to run in parallel is

$$2\,core \times 2\left(Intel\,HTT\right) = 4\,threads$$

Therefore, this machine supports multithreaded optimization, and the maximum number of threads (threads running concurrently) is equal to four.

For a Motorola MT788 target machine, which uses a single-core Intel Atom Z2480 processor with HT, the optimal number of threads is two. If the target machine is a Lenovo K900 with a dual-core Intel Atom Z2580 processor with Intel HT, the optimal number of threads is four.

In general, when you consider multithreaded optimization on the Android platform, it is necessary to look carefully at the processor information to see if it supports hyperthreading or multi-core technology.

Case Study: Intel GPA-Assisted Multithreaded Optimization for an Android Application

The previous section explained several optimization techniques and principles. This section uses a comprehensive example to explain optimization. In this case, multithreaded optimization is combined with optimization assisted by Intel GPA to make the application run faster.

The example app calculates pi (π). Let's look at some background for the app. The mathematical formula is as follows:

$$\int_0^1 \frac{1}{x^2+1} dx = \arctan(1) - \arctan(0) = \frac{\pi}{4}$$

The integration formula can be expressed using the infinitive:

$$\pi = 4\int_0^1 \frac{1}{x^2+1} dx = 4\lim_{\Delta x \to 0}\sum \frac{1}{x^2+1}\Delta x$$

Δx cannot be infinitely small—you can only make Δx as small as possible. So, the result of the formula is closer to p. Using $step$ to represent Δx,

$$num\_steps = \frac{1}{step}$$

The value of step must be maximum to get an accurate value of pi. Consider that

$$f(x) = \frac{1}{x^2+1}$$

While f(x) is a raised function. Here you take a median value to calculate the sum. That is, you use

$$f\left(\frac{i+0.5}{num\_steps}\right)$$

to replace

$$f\left(\frac{i}{num\_steps}\right)$$

to calculate the sum. The result calculated by this formula is not always smaller than the actual value of π. So, eventually, you get the final formula on which this app is based:

$$\frac{\pi}{4} \approx \sum_{i=0}^{num\_steps} f(x) \times step = \sum_{i=0}^{num\_steps} f\left(\frac{i+0.5}{num\_steps}\right) \times step = step \times \sum_{i=0}^{num\_steps} f[(i+0.5) \times step]$$

It is not difficult to write the source code based on this formula.

Original Application and Intel GPA Analysis

You begin by deriving the app's un-optimized computing source code from the formula in the previous section. This application is named SerialPi.

The design of this app is the same as that in the "Thread Example" section earlier. The task of calculating π is put in a worker thread (here called a task thread) to run. A button is set on main activity to control the running of the thread, and a TextView is used to display the result of the task thread. The interface showing the app's single run is shown in Figure 11-18.

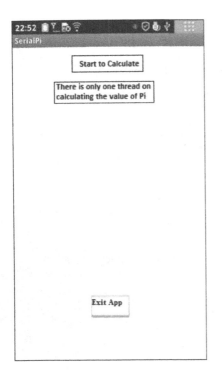

(a) App start

(b) Click Start to Calculate and output of Pi value after 22 seconds

Figure 11-18. *SerialPi app interface*

The interface after the application starts is shown in Figure 11-18(a). When you click the Start Calculating button, all buttons on the interface gray out until the computation is complete. The interface then displays the computation result as well as the thread's total running time. Clicking Exit App, as shown in Figure 11-18(b) exits the application. From the interface screen, you can see that it takes about 22 seconds for this app to calculate π. Running the application repeatedly, the calculation time remains about the same (22 seconds).

The steps to build the application and write the key code are as follows:

1. Create a new application called `SerialPi`. The proposed project property should use the default value. Set [Build SDK] to support x86 API.

2. Edit `activity_main.xml`. Place two `Button` components and two `TextView` components in the layout. Set the ID attribute of one `TextView` to `@+id/taskOuputInfo`: it will display the results of the task thread, as shown in Figure 11-19.

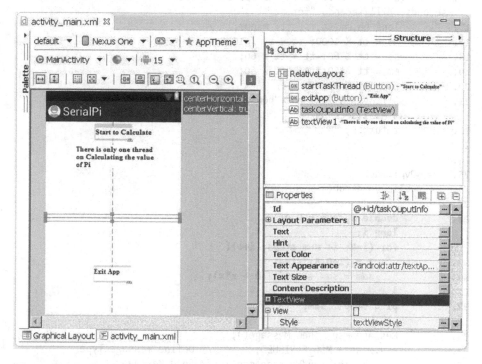

Figure 11-19. *Layout for the* `SerialPi` *App*

3. Create new thread class `MyTaskThread` in the project, and edit the source code file `MyTaskThread.java` as follows:

```
1. package com.example.serialpi;
2. import android.os.Handler;
3. import android.os.Message;

4. public class MyTaskThread extends Thread {
5.     private Handler mainHandler;
6.     public static final int MSG_FINISHED = 1;
```

```
7. // Defined the message type  for the end of the calculation
8.     private static final long num_steps = 200000000;
9. // num_steps variables in Formula, the total number of steps
       private static final double step = 1.0 / num_steps;
10. // Step variable  in formula, step length
11.    public static double pi = 0.0;
12. // the calculation of results of π
13.
14.     static String msTimeToDatetime(long msnum){
15. // The function converts the number of milliseconds into hours: minutes:
    seconds. Milliseconds "format
16.        long hh,mm,ss,ms, tt= msnum;
17.        ms = tt % 1000; tt = tt / 1000;
18.        ss = tt % 60; tt = tt / 60;
19.        mm = tt % 60; tt = tt / 60;
20.        hh = tt % 60;
21.        String s = "" + hh +"hour "+mm+"minute "+ss + "Second" + ms
           +"Milliseconds";
22.        return s;
23.     }
24.
25.     @Override
26.     public void run()
27.     {
28.         double x, sum = 0.0;
            long i;
            for (i=0; i< num_steps; i++){
29.             x = (i+0.5)*step;
30.             sum = sum + 4.0/(1.0 + x*x);
31.         }
32.         pi = step * sum;

33.         Message msg = new Message();
34.         msg.what = MSG_FINISHED;        // Define message Type
35.         mainHandler.sendMessage(msg);   // Send Message
36.     }
37.
38.     public MyTaskThread(Handler mh)     // Constructor
39.     {
40.         super();
41.         mainHandler = mh;
42.     }
43. }
```

Similar to the framework and the example code listed in the thread example earlier, thread-inheritance laws are used to initialize the thread. Pay close attention to the code segments in bold, which are most directly related to the calculation of π. Lines 7 and 8 define a static variable with the same name used in the formula that calculates π. Line 9 defines the variable for saving the results of the π calculation. Note that this variable is public so that the main thread can access it.

Lines 22–28 calculate π according to the formula. The x variable is an independent variable of function

$$f(x) = \frac{1}{x^2 + 1}$$

and sum is a cumulative variable of Σ. Line 28 calculates the final results. Refer to the code framework mentioned in the earlier section of this chapter on page 32 titled. "Thread Example"; it should not be difficult to understand.

Note that in the thread's run function, once the calculation is complete, the message is sent to the main thread (interface) in line 29.

4. Edit the source code in the main activity class file MainActivity.java. This code controls the run of the thread and displays the calculated results:

```
1.  package com.example.serialpi;
2.  import android.os.Bundle;
3.  import android.app.Activity;
4.  import android.view.Menu;
5.  import android.widget.Button;
6.  import android.view.View;
7.  import android.view.View.OnClickListener;
8.  import android.os.Process;
9.  import android.widget.TextView;
10. import android.os.Handler;
11. import android.os.Message;

12. public class MainActivity extends Activity {
13.     private MyTaskThread myThread = null;
14.     private TextView tv_TaskOutputInfo;  // Display (Calculated) Task
            thread output
15.     private Handler mHandler;;
16.     private long end_time;
17.     private long time;
18.     private long start_time;

19.     @Override
20.     public void onCreate(Bundle savedInstanceState) {
21.         super.onCreate(savedInstanceState);
22.         setContentView(R.layout.activity_main);
23.         tv_TaskOutputInfo = (TextView)findViewById(R.id.taskOuputInfo);
24.         final Button btn_ExitApp = (Button) findViewById(R.id.exitApp);
```

```
25.        btn_ExitApp.setOnClickListener(new /*View.*/OnClickListener(){
26.            public void onClick(View v) {
27.                exitApp();
28.            }
29.        });
30.        final Button btn_StartTaskThread =
           (Button) findViewById(R.id.startTaskThread);
31.        btn_StartTaskThread.setOnClickListener(new /*View.*/
           OnClickListener(){
32.            public void onClick(View v) {
33.                btn_StartTaskThread.setEnabled(false);
34.                btn_ExitApp.setEnabled(false);
35.                startTask();
36.            }
37.        });
38.        mHandler = new Handler() {
39.            public void handleMessage(Message msg) {
40.                switch (msg.what)
41.                {
42.                case MyTaskThread.MSG_FINISHED:
43.                    end_time = System.currentTimeMillis();
44.                    time = end_time - start_time;
45.                    String s = " The end of the run,Pi="+ MyTaskThread.
                       pi+ "  Time consumed:"
46.                                +
47. MyTaskThread.msTimeToDatetime(time);
48.                    tv_TaskOutputInfo.setText(s);
49.                    btn_ExitApp.setEnabled(true);
50.                    break;
51.                default:
52.                    break;
53.                }
54.            }
55.        };
    }
56.
57.    @Override
58.    public boolean onCreateOptionsMenu(Menu menu) {
59.        getMenuInflater().inflate(R.menu.activity_main, menu);
60.        return true;
    }
61.
62.    private void startTask() {
63.        myThread = new MyTaskThread(mHandler);    // Create a thread
64.        if (! myThread.isAlive())
```

```
65.          {
66.              start_time = System.currentTimeMillis();
67.              myThread.start();   // Start thread
68.          }
    }
69.
70.      private void exitApp() {
71.          try {
72.              if (myThread!=null)
73.              {
74.                  myThread.join();
75.                  myThread = null;
76.              }
77.          } catch (InterruptedException e) {
78.          }
79.          finish();   // Exit the activity
80.          Process.killProcess(Process.myPid());   // Exit the application
             process
81.      }
    }
```

This code is similar to the code framework of the example MainActivity class in the "Thread Example" section. The lines of code shown with a gray background are added to estimate the task's running time. Three variables are defined in line 16-18: start_time is the task's start time, end_time as the task's end time, and time is the task's running time. These three variables are parts of the following formula:

time = end_time - start_time

In line 65, when you start the task threads, the machine's current time is recorded in the start_time variable at the same time. In lines 43-44, when the message is received that the task thread has finished running, the machine's time is recorded in end_time. The currentTimeMillis function is a static function provided by the Java System class in the java.lang package; it returns the current time in milliseconds.

5.   Referring to the "Thread Communication" section's example,
     modify the project's AndroidManifest.xml file to make it
     comply with the requirements of Intel GPA monitoring.

After the coding is completed and you've compiled and generated the app, deploy it to the target device.

Now you can use Intel GPA to analyze this application. See the steps in the "Thread Communication" section. First you monitor and analyze the two CPU loads (CPU XX Load indicators). During monitoring, click the Start button to begin running and monitoring information recorded under Intel GPA. The results of the analysis are shown in Figure 11-20.

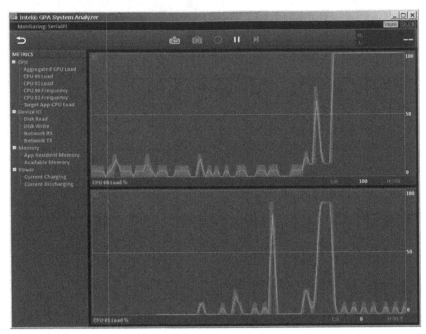

(a) After clicking the Start button

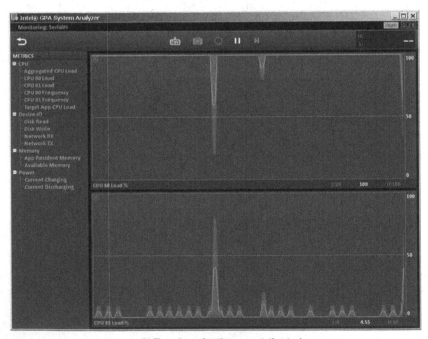

(b) Thread running the computation task

Figure 11-20. Intel GPA analysis screen for SerialPi

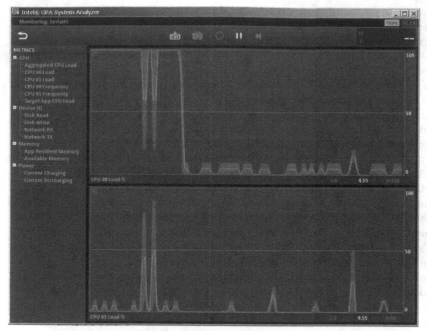

(c) End of the thread's run

Figure 11-20. (*continued*)

Figure 11-20(a) shows the analysis when you click the Start button, Figure 11-20(b) shows the task thread running and Figure 11-20(c) shows the task thread at the end of the run. From the three screens, you can see that the load on the CPU stays at a low level before the app begins to run and after the end of the run. Once the computing task thread starts to run, the load on the CPU rises sharply to 100% of load. You can also see that while the task thread is running, only one of the two CPUs is at full capacity; the other is at low load levels. By analyzing the graph, you can see that the 100% load does not always occur on a specific CPU. Instead, the 100% load alternates between the two CPUs, which reflects the Java Runtime time support for task scheduling: the processor system is transparent to applications. Although a two-CPU load rate is subject to rotation, the load rate is a complementary state: a rising load on one CPU means a decreasing load on another. Thus the total load (sum of the loads of two CPUs at any time) does not exceed the 100% load of a single CPU.

Optimized Application and Intel GPA Analysis

The preceding example uses code derived directly from the formula for calculating π. Is there room for optimization? The answer is definitely yes. Doing so requires you to examine the app's algorithm and apply the optimization principles you've learned, making full use of the Intel Atom processor's hardware features.

How do you tap the full performance potential of the Intel Atom processor? As explained earlier, multi-core Intel Atom processors with Intel Hyper-Threading Technology support multithreading running in parallel on multiple physical cores. For example, the Lenovo K900 phone uses an Intel Atom Z2580 processor and supports two threads running in parallel. This is the entry point for your algorithm optimization: you can divide and conquer. By carefully analyzing the run function in the example MyTaskThread class in the previous section, you can make computing tasks allocated to multiple (in this case, two) threads run; and the threads running in parallel can make the app run faster.

To calculate the cumulative value of the integral area for π, in line 24 you calculated the integral area one step at a time and added the cumulative sum. In this section you take a different approach: you divide the integral area into many blocks and let each thread be responsible for calculating a block. You get the π value by adding the cumulative area of the blocks calculated by the threads. This way, you use a divide-and-conquer strategy to complete the task distribution and get the final results. The optimized app is called ThreadPi. When ThreadPi is calculating the cumulative value of the integral area (which is the π value), each thread's calculation step accumulates the step size to increase the total number of threads so that each thread is responsible for the sum of their own area of the block.

The UI of the running ThreadPi app is shown in Figure 11-21.

The interface of this optimized application (ThreadPi) is the same as the original application (SerialPi). In Figure 11-21(b), you can see that this application takes 13 seconds to calculate the value of π. The time is reduced to almost half that of the original application (22 seconds). The only difference is that the application uses two threads to calculate π.

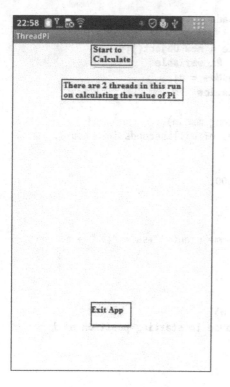
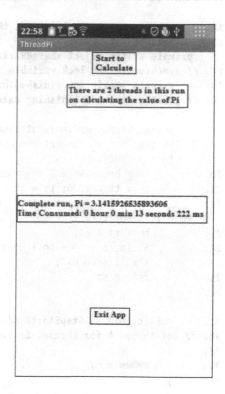

(a) UI when the app starts   (b) Click Start to Calculate to run the app

Figure 11-21. User interface of ThreadPi

This application is based on modifying the original application code. The key changes are as follows.

1.   Modify the thread class of the computing tasks' MyTaskThread source code file MyTaskThread.java as follows:

```
1. package com.example.threadpi;
2. import android.os.Handler;
3. import android.os.Message;

4. public class MyTaskThread extends Thread {
5.     private Handler mainHandler;
6.     public static final int MSG_FINISHED = 1;
7.     private static final long num_steps = 200000000;
8. // num_steps variable in formula, total steps
9.     private static final double step = 1.0 / num_steps;
10. // step variable in formula, step length
11.     public static double pi = 0.0;    //  Calculated result of π
```

383

```
12.     public static final int num_threads = 2;    // Thread count
13.     private int myNum;                           // Thread #
   private static Object sharedVariable = new Object();
14. // synchronization lock variable for Pi variable
15.     private static int finishedThreadNum = 0;
16. // count of threads finishing calculation
17.
18.     static String msTimeToDatetime(long msnum){
19. // The function to convert the number of milliseconds into hours:
   minutes: seconds. Millis
20.         long hh,mm,ss,ms, tt= msnum;
21.         ms = tt % 1000; tt = tt / 1000;
22.         ss = tt % 60; tt = tt / 60;
   mm = tt % 60; tt = tt / 60;
23.         hh = tt % 60;
24.         String s = "" + hh +"hour "+mm+"minute "+ss + "秒 " + ms
            +"milliseconds";
25.         return s;
26.     }

27.     public void setStepStartNum(int n)
28. // set thread # for thread, in response to starting position of i
29.     {
30.         myNum = n;
31.     }
32.
33.     @Override
34.     public void run()
35.     {
36.         double x, partialSum = 0.0;
37.         long i;
38.         for (i = myNum; i < num_steps; i += num_threads) {
39.             x = (i + 0.5) * step;
40.             partialSum += 4.0 / (1.0 + x * x);
41.         }
42.         synchronized (sharedVariable) {
43.             pi += partialSum * step;
44.             finishedThreadNum++;
45.             if (finishedThreadNum >=num_threads) {
   // waiting all threads finishing run and send message
46.                 Message msg = new Message();
47.                 msg.what = MSG_FINISHED; //Define message type
48.                 mainHandler.sendMessage(msg);    //Send message
49.             }
50.         }
51.     }
```

```java
public MyTaskThread(Handler mh)   // constructor
{
    super();
    mainHandler = mh;
}
}
```

The code segments shown with in bold are the main difference between ThreadPi and SerialPi. Lines 10–13 define the variables required for multithreaded computing tasks. The variable num_threads computes the number of threads when the computing task starts. In this case, the Lenovo K900 has an Intel Atom processor with two logical CPUs, so this value is set to 2. The myNum variable computes the thread number, which is in the range 0 to num_threads - 1. The variable sharedVariable is introduced by a synchronization lock applied to variable pi. Because pi is a simple variable, it cannot be directly locked. The finishedThreadNum variable is the number of threads used to complete the calculation. When the value of finishedThreadNum is equal to that of num_threads, all the computing threads have finished running.

Lines 23–26 are a function you add specifically for MyTaskThread, the computing thread. It marks the thread's index number.

Lines 30–44 are the prototype code of the computing thread. Lines 30–35 are the direct code to calculate π. Compared with the corresponding code in the original application, you can see that the sum variable in the original app has been replaced with partialSum, which reflects the fact that the area of this thread is only part of the total area. The most important difference is in line 32: the step-length variable i is not 1 but num_threads, which means the thread moves forward a few steps every time. The initial position of variable I is not 0 but is derived from the thread number. This is a little like a track and field competition, where each athlete (thread) starts at the beginning of their lane rather than from the same starting point. The thread computation is like athletes running in their own lanes on their own track.

Each thread calculates its sum and needs to add this data to the total cumulative sum (the pi variable). This variable is shared by multiple threads, so you need to add a synchronization lock. This step corresponds to lines 36–44. Line 36 adds the synchronization lock, and line 37 adds the result of the thread's calculation to the public results of pi. Line 38 adds 1 to the number of threads at the end of the calculation. In line 39, by comparing the number of threads that have finished the calculation to the total number of threads, you determine whether all the threads have finished running. Only at after all threads have finished is the message sent to the main thread.

2.   Modify the source code file of the main activity class MainActivity.java as follows:

```java
1. package com.example.threadpi;
2. import android.os.Bundle;
3. import android.app.Activity;
4. import android.view.Menu;
5. import android.widget.Button;
6. import android.view.View;
7. import android.view.View.OnClickListener;
```

```
 8. import android.os.Process;
 9. import android.widget.TextView;
10. import android.os.Handler;
11. import android.os.Message;

12. public class MainActivity extends Activity {
13.     private MyTaskThread thrd[] = null;
14.     private TextView tv_TaskOutputInfo;
15.     private Handler mHandler;;
16.     private long end_time;
17.     private long time;
18.     private long start_time;

19.     @Override
20.     public void onCreate(Bundle savedInstanceState) {
21.         super.onCreate(savedInstanceState);
22.         setContentView(R.layout.activity_main);
23.         tv_TaskOutputInfo =
                (TextView)findViewById(R.id.taskOuputInfo);
24.         TextView tv_Info = (TextView)findViewById(R.id.textView1);
25.         String ts = "This example currently has"+ MyTaskThread.num_
                threads + "threads in this run on calculating the value of Pi";
26.         tv_Info.setText(ts);
27.         final Button btn_ExitApp = (Button) findViewById(R.id.exitApp);
29.         btn_ExitApp.setOnClickListener(new /*View.*/OnClickListener(){
30.             public void onClick(View v) {
31.                 exitApp();
32.             }
33.         });
34.         final Button btn_StartTaskThread = (Button) findViewById(R.
                id.startTaskThread);
35.         btn_StartTaskThread.setOnClickListener(new /*View.*/
                OnClickListener(){
36.             public void onClick(View v) {
37.               btn_StartTaskThread.setEnabled(false);
38.               btn_ExitApp.setEnabled(false);
39.                 startTask();
40.             }
41.         });
42.         mHandler = new Handler() {
43.             public void handleMessage(Message msg) {
44.               switch (msg.what)
45.               {
46.               case MyTaskThread.MSG_FINISHED:
47.                   end_time = System.currentTimeMillis();
```

```
48.                    time = end_time - start_time;
49.                    String s = "Run End,Pi="+ MyTaskThread.pi+ " Time
                       spent:"
50.                          + MyTaskThread.msTimeToDatetime(time);
51.                    tv_TaskOutputInfo.setText(s);
52.                    btn_ExitApp.setEnabled(true);
53.                    break;
54.                default:
55.                    break;
56.                }
57.            }
58.        };
59.    }
60.
61.    @Override
62.    public boolean onCreateOptionsMenu(Menu menu) {
63.        getMenuInflater().inflate(R.menu.activity_main, menu);
    return true;
64.    }
65.
66.    private void startTask() {
67.        thrd = new MyTaskThread[MyTaskThread.num_threads];
68.        start_time = System.currentTimeMillis();
69.        for( int i=0; i < MyTaskThread.num_threads; i++){
70.            thrd[i] = new MyTaskThread(mHandler);  // Create a thread
71.            thrd[i].setStepStartNum(i);
72.            thrd[i].start();
        }
73.    }
74.
75.    private void exitApp() {
76.        for (int i = 0; i < MyTaskThread.num_threads && thrd
        != null; i++) {
77.            try {
78.                thrd[i].join();   // Wait for thread running to end
79.            } catch (InterruptedException e) {
80.            }
81.        }
82.        finish();
83.        Process.killProcess(Process.myPid());
        }
    }
```

The code segments in bold are the main difference between this application and the original application. In line 13, the single thread object variable of the original application changes to an array of threads. In lines 67–71, starting a single thread in the original application is changed to starting all the threads in the array and setting the index number of the thread when the app starts. The meaning of the thread number is introduced in the MyTaskThread code description. And instead of waiting for the end of a single thread, you wait for the end of the thread array (lines 74–79).

After finishing these optimizations, you need to compile, generate, and deploy the application to on the target device, just as you did the original application. You can run the application independently and measure its run time. The computing time is reduced to almost half of its original length.

Next you can use Intel GPA to analyze the optimized application (ThreadPi). The analysis process is the same as the process used for SerialPi. The results are shown in Figure 11-22.

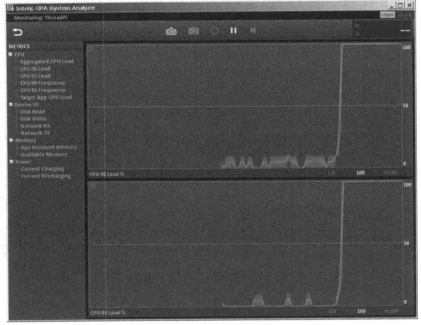

(a) After clicking the Start button

Figure 11-22. Intel GPA analysis of ThreadPi

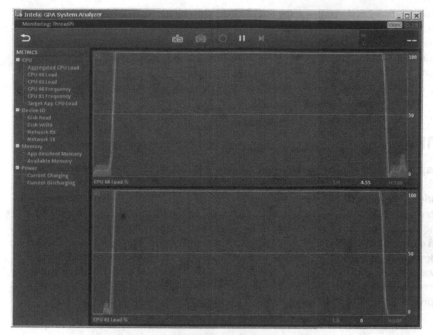

(b) Threads running

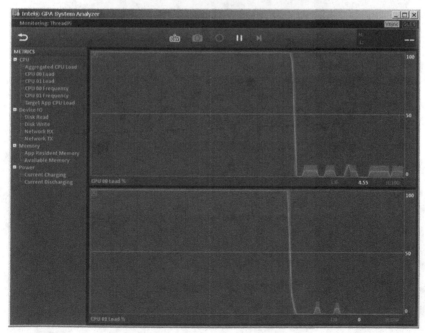

(c) After the threads have finished the calculation

Figure 11-22. (*continued*)

As you can see, when you click the Start button, the calculation (task) threads start running. Both CPU loads raise from low load to 100% capacity. When the calculation is complete, the CPU loads drop back to a low load condition. Unlike in the original application, while the computing task is running, both CPUs are 100% loaded. There is no longer any load rotation. This indicates that the optimized application has two parallel CPUs working at full capacity on the calculation task, which makes the application runs faster.

Summary

This chapter introduced the basic principles of performance optimization, optimization methods, and related tools for Android application development. Because Java is the application development language of choice for Android developers, the optimization tools presented in the previous chapter are mainly for Java. Java applications run in a virtual machine and are inherently slower than C/C++ applications, which are directly compiled and run on hardware instructions. In addition, due to the fundamental nature of C/C++, many developers have more experience with C/C++ applications and have created more optimization tools. As a result, C/C++ development shouldn't be excluded from Android app development. The next chapter introduces the Android NDK for C/C++ application development along with related optimization methods and optimization tools.

CHAPTER 12

■ ■ ■

NDK and C/C++ Optimization

The previous chapter introduced the basic principles of performance optimization, optimization methods, and related tools for Android application development. Because Java is the recommended application development language for Android developers, the optimization tools presented in Chapter 11 were mainly for Java. However, C/C++ development shouldn't be excluded from Android app development. This chapter introduce the Android NDK for C/C++ application development along with related optimization methods and optimization tools.

Introduction to JNI

Java applications do not run directly on the hardware—they run in a virtual machine. The source code of an application is not compiled to get hardware instructions, but is instead compiled to allow a virtual machine interpret and execute code. For example, Android applications run in the Dalvik virtual machine (DVM); its compiled code is executable code for the DVM in .dex format. This feature means Java runs on the virtual machine and ensures its cross-platform capability: that is, its "compile once, run anywhere" feature. Dalvik has a just-in-time (JIT) compiler and is optimized to have a low memory requirement.

Everything has pros and cons. Java's cross-platform capability causes it to be less connected to and limits its interaction with the local machine's internal components, making it difficult to use local machine instructions to take advantage of the machine's performance potential. It is difficult to use locally based instructions to run a huge existing software library, and this limits its functionality and performance. Starting in Android 4.4 (KitKat), Google introduced Android Runtime (ART), which is an application runtime environment that replaces Dalvik. ART transforms the application's bytecode into native instructions that are later executed by the device's runtime environment. ART introduces ahead-of-time (AOT) compilation by performing it when an application is installed.

Is there a way to make Java code and native code software collaborate and share resources? The answer is yes, using the Java Native Interface (JNI), which is an implementation method for a Java local operation. JNI is a Java platform defined by the Java standard to interact with the code on the local platform, generally known as the *host platform*. But this chapter is about the mobile platform; and in order to distinguish it from the mobile cross-development host, we call it the *local platform*. The interaction between Java Code and native application includes two directions: Java code calling native functions (methods), and local application calls to the Java code. Relatively speaking, the former method is used more in Android application development. So this chapter's emphasis is on the approach in which Java code calls native functions.

Java calls native functions through JNI by having the local method stored in the form of library files. For example, on a Windows platform, the files are in .dll file format, and on Unix/Linux machines, the files are in .so file format. An internal method of calling the local library file enables Java to establish close contact with the local machine: this is called the *system-level* approach for various interfaces.

JNI usually has two usage scenarios: first, to be able to use legacy code (for example, prior to use C/C++, Delphi and other development tools); second, in order to better, more directly interact with the hardware for better performance.

JNI's general workflow is as follows: Java initiates calls so that the local function's side code (such as a function written in C/C++) runs. This time the object is passed over from the Java side and run a local function Then the result value is returned to the Java code. Here JNI is an adapter, completing mapping between the variables and functions (Java method) between the Java language and native compiled languages (such as C/C++). Java and C/C++ are very different in terms of function prototype definitions and variable types. In order to make the two match, JNI provides a jni.h file to complete the mapping between them. This process is shown in Figure 12-1.

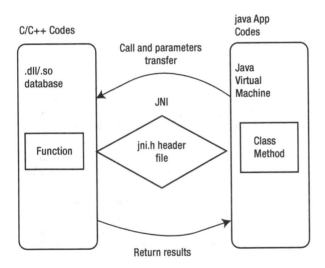

Figure 12-1. *JNI general workflow*

The general framework of a C/C++ function call via JNI and a Java program (in particular, an Android application) is as follows:

1. A method of compiling native declared in a Java class (C/C++ function).

2. The .java source code file containing the native method is compiled.

3. The javah command generates a .h file, including a function prototype for implementing the native method based on the .class files.

4. C/C++ is used to implement the local method.

5. The recommended method for this step is to first copy the function prototypes in the .h file and then modify the function prototypes and add the function body. In this process, the following points should be noted:

   • The JNI function call must use the C function. If it is a C++ function, do not forget to add the extern C keyword.

   • Method names should use the following template:

     Java_package_class_method, or Java_ package name _ class name _ function method name.

6. The C/C++ file is compiled into a dynamic library (under Windows, a .dll file; under Unix/Linux, a .so file).

Use the System.loadLibrary() or System.load() method in Java to load the dynamic library that is generated. These two functions are slightly different:

> System.loadLibrary() loads the default directory under the local link library.

> System.load() requires an absolute path, depending on the local directory to add a cross-link library.

In the first step, Java calls the native C/C++ function; the format is not the same for both C and C++. For example, for Java methods such as non-passing parameters and returning a String class, C and C++ code for the function differ in the following ways:

   • C code:

```
Call function:(*env) -> <jni function> (env, <parameters>)
Return jstring:return (*env)->NewStringUTF(env, "XXX");
```

   • C++ code:

```
Call function:env -> <jni function> (<parameters>)
Return jstring:return env->NewStringUTF("XXX");
```

NewStringUTF is the Java String object's function generated in C/C++, provided by JNI.

Java Methods and C Function Prototype Java

Earlier you saw that in the code framework for Java programs to call a C/C++ function, you can use the javah command, which generates the corresponding .h file for native methods based on the .class files. The .h file is generated in accordance with certain rules, to make the correct Java code to find the corresponding C function to execute. Another good solution is to use env->RegisterNatives function to manually do the mapping and avoid using javah.

For example, suppose you have the following Java code for Android:

```
    public class HelloJni extends Activity
1.  {
2.      public void onCreate(Bundle savedInstanceState)
3.      {
4.          TextView tv.setText(stringFromJNI() );   // Use C function Code
5.      }
6.      public native String  stringFromJNI();
7.  }
```

For the C functions stringFromJNI() used on line 4, the function prototype in the .h file generated by javah is

```
1.  JNIEXPORT jstring JNICALL Java_com_example_hellojni_HelloJni_stringFromJNI
2.      (JNIEnv *, jobject);
```

The C source code files to define the function code are roughly as follows:

```
1.  /*
2.  ......
3.  Signature: ()Ljava/lang/String;
4.  */
5.  jstring Java_com_example_hellojni_HelloJni_stringFromJNI
    (JNIEnv* env,  jobject thiz )
6.    {
7.        ......
8.        return (*env)->NewStringUTF(env, "......");
9.  }
```

From this code, you can see that the function name is quite long but still regular, in full accordance with the naming convention java_package_class_method. That is, the stringFromJNI() method in Hello.java corresponds to the Java_com_example_ hellojni_HelloJni_stringFromJNI() method in C/C++.

Notice the comment for Signature: ()Ljava/lang/String;. Here the () in ()Ljava/lang/String; indicates the function parameter is empty, which means, other than the two parameters JNIEnv * and jobject, there are no other parameters. JNIEnv * and jobject are two parameters that all JNI functions must have for the JNI environment and corresponding Java class (or object), respectively. Ljava/lang/String; indicates that the function's return value is a Java String object.

Java and C Data Type Mapping

As mentioned, Java and C/C++ have very different variable types. In order to make the two match, JNI provides a mechanism to complete the mapping between Java and C/C++. The relationships of the main types are shown in Table 12-1.

Table 12-1. *The Correspondence between Java Types and Local (C/C++) Types*

Java Type	Native Type	Description
boolean	jboolean	C/C++ 8-bit integer
byte	jbyte	C/C++ unsigned 8-bit integer
char	jchar	C/C++ unsigned 16-bit integer
short	jshort	C/C++ signed 16-bit integer
int	jint	C/C++ signed 32-bit integer
long	jlong	C/C++ unsigned 64-bit integer
float	jfloat	C/C++ 32-bit floating point
double	jdouble	C/C++ 64-bit floating point
void	void	N/A
Object	jobject	Any Java object, or does not correspond to an object of Java type
Class	jclass	Class object
String	jstring	String object
Object[]	jobjectArray	Array of any object
boolean[]	jbooleanArray	Boolean array
byte[]	jbyteArray	Array of bits
char[]	jcharArray	Character array
short[]	jshortArray	Short integer array
int[]	jintArray	Integer array
long[]	jlongArray	Long integer array
float[]	jfloatArray	Floating-point array
double[]	jdoubleArray	Double floating-point array

When a Java parameter is passed, you can use C code as follows:

- *Basic types can be used directly*: For example, double and jdouble are interchangeable. Basic types are those from boolean through void in Table 12-1. In such a type, if the user passes a boolean parameter into the method, then there is a local method jboolean corresponding to the boolean type. Similarly, if the local methods return a jint, then an int is returned in Java.

- *Java object usage*: An Object object has String objects and a generic object. The two objects are handled a little differently:

  - String *object*: The String object passed by Java programs is the corresponding jstring type in the local method. The jstring type and char * in C are different. So if you just use it as a char *, an error will occur. Therefore, jstring nust be converted into a char * in C/C++ prior to use. Here you use the JNIEnv method for conversion.

  - Object *object*: Use the following code to get the object handler for the class:

```
jclass objectClass = (env)->FindClass("com/ostrichmyself/jni/Structure");
```

  - Use the following code to get the required domain handler for the class:

```
jfieldID str = (env)->GetFieldID(objectClass,"nameString","Ljava/lang/String;");
jfieldID ival = (env)->GetFieldID(objectClass,"number","I");
```

  - Then use the following similar code to assign values to the incoming fields of the jobject object:

```
(env)->SetObjectField(theObjet,str,(env)->NewStringUTF("my name is D:"));
(env)->SetShortField(theObjet,ival,10);
```

  - If there is no incoming object, then C code can use the following code to generate a new object:

```
jobject myNewObjet = env->AllocObject(objectClass);
```

■ **Note**   NewObject() needs to be called instead if you want the object constructor to be called.

Java Array Processing

For an array type, JNI provides some operaable functions. For example, GetObjectArrayElement can take the incoming array and use NewObjectArray to create an array structure.

Resource Release

The principle of resource release is as follows:

- Objects of C/C++ new or object of malloc need to use the C/C++ to release.

- If the new object of the JNIEnv method is not used by Java, it must be released.

- To convert a string object from Java to UTF using GetStringUTFChars, you need to open the memory, and you must use ReleaseStringUTFChars method to release the memory after you are finished using char *.

These are brief descriptions of the basic ideas of type mapping when Java exchanges data with C/C++. For more information about Java and C/C++ data types, please refer to related Java and JNI books, documentation, and examples.

Introduction to NDK

You now know that the Java code can access local functions (such as C/C++) using JNI. To achieve this, you need development tools. As stated earlier, an entire set of development tools based on the core Android SDK are available that you can use to cross-compile Java applications to applications that can run on the target Android device. Similarly, you need cross-development tools to compile C/C++ code into applications that can run on an Android device. This tool is the Android Native Development Kit (NDK), which you can download from http://developer.android.com.

Prior to the NDK, third-party applications on the Android platform were developed on a special Java-based DVM. The announcement of the native SDK allows developers to directly access Android system resources and to implement parts of apps using native-code languages such as C and C++. The application package file (.apk) can be directly embedded into the local library. In short, with the NDK, Android applications originally run on the DVM can use native languages like C/C++ for program execution. This brings the following benefits:

- Performance improvements from using native code to develop parts of programs that require high performance, and by directly accessing the CPU and hardware

- The ability to reuse existing native code

Of course, compared to the DVM, using native SDK programming also has some disadvantages, such as added program complexity, difficulty in guaranteeing compatibility, the inability to access the Framework API, more difficult debugging, decreased flexibility, and so on. In addition, access to JNI requires additional performance overhead.

In short, NDK application development has pros and cons. You need to use NDK at your own discretion. The best strategy is to use NDK to develop parts of the application for which native code will improve performance.

NDK includes the following major components:

- Tools and build file needed to generate native code libraries from C/C++ sources. These include a series of NDK commands, including javah (use the .class files to generate the corresponding .h files) and gcc (described later)

- A consistent local library embedded in the application package (.apk files) that can be deployed in Android devices

- Support for some native system header files and libraries for all future Android platforms

- Documentation, samples, and tutorials

The process framework of NDK application development is shown in Figure 12-2. An Android application consists of three parts: Android application files, Java native library files, and dynamic libraries. These three parts are generated from different sources through the respective generation path. For an ordinary Android application, the Android SDK generates Android applications files and Java native library files. The Android NDK generates the dynamic library files (the file with the .so extension) using native code (typically C source code files). Finally, Android application files, Java native library files, and dynamic libraries are installed on the target machine, and complete collaborative applications run.

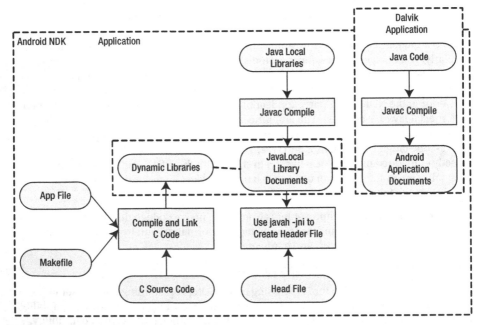

Figure 12-2. Flowchart of Android NDK application development

Application projects developed with NDK (referred to as *NDK application projects*) have the components shown in Figure 12-3. Unlike typical applications developed using the Android SDK, in addition to the Dalvik class code, manifest files, and resources, NDK application projects also include JNI and a shared library generated by NDK.

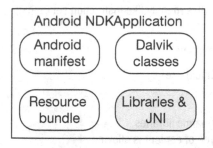

Figure 12-3. Application components for an Android NDK application

Android adds NDK support in its key API version. Each version includes some new NDK features, simple C/C++, a compatible Standard Template Library (STL), hardware expansion, and so on. These features make Android more open and more powerful. The mapping of the Android API and its corresponding relationship with the NDK are shown in Table 12-2.

Table 12-2. Relationship between the Main Android API and NDK Versions

API Version	Supported NDK Version
API Level 3	Android 1.5 NDK 1
API Level 4	Android 1.6 NDK 2
API Level 7	Android 2.1 NDK 3
API Level 8	Android 2.2 NDK 4
API Level 9	Android 2.3 NDK 5
API Level 12	Android 3.1 NDK 6
API Level 14	Android 4.0.1 NDK 7
API Level 15	Android 4.0.3 NDK 8
API Level 16	Android 4.1 NDK 8b
API Level 16	Android 4.2 NDK 8d
API Level 17	Android 4.2 NDK 9
API Level 18	Android 4.3 NDK 9d
API Level 19	Android 4.4 NDK 10

TIP: THE MEANING OF APPLICATION BINARY INTERFACE (ABI)

Each piece of native code generated using the Android NDK is given a matching application binary interface (ABI). The ABI precisely defines how the application and its code interact with the system at runtime. An ABI is roughly like instruction set architecture (ISA) in computer architecture.

A typical ABI usually contains the following information:

- Machine code the CPU instruction set should use

- Runtime memory access ranking

- The format of executable binary files (dynamic libraries, programs, and so on) as well as what type of content is allowed and supported

- Different conventions used in passing data between the application code and systems (for example, when the function call registers and/or how to use the stack, alignment restrictions, and so on)

- Alignment and size limits of enumerated types, structure fields, and array

- A unique name; the available list of function symbols for application machine code at runtime usually comes from a very specific set of libraries

Android currently supports the following ABI types:

- *armeabi*: ABI name for the ARM CPU, which supports at least the ARMv5TE instruction set.

- *armeabi-v7a*: Another ABI name for ARM-based CPUs; it extends the armeabi CPU instruction set extensions, such as Thumb-2 instruction set extensions and floating-point processing unit directives for vector floating-point hardware.

- *x86*: ABI name generally known for supporting the x86 or IA-32 instruction set of the CPU. More specifically, its target is often referred to in the following sections as the i686 or Pentium Pro instruction set. Intel Atom processors belong to this ABI type.

- *MIPS*: ABI for MIPS-based CPUs that support the MIPS32r1 instruction set. The ABI includes the following features: MIPS32 revision 1 ISA, little-endian, O32, hard-float, and no DSP applicationThese types have different compatibilities. x86 is incompatible with armeabi and armeabi-v7a. The armeabi-v7a machine is compatible with armeabi, which means the armeabi framework instruction set can run on an armeabi-v7a machine, but not necessarily the other way around, because some ARMv5 and ARMv6 machines do not support armeabi-v7a code. Therefore, when you build the application, users should be chosen carefully based on their corresponding ABI machine type.

Installing NDK and Setting Up the Environment

The NDK is included in Intel Beacon Mountain for Linux, Intel Beacon Mountain for OS X and Intel Integrated Native Developer Experience (INDE) for Windows host system, and is installed when you install one of those Intel tools. The installation is detailed in Chapter 3. An environment setup program is also included in Intel INDE; you can download it and run the setup automatically.

Installing CDT

CDT is an Eclipse plug-in that compiles C code into .so shared libraries. After installing the Cygwin and NDK module, you already can compile C code into .so shared libraries at the command line, which means the core component of Windows NDK is already installed. If you prefer to use the Eclipse IDE rather than a command-line compiler to compile the local library, you need to install the CDT module.

If you need to install it, follow these steps.

1. Visit the official Eclipse web site (www.eclipse.org/cdt/downloads.php) and download the latest CDT package.

2. Start Eclipse. Select Help ➤ Install New Software ➤ Start to install CDT.

3. In the pop-up Install dialog box, click Add.

4. In the pop-up Add Repository dialog box, enter a name.

5. For Location, you can enter the local address or the Internet address. If you use an Internet address, Eclipse goes to the Internet to download and install the package; a local address directs Eclipse to install the software from the local package. In this case, enter the local address; then click the Archive button in the pop-up dialog box and enter the directory and file name for the CDT file you downloaded. If you downloaded it from the Internet, the address is http://download.eclipse.org/tools/cdt/releases/galileo/.

6. After returning to the Install dialog box, click to select the software components that need to be installed. In this example, CDT Main Feature is the required component you need to select. A list of detailed information about CDT components to install is displayed, as shown in Figure 12-4.

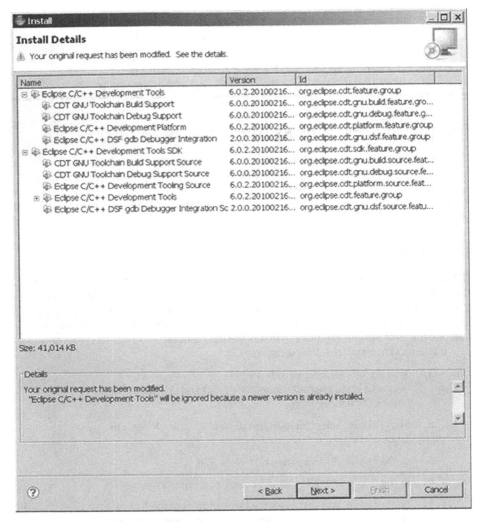

Figure 12-4. *Detailed information for the CDT component installation*

7. Review the License dialog box, and click "I accept the terms of the license agreement" to continue.

8. The installation process starts. When it is finished, restart Eclipse to complete the installation.

NDK Examples

This section provides an example to illustrate the use of JNI and NDK. As described previously, NDK can be run from both the command line and in the Eclipse IDE. The example uses both methods to generate the same NDK application.

Using the Command Line to Generate a Library File

The app name in this example is jnitest. It is a simple example to demo the JNI code framework. The steps are as follows:

1. Create an Android app project, compile the code, and generate the .apk package. You first create a project in Eclipse, and name the project jnitest. Choose Build SDK to support the x86 version of the API, as shown in Figure 12-5. For the other options, use the default values. Then generate the project.

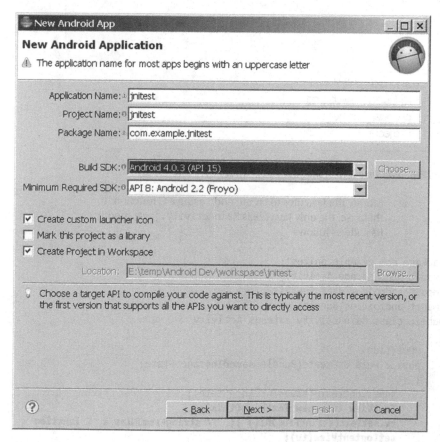

Figure 12-5. Setting up the jnitest *project parameters*

After the project has been generated, the file structure is created as shown in Figure 12-6. Note the directory where the library file (in this case, android.jar) is located, because later steps use this parameter.

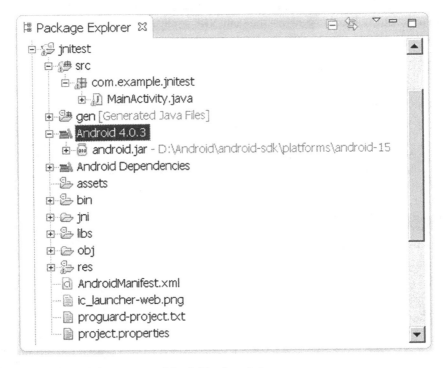

Figure 12-6. *File structure of the jnitest project*

    a.   Modify the Java files to create code using a C function. In this case, the only Java file is MainActivity.java; modify its code as follows:

```
1.   package com.example.jnitest;
2.   import android.app.Activity;
3.   import android.widget.TextView;
4.   import android.os.Bundle;
5.   public class MainActivity extends Activity
6.   {
7.       @Override
8.       public void onCreate(Bundle savedInstanceState)
9.       {
10.          super.onCreate(savedInstanceState);
11.          TextView tv = new TextView(this);
12.          tv.setText(stringFromJNI() );  // stringFromJNIas a  C function
13.          setContentView(tv);
14.      }
```

```
15.    public native String stringFromJNI();
16.
17.    static {
18.        System.loadLibrary("jnitestmysharelib");
19.    }
20. }
```

The code is very simple. In lines 11–13, you use a TextView to display a string returned from the stringFromJNI() function. But unlike in the Android application discussed earlier, nowhere in the entire project can you find the implementation code for this function. So where does the function implementation occur? Line 15 declares that the function is not a function written in Java, but is instead written by the local (native) libraries, which means the function is outside of Java. Because it is implemented in the local library, the question is, what libraries? The answers are described in lines 17–20. The parameter of the static function LoadLibrary of the System class describes the name of the library: the library is one of shared libraries in Linux named libjnitestmysharelib.so. The application code declared in the static area will be executed before Activity.onCreate. The library will be loaded into memory at the first use.

Interestingly, when the loadLibrary function loads the library name, it automatically adds the lib prefix before the parameters and the .so suffix at the end. Of course, if the name of the library file specified by parameter starts with lib, the function does not add the lib prefix.

    b.   Generate the project in Eclipse. Only build it—do not run it. This compiles the project, but the .apk file is not deployed to the target machine.

When this step is completed, the corresponding .class files are generated in the project directory bin\classes\com\example\jnitest. This step must be completed before the next step, because the next step needs to use the appropriate .class files.

    2.   Create a jni subdirectory in the project root directory. For example, if the project root directory is E:\temp\AndroidDev\ workspace\jnitest, then you can use the md command to create the jni subdirectory:

```
E:\temp\Android Dev\workspace\jnitest>mkdir jni
```

Test whether the directory has been built:

```
E:\temp\Android Dev\workspace\jnitest>dir
......
2013-02-01  00:45    <DIR>         jni
```

3. Create a C interface file. This is the C function prototype that works with the local (external) function. Specific to this case are the C function prototypes of the stringFromJNI function. You declare in Java that you need to use the prototype of the external function; but it is in the Java format, so you need to change it to C format, which means building a C JNI interface file. This step can be done with the javah command:

```
$ javah -classpath <directory of jar and .class documents> -d <directory of
.h documents>  <the package + class name of class>
```

The command parameters are as follows:

-classpath: The class path

-d: The storage directory for the generated header file

<class name>: The complete .class class name of a native function being used, which consists of "the package + class name of class" component.

For this example, follow these steps:

a. Enter the root directory using the command line (for this example, E:\temp\Android Dev\workspace\jnitest).

b. Run the following command:

```
E:> javah -classpath "D:\Android\android-sdk\platforms\android-15\android.jar";
bin/classes  com.example.jnitest.MainActivity
```

In this example, the class of the native function stringFromJNI's used is MainActivity; and the resulting file after compiling this class is MainActivity.class, which is located in the root directory of the project bin\classes\com\example directory. The first line of the source code file of its class MainActivity.java shows where the package of the class is:

```
package com.example.jnitest;
```

Therefore, this is the command: "class name = package name.Class name" (be careful not to use the .class suffix).

-classpath first needs to explain the Java library path of the entire package (in this case, the library file is android.jar; its location is at D:\Android\android-sdk\platforms\android-15\android.jar). Second, it needs to define the target class (MainActivity.class) directory. In this case, it is bin\classes under bin\classes\com\example\MainActivity.class, both separated by semicolons (C).

    c.   Now the .h file is generated in the current directory (the project root directory). The file defines the C language function interface. You can test the output:

```
E:\temp\Android Dev\workspace\jnitest>dir
......
2013-01-31  22:00          3,556 com_example_jnitest_MainActivity.h
```

It is apparent that a new .h file has been generated. The document reads as follows:

```
1.  /* DO NOT EDIT THIS FILE - it is machine generated */
2.  #include <jni.h>
3.  /* Header for class com_example_jnitest_MainActivity */
4.
5.  #ifndef _Included_com_example_jnitest_MainActivity
6.  #define _Included_com_example_jnitest_MainActivity
7.  #ifdef __cplusplus
8.  extern "C" {
9.  #endif
10. #undef com_example_jnitest_MainActivity_MODE_PRIVATE
11. #define com_example_jnitest_MainActivity_MODE_PRIVATE 0L
12. #undef com_example_jnitest_MainActivity_MODE_WORLD_READABLE
13. #define com_example_jnitest_MainActivity_MODE_WORLD_READABLE 1L
14. #undef com_example_jnitest_MainActivity_MODE_WORLD_WRITEABLE
15. #define com_example_jnitest_MainActivity_MODE_WORLD_WRITEABLE 2L
16. #undef com_example_jnitest_MainActivity_MODE_APPEND
17. #define com_example_jnitest_MainActivity_MODE_APPEND 32768L
18. #undef com_example_jnitest_MainActivity_MODE_MULTI_PROCESS
19. #define com_example_jnitest_MainActivity_MODE_MULTI_PROCESS 4L
20. #undef com_example_jnitest_MainActivity_BIND_AUTO_CREATE
21. #define com_example_jnitest_MainActivity_BIND_AUTO_CREATE 1L
22. #undef com_example_jnitest_MainActivity_BIND_DEBUG_UNBIND
23. #define com_example_jnitest_MainActivity_BIND_DEBUG_UNBIND 2L
24. #undef com_example_jnitest_MainActivity_BIND_NOT_FOREGROUND
25. #define com_example_jnitest_MainActivity_BIND_NOT_FOREGROUND 4L
26. #undef com_example_jnitest_MainActivity_BIND_ABOVE_CLIENT
27. #define com_example_jnitest_MainActivity_BIND_ABOVE_CLIENT 8L
28. #undef com_example_jnitest_MainActivity_BIND_ALLOW_OOM_MANAGEMENT
29. #define com_example_jnitest_MainActivity_BIND_ALLOW_OOM_MANAGEMENT 16L
30. #undef com_example_jnitest_MainActivity_BIND_WAIVE_PRIORITY
31. #define com_example_jnitest_MainActivity_BIND_WAIVE_PRIORITY 32L
32. #undef com_example_jnitest_MainActivity_BIND_IMPORTANT
33. #define com_example_jnitest_MainActivity_BIND_IMPORTANT 64L
34. #undef com_example_jnitest_MainActivity_BIND_ADJUST_WITH_ACTIVITY
35. #define com_example_jnitest_MainActivity_BIND_ADJUST_WITH_ACTIVITY 128L
36. #undef com_example_jnitest_MainActivity_CONTEXT_INCLUDE_CODE
37. #define com_example_jnitest_MainActivity_CONTEXT_INCLUDE_CODE 1L
```

```
38. #undef com_example_jnitest_MainActivity_CONTEXT_IGNORE_SECURITY
39. #define com_example_jnitest_MainActivity_CONTEXT_IGNORE_SECURITY 2L
40. #undef com_example_jnitest_MainActivity_CONTEXT_RESTRICTED
41. #define com_example_jnitest_MainActivity_CONTEXT_RESTRICTED 4L
42. #undef com_example_jnitest_MainActivity_RESULT_CANCELED
43. #define com_example_jnitest_MainActivity_RESULT_CANCELED 0L
44. #undef com_example_jnitest_MainActivity_RESULT_OK
45. #define com_example_jnitest_MainActivity_RESULT_OK -1L
46. #undef com_example_jnitest_MainActivity_RESULT_FIRST_USER
47. #define com_example_jnitest_MainActivity_RESULT_FIRST_USER 1L
48. #undef com_example_jnitest_MainActivity_DEFAULT_KEYS_DISABLE
49. #define com_example_jnitest_MainActivity_DEFAULT_KEYS_DISABLE 0L
50. #undef com_example_jnitest_MainActivity_DEFAULT_KEYS_DIALER
51. #define com_example_jnitest_MainActivity_DEFAULT_KEYS_DIALER 1L
52. #undef com_example_jnitest_MainActivity_DEFAULT_KEYS_SHORTCUT
53. #define com_example_jnitest_MainActivity_DEFAULT_KEYS_SHORTCUT 2L
54. #undef com_example_jnitest_MainActivity_DEFAULT_KEYS_SEARCH_LOCAL
55. #define com_example_jnitest_MainActivity_DEFAULT_KEYS_SEARCH_LOCAL 3L
56. #undef com_example_jnitest_MainActivity_DEFAULT_KEYS_SEARCH_GLOBAL
57. #define com_example_jnitest_MainActivity_DEFAULT_KEYS_SEARCH_GLOBAL 4L
58. /*
59.  * Class:      com_example_jnitest_MainActivity
60.  * Method:     stringFromJNI
61.  * Signature:  ()Ljava/lang/String;
62.  */
63. JNIEXPORT jstring JNICALL Java_com_example_jnitest_MainActivity_
    stringFromJNI
64. (JNIEnv *, jobject);
65.
66. #ifdef __cplusplus
67. }
68. #endif
69. #endif
```

In this code, pay special attention to lines 63–64, which are C function prototypes of a local function stringFromJNI.

    4.   Compile the corresponding C file. This is the true realization of a local function (stringFromJNI). The source code file is obtained by modifying the .h file based on the previous steps.

Create a new .c file under the jni subdirectory in the project. The file name can be anything; in this case, it is jnitestccode.c. The contents are as follows:

```
1. #include <string.h>
2. #include <jni.h>
3. jstring Java_com_example_hellojni_HelloJni_stringFromJNI( JNIEnv* env,
   jobject thiz )
```

```
4. {
5.     return (*env)->NewStringUTF(env, "Hello from JNI !");  // Newly added
       code
6. }
```

The code that defines the function implementation is very simple. Line 3 is the Java code used in the prototype definition of the function stringFromJNI; it is basically a copy of the corresponding contents of the .h file obtained from lines 63–64 of com_example_jnitest_MainActivity.h), slightly modified to make the point. The prototype formats of this function are fixed; JNIEnv* env and jobject thiz are inherent parameters of JNI. Because the parameter of the stringFromJNI function is empty, there are only two parameters in the generated C function. The role of the code in the fifth line is to return the string "Hello from JNI!" as the return value.

The code in line 2 is the header file that contains the JNI function, which is required for any functions that use JNI. As it relates to the string function, line 1 contains the corresponding header file in this case. After completing these steps, the .h file has no use and can be deleted.

5. Create the NDK makefile file in the jni directory. These documents are mainly Android.mk and Application.mk: Android.mk is required, but if you use the default application configuration, you do not need Application.mk. The specific steps are as follows:

    a. Create a new Android.mk text file under the jni directory in the project. This file is used to tell the compiler about some requirements, such as which C files to compile, what file name to use for compiled code, and so on. Enter the following:

    ```
    1. LOCAL_PATH      := $(call my-dir)
    2. include $(CLEAR_VARS)
    3. LOCAL_MODULE    := jnitestmysharelib
    4. LOCAL_SRC_FILES := jnitestccode.c
    5. include $(BUILD_SHARED_LIBRARY)
    ```

Line 3 represents the generated .so file name (identifying each module described in your Android.mk file). It must be consistent with parameter values of the System.loadLibrary function in the Java code. This name must be unique and may not contain any spaces.

■ **Note** The build system automatically generates the appropriate prefix and suffix; in other words, if one is the shared library module named jnitestmysharelib, then a libjnitestmysharelib.so file is generated. If you name the library libhello-jni, the compiler does not add a lib prefix and generates libhello-jni.so too.

The LOCAL_SRC_FILES variable on line 4 must contain the C or C++ source code files to be compiled and packaged into modules. The previous steps create a C file name.

■ **Note** You do not have to list the header files and include files here, because the compiler automatically identifies the dependent files for you—just list source code files that are directly passed to the compiler. In addition, the default extension name of C++ source files is .cpp. It is possible to specify a different extension name, as long as you define the LOCAL_DEFAULT_CPP_EXTENSION variable. Don't forget the period character at the start (.cxx, rather than cxx).

The previous code in lines 3 and 4 is very important and must be modified for each NDK application based on its configuration. The contents of the other lines can be copied from the example.

> b. Create an Application.mk text file under the jni directory in the project. This file is used to tell the compiler the specific settings for this application. Enter the following:

```
APP_ABI := x86
```

This file is very simple; the object code generated by the application instructions is for 86 architecture, so you can run the application on Intel Atom machines. For APP_ABI parameters, you can use any architecture (x86, armeabi, armeabi-v7a or MIPS) that you want to support.

> 6. Compile the .c file to the .so shared library file. Go to the project root directory (where AndroidManifest.xml is located) and run the ndk-build command:

```
E:\temp\Android Dev\workspace\jnitest>ndk-build
D:/Android/android-ndk-r8d/build/core/add-application.mk:128: Android NDK:
WARNING: APP_PLATFORM android-14 is larger than android:minSdkVersion 8 in
./AndroidM
anifest.xml
"Compile x86  : jnitestmysharelib <= jnitestccode.c
SharedLibrary : libjnitestmysharelib.so
Install       : libjnitestmysharelib.so => libs/x86/libjnitestmysharelib.so
```

This command adds two subdirectories (libs and obj) in the project folder and creates a .so file (command execution information prompt file named libjnitestmysharelib.so) under the obj directory.

If these steps do not define the specified ABI in the Application.mk file, the ndk-build command generates object code for the ARM architecture (armeabi). If you want to generate the x86 architecture instructions, you can do so using the ndk-build APP_ABI = x86 command to remedy the situation. The architecture of the object code generated by this command is still x86.

7. Run the project. Figure 12-7 shows the application running on the target device.

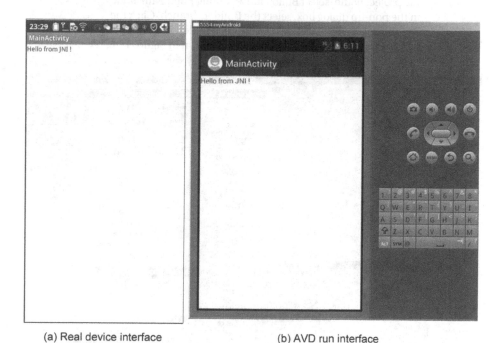

(a) Real device interface   (b) AVD run interface

Figure 12-7. jnitest *application interface*

Generating a Library File in the IDE

The previous section described the process of compiling C files into dynamic library .so files that can be run on the Android target device. To do this, you run the ndk-build command in the command line. You can also complete this step in the Eclipse IDE.

Eclipse supports direct NDK integration. You can install CDT into Eclipse, create an Android project to which you want to add C/C++ code, create a jni/ directory in your project directory, place your C/C++ sources file in the same directory, and put the Android.mk file into it—this is a makefile that tells the Android build-system how to build your files.

411

If for some reason, you need to manually build the code, you can use the following process to generate the library files in the IDE. The code in steps 1–7 is exactly the same as in the previous section, except that in step 6, you compile .c files into .so shared library files. This is explained in detail in a moment:

1. Compile the .c file into the .so shared library file. Right-click the project name, select Build Path ➤ Config Build Path, and, in the pop-up dialog box, select the Builders branch. Click the New button in the dialog box, and then; double-click Program in the prompt dialog box. This process is shown in Figure 12-8.

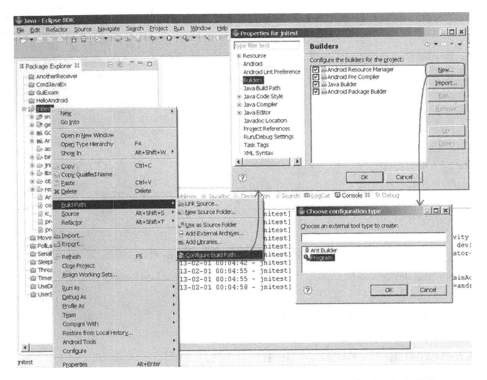

Figure 12-8. Entering parameters settings for the interface to compile C code in Eclipse

2. In the pop-up Edit Configuration dialog box, for the Main tab settings, enter the following:

   Location: The path to the Cygwin bash.exe

   Working Directory: The bin directory of Cygwin

Arguments:

```
--login -c "cd '/cygdrive/E/temp/Android
Dev/workspace/jnitest' && $ANDROID_NDK_ROOT/ndk-build"
```

`E/temp/Android Dev/workspace/jnitest` is the drive letter
and path for the project. The settings are shown in Figure 12-9.

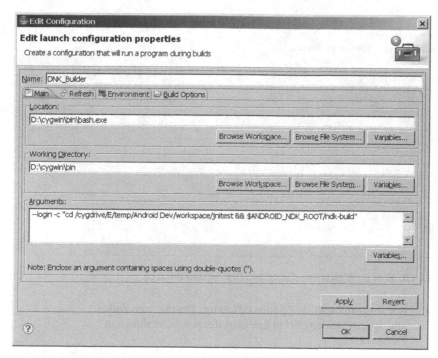

Figure 12-9. Main tab setting in the Edit Configuration dialog box

3.   Configure the Refresh tab, ensuring that the The Entire
     Workspace and Recursively Include Sub-folders items are
     selected, as shown in Figure 12-10.

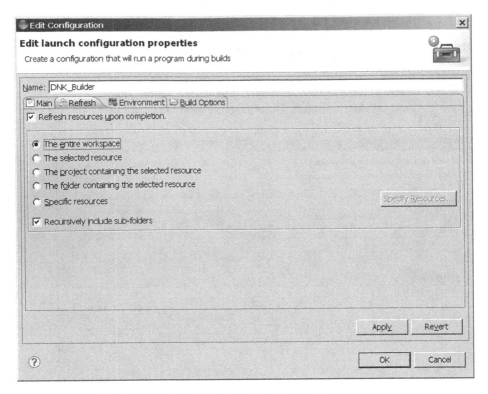

Figure 12-10. Edit Configuration dialog box Refresh tab settings

    4.   Reconfigure the Build Options tab. Select During Auto Builds
and Specify Working Set of Relevant Resources, as shown in
Figure 12-11.

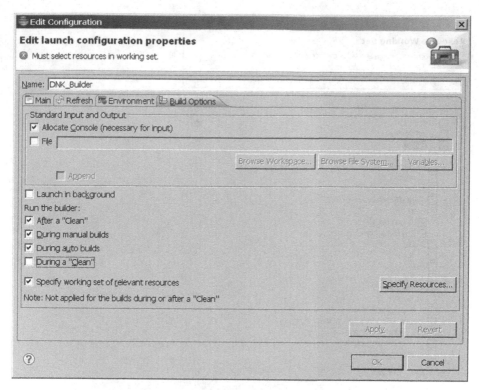

Figure 12-11. Edit Configuration dialog box Build Options tab settings

5. Click the Specify Resources button. In the Edit Working Set dialog box, select the jni directory, as shown in Figure 12-12.

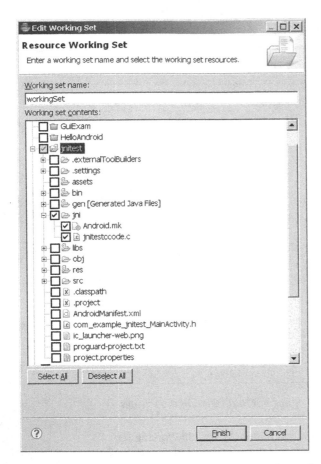

Figure 12-12. *Select source code and directories where related files are located*

6. Save the configuration. It will automatically compile C-related code under the jni directory and output the corresponding .so library files to the project's libs directory. The libs directory is created automatically. In the Console window, you can see the output of the build is as follows:

```
/cygdrive/d/Android/android-ndk-r8d/build/core/add-application.mk:128:
Android NDK: WARNING: APP_PLATFORM android-14 is larger than
android:minSdkVersion 8 in ./AndroidManifest.xml
Cygwin       : Generating dependency file converter script
Compile x86  : jnitestmysharelib <= jnitestccode.c
SharedLibrary : libjnitestmysharelib.so
Install      : libjnitestmysharelib.so => libs/x86/libjnitestmysharelib.so
```

Workflow Analysis for NDK Application Development

The process of generating an NDK project as described works naturally to achieve C library integration with Java. You compile .c files into .so shared library files. The intermediate version of the libraries is put into the obj directory, and the final version is put into the libs directory. When this is completed, the project file structure is created as shown in Figure 12-13.

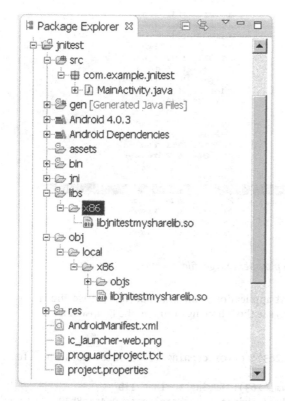

Figure 12-13. The jnitest project structure after NDK library files are generated

When you run the project, the shared library .so files are in the project directory on the host machine and are packed in a generated .apk file. The .apk file is essentially a compressed file; you can use compression software like WinRAR to view its contents. For this example, you can find the .apk file in the bin subdirectory of the project directory; open it with WinRAR to show the file structure. The content of the lib subdirectory of the .apk is a clone of the content of the project's lib subdirectory.

When the .apk is deployed to the target machine, it is unpacked. The .so files are placed in the /data/dat/XXX/lib directory, where XXX is the application package name. For this example, the directory is /data/data/com.example.jnitest/lib. You can view the file structure of the target machine under the Eclipse DDMS; the file structure for

417

the example is shown in Figure 12-14. If you are interested, you can try it on the command line, using the adb shell command to view the corresponding contents in the target file directory.

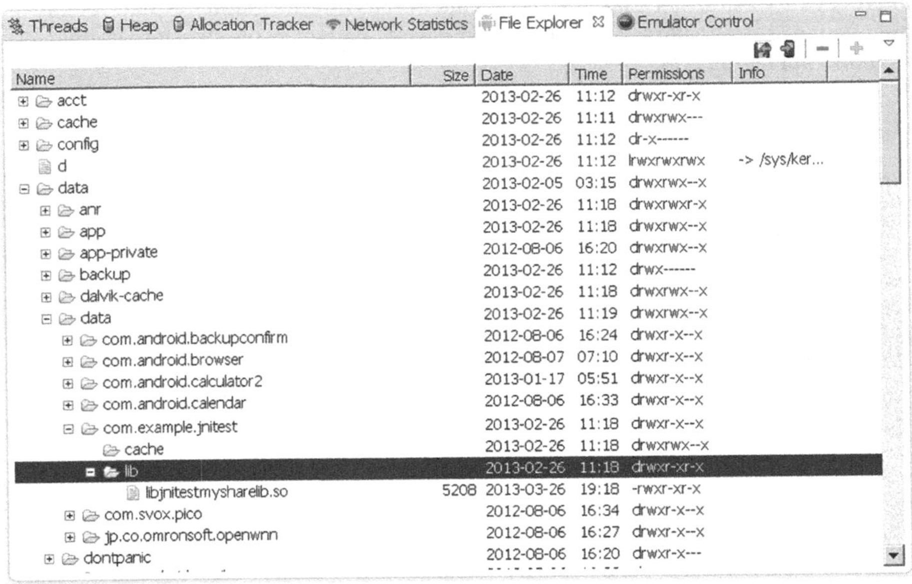

Figure 12-14. jnitest *application deployment target file structure*

In addition, if you run the jnitest application in an emulator (in this case, the target machine is a virtual machine), you can see the following output in the Eclipse Logcat window:

```
1. 07-10 05:43:08.579: E/Trace(6263): error opening trace file: No such file
or directory (2)
2. 07-10 05:43:08.729: D/dalvikvm(6263): Trying to load lib
/data/data/com.example.jnitest/lib/libjnitestmysharelib.so 0x411e8b30
3. 07-10 05:43:08.838: D/dalvikvm(6263): Added shared lib
/data/data/com.example.jnitest/lib/libjnitestmysharelib.so 0x411e8b30
4. 07-10 05:43:08.838: D/dalvikvm(6263): No JNI_OnLoad found in
/data/data/com.example.jnitest/lib/libjnitestmysharelib.so 0x411e8b30,
skipping init
5. 07-10 05:43:11.773: I/Choreographer(6263): Skipped 143 frames!  The
application may be doing too much work on its main thread.
6. 07-10 05:43:12.097: D/gralloc_goldfish(6263): Emulator without GPU
emulation detected.
```

Lines 2–3 are reminders of the .so shared library loaded in the application.

NDK Compiler Optimization

From the example, you can see that the NDK tool's core role is to compile source code into a .so library file that can run on an Android machine. The .so library file is put into the lib subdirectory of the project directory, so that when you use Eclipse to deploy applications, you can deploy the library files to the appropriate location on a target device, and the application can using the library function.

■ **Note**   The nature of the NDK application is to establish a code framework that complies with the JNI standard, to let Java applications use a local function beyond the scope of the virtual machine.

The key NDK command to compile the source code into a .so library file is ndk-build. This command is not actually a separate command, but an executable script. It calls the make command in the GNU cross-development tools to compile a project; and make calls, for example, the gcc compiler to compile the source code to complete the process, as shown in Figure 12-15. Of course, you can also directly use .so shared libraries developed by third parties that are already in Android applications, thus avoiding the need to write your own library (function code).

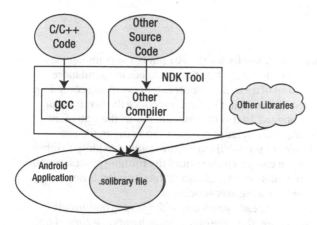

Figure 12-15. *The working mechanism of NDK tools*

As Figure 12-15 shows, the GNU compiler gcc is the core tool in NDK to complete C/C++ source code compilation. gcc is the standard Linux compiler, which can compile and link C, C++, Object-C, FORTRAN, and other source code on the local machine. Not only can the gcc compiler do local compiling, but it can also do cross-compiling. This feature has been used by Android NDK and other embedded development tools. In compiler usage, gcc cross-compiling is compatible with native compiling; that is, command parameters and switches of locally compiled code can essentially be ported without modification to cross-compiling code. Therefore, the gcc compiling method described next is generic for both local and cross-compiling.

Chapter 11 mentioned that some optimizations can be done automatically by the compiler, which is referred to as *compiler optimization*. For systems based on Intel x86 architecture processors, in addition to the GNU gcc compiler, the Intel C/C++ compiler is also good. Relatively speaking, because the Intel C/C ++ compiler fully utilizes the features of Intel processors, the code-optimization results are better. For Android NDK, both the Intel C/C++ compiler and gcc can complete the C/C++ code compilation. Currently, the Intel C/C ++ compiler provides the appropriate usage mechanisms. Ordinary users need a professional license, whereas gcc is open source, free software and is more readily available. So, this section uses gcc as an experimental tool to explain how to perform C/C++ module compiler optimization for Android applications.

The gcc optimization is controlled by options in the compiler switches. Some of these options are machine independent, and some are associated with the machine. This section discusses some important options. Machine-related options are described only if relevant to Intel processors.

Machine-Independent Compiler Switch Options

The machine-independent options for gcc compiler switches are the -Ox options, which correspond to different optimization levels. Following are the details.

-O or -O1

Level 1 optimization, which is the default level, uses the -O option; the compiler tries to reduce code size and execution time. For large functions, it needs to spend more compiling time and use a large amount of memory resources for optimizing compiling.

When the -O option is not used, the compiler's goal is to reduce the overhead of compiling so that results can be debugged. In this compilation mode, the statement is independent. By inserting a breakpoint interrupt program run between the two statements, you can reassign variables or modify the program counter to jump to other currently executing statements, so you can precisely control the running process and the user can get results when they want to debug. In addition, if the -O option is not used, only declared register variables can have a register allocation.

If you specify the -O option, the -fthread-jumps and -fdefer-pop options are turned on. On a machine with a delay slot, the -fdelayed-branch option is turned on. Even for machines that support debugging without a frame pointer, the -fomit-frame-pointer option is turned on. Some machines may also open other options.

-O2

This option optimizes even more. gcc performs nearly all supported optimizations that do not involve a space-speed tradeoff. As compared to -O, this option increases both compilation time and the performance of the generated code.

-O3

This option optimizes still more. It turns on all optimizations specified by -O2 and also turns on the -finline-functions, -funswitch-loops, -fpredictive-commoning, -fgcse-after-reload, -ftree-vectorize, -fvect-cost-model, -ftree-partial-pre, and -fipa-cp-clone options.

-O0

This option reduces compilation time and makes debugging produce the expected results. This is the default.

An automatic inline function is often used as a function-optimization measure. C99 (C language ISO standard developed in 1999) and C++ both support the inline keyword. The inline function uses inline space in exchange for time. The compiler does not compile an inline-described function into a function, but directly expands the code for the function body, thereby eliminating the function call For example, consider the following function:

```
inline long factorial (int i)
{
    return factorial_table[i];
}
```

Here all occurrences of all the code in the factorial() call are replaced with the factorial_table [] array references.

In the optimizing state, some compilers treat that function as an inline function even if the function does not use inline instructions, if appropriate in the circumstances (such as if the body of the function code is relatively short and the definition is in the header file), in exchange for execution time.

Loop unrolling is a classic speed-optimization method and is used by many compilers as the automatic optimization strategy. For example, the following code needs to loop 100 cycles:

```
for (i = 0; i < 100; i++)
{
    do_stuff(i);
}
```

At the end of each cycle, the cycle conditions have to be checked to do a comparative judgment. By using a loop-unrolling strategy, the code can be transformed as follows:

```
for (i = 0; i < 100; )
{
    do_stuff(i); i++;
    do_stuff(i); i++;
    do_stuff(i); i++;
    do_stuff(i); i++;
```

```
    do_stuff(i); i++;
    do_stuff(i); i++;
    do_stuff(i); i++;
    do_stuff(i); i++;
    do_stuff(i); i++;
    do_stuff(i); i++;
}
```

The new code reduces the comparison instruction from 100 to 10 times, and the time used to compare conditions can be reduced by 90%.

Both methods described here improve the code efficiency and accomplish the optimization of the object code. This is a typical way of optimizing the object code to make it more time efficient

Intel Processor-Related Compiler Switch Options

The m option of gcc is defined for the Intel i386 and x86-64 processor family. The main command options and their effects are shown in Table 12-3.

Table 12-3. *Intel Processor-Related gcc Switch Options*

Switch Option	Notes	Description
-march=cpu-type -mtune=cpu-type		Generates code for the specified type of CPU. cpu-type can be i386, i486, i586, Pentium, i686, Pentium 4, and so on.
-msse		Compiler automatic vectorization: use or do not use MMX, SSE, and SSE2 instructions. For example, -msse means programming into the instruction, and -mno-sse means not programmed into the SSE instruction.
-msse2		
-msse3		
-mssse3	gcc-4.3 new addition	
-msse4.1	gcc-4.3 new addition	
-msse4.2	gcc-4.3 new addition	
-msse4	Include 4.1 and .2, gcc-4.3 new addition	
-mmmx		
-mno-sse		
-mno-sse2		
-mno-mmx		
-m32 -m64		Generate 32/64 machine code.

In Table 12-3, -march is the CPU type of the machine, and -mtune is the CPU type that the compiler wants to optimize; by default it is the same as for -march. The -march option is a *tight constraint,* and -mtune is a *loose constraint.* The -mtune option can provide backward compatibility.

For example, a compiler with the options -march = i686, -mtune = pentium4 is optimized for the Pentium 4 processor but can be run on any i686 as well. And for -mtune = pentium-mmx compiled procedures, the Pentium 4 processor can be run.

The following option generates cpu-type instructions that specify the type of machine:

-march=cpu-type

The -mtune = cpu-type option is only available if you are optimizing code generated for cpu-type. By contrast, -march = cpu-type generates code not run on non-gcc for the specified type of processor, which means -march = cpu-type implies the -mtune = cpu-type option.

The cpu-type option values related to Intel processors are listed in Table 12-4.

Table 12-4. The Main Option Values of gcc -march Parameters for cpu-type

cpu-type Value	Description
native	Selects the CPU to generate code at compilation time by determining the processor type of the compiling machine. Using -march=native enables all instruction subsets supported by the local machine (hence the result might not run on different machines). Using -mtune=native produces code optimized for the local machine under the constraints of the selected instruction set.
i386	Original Intel i386 CPU.
i486	Intel i486 CPU. (No scheduling is implemented for this chip.)
i586 Pentium	Intel Pentium CPU with no MMX support.
pentium-mmx	Intel Pentium MMX CPU, based on a Pentium core with MMX instruction set support.
pentiumpro	Intel Pentium Pro CPU.
i686	When used with -march, the Pentium Pro instruction set is used, so the code runs on all i686 family chips. When used with -mtune, it has the same meaning as generic.
pentium2	Intel Pentium II CPU, based on a Pentium Pro core with MMX instruction set support.
pentium3 pentium3m	Intel Pentium III CPU, based on a Pentium Pro core with MMX and SSE instruction set support.

(continued)

423

Table 12-4. (*continued*)

cpu-type Value	Description
pentium-m	Intel Pentium M; low-power version of the Intel Pentium III CPU with MMX, SSE, and SSE2 instruction set support. Used by Intel Centrino-based notebooks.
pentium4 pentium4m	Intel Pentium 4 CPU with MMX, SSE, and SSE2 instruction set support.
prescott	Improved version of Intel Pentium 4 CPU with MMX, SSE, SSE2, and SSE3 instruction set support.
nocona	Improved version of Intel Pentium 4 CPU with 64-bit extensions and MMX, SSE, SSE2, and SSE3 instruction set support.
core2	Intel Core 2 CPU with 64-bit extension and MMX, SSE, SSE2, SSE3, and SSSE3 instruction set support.
corei7	Intel Core i7 CPU with 64-bit extensions and MMX, SSE, SSE2, SSE3, SSSE3, SSE4.1, and SSE4.2 instruction set support.
corei7-avx	Intel Core i7 CPU with 64-bit extensions and MMX, SSE, SSE2, SSE3, SSSE3, SSE4.1, SSE4.2, AVX, AES, and PCLMUL instruction set support.
core-avx-i	Intel Core CPU with 64-bit extensions and MMX, SSE, SSE2, SSE3, SSSE3, SSE4.1, SSE4.2, AVX, AES, PCLMUL, FSGSBASE, RDRND, and F16C instruction set support.
atom	Intel Atom CPU with 64-bit extensions and MMX, SSE, SSE2, SSE3, and SSSE3 instruction set and Atom Silvermont (SLM) architecture support.

Traditional gcc is a local compiler. These command options can be added to gcc to control gcc compiler options. For example, suppose you have an int_sin.c file:

```
$ gcc int_sin.c
```

This command uses the O1 optimization level (default level) and compiles int_sin.c into an executable file named by default a.out.

This command uses O1 optimization (default level) to compile int_sin.c into an executable file; the executable file name is specified as sinnorm:

```
$ gcc int_sin.c -o sinnorm
```

This command uses O1 optimization (default level) to compile int_cos.c into a shared library file coslib.so. Unlike source code files compiled into an executable program, this command requires that the source code file int_cos.c does not contain the main function:

```
$ gcc int_cos.c -fPIC -shared -o coslib.so
```

This command compiles int_sin.c into the executable file with the default file name. The compiler does not perform any optimization:

```
$ gcc -O0 int_sin.c
```

This command uses the highest optimization level O3 to compile the int_sin.c file to the executable file with the default file name:

```
$ gcc -O3 int_sin.c
```

This command compiles int_sin.c into an executable file using SSE instructions:

```
$ gcc -msse int_sin.c
```

This command compiles int_sin.c into an executable file without any SSE instructions:

```
$ gcc -mno-sse int_sin.c
```

This command compiles int_sin.c into an executable file that can use Intel Atom processor instructions:

```
$ gcc -mtune=atom int_sin.c
```

From the example compiled by gcc locally, you have some experience using the compiler switch options for gcc compiler optimizations. For the gcc native compiler, the gcc command can be used directly in the switch options to achieve compiler optimization. However, from the previous example, you know that the NDK does not directly use the gcc command. Then how do you set the gcc compiler switch option to achieve NDK optimization?

Recall that in the NDK example, you used the ndk-build command to compile C/C++ source code; the command first needed to read the makefile Android.Mk. This file contains the gcc command options. Android.mk uses LOCAL_CFLAGS to control and complete the gcc command options. The ndk-build command passes LOCAL_CFLAGS runtime values to gcc as its command option to run the gcc command. LOCAL_CFLAGS passes the values to gcc and uses them as the command option to run gcc commands:

For example, in section 3, you amended Android.mk as follows:

```
1. LOCAL_PATH      := $(call my-dir)
2. include $(CLEAR_VARS)
3. LOCAL_MODULE    := jnitestmysharelib
4. LOCAL_SRC_FILES := jnitestccode.c
5. LOCAL_CFLAGS    := -O3
6. include $(BUILD_SHARED_LIBRARY)
```

Line 5 is new: it sets the LOCAL_CFLAGS variable script.

When you execute the ndk-build command, which is equivalent to adding a gcc -O3 command option, it instructs gcc to compile the C source code at the highest optimization level, O3. Similarly, if you edit the line 5 to

```
LOCAL_CFLAGS      := -msse3
```

you instruct gcc to compile C source code into object code using SSE3 instructions that Intel Atom supports.

You can set LOCAL_CFLAGS to a different value and compare the target library file size and content differences. Note that this example jnitest C code is very simple and does not involve complex tasks. As a result, the size and content of the library files are not very different when compiled from different LOCAL_CFLAGS values.

Is there an example where there is a significant difference in the size or content of the library file? Yes, as you will see in the following sections.

Optimization with Intel Integrated Performance Primitives (Intel IPP)

Figure 12-15 shows that Android applications can bypass NDK development tools and use existing .so shared libraries developed by third parties directly, including third-party shared libraries provided by Intel Integrated Performance Primitives (Intel IPP). Intel IPP is a powerful function library for Intel processors and chipsets, and it covers math, signal processing, multimedia, image and graphics processing, vector computing, and other areas. A prominent feature of Intel IPP is that its code has been extensively optimized based on the features of the Intel processor, using a variety of methods. It is a highly optimized, high-performance service library. Intel IPP has cross-platform features; it provides a set of cross-platform and OS general APIs, which can be used for Windows, Linux, and other operating systems; and it supports embedded, desktop, server, and other processor-scale systems.

Intel IPP is really a set of libraries, each with different function areas within the corresponding library, and it differs slightly according to the number of functions supported in different processor architectures. For example, Intel IPP 5.X image-processing functions can support 2,570 functions in Intel architecture, whereas it supports only 1,574 functions in the IXP processor architecture.

The services provided by a variety of high-performance libraries, including Intel IPP, are multifaceted and multilayered. Applications can use Intel IPP directly or indirectly. It can provide support not only for applications, but also for other components and libraries.

Applications using Intel IPP can use its function interface directly or use sample code to indirectly use Intel IPP. In addition, using the OpenCV library (a cross-platform Open Source Computer Vision Library) is equivalent to indirectly using the Intel IPP library. Both the Intel IPP and Intel MKL libraries run on high-performance Intel processors on various architectures.

Taking into account the power of Intel IPP, and in accordance with the characteristics of optimized features of the Intel processor, you can use the Intel IPP library to replace some key source code that runs more often and consumes time. This way, you can obtain much higher performance acceleration than with general code. This is simply a "standing on the shoulders of giants" practical optimization method: you can achieve optimization without manually writing code in critical areas.

Intel recently released the Intel Integrated Native Development Experience (INDE), which provides both Intel IPP and Intel Threaded Building Blocks (Intel TBB) for Android application developers. You can easily use Intel IPP, Intel TBB, Intel GPA, and other tools for Android application development.

NDK Integrated Optimization Examples

This section uses a case study to demonstrate comprehensive optimization techniques by integrating NDK with C/C++. The case is divided into two steps. The first step is to compile a local function from C/C++ code to accelerate the computing tasks in a traditional Java-based program; the second step demonstrates using NDK compiler optimizations to achieve C/C++ optimization. Each step is introduced in its own section; the two sections are closely linked.

C/C++: Accelerating the Original Application

The previous chapter introduced a Java code example (SerialPi) that calculates π. In this section, you change the computing tasks from Java to C code, using NDK to turn it into a local library. You then compare it with the original Java code tasks and get some firsthand experience with using C/C++ native library functions to achieve traditional Java-based task acceleration.

The application used for this case study is named NdkExp; see Figure 12-16.

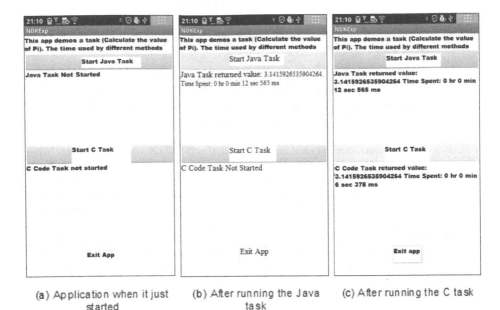

(a) Application when it just started   (b) After running the Java task   (c) After running the C task

Figure 12-16. *Original version of* NdkExp

Figure 12-16(a) shows the application's main interface, including three buttons: Start Java Task, Start C Task, and Exit Application. Clicking the Start Java Task button starts a traditional Java task that calculates π. When the task is completed, the calculated results are displayed below the button along with the time spent, as shown in Figure 12-16(b). Clicking the Start C Task button starts a computing task written in C, using the same math formula to calculate π. When the task is completed, the calculated results are displayed below the button along with the time spent, as shown in Figure 12-16(c).

For the same task, the application written in traditional Java takes 12.565 seconds to complete; the application written in C and compiled by the NDK development tool takes only 6.378 seconds to complete. This example shows you the power of using NDK to achieve performance optimization.

This example is implemented as follows:

1. Generate the project in Eclipse, name it NdkExp, and choose the Build SDK option to support the x86 version of the API. Use the default values for the other options. Then generate the project.

2. Modify the main layout file. Put three TextView widgets and three Button widgets in the layout, set the Text and ID attributes, and adjust their size and position, as shown in Figure 12-17.

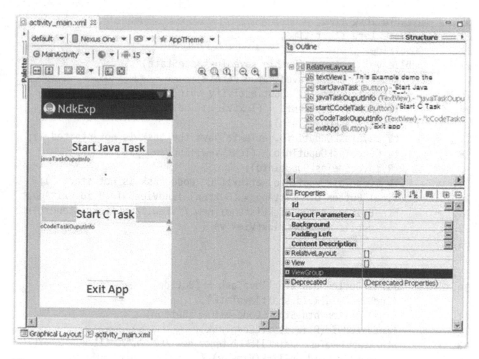

Figure 12-17. *Layout of the original NdkExp*

3. Modify the main layout of the class source code file
   `MainActivity.java` as follows:

```
1.  package com.example.ndkexp;
2.  import android.os.Bundle;
3.  import android.app.Activity;
4.  import android.view.Menu;
5.  import android.widget.Button;
6.  import android.view.View;
7.  import android.view.View.OnClickListener;
8.  import android.os.Process;
9.  import android.widget.TextView;
10. import android.os.Handler;
11. import android.os.Message;
12.
13. public class MainActivity extends Activity {
14.     private JavaTaskThread javaTaskThread = null;
15.     private CCodeTaskThread cCodeTaskThread = null;
16.     private TextView tv_JavaTaskOuputInfo;
17.     private TextView tv_CCodeTaskOuputInfo;
18.     private Handler mHandler;;
19.     private long end_time;
```

```
20.     private long time;
21.     private long start_time;
22.     @Override
23.     public void onCreate(Bundle savedInstanceState) {
24.         super.onCreate(savedInstanceState);
25.         setContentView(R.layout.activity_main);
26.         tv_JavaTaskOuputInfo = (TextView)findViewById(R.
            id.javaTaskOuputInfo);
27.         tv_JavaTaskOuputInfo.setText("Java the task is not started ");
28.         tv_CCodeTaskOuputInfo = (TextView)findViewById
            (R.id.cCodeTaskOuputInfo);
29.         tv_CCodeTaskOuputInfo.setText("C  code task is not start ");
30.         final Button btn_ExitApp = (Button) findViewById(R.id.exitApp);
31.         btn_ExitApp.setOnClickListener(new /*View.*/OnClickListener(){
32.             public void onClick(View v) {
33.                 exitApp();
34.             }
35.         });
36.         final Button btn_StartJavaTask = (Button)
            findViewById(R.id.startJavaTask);
37.         final Button btn_StartCCodeTask = (Button)
            findViewById(R.id.startCCodeTask);
38.         btn_StartJavaTask.setOnClickListener(new /*View.*/OnClickListener(){
39.             public void onClick(View v) {
40.                 btn_StartJavaTask.setEnabled(false);
41.                 btn_StartCCodeTask.setEnabled(false);
42.                 btn_ExitApp.setEnabled(false);
43.                 startJavaTask();
44.             }
45.         });
46.         btn_StartCCodeTask.setOnClickListener(new /*View.*/OnClickListener(){
47.             public void onClick(View v) {
48.                 btn_StartJavaTask.setEnabled(false);
49.                 btn_StartCCodeTask.setEnabled(false);
50.                 btn_ExitApp.setEnabled(false);
51.                 startCCodeTask();
52.             }
53.         });
54.         mHandler = new Handler() {
55.             public void handleMessage(Message msg) {
56.             String s;
57.                 switch (msg.what)
58.                 {
59.                 case JavaTaskThread.MSG_FINISHED:
60.                     end_time = System.currentTimeMillis();
61.                     time = end_time - start_time;
```

```
62.                       s = " The return value of the Java task "+ (Double)
                              (msg.obj) +"  Time consumed:"
63.                           + JavaTaskThread.msTimeToDatetime(time);
64.                       tv_JavaTaskOuputInfo.setText(s);
65.                       btn_StartCCodeTask.setEnabled(true);
66.                       btn_ExitApp.setEnabled(true);
67.                    break;
68.                 case CCodeTaskThread.MSG_FINISHED:
69.                       end_time = System.currentTimeMillis();
70.                       time = end_time - start_time;
71.                       s = " The return value of the C code task"+ (Double)
                              (msg.obj) +"  time consumed:"
72.                           + JavaTaskThread.msTimeToDatetime(time);
73.                       tv_CCodeTaskOuputInfo.setText(s);
74.                       btn_StartJavaTask.setEnabled(true);
75.                       btn_ExitApp.setEnabled(true);
76.                    break;
77.                 default:
78.                    break;
79.                 }
80.             }
81.         };
82.     }
83.
84.     @Override
85.     public boolean onCreateOptionsMenu(Menu menu) {
86.         getMenuInflater().inflate(R.menu.activity_main, menu);
87.         return true;
88.     }
89.
90.     private void startJavaTask() {
91.         if (javaTaskThread == null)
92.             javaTaskThread = new JavaTaskThread(mHandler);
93.         if (! javaTaskThread.isAlive())
94.         {
95.                 start_time = System.currentTimeMillis();
96.                 javaTaskThread.start();
97.                 tv_JavaTaskOuputInfo.setText
                        ("The Java task is running...");
98.         }
99.     }
100.
101.     private void startCCodeTask() {
102.         if (cCodeTaskThread == null)
103.             cCodeTaskThread = new CCodeTaskThread(mHandler);
```

```
104.          if (! cCodeTaskThread.isAlive())
105.          {
106.                  start_time = System.currentTimeMillis();
107.                  cCodeTaskThread.start();
108.                  tv_CCodeTaskOuputInfo.setText
                      ("C code task is running...");
109.          }
110.      }
111.      private void exitApp() {
112.          try {
113.              if (javaTaskThread !=null)
114.              {
115.                  javaTaskThread.join();
116.                  javaTaskThread = null;
117.              }
118.          } catch (InterruptedException e) {
119.          }
120.          try {
121.              if (cCodeTaskThread   !=null)
122.              {
123.                  cCodeTaskThread.join();
124.                  cCodeTaskThread = null;
125.              }
126.          } catch (InterruptedException e) {
127.          }
128.          finish();
129.          Process.killProcess(Process.myPid());
130.      }
131.
132.      static {
133.          System.loadLibrary("ndkexp_extern_lib");
134.      }
135. }
```

This code is basically the same as the example code for SerialPi. Only the code in lines 123–134 is ew. This code requires that the libndkexp_extern_lib.so shared library file be loaded before the application runs. The application needs to use local functions in this library.

4. The new thread task class JavaTaskThread in the project is used to calculate π. The code is similar to the MyTaskThread class code in the SerialPi example and is omitted here.

5. The thread task class CCodeTaskThread in the new project calls the local function to calculate π; its source code file CCodeTaskThread.java reads as follows:

```
1.  package com.example.ndkexp;
2.  import android.os.Handler;
3.  import android.os.Message;

4.  public class CCodeTaskThread extends Thread {
5.      private Handler mainHandler;
6.      public static final int MSG_FINISHED = 2;   // The message after the
                                                     end of the task
7.      private native double cCodeTask();    // Calling external C functions
                                              to accomplish computing tasks

8.      static String msTimeToDatetime(long msnum){
9.          long hh,mm,ss,ms, tt= msnum;
10.         ms = tt % 1000; tt = tt / 1000;
11.         ss = tt % 60; tt = tt / 60;
12.         mm = tt % 60; tt = tt / 60;
13.         hh = tt % 60;
14.         String s = "" + hh +" Hour "+mm+" Minute "+ss + " Second " + ms
            +" Millisecond ";
15.         return s;
16.     }

17.     @Override
18.     public void run()
19.     {
20.         double pi = cCodeTask();   // Calling external C function to
                                       complete the calculation
21.         Message msg = new Message();
22.         msg.what = MSG_FINISHED;
23.         Double dPi = Double.valueOf(pi);
24.         msg.obj = dPi;
25.         mainHandler.sendMessage(msg);
26.     }

27.     public CCodeTaskThread(Handler mh)
28.     {
29.         super();
30.         mainHandler = mh;
31.     }
32. }
```

This code is similar to the code framework of the MyTaskThread class of the SerialPi example. The main difference is at line 20. The original Java code for calculating π is replaced by calling a local function cCodeTask to achieve the task. To indicate that cCodeTask is a local function, you add the local declaration in line 7.

6. Build the project in Eclipse. Again, just build, rather than run.

7. Create the jni subdirectory in the project root directory.

8. Write the C implementation code for the cCodeTask function.

9. Compile the file into a .so library file. The main steps are as follows.

   a. Create a C interface file. Because it is a cCodeTaskThread class using a local function, you need to generate the class header file based on the class file of this class. At the command line, go to the project directory and run the following command:

   ```
   E:\temp\Android Dev\workspace\NdkExp> javah
   -classpath "D:\Android\android-sdk\platforms\
   android-15\android.jar";bin/classes com.example.
   ndkexp.CCodeTaskThread
   ```

This command generates a file in the project directory named com_example_ndkexp_CCodeTaskThread.h. The main content of the document is as follows:

```
······
23. JNIEXPORT jdouble
    JNICALL Java_com_example_ndkexp_CCodeTaskThread_cCodeTask
24. (JNIEnv *, jobject);
    ······
```

In lines 23-24, the prototype of the local function cCodeTask is defined.

   b. Based on these header files, create a corresponding C code file in the jni directory of the project. In this case, name it mycomputetask.c it reads as follows:

```
1.  #include <jni.h>
2.  jdouble Java_com_example_ndkexp_CCodeTaskThread_cCodeTask
    (JNIEnv* env, jobject thiz )
3.  {
4.      const long num_steps = 100000000;    // The total step length
5.      const double step = 1.0 / num_steps;
6.      double x, sum = 0.0;
7.      long i;
8.      double pi = 0;
9.
```

```
10.     for (i=0; i< num_steps; i++){
11.         x = (i+0.5)*step;
11.         sum = sum + 4.0/(1.0 + x*x);
12.     }
13.     pi = step * sum;
14.
15.     return (pi);
16. }
```

Lines 4–16 are the body of the function—the code calculating π, which is the code that corresponds to the MyTaskThread class in SerialPi. It is not difficult to understand. Note that in line 4, the value of the variable num_steps (the total step length) must be the same as the value of the step size the JavaTaskThread class represents. Otherwise, it make no sense to compare the performance here.

The first line of each Jni file must contain the headers. Line 2 is the cCodeTask function prototype and is based on slightly modified header files obtained in the previous step.

Line 16 returns the results. With the Java double type, which corresponds to the C jdouble type, C can have a pi variable of type double returned directly to it. This is discussed in the introduction to this chapter.

      c. In the project jni directory, by following the method Section: Using the Command Line Method to Generate a Library File on page 12 of this chapter3, create Android. mk and Application.mk files. The content of Android.mk reads as follows:

```
1.  LOCAL_PATH := $(call my-dir)
2.  include $(CLEAR_VARS)
3.  LOCAL_MODULE        := ndkexp_extern_lib
4.  LOCAL_SRC_FILES     := mycomputetask.c
5.  include $(BUILD_SHARED_LIBRARY)
```

Line 4 specifies the C code in the case file. Line 3 indicates the file name of the generated library; its name must be consistent with the parameters of the System.loadLibrary function in line 133 of the project file MainActivity.java.

      d. Based on the method described in Section: Using the Command Line Method to Generate a Library File on page 12 of this chapter compile the C code into the .so library file under the lib directory of the project.

    10. Run the project.

The application's running interface is shown in the next section, in Figure 12-18.

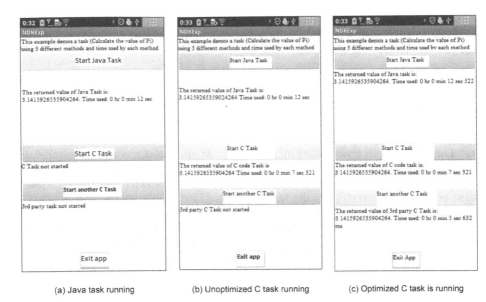

(a) Java task running   (b) Unoptimized C task running   (c) Optimized C task is running

Figure 12-18. *Extended version of NdkExp*

Extending Compiler Optimization

The example demonstrates the capabilities of NDK for application acceleration. However, the application implements only one local function and is unable to provide information to compare the effects of compiler optimizations. For this purpose, in this section you rebuild the application and use it to experiment with the effects of compiler optimizations; see Figure 12-18.

The application has four buttons. When you click the Start Java Task button, the response code does not change. When you click the Start C Task or Start another C Task button, the application starts a local function running.

The code (the function body) of the two functions is the same. It calculates the values of π, but using different names. The first button calls the cCodeTask function, and the second button calls the anotherCCodeTask function. These functions are located in the mycomputetask.c and anothertask.c files, respectively, and they correspond to the library files libndkexp_extern_lib.so and libndkexp_another_lib.so after being compiled. In this case, you compile libndkexp_extern_lib.so using the -O0 option and libndkexp_another_lib.so using the -O3 option, so one is compiled unoptimized and the other is compiled optimized.

Clicking Start C Task runs the unoptimized version of the C function, as shown in Figure 12-20(b); and clicking Start Another C Task runs the optimized version, as shown in Figure 12-20(c). After task execution, the system displays the calculated results to the consumption of time.

As you can see in Figure 12-18, regardless of whether the compiler optimizations are used, the running time of the local function is always shorter than the running time (12.522 seconds) of the Java function. The execution time (5.632 seconds) of the -O3 optimization function is less than the execution time (7.321 seconds) of the unoptimized (-00 compiler option) function. From this result comparison, you can see that using compiler optimizations actually reduces application execution time. Not only that, it is even less than the original application running time (6.378 seconds) in section C/C++: The Original Application Acceleration. This is because the original application without compiler options defaults to the -01 level of optimization, whereas the -03 optimization level is even higher than the original application, so it's not surprising that it has the shortest running time.

This application is a modified and extended version of the original application NdkExp. The steps are as follows:

1. Modify the main layout file. Add a TextView widget and a Button widget in a layout. Set the Text and ID properties, and adjust their size and position, as shown in Figure 12-19.

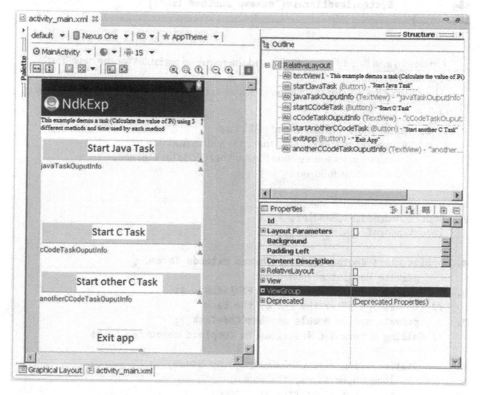

Figure 12-19. Extended NdkExp layout

2. Modify the class source code file MainActivity.java of the main layout. The main changes are as follows:

```
     ...
13.  public class MainActivity extends Activity {
14.      private JavaTaskThread javaTaskThread = null;
15.      private CCodeTaskThread cCodeTaskThread = null;
16.      private AnotherCCodeTaskThread anotherCCodeTaskThread = null;
17.      private TextView tv_JavaTaskOuputInfo;
18.      private TextView tv_CCodeTaskOuputInfo;
19.      private TextView tv_AnotherCCodeTaskOuputInfo;
     ......
182.     static {
183.         System.loadLibrary("ndkexp_extern_lib");
184.         System.loadLibrary("ndkexp_another_lib");
185.     }
186. }
```

On line 16 and line 19 respectively, add the required variables for the new Start Other C Task button.

The key change is in line 184; here, in addition to loading the original shared library files, you also add another library file.

3. In the project, add a thread task class AnotherCCodeTaskThread that calls a local function to calculate π. Its source code file AnotherCCodeTaskThread.java reads as follows:

```
1.  package com.example.ndkexp;
2.  import android.os.Handler;
3.  import android.os.Message;

4.  public class AnotherCCodeTaskThread extends Thread {
5.      private Handler mainHandler;
6.      public static final int MSG_FINISHED = 3;
    // The message after the end of the task
7.      private native double anotherCCodeTask();
    // Calling external C functions to complete computing tasks

8.      static String msTimeToDatetime(long msnum){
9.          long hh,mm,ss,ms, tt= msnum;
10.         ms = tt % 1000; tt = tt / 1000;
11.         ss = tt % 60; tt = tt / 60;
12.         mm = tt % 60; tt = tt / 60;
13.         hh = tt % 60;
```

```
14.        String s = "" + hh +"Hour "+mm+"Minute "+ss + "Second " + ms
           +"Millisecond";
15.        return s;
16.    }

17.    @Override
18.    public void run()
19.    {
20.        double pi = anotherCCodeTask();  // Calling external C function
                                            //    to complete the calculation
21.        Message msg = new Message();
22.        msg.what = MSG_FINISHED;
23.        Double dPi = Double.valueOf(pi);
24.        msg.obj = dPi;
25.        mainHandler.sendMessage(msg);
26.    }

27.    public CCodeTaskThread(Handler mh)
28.    {
29.        super();
30.        mainHandler = mh;
31.    }
32. }
```

This code is almost identical to the code of the CCodeTaskThread class. It does a little processing by calling another external C function anotherCCodeTask to complete computing tasks in line 20. For this, in line 7 it provides appropriate instructions for local functions and changes the value of the message type in line 6. This way, it distinguishes itself from the previous C with a message. Line 4 shows the task class, inherited from the Thread class.

4. Build the project in Eclipse: just a build, not a run.

5. Modify the makefile file of mycomputetask.c, and rebuild library files. To do so, first modify the Android.mk file under the jni directory of the project, which reads as follows:

```
1.  LOCAL_PATH      := $(call my-dir)
2.  include $(CLEAR_VARS)
3.  LOCAL_MODULE    := ndkexp_extern_lib
4.  LOCAL_SRC_FILES := mycomputetask.c
5.  LOCAL_CFLAGS    := -O0
6.  include $(BUILD_SHARED_LIBRARY)
```

Unlike the original application, in line 5 you add parameters for the command LOCAL_CFLAGS passed to gcc. The value -O0 means no optimization.

6. compile the C code file into the .so library file in the lib directory of the project.

7. Save the .so library files in the lib directory of the project (in this example, the file is libndkexp_extern_lib.so) to some other directory, because the following operations will delete this .so library file.

8. Write the C implementation code for the anotherCCodeTask function. Copy the processing steps for the cCodeTask function in the previous section. Using the method in the section "NDK Examples," compile the file into the .so library file. The main steps are as follows:

    a. Create a C interface file. At the command line, go to the project directory, and then run the following command:

        ```
        E:\temp\Android Dev\workspace\NdkExp> javah
        -classpath "D:\Android\android-sdk\platforms\
        android-15\android.jar";bin/classes com.example.
        ndkexp.AnotherCCodeTaskThread
        ```

This command generates a com_example_ndkexp_AnotherCCodeTaskThread.h file. The main contents of the file are as follows:

```
      ......
23. JNIEXPORT jdouble JNICALL Java_com_example_ndkexp_
    AnotherCCodeTaskThread_anotherCCodeTask
24.   (JNIEnv *, jobject);
      ......
```

Lines 23–24 define the local function, which is anotherCCodeTask prototype.

    b. Based on the previously mentioned header files in the project Jni directory, establish corresponding C code files, in this case anothertask.c. The content is a modification of mycomputetask.c:

        ```
        1.  #include <jni.h>
        2.  jdouble Java_com_example_ndkexp_
            AnotherCCodeTaskThread_anotherCCodeTask
            (JNIEnv* env,  jobject thiz )
        3.  {
              ......
        17. }
        ```

The second line of mycomputetask.c is replaced by the prototype of the anotherCCodeTask function. This is the same function prototype copied from that in the .h file created in the previous step, with minor revisions. The final form is in line 2.

c. Modify the Android.mk file in the jni directory as follows:

```
1.  LOCAL_PATH       := $(call my-dir)
2.  include $(CLEAR_VARS)
3.  LOCAL_MODULE     := ndkexp_another_lib
4.  LOCAL_SRC_FILES := anothertask.c
5.  LOCAL_CFLAGS     := -O3
6.  include $(BUILD_SHARED_LIBRARY)
```

In line 4, the value is replaced with the new C code file anothertask.c. In line 3, the value is replaced with a new library file name consistent with the parameters of the System.loadLibrary function, which is in line 184 of the MainActivity.java file. In line 5, the value of the LOCAL_CFLAGS parameter for the passed gcc command is replaced with -O3, which represents the highest level of optimization.

d. Follow the method described in section 3.1 to compile the C code file into the .so library file under the lib directory of the project. The libndkexp_extern_lib. so documents in the lib directory disappear and are replaced by a newly generated libndkexp_another_lib. so file. So, it is very important to save the library files.

9. Put the previously saved libndkexp_extern_lib.so library file back into the libs directory. There are now two files in the directory. You can use the dir command to verify:

```
E:\temp\Android Dev\workspace\NdkExp>dir libs\x86
2013-02-28  00:31     5,208 libndkexp_another_lib.so
2013-02-28  00:23     5,208 libndkexp_extern_lib.so
```

10. Run the project.

Comparing Compiler Optimizations

Through this case study, you have learned the effects of compiler optimization. The task execution time was shortened from 7.321 seconds before optimization to 5.632 seconds after optimization. But you only compared the difference between the gcc -O3 and -O0 command options in the example. You can extend this configuration by modifying the Android.mk file content when compiling the two files mycomputetask.c and anothertask.c, and compare the difference in the optimizing effects when using different compiler command options. To modify the Android.mk file, you only need to modify the value of the LOCAL_CFLAGS item; you can select many gcc command options to compare. Let's look at an example.

Example 1. Comparing Optimization Results Using SSE Instructions

Compile the Start C Task button corresponding to the Android.mk file of mycomputetask.c:

```
LOCAL_CFLAGS := -mno-sse
```

And compile the Start other C Task button corresponding to the Android.mk file of anothertask.c:

```
LOCAL_CFLAGS := -msse3
```

The former tells the compiler not to compile SSE instructions; the latter allows the compiler to program into SSE3 instructions. The reason to choose SSE3 instructions is that SSE3 is the highest level of instructions the Intel Atom processor supports.

The results of running the application are shown in Figure 12-20.

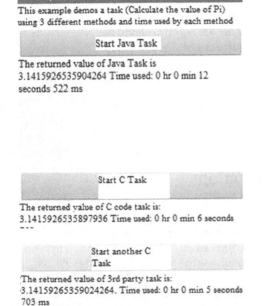

Figure 12-20. *Optimization comparison of compiler SSE instructions for NdkExp*

The same task using an SSE instruction has a shorter execution time than not using an SSE instruction. The execution time is shortened from the original 6.759 seconds to 5.703 seconds.

Noted that, in this example, we finished modifying Android.mk and reran ndk-build to generate the .so library file. We immediately deployed and ran the NdkExp project but found out that we could not achieve the desired effect because only the .so library files are updated. The Eclipse project manager does not detect that that the project needs to rebuild. As a result, the .apk was not updated, and NdkExp on the target machine would not run updates or the original code. Considering this situation, you can use the following methods to avoid this problem:

1. Uninstall the application from the phone.

2. Delete the three documents classes.dex, jarlist.cache, and NdkExp.apk in the bin subdirectory of the host project directory.

3. Delete the project in Eclipse.

4. In Eclipse, re-import the project.

5. Re-deploy and run the projects.

Here you only compared the effect of SSE instructions. You can try other gcc compiler options and compare their operating results.

In addition, the previous examples are only concerned with the NDK effect, so the C functions still use single-threaded code. You can combine the NDK optimization knowledge from this chapter with the multithreading optimization from the previous chapter and change the C function to multithreading, and implement it along with the compiler optimization. Such a set of written optimization techniques in a variety of applications will allow the applications to run faster.

Summary

This chapter introduced the Android NDK for C/C++ application development, along with related optimization methods, and optimization tools. The Intel mobile hardware and software provide a basis for low-power design. The Intel Atom processor provides hardware support for low power, which is a major feature of the Android operating system.

The next chapter presents an overview of low-power design. It also discusses the Android power-control mechanisms and how to achieve the goal of low-power application design.

CHAPTER 13

■ ■ ■

The Low-Power Design of Android Application and Intel Graphics Performance Analyzers (Intel GPA): Assisted Power Optimization

Unlike general-purpose computers that use an AC power supply, not all mobile devices can be directly connected to AC power; it cannot be assumed that the power supply is inexhaustible. In addition, heat dissipation must be considered for mobile devices. If power consumption is too high, it requires the system to increase heat dissipation, and at some point it may reach a point where this is not allowed. Due to strict constraints on the system's overall power consumption, *low-power design*, commonly known as *power saving*, is an important element of applications for mobile devices; in many cases it is a rigid requirement or the basis for survival. For example, it would be difficult to imagine a mobile phone the market would accept that could support only a few hours' time.

On the other hand, Intel Mobile hardware and software provide a basis for low-power design. The Intel Atom processor provides hardware support for low power, and low-power support is a major feature of Android. Both provide a good platform for low-power design for mobile applications.

This chapter is organized as follows: first an overview of and introduction to low-power design, then a discussion of the Android power-control mechanisms, and finally a discussion of how to achieve the goal of low-power application design.

Overview of Low-Power Design

Let's look at the power-consumption characteristics of mobile systems. For a mobile device, the processor, radio communication, and the screen are the three main components of its power consumption (power). The processor and its ancillary

445

equipment are responsible for most of the battery power consumption. Therefore, this chapter focuses on the power consumption of the processor and its ancillary equipment (abbreviated here as *processor power consumption*).

The Basics of Consumption

Battery life mainly refers to the running time that a mobile device such as a laptop, an MP3 player, or a mobile phone, equipped with its own battery alone, can maintain without an external power adapter. In general, the factors that affect the machine's battery life include the battery itself as well as the machine power consumption (watts/hour).

For a semiconductor product, the power consumption of a digital circuit is composed of two parts. The first part is *static power consumption*, from the perspective of integrated circuit technology, which is power consumption caused by *drain current* (leakage current), which is part of the electronic circuit (such as CMOS). The ability to control this power consumption is mainly determined by the production processes and materials used. The second part of a digital circuit's power consumption is *dynamic power dissipation*. Many factors affect this part, such as circuit design, circuit complexity, and working clock frequency.

The dynamic power of the processor (or CPU), also known as *switching power*, referred to as *power consumption*, is determined by the following empirical equation:

$$P = a \times C \times F \times V^2$$

In this formula, P is the processor power consumption, a is an adjustment parameter relating to the circuit, C is total gate capacitance of a single clock cycle (which is fixed for a processor), F is the processor operating frequency, and V is operating voltage. As you can see, the processor's power consumption is proportional to the square of the operating voltage, proportional to the operating frequency.

■ **Tip**   With regard to processor power consumption, there is a related concept called *thermal design power (TDP)*. TDP is easy to confuse with CPU power consumption. Although both are indicators used to measure processor power, and both use watts (W) as a unit, TDP has a different meaning than processor power consumption.

TDP is a heat-release indicator's reflection of a processor. By definition, it is the heat released by a processor when it reaches maximum load. The processor TDP power consumption is not the real power consumption of the processor. Processor power (power) is a physical parameter, which is equal to the value of current flowing through the processor core and the product of the voltage value of the processor core, and it reflects the actual power consumption of energy in the unit of time. TDP is the heat generated by the processor's thermal effect of current and other forms of heat release. Obviously, the processor TDP is less than the power consumption of the processor.

TDP cooling system requirements are an important factor for hardware designers and manufacturers to consider. But this chapter discusses the actual consumption of electrical power—processor power consumption—not TDP.

From the processor power-consumption formula, the adjust parameter a and total gate capacitance C are determined by the processor design and materials. For a processor, parameters a and C are fixed; if you want to reduce power consumption, you must start from the operating frequency (F) and operating voltage (V), which are the starting point for many low-power technologies.

In general, the methods to achieve the greater energy efficiency for a CMOS processor are as follow:

1. Reduce the voltage or the processor clock frequency.

2. Internally disable some of the currently executing functions that do not require a functional unit.

3. Allow part of the processor to be fully disconnected from the main power supply to eliminate leakage.

4. Improve processor circuit design and manufacturing processes; obtain energy efficiency by applying the principles of physics.

There are two types of tactics for managing processor power (power consumption). One is the use of static power-management mechanisms. Such mechanisms are invoked by the user and do not depend on processor activity. One example of a static mechanism is a power-saving mode to conserve power. The power-saving mode can be entered with a single instruction and exited through receipt of an interrupt or other event.

Another tactic for managing processing power is to use dynamic power-management mechanisms. Such mechanisms are based on the dynamic activity of the processor power-consumption control. For example, when the command is run, if some part of the processor logic does not need to run, the processor may switch off these specific sections.

Power Consumption Control Technology

To help you understand the power-consumption basics for semiconductors (including processors), let's look at the ways you can implement power consumption control technology in hardware. These pathways are discussed in the following sections.

Dynamic Voltage/Frequency Scaling Technology

Dynamic frequency scaling (DFS) is a way of controlling power consumption by adjusting (reducing) the operating frequency of the processor so that it runs at less than the peak frequency, thus reducing processor power. This technology was first used on laptops and is now more and more widely used in mobile devices.

DFS technology has other uses besides saving energy on the processor. It can be used in a quiet computing environment on the machine or in a light load condition to reduce cooling costs as well as the overall energy demand. When a system has inadequate cooling and the temperature is close to a critical value, this technology helps to reduce heat buildup, thus preventing the machine from experiencing critical temperature problems. Many overclocking systems also use this technique to achieve temporary supplemental cooling.

■ **Tip**   In contradiction to, but related to, DFS technology is *overclocking*. This technology upgrades processor (dynamic) power to exceed the manufacturer's prescribed design limits and improve processor performance. There is an important difference between DFS and overclocking: overclocking is in the front-side bus (mainly because multiples usually are locked) in a modern computer system, whereas DFS is used in the multiplier to completion. Moreover, overclocking is often static; DFS is usually dynamic.

In practice, the Advanced Configuration and Power Interface (ACPI) specifies that the C0 working state of modern processors can be divided into named performance states (P-states) and throttling states (T-states). The P-state allows you to reduce the clock frequency, and the T-state does so by inserting a STPCLK (stop the clock) signal to temporarily close the clock signal and further suppress processor power consumption (but not the actual clock frequency). Intel is also working with Google on improving power management for Android and has created drivers for three CPU standby states: Active Standby (S0i1), Always On Always Connected (AOAC) Standby (S0i2), and Deep Sleep Standby (S0i3).

As described, power consumption is mainly caused by leakage current due to the presence of static power; dynamic power is only part of the total power of the chip. When the chip size becomes smaller, the CMOS threshold level is lowered, and the influence of the leakage current appears more obvious. Especially for the current chip-manufacturing process, which is under the micron level, dynamic power is only about two thirds of the total power of the chip, which limits the effect of frequency scaling.

Dynamic voltage scaling (DVS) is another way to control processor power consumption. This is accomplished by adjusting (lowering) the operating voltage of the processor to reduce processor power.

DFS does not have much value simply as a way to save dynamic power. Taking into account the important role of V^2 in the dynamic power formula, as well as the fact that there has been in-depth optimization of the low-power idle state for modern processors to save a lot of power consumption in DFS, you need to consider DVS. Reducing the processor clock frequency also provides voltage reduction space (because in a certain range, the maximum operating frequency a processor can support is increased with the increase of the processor's supply voltage). Voltage scaling and frequency scaling can be used in conjunction to form a comprehensive power-control method: dynamic voltage/frequency discharge reduction, or *dynamic voltage and frequency scaling (DVFS)*. This technology is also known as *Intel processor CPU throttling*.

Dynamic voltage/frequency scaling technology affects performance. This technique reduces the number of instructions issued by the processor at a given time, thereby causing a decline in processing performance (speed). Therefore, it is usually used at a lower processor load (such as when the system is running in the idle state).

Clock Gating

Clock gating is another way to achieve energy savings, in this case by closing and opening the module clock and power control. This technology was applied in the first family of applications, such as the OMAP3-like traditional phone chip; the Intel Pentium 4 processor also used it.

For CMOS processor components, the power consumed to change the level state is much greater than the power consumed to maintain the level state, because the clock signal is extremely frequent when changing level state. If you use clock-gating technology in the current clock cycle, if the system does not use some of the logic module, the module clock signal is cut off, creating a closed circuit in the module so the logic switch does not change state. You only need to retain the leakage current while the switching power consumption is close to zero, to reduce power consumption. When there is work to be done, the module clock is reactivated. This process is also known as *clipping* (or *pruning*) *the clock tree*. In a sense, clock gating is an extreme case of the variable frequency clock, but the two values are zero and the maximum frequency.

This technique requires that each module—known as a *functional unit block (FUB)*—contain the clock gate logic circuit. That is, the technique of clipping the clock tree must be ensured by the additional logic components.

Clock gating has several forms. With the software manual clock-gating method, the driver controls when to turn on or off the various clocks used by the specified idle controller. The other method is automatic clock gating: the hardware can be informed or can detect whether there is work to do and then close the gate if you specify that the clock is no longer needed. For example, an internal bridge or bus may use the automatic clock-gating method so that it is always gated off until the processor or DMA engines need to use it. Peripheral devices on the bus may be closed by the driver in the gated code if the software did not use them.

Energy-Saving Circuit Design and Manufacturing Processes

Chip circuit design choices and manufacturing processes can improve energy savings on a physical level. One of these design choices is to use an ultra-low voltage (ULV) processor. ULV series processors reduce the processor core voltage and reduce the number of processor cores and even size, to realize power-consumption control from the hardware (at the physical level).

In addition, similar to the ULV processor, a 45-nanometer manufacturing process reduces processor power consumption at the hardware level. The chip consumes less power and has longer battery life, has more transistors, and is smaller. The Intel Atom Bay Trail processor uses a 22-nanometer manufacturing process for energy-saving technologies (14nm technology will be used on the next generation of processors).

449

With the further enhancement of manufacturing processes and manufacturing precision, chips are getting smaller and smaller, while at the same time, physical power consumption is becoming lower and lower.

With an understanding of hardware power control, you can look at system power-control technology. Some of these techniques are at the hardware level, some are at the operating system layer, and some are at the system layer and include both software and hardware.

Intel SpeedStep and Enhanced Intel SpeedStep Technology

Intel SpeedStep Technology was developed to provide power control for Intel CPUs; the technology is now generally referred to as Enhanced Intel SpeedStep Technology (EIST). It was first used in the Intel Pentium M, Pentium 4 6xx Series, and Pentium D processors. Intel Core, Intel Atom, and other processor series have also adopted it. EIST mainly takes advantage of dynamic voltage and frequency scaling; the basic principle is to adjust processor voltage and frequency to reduce power consumption and heat. Of course, with the reduction of voltage and frequency, processing speed is also reduced. This technology has undergone several generations of development, as discussed next.

First-Generation Intel SpeedStep Technology

The original Intel SpeedStep Technology allows the processor to switch freely between two modes of operation: AC status, which offers the highest performance mode (Maximum Performance mode); and battery status (Battery Optimized mode).
These two modes are automatically selected according to the computer's power source: external power supply or battery. Maximum Performance mode is the approximate performance when the computer is connected to AC power (that is, always powered by an external power supply). Battery Optimized mode is used when the computer is using the minimum battery power to achieve the best performance. Usually, when switching modes with Intel SpeedStep Technology, the power of the processor is reduced by 40% while still maintaining the 80% of peak performance.

The conversion speed of mode switching is very fast—only 1/2000 of a second, so the user does not feel the transformation. Even if a program's performance requirements are sensitive (for example, playing DVD movies), this conversion process does not affect program operation. In addition, users can set up their own mode to use the battery in Maximum Performance mode or an external power supply in Battery Optimized mode. To do so, the user selects a mode onscreen, without having to restart the computer.

Second-Generation Intel SpeedStep Technology (EIST)

EIST begins dynamic switching between the two modes of performance for voltage and frequency, according to the processor load in real time. Using this technique, the battery-powered processor load automatically switches to the maximum operating frequency and voltage. It can also switch to the lowest operating frequency and voltage automatically, according to the processor load in the external power supply. In other words, the technical processing of the operating frequency and voltage change is no longer determined by the type of power source.

Third-Generation Intel SpeedStep Technology (Improved EIST)

In addition to the two basic modes of operation, the improved EIST provides a variety
of intermediate modes and supports multiple frequencies, speeds, and voltage settings
(controlled by the processor voltage adjustment mechanism), according to the strength of
the processor's current load. It automatically switches the operating mode.

EIST includes a number of software and hardware technologies to ensure that it
runs smoothly, including the system BIOS, the user terminal software, ASIC control, and
chipset support. The software program itself does not need to make any changes; it can
easily use this technique. At the same time, EIST also requires the operating system to
cope with, for example, its processor load detection, which is accomplished through the
operating system.

APM and the ACPI Standard

To make low power consumption possible for mobile computing systems, hardware
and operating systems need to work together. Coordinating operating systems and
hardware for both power consumption and power management requires a unified set
of interface specifications. The earliest specification was Advanced Power Management
(APM), released by Intel and Microsoft; it is a set of APIs, running on IBM-compatible
PC operating systems and BIOS synergy to manage power consumption. The current
specification is Advanced Configuration and Power Interface (ACPI), which comes from
the development of APM.

ACPI is an open industry standard for power-management services. It is compatible
with multiple operating systems; the initial goal is to use it with personal computers.
ACPI has power-management tools and a hardware abstraction layer. The operating system
has its own power-management model. It sends demand controls to hardware via ACPI
and then observes the hardware status as an input, to control the power of computers and
peripherals. ACPI in the entire computer system structure is illustrated in Figure 13-1.

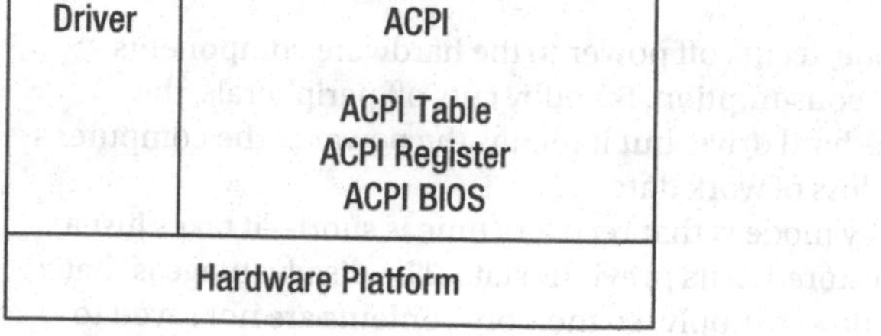

Figure 13-1. ACPI structure

ACPI supports the following five basic global power states:

- *G3*: Mechanical off state; the system does not consume power.

- *G2*: Soft off state; the entire operating system restarts to restore the machine to working conditions. This state has four substates:

  - *S1*: No system context; the missing low wake-up delay state.

  - *S2*: Lost low CPU and system cache status wake-up delay state.

  - *S3*: In addition to the main memory, all other system status is lost; low wake-up delay state.

  - *S4*: Low-power sleep mode; all devices are turned off.

- *G1*: Sleep state; the system appears to be off; the low-power state. The time required to return to the normal operating state is inversely proportional to the power consumption of the low-power state.

- *G0*: The working state; the system is fully available.

- *Retention state*: The system does not comply with ACPI.

The typical power-management program includes a viewer for messages received by ACPI that describe the behavior of the system. Also included is a decision model based on observations to determine power-management behavior.

Popular operating systems and software platforms, such as Windows and Android, all support ACPI.

Low-Power Operating System States

When the task is idle (or in an inactive state), the computer system achieves energy savings by entering the various low-power operating modes. These low-power modes are sometimes collectively referred to as *sleep mode*. They are between the states in which system is fully booted and completely closed, with a variety of forms; each form has its own characteristics to meet users' various needs. These modes are described in the following sections.

Standby

When the system is in standby mode, it cuts off power to the hardware components, thereby reducing computer power consumption. Standby cuts off peripherals, the monitor, and even the power of the hard drive, but it retains the power of the computer's memory to ensure that there is no loss of work data.

The main advantage of standby mode is that recovery time is short—it takes just a few seconds for the system to be restored to its previous state. The disadvantage is that standby mode needs the memory power supply, so memory contents are not saved to the folder and therefore do not affect the running speed of memory reload. However, if a power failure occurs in this mode, all unsaved memory contents are lost. Therefore, standby is also known as *suspend to RAM* (STR).

When the system is in standby mode, the hard disk and other equipment are in the power-wait state until a wakeup call is received. The power supply, processor, graphics, and other fans are working, and the keyboard indicator is lit. You can press any keyboard key or move the mouse to wake up the computer. The hard disk is repowered, and allows memory, processors, and other devices to exchange data and return to the original mode of operation.

Hibernate

When the system is in hibernate mode, an image of the operating mode is saved to external memory and then the computer is turned off. When you turn on the power and reboot, operation reverts to the earlier look: files and documents are arranged as you left them on the desktop.

Hibernate mode is deeper than standby mode and thus helps save more power, but the computer takes longer to restart. In addition, hibernate mode includes higher security. This is because this mode not only closes the power supply to the peripherals and hard disk but also cuts off the power supply of the RAM memory chips. This mode is also known as *suspend to disk* (STD).

As the computer enters hibernate mode, before the power is turned off, all data is stored (written) in external memory (usually a hard disk) to the reference file. On coming out of hibernate mode, the system is restored (read) from the reference file, and data is reloaded into memory. In this way, the system reverts to the previous operating mode. Because hibernate mode needs to save memory data, the recovery (wake-up) time is longer than with standby mode.

The advantage of this mode is that no power is consumed, and thus you need not be afraid of power anomalies during sleep. It can also save and restore the user state, but this requires the same space on the hard disk as the physical memory size.

Hibernation of a computer system is almost as quiet as regular shutdown; you can completely remove power, and memory data (running) won't be lost due to a power failure. Compared to standby, hibernation is generally difficult to wake up with an external device; it needs to start the system with a normal boot. However, hibernate mode boots the system without triggering a regular start process: it only needs the hard disk memory mirroring read taken into memory, so it is much faster than a standard boot.

Sleep

Sleep mode combines all the advantages of standby and hibernation. The system switches to the sleep state; all the data in system memory dumps into the hibernation file on the hard disk, and then all power to the equipment in addition to memory is turned off so data in memory is maintained. Thus, restoring power during sleep is not an exception; you can quickly recover directly from the data in memory. If there are power anomalies and the data in memory is lost during sleep, data can also be recovered from the hard disk, but the speed is a little slower. In any case, this model does not result in data loss.

Sleep mode is not always continuously maintained. If the system enters sleep mode for a period of time without being awakened, it may automatically change to hibernate mode and turn off the power supply to the memory to further reduce energy consumption.

Achieving these low-power energy-saving features requires both operating system support and hardware support, such as support for ACPI. Only by combining these features can you achieve the energy savings described. When the idle time (also known as non-active time) reaches a specified length or the battery power is low, the operating system can automatically put your computer system in a low-power state, saving energy for the entire system.

Linux Power-Control Mechanism

Android is based on Linux. Linux has a lot of practical tools for analyzing and reducing power consumption, some of which have been adopted by Android. The following sections describe several types of Linux power control and management, including many aspects of the technology and its components.

Tickless Idle

Tickless idle, sometimes called *non-fixed frequency* or *no empty circulation*, is the technology used in the Android Linux kernel to improve its power-saving ability.

The traditional Linux kernel processor uses a periodic timer to record the state of the system, load balance, schedule, and maintain a variety of processor timer events. Early timer frequencies were generally 100 Hz. The new kernel uses 250 Hz or up to 1,000 Hz. However, when the processor is idle, these periodic timed events consume a lot of power. Tickless idle eliminates this periodic timer event in the processor and is also related to the optimization of other timers.

After using tickless idle, the Linux kernel is an empty cycle-free kernel. The kernel still records the time, but using a different approach. There is no longer frequent checking to see if there is work to be done. When the kernel knows there is work to be done, it schedules hardware to issue an interrupt request. Tickless idle technology has another indirect benefit in energy efficiency: you can make better use of virtual technology, which means the virtualization software is not interrupted unnecessarily or too often.

Tickless idle provides the necessary kernel foundation for excellent power savings. However, it also requires collaboration with the application. If the application does not follow the principle of low-power design, is badly written, or is using the wrong behavior, it may easily consume or waste the power savings created by tickless idle.

PowerTOP

PowerTOP helps users find applications that consume additional power when the computer is idle. It has a more prominent role for advanced software. Here are PowerTOP's features:

- Gives recommendations to help users make better use of the system's various hardware power-saving features

- Identifies culprit software modules that prevent hardware power savings from achieving optimal performance

- Helps developers test their applications and achieve optimal behavior

- Provides adjustment proposals to access low power

A screenshot of PowerTOP running is shown in Figure 13-2.

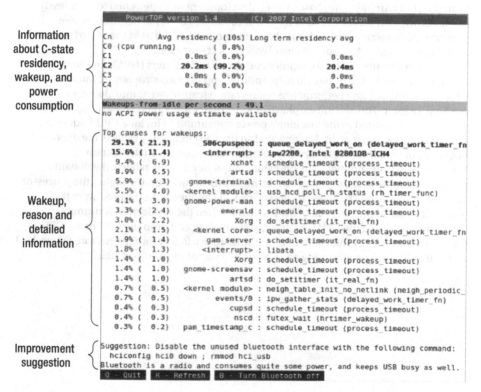

Figure 13-2. PowerTOP interface example

Many Linux systems on the Intel Atom platform, such as Ubuntu, support the PowerTOP tool. Figure 13-2 shows PowerTOP running in Ubuntu. Android does not support this tool yet (it is not known if Android will support it in the future). However, Intel has recently provided tools on Android with functionality similar to that of PowerTOP, as introduced in the following sections.

Intel Power-Optimization Aids

Intel has introduced some aids to help with low-power design for Android applications. The role of these auxiliary tools is similar to the profiler with regard to performance optimization, VTune, and so on. With these tools, you can do tool-assisted optimization on the application's power consumption. In other words, the aids offer guidance or counseling. To achieve real optimization, you must rewrite the code in accordance with low-power design principles (described in the following sections).

Intel developed the Intel Mobile Development Kit for Android for system or middleware developers to create Android system or middleware software that takes advantage of the latest innovations Intel platforms have to offer. This kit provides access to an x86 (Intel Architecture) based tablet, development tools designed to seamlessly create software for this device, and technical collateral about the OS, tools, system software, middleware, and hardware. You can purchase the kit at https://software. intel.com/en-us/intel-mobile-development-kit-for-android.

You can also use the Intel Graphics Performance Analyzers (GPA): free, low-power auxiliary tools provided by Intel to help Android applications save power. Intel GPA–assisted speed and performance optimization features were introduced in the previous chapter. This section emphasizes its auxiliary functions for power optimization.

Indicators related to the machine's power consumption include CPU frequency, current charging, current discharging, and so on. CPU frequency reflects the operating frequency of the processor in the CPU column. As mentioned in the section "The Basics of Consumption," the operating frequency directly reflects the dynamic power consumption of the processor: the higher the frequency, the higher the processor power consumption. Therefore, by observing CPU frequency, you can analyze the (dynamic) power consumption of the processor when the application is running.

When analyzing the CPU frequency, you can drag and drop the CPU in the CPU Column XX Frequency indicator items to the display window for observation. Figure 13-3 shows the CPU frequency during an analysis of a sample app, MoveCircle.

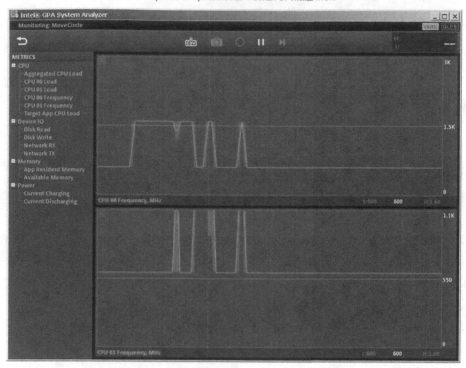

Figure 13-3. Intel GPA CPU frequency analysis

The vertical axis in Figure 13-3 is the operating frequency of the CPU; the unit is
megahertz (MHz). In this example, the target machine is a Lenovo K800 Smartphone
with an Intel Atom processor, two logical CPUs, and two display windows. As you can
see, when the application has a computing task, the CPU increases the frequency to cater
to the needs of the calculation; when computing tasks are light, the CPU reduces the
operating frequency to save power.

The Current Charging and Current Discharging indicators reflect the charge and
discharge conditions. Unlike CPU frequencies, these reflect the machine's overall
power consumption. Current Discharging indicates the discharge status; this is a direct
reflection of the machine's power consumption, and it is the direct target you want to
observe. However, during the Intel GPA analysis, the target machine is connected to
the host via a USB cable, so the host becomes a power supply and is charging the target
machine (phone). Thus you should not ignore the Current Charging indicator when
analyzing overall machine power consumption.

While analyzing overall machine power consumption, you can drag and drop
the power bar under the corresponding Current Charging (top graph) and Current
Discharging (bottom graph) index entries to the display window to observe them.
Figure 13-4 shows an analysis of the machine's charging and discharging using the
sample MoveCircle app.

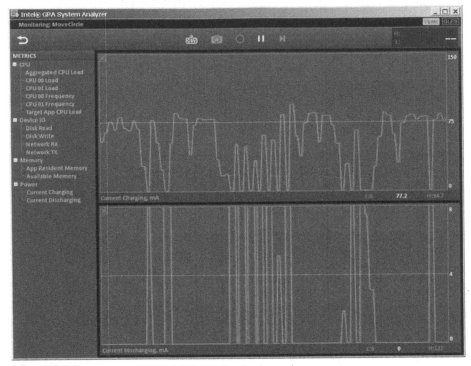

(a) The application is running

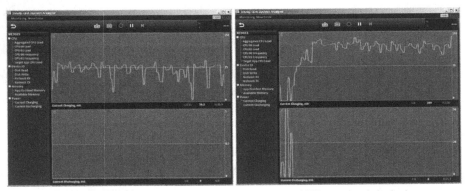

(b) The application is not running

(c) The screen is locked

Figure 13-4. Intel GPA machine overall power analysis

The vertical axis in Figure 13-4 is in the current in milliamperes (mA). When the voltage is constant, it is a direct reflection of power consumption. When no application is running, the charge (Current Charging) maintains a natural fluctuation of the state, and the discharge (Current Discharging) stays almost 0 for the low state, as shown in Figure 13-4(b). When the application is running, due to the increase in the dynamic power consumption of the CPU, the discharge no longer maintains the 0 state. Discharge at the same time lowers the value of the charge; this is visible in Figure 13-4(a).

When the user locks the screen, the screen may go blank and running applications may also be suspended, quickly reducing the CPU's dynamic power consumption; this brings the discharge almost back to the 0 state, and the charge rises. This process is shown in Figure 13-4(c).

As you can also see in the previous figures, the Intel Atom processor and Android have load-sensing power-management capabilities, and they work together on dynamic power management. When the application is not running or is completing low-power computing tasks, the system perceives this change, and the hardware (processor) control technology jumps in and reduces power consumption. It usually does so by lowering the operating frequency/voltage using EIST.

Low-Power Considerations in Application Design

Hardware and operating systems provide good technical support for low power consumption by the system, and this can also be accomplished using appropriate management mechanisms and means of control. However, the ultimate low-power target requires the close cooperation of the application. If the application is developed without following the principle of low-power design, the final program may either not use the system's low-power potential or waste power, cancelling out the power savings from the low-power technology provided by the hardware and operating system. Therefore, this chapter emphasizes the importance of low-power requirements and principles in application design.

Low-power design requirements and principles in application development involve many technologies and methodologies. Let's examine the major principles and recommendations.

The Most Basic Principle of Low-Power Optimization

The most basic principle of low-power optimization is to minimize the working hours of the processor and various peripherals. When a peripheral is not required and processor operation is not required, the best way to reduce their power consumption is to turn them off.

Because the processor uses a larger proportion of the total power consumption of the system, the processor's working hours need to be as short as possible; it should spend longer in idle mode or power-down mode. This is a software design key to reducing the mobile system's power consumption.

General Recommendations: High Performance = Low Power Consumption

In most cases with fixed voltage, running at peak velocity (high frequency) for a short period of time with a long time in a deep idle state is much more energy efficient than a long run at a medium operating frequency with a mild idle state. Therefore, for the same task, much less electricity is consumed if your app runs to completion in the shortest possible time and then enters an idle state, rather than runs over a longer time to completion before entering a short idle state.

A fast algorithm can also reduce power consumption, which follows the recommendation that high performance is equal to low power consumption.

Use Low-Power Hardware as Much as Possible to Achieve the Task

The same task can be accomplished with different types of hardware, and different hardware has different power-consumption overhead. When your app has the option to choose different hardware to run the same task, you should choose low-power hardware.

In general, the energy consumption of the register access is the lowest; and the energy consumption of cache access is lower than the energy consumption of main memory access. Therefore, the program design should try to follow these suggestions:

- Use the register as effectively as possible.

- Analyze the behavior of the cache to discover the main cache conflict.

- Use page-mode access as much as possible in the storage system.

Polling Is the Enemy of Low-Power Optimization

Programs waiting for state changes or accessing peripheral devices may use polling; this method is sometimes referred to as *rapid rotation* or *spinning* code. Polling allows the processor to perform a few instructions repeatedly. Power consumption is roughly equal to heavy computing tasks, and its role is just waiting for a status change; but the waiting period cannot allow the processor to enter an idle state, resulting in a lot of wasted power. Therefore, in low-power design, you should try to avoid using polling and instead use alternative methods. For example, you should use interrupts instead of polling access peripherals. In the client/server collaboration model, you should change the client inquiry service to have the server actively push services to the client. For thread synchronization, if you need to query the status change, you should use the operating system event or semaphore.

For example, suppose Thread 2 wants to access a resource. The ability to access is determined by the access-control variable canGo. Thread 1 is responsible for on or off access control of variables canGo. If this is achieved by the polling statement, the thread code may be as follows:

```
volatile boolean canGo = false;        // Shared variables
// The code of thread 1                // The code of thread 2
void run()                             void run()
{                                      {
    ......
    canGo = true;                          while (!canGo);
    // Allow thread 2 to access a resource     // Wait canGo Change to true
    ......                                 ...... // Access to the resource code
}                                      }
```

In the previous code, the Thread 2 while statement is typical of polling; it consumes a lot of processor time to prevent entry into the idle sleep state. You can change to a Java wait-notify mechanism to achieve the same functions:

```
volatile boolean canGo = false;
Object sema;                           // The synchronization lock canGo variable
// The code of thread 1                // The code of thread 2
void run()                             void run()
{                                      {
    synchronized(sema){                    synchronized(sema){
        canGo = true; // Allow
        thread 2 to access a resource      while (!canGo)
        sema.notifyAll()                   sema.wait();
    }                                  }
    .....                                  ...... // Access to the resource code
}                                      }
```

After being replaced by the wait-notify code, thread 2 has no rapid rotation of the polling statement: each time it checks the canGo variable in a loop, if the conditions are not met, it enters the suspend state and releases the CPU. So, the CPU load is not wasted on the thread. When the CPU has no other tasks, the load soon drops to a low state. When low load to the processor is detected, the system takes measures to reduce power consumption. This could not be done with the rapid rotation of polling mode before the optimization.

Event-Driven Programming

In addition to implementing the software design methodology, low-power programs should always follow the *event-driven model* of program design if possible. Event-driven programming means the program is designed to respond to events: when an event arrives, the application runs to handle the event; when no event arrives or the event is finished, the program gives up the processor and changes to a sleep state. Here the event is referred to as a *generalized event*, including user input, network communication events, and process/thread synchronization events.

When the event-driven design process is used, processor utilization is particularly high: programs only run when there are real things to deal with, and they free the processor when there is nothing to do. When the processor is in an idle state, the operating system and hardware can detect the idle in a timely manner and initiate the operation to reduce power consumption.

Reduce Periodic Operations Similar to Polling in Application Programs

Earlier you saw that the polling operation consumes unnecessary energy. Unnecessary programming of periodic triggers or running operations can have an effect similar to polling and consume power unnecessarily.

Tickless idle, as discussed earlier, is an operating system kernel improvement that follows this principle; it removes periodic timed operations from the kernel. In addition, Linux applications have many unnecessary periodic triggers or running operations, such as these:

- Mouse movement, once per second. This is commonly used in screensavers.

- Changes in volume, 10 times per second. This is commonly used in the mixer program.

- The next minute, once per second. This clock program is commonly used.

- USB reader, 10 times per second. This daemon is commonly used.

- Other application data and conditions that change:

  - More than 10 times per second (web browser)

  - More than 30 times per second (GPS signal acquisition applications)

  - More than 200 times per second (the Flash plug-in)

These unnecessary triggers and operations cause the system to wake up from an idle state. When ported to Android, such operations should be noted and carefully avoided or improved; otherwise they can easily offset power-consumption savings.

Low-Power Recommendations for Data Acquisition and Communications

When designing communication modules, try to improve the communication rate. When the communication rate is increased, it means communication time is shortened and fewer high-power communications, reducing total power consumption.

Similarly, when using Wi-Fi communication, you should use burst mode to transmit data, which can shorten the communication time (especially when sending data). It is easy for Wi-Fi devices to enter an idle state as soon as possible.

Establishing a Power-Aware Program

Power for Android devices often toggles between being connected to an external power supply and using battery power. The power requirements of the software for both power states are completely different: the former is power-insensitive but requires that priority be put on performance most of time; the latter is power-consumption-sensitive and therefore needs to strike a balance between performance and power consumption. Thus the application should detect the type of power supply and make adjustments to adapt to power-related changes.

In addition, some power-management factors may affect software behavior, such as when the device's battery is below a certain threshold and the device enters the closed state and automatic sleep, and so on. Application design should take into account environmental changes brought about by these power-management events, pay attention to the possible impact of these factors, and respond appropriately. For example, ongoing processing of time-consuming operations (such as lengthy floating-point operations, the query circulating system, and complex graphics reproduction) can be interrupted or suspended by power-management events. One of the countermeasures is to save the scene and make sure the environment is allowed time to recover from the interrupt status.

In addition, you can develop a kind of defensive programming for power, such as advance consideration or prediction of what kind of task or application the user will start (for example, playing a movie); or determining in advance whether there is enough battery power to complete the task, and if not, alerting the user at the start of the task.

Case Study 1: Intel GPA Assisted Power Optimization for an Android Application

Following is a case study to demonstrate a comprehensive approach that uses the Intel GPA power-analysis tools to rewrite and optimize an application that has high power consumption, in accordance with low-power design principles.

Original Application and Intel GPA Power Analysis

The example application runs for a specified period of time (20 seconds). This application, without low-power optimized code, is called PollLast. The application design calls for it to get the current time through the static function currentTimeMillis of the Java System class; the current time plus the duration of the runtime specified in the program is equal to the end of the program run. The program then gets the current time in the looping function currentTimeMillis and compares it with the program end time. If the current time exceeds the program end time, the program ends the loop and finishes the program. Because the entire task takes a long time to process, you run the program as a worker thread so it does not affect the response of the main interface. The main interface controls the start of the task.

The application's operation interface is shown in Figure 13-5.

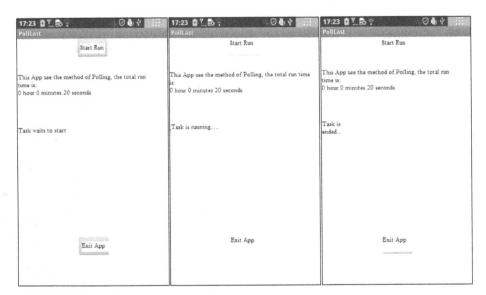

(a) The application has just started   (b) After clicking the Start Run button   (c) After the task has finished running

Figure 13-5. *Separate* PollLast *applications running in the interface*

The main steps to create the application are as follows:

1. Create a new project called PollLast. Set the proposed project property to use the default value, and select the Build SDK version which supports the x86 API.

2. Edit the main layout file, and place two Buttons and two TextViews on the layout; one is used to display the operating status of the task thread, as shown in Figure 13-6.

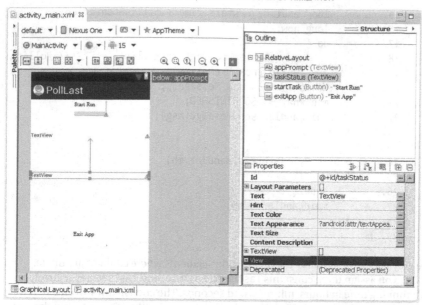

Figure 13-6. *The main layout of the* `PollLast` *application*

3. Create a new task thread class `MyTaskThread`, which will run a specified time. Edit the source code file `MyTaskThread.java` as follows:

```
1. package com.example.polllast;
2. import android.os.Handler;
3. import android.os.Message;

4. public class MyTaskThread extends Thread {
5.   private Handler mainHandler;
6.   public static final int MSG_FINISHED = 1;
7.   public static final int lasthour = 0;
      // The number of hours the program is running
8.   public static final int lastmin = 0;
      // The number of minutes of the program to run
9.   public static final int lastsec = 20;
      // The number of seconds the program is running

10. @Override
11. public void run()
12. {
13.     long start_time = System.currentTimeMillis();
14.     long millisecduration = ((lasthour * 60 + lastmin) * 60 +
        lastsec)*1000;
```

```
15.        long endtime = start_time + millisecduration;
16.        long now;
17.        do {
18.            now = System.currentTimeMillis();        // Polling
19.        }    while (now < endtime);
20.        Message msg = new Message();
21.        msg.what = MSG_FINISHED;
22.        mainHandler.sendMessage(msg);
23.    }

24.    public MyTaskThread(Handler mh)
25.    {
26.        super();
27.        mainHandler = mh;
28.    }
29. }
```

The gray background marks the major code segments where changes are made.
In lines 7–9, you assign three constants lasthour, lastmin, and lastsec, respectively, as
the task's running time in hours, minutes, and seconds. The code in lines 13 and 14 is a
core part of the task. In lines 13–15, you set the task start time, duration, and end time, in
milliseconds. Line 16 defines the current-time variable now. In lines 17–19, you use a loop
to poll and compare time. Each cycle first gets the current time and then compares it with
the end time; if the current time is greater than the end time, the loop is ended.

This is typical polling code. The loop body is only a statement to query the current
time, so the loop is very fast and consumes lots of processor computing resources.

4.   Edit the main activity class source code file MainActivity.
      java, and let it control running the task thread. The code
      sections are almost the same as the MainActivity example's
      SerialPi class code (see Chapter 8).

5.   Modify the project's AndroidManifest.xml file to meet the
      Intel GPA monitoring requirements.

Now you can deploy the application to the target machine. This example uses the
Lenovo K800 mobile phone as a test target.

Figure 13-7 and Figure 13-8 show the analysis using Intel GPA. This example
analyzes the main monitor CPU frequency (the CPU XX Frequency indicator) and the
charge or discharge (Current Charging and Current Discharging indicators). You click
the Start Run button to start running the task and recording the Intel GPA monitoring
information.

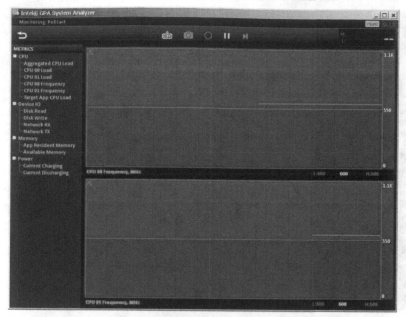

(a) The application has just started

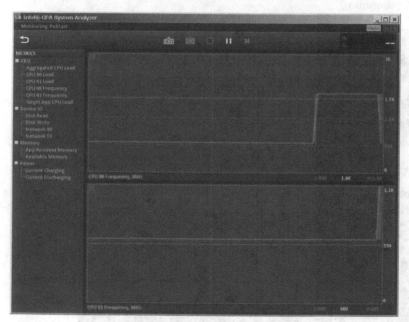

(b) After clicking the Start Run button

Figure 13-7. PollLast *Intel GPA CPU frequency analysis*

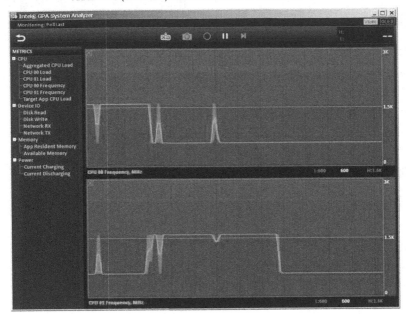

(c) After the task has finished running

Figure 13-7. (*continued*)

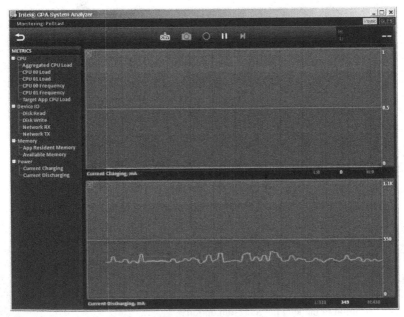

(a) The application has just started

Figure 13-8. PollLast *Intel GPA charge/discharge analysis*

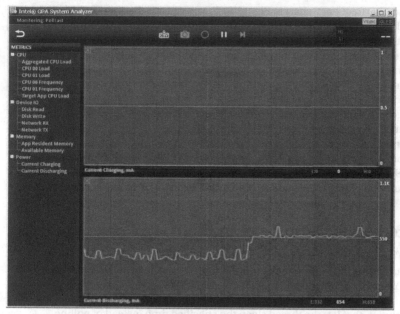

(b) After clicking the Start Run button

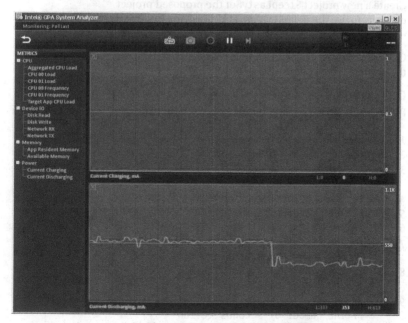

(c) After the task has finished running

Figure 13-8. (*continued*)

From the CPU frequency chart in Figure 13-7, you can see that CPU frequency jumps from 600 MHz up to 1.6 GHz after starting the task and drops back to 600 MHz after running the task. Of course, both logical CPU frequencies do not jump up to 1.6 GHz when the task is running: they have a complementary relationship. When the task is running, only one CPU frequency jumps to the highest values. The main reason for this complementary effect is that this example task has only one worker thread.

The machine's charge is shown in Figure 13-8 in a map view of discharge conditions. The discharge maintained a level below 400 mA before starting the task, as shown in Figure 13-8(a). After starting the task, the discharge jumped to levels above 550 mA. After running the task, discharge level returned to 400 mA or less. The phone was fully charged before running, so the entire example process was always charged in a low state of approximately 0. Discharge reflects the charge level of the machine under the same total power consumption. Running the task led to a dramatic increase in power consumption.

Optimized Applications and an Intel GPA Power Analysis

Through the code analysis of the PollLast application, you know that using a polling statement causes machine power consumption to rise, especially in MyTaskThread.java lines 17–19. You need to rewrite this segment by applying the low-power application design principles as previously described and change the polling code. You can create an optimized solution that lets the thread sleep the specified time instead of polling. This application is an improved version based on PollLast, with these changes:

1. Create a new project SleepLast. Set the proposed project property to use the default value, and select the Build SDK which supports the x86 API.

2. Copy the PollLast main layout file to the project, and replace the original layout of the project file.

3. Copy the original application MyTaskThread.java to this project, and modify its contents as follows:

```
1. package com.example.sleeplast;
2. import android.os.Handler;
3. import android.os.Message;

4. public class MyTaskThread extends Thread {
5.     private Handler mainHandler;
6.     public static final int MSG_FINISHED = 1;
7.     public static final int lasthour = 0;
        // The number of hours run
8.     public static final int lastmin = 0;
        // The number of minutes run
9.     public static final int lastsec = 20;
        // The number of seconds to run
```

```
10.     @Override
11.     public void run()
12.     {
13.         long millisecduration = ((lasthour * 60 + lastmin) *
            60 + lastsec)*1000;
14.         try {
15.             Thread.sleep(millisecduration);
16.         } catch (InterruptedException e) {
17.             e.printStackTrace();
18.         }
19.         Message msg = new Message();
20.         msg.what = MSG_FINISHED;
21.         mainHandler.sendMessage(msg);
22.     }

23.     public MyTaskThread(Handler mh)
24.     {
25.         super();
26.         mainHandler = mh;
27.     }
28. }
```

The first line of code is the declaration of the application package.

The main changes are from lines 13–18. Here you use the static function sleep of the Thread class to specify how long the thread should sleep. The application calculates the sleep time in milliseconds in line 13. Because sleep may throw an InterruptedException exception, you put the function into a try-catch statement block.

4. Copy the MainActivity.java from the original application to cover the same documents. Change its package-declaration line to

   package com.example.sleeplast;

5. Modify the project's AndroidManifest.xml file to match the Intel GPA monitoring requirements.

Now you can deploy the application to the target machine. Again, this example uses a Lenovo K800.

In the real world, you only need to modify the source code of the original application to achieve the optimization for low-power consumption—you don't need to create a separate application. For example, in this case, you would only need to do step 3. This example creates an optimized version of the application to highlight the differences.

Following the same procedure as with the original application, you can use Intel GPA to analyze the optimized application. The results are shown in Figure 13-9 and Figure 13-10.

(a) The application has just started

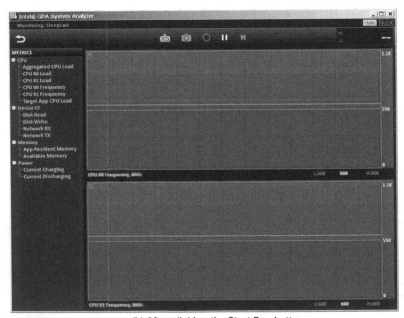

(b) After clicking the Start Run button

Figure 13-9. *Intel GPA CPU frequency analysis of the* SleepLast *application*

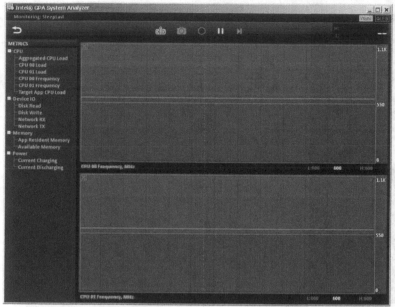

(c) After the task has finished running

Figure 13-9. (*continued*)

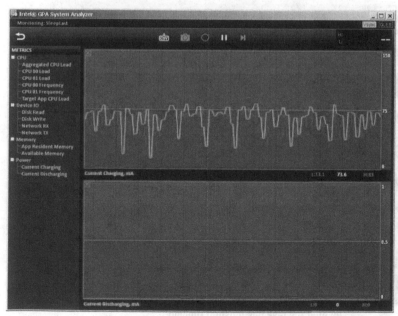

(a) The application has just started

Figure 13-10. *Intel GPA charge/discharge analysis of* SleepLast

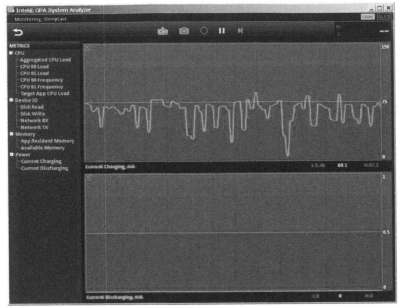

(b) After clicking the Start Run button

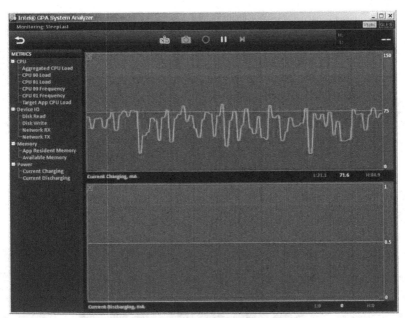

(c) After the task has finished running

Figure 13-10. (*continued*)

In Figure 13-9, compare the graph when the task has not yet started (Figure 13-9(a))
and graph when the task is complete Figure 13-9(c)): the processor frequency does not
change (Figure 13-9(b)) when the task runs. Essentially, all three states have the same
frequency and remain at a low level of 600 MHz. This reflects the fact that the processor's
dynamic power consumption before, during, and after the process did not change
significantly and maintained low load levels.

Figure 13-10 reflects overall machine power consumption, which is also consistent.
Before starting the task (Figure 13-10(a)), during the running of the application
(Figure 13-10(b)), and at the end (Figure 13-10(c)), discharge maintained a low level of
approximately 0. The graph representing charging did not change significantly before,
during, or after the application ran. Compared with PollLast, which caused significant
overall power consumption, the optimized SleepLast application achieves an optimized
power-saving result.

Case Study 2: Timer Optimization and Intel GPA Power Analysis

This section introduces another power-optimization solution: the timer method. You use
Java's Timer and TimerTask to implement a timer. The timer measure the specified time
and notifies the task that it should end when a specified time has passed.

Follow these steps to create the application:

1. Create a new project called TimerLast. Set the proposed
    project property to use the default value, and select the Build
    SDK version that supports the x86 API.

2. Copy the main layout file from PollLast to this project, and
    replace the layout file.

3. Copy MainActivity.java from PollLast to this project, and
    modify its contents as follows:

```
1.  package com.example.timerlast;
2.  import android.os.Bundle;
3.  import android.app.Activity;
4.  import android.view.Menu;
5.  import android.widget.Button;
6.  import android.view.View;
7.  import android.view.View.OnClickListener;
8.  import android.os.Process;
9.  import android.widget.TextView;
10. import android.os.Handler;
11. import android.os.Message;
12. import java.util.Timer;
13.
```

```
14. public class MainActivity extends Activity {
15.      private TextView tv_TaskStatus;
16.      private Button btn_ExitApp;
17.      private Handler mHandler;
18.      private Timer timer =null;              // Timer
19.
20.      @Override
21.      public void onCreate(Bundle savedInstanceState) {
     ......
35.          final Button btn_StartTask = (Button) findViewById(R.
             id.startTask);
36.          btn_StartTask.setOnClickListener(new /*View.*/
             OnClickListener(){
37.              public void onClick(View v) {
38.                  btn_StartTask.setEnabled(false);
39.                  btn_ExitApp.setEnabled(false);
40.                  tv_TaskStatus.setText("Task operation...");
41.                   startTask();
42.              }
43.          });
     ......
58.      }
     ......
66.      private void startTask() {
67.            long millisecduration =
68.            ((MyTaskTimer.lasthour * 60 + MyTaskTimer.
               lastmin) * 60 + MyTaskTimer.lastsec)*1000;
69.          timer = new Timer();               // Creating Timer
70.          timer.schedule(new MyTaskTimer(mHandler),
             millisecduration);               // Set the timer
71.      }
     ......
79. }
```

Lines 35–43 are the response code when the Start Run button is clicked. The key code line is line 41, which calls the custom function startTask. Lines 66–71 implement this function code. The program first calculates the total number of milliseconds for the timing. In line 69, the timer is created. Line 70 sets the timer and calls back the MyTaskTimer object when timing ends.

4. Create a new MyTaskTimer class, and let it inherit from the
   TimerTask class. It is responsible for notifying the activity
   interface that the task has been completed. Edit the source
   code file MyTaskTimer.java as follows:

```
1. package com.example.timerlast;
2. import java.util.TimerTask;        // TimerTask classes using Java
3. import android.os.Handler;
4. import android.os.Message;
5.
6. public class MyTaskTimer extends TimerTask {
7.     private Handler mainHandler;
8.     public static final int MSG_FINISHED = 1;
9.     public static final int lasthour = 0;
       // The task of operating hours
10.    public static final int lastmin = 0;
       // The task of operating minutes
11.    public static final int lastsec = 20;
       // The task of operating seconds
12.
13.    public MyTaskTimer(Handler mh)
14.    {
15.        super();
16.        mainHandler = mh;
17.    }
18.
19.    @Override
20.    public void run(){
21.        Message msg = new Message();
22.        msg.what = MSG_FINISHED;           // Defined message
           types
23.        mainHandler.sendMessage(msg);       // Send a message
24.    }
25. }
```

According to the Java timer framework, when the timer expires, the program callback
function of TimerTask runs. The previous code lets the MyTaskTimer class inherit from
TimerTask and allows the code for the self-timing timer to expire in the run function. In
this case, lines 19–24 hold the callback code that indicates timing is complete and sends a
"finished" message to the main interface. The main interface responds to this message in
its own handler and displays a message that the task is ended.

Now you can deploy the application to the target machine. As before this example
uses a Lenovo K800 smartphone with an Intel Atom processor.

Following the same procedure as previously, you can use Intel GPA to analyze the
optimized application, record the GPA monitoring information, and analyze the results,
as shown in Figure 13-11 and Figure 13-12.

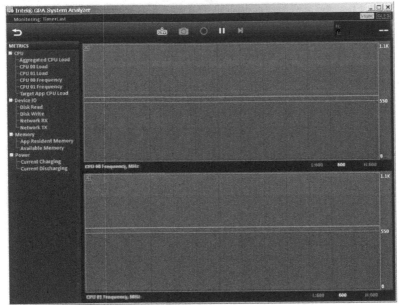

(a) The application has just started

(b) After clicking the Start Run button

Figure 13-11. *Intel GPA CPU frequency analysis of* TimerLast

(c) After the task has finished running

Figure 13-11. (*continued*)

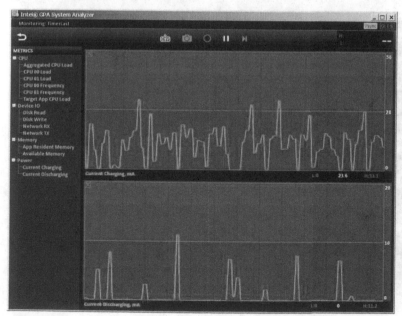

(a) The application has just started

Figure 13-12. *Intel GPA charge/discharge analysis of* TimerLast

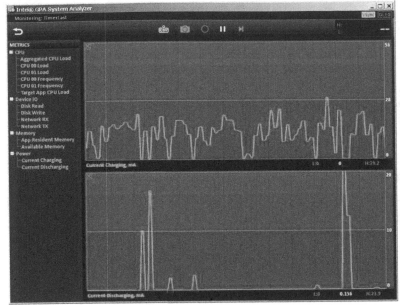

(b) After clicking the Start Run button

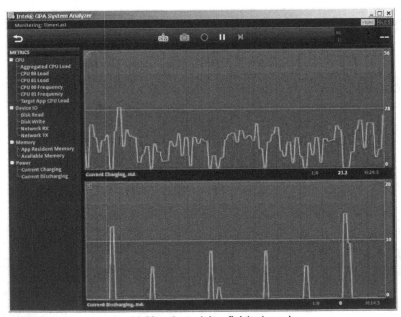

(c) After the task has finished running

Figure 13-12. (*continued*)

The frequency graph shown in Figure 13-11 is similar to the SleepLast graph from Figure 13-9. The processor frequency does not change in Figure 13-11(b) after running the task and has essentially the same frequency as before the task started (Figure 13-11(a)) and after it ended (Figure 13-11(c)). It stayed in the low 600 MHz range. The only difference is a rise in occasional glitches at the end of the task (Figure 13-11(c)). The processor's dynamic power consumption did not change significantly before, during, and after the process: it maintained low load levels.

Figure 13-12 shows that overall machine power consumption is consistent with Figure 13-11. Of course, the TimerLast graph is not as pretty as the display in Figure 13-10, which shows the performance of SleepLast—discharge graphs always have some glitches. However, the indicator did not change significantly before the task, while the task ran, and after task completion. This proves that running the task did not cause the extra power consumption. Compared with PollLast, which caused significant overall power consumption, the optimized TimerLast application achieved an optimized power-saving result.

Book Summary

In this book, you learned how to develop and optimize Android applications on Intel Atom platforms, as well as how to develop power-efficient applications. Here is a summary of the key concepts:

- Most Android applications written in Java can execute on the Intel Atom platform directly. NDK applications need to recompile native code. If assembly code is included in the application, this portion of the code must be rewritten.

- Make full use of Intel Architecture features to improve your Android application performance.

- Add platform-specific compile switches to make the GCC build code more effective.

- Intel provides various useful tools to help Android developers. Many of them focus on improving performance and can help you optimize your applications.

The common methods of creating Android apps are as follows:

- Java compiled using the Android SDK APIs, to run in the Dalvik VM. Google is releasing a new Android Runtime (ART) for the new Android L OS at the end of 2014.

- Using the latest SDK, testing goes faster if you speed up your Android emulation software with Intel HAXM.

- Created in or ported to NDK. This is the preferred method if you have the C++ code. Native C++ code is compiled into a binary before execution and doesn't require interpretation into machine language.

If you don't have an Android development environment (IDE), the new tool suite Intel Integrated Native Developer Experience (INDE) loads a selected Android IDE and also downloads and installs multiple Intel tools to help you make, compile, troubleshoot, and publish Android applications. Go to `https://software.intel.com/en-us/android` to download and use those tools. You can also visit this book's Apress web page to keep up with updates and any posted errata: `www.apress.com/9781484201015`.

Index

■ A, B

Advanced Linux Sound
 Architecture (ALSA), 131
Android application
 ART, 232
 components
  activities, 228
  broadcast intent receiver, 230
  intent and intent filters, 229
  service process, 229
 content provider, 231
 Dalvik virtual machine, 231
 file structure, 214
  AndroidManifest.xml, 218
  constant definitions, 222
  layout files, 224
  R.java file, 221
  source code file, 227
Android application
 cross-development, 341
Android application development, 47
 debugging and simulation
  cross-debugging, 57
  debugging tools, 57
  system simulators, 55
 development environment, 48
  cross-development
   configuration, 48
  programming languages, 49
 development process, 51
  construction stage, 52
  debugging and optimizing stage, 54
  deployment stage, 53
  encoding, 52
 emulator
  DDMS interface, 98–99, 102
  Eclipse interface, 97

home page, 100
IDE interface, 104
initial page, 103
Intel HAXM, 97
MainActivity application, 100–101
message box, 96
runtime configuration, 95
GNU toolsets, 61–62
GPL toolsets, 61
Intel GPA, 126
Intel ICC, 125
Intel INDE (see Intel Integrated
 Native Developer Experience
 (Intel INDE))
Intel performance libraries, 129
Intel Project Anarchy, 129
Intel system studio, 127, 129
LGPL toolsets, 61
new project creation
 activity setting, 92–93
 dialog box setup, 89–90
 directory structure, 94
 Eclipse, 88
 icon setting, 91
real device, 104
tool chains, 60
 aapt.exe, 71
 adb.exe, 70
 aidl.exe, 71
 android.bat, 71
 android.jar, 68
 build manager, 63
 in command-line format, 66
 command line toolsets, 61
 compiler and linker, 62
 ddms.bat, 69
 debugger, 63
 dx.bat, 71

Android application development (*cont.*)
full-screen editors, 62
gproof, 64
IDEs, 61
libraries, 66
line editors, 62
makefile, 63
sqlite3.exe, 71
vs. GNU toolsets, 65
Android customization
flash_device.sh, 201
generation and installation, 199–200
Intel Build Tools Suite features, 201
recovery, 199
reflashing, 199
ROM package/image
creation, 196
data\app directory, 197
development process, 193
embedded system, 194
files and folders, 195
file structure of, 195
Java environment, 198
Lenovo K900 Website, 197
process of, 196
system\app directory, 197
system\bin directory, 197
system\media directory, 197
zip packages, 198
SD card, 200
wiping, 199
Android Debug Bridge (adb)
command prompt, 70
device/phone simulator, 177
functions, 183
host machine's Windows
command line, 177
installation command, 179
kill-server command, 183
push command, 183
shell command rm, 182
target machine, 178–179
Android devices *vs.* desktop computers
application windows, 209
copyright protection
problems, 214
keyboard input problems, 213
keys and buttons, 205
multimodal interactions, 208
onscreen keyboards, 208

screen size, 208
buttons and graphical
elements, 209
text and icon size, 209
screen size and densities, 204
software distribution, 214
storage devices, 208
tap-only touch screens
hover-over operations, 212
mapping errors, 210
moving the cursor without
clicking, 210
right-click functions, 212
touch screens and stylus, 207
Android interface design, 235. *See also*
GuiExam application
Android multithreaded design
in activity_main.xml, 363
extensions and support
assistive thread, 358
handler, 360
interface thread, 358
looper-message
mechanism, 358, 360
message queue, 359–360
UI thread, 358
GuiExam application, 361
button status, 366
demo app, 362
Handler class, 365
mainHandler variable, 367
MyTaskThread, 367
myThread, 365
response code, 365
setButtonAvailable function, 365
stepTime constant, 367
stop-the-thread prototype
function, 366
TextView widget, 365
Java thread programming
interface, 356
parallel execution, 355
programming framework, 356
thread communication
notifyAll function, 370
notify function, 370
wait function, 370
thread synchronization
competition, 367
critical section, 367

generalized rules, 369
genlock, 368
static synchronization
  method, 369
synchronization (general)
  method, 369
Android OS, 131
  adb command prompt (*see* Android
    Debug Bridge (adb) command
    prompt)
  architecture, 133–134
  AVD, 151
  class reference page, 157
  DDMS (*see* Dalvik Debug Monitor
    Service (DDMS))
  drivers and technologies, 131
  emulator, 151
    APIs, 184
    creation, 186
    event command, 187
    geo command, 187–188
    gsm command, 188
    installation, 184
    kill command, 188
    network command, 189
    power command, 189
    redir Command, 189
    scale command, 190
    sms command, 190
    Telnet command, 186
  index.html file, 157
  Lenovo K900 smartphone
    DDMS, 139
    drop-down menu options, 136
    four-leaf clover design, 134
    menu interface, 136
    mobile device menu, 138
    multiscreen interface, 136
    parameters of, 138
    Web browser, 139
  Linux commands and operations
    (*see* Linux commands and
    operations)
  online reading function, 158
  SDK entry page, 159
  UI subsystem, 132
Android Run Time (ART), 50, 232, 391
Android Virtual Device (AVD)
  interface, 57, 151
Application binary interface (ABI), 400

■ **C**

Cloud computing, 43
CMOS processor, 447
Complex instruction set
  computer (CISC), 9
Customization
  Android customization (*see* Android
    customization)
  Embedded OS
    modes of, 192
    principle of, 191

■ **D**

Dalvik Debug Monitor Server (DDMS), 139
Dalvik Debug Monitor Service (DDMS)
  command line, 160
  editing and debug interfaces, 161–163
  emulator
    control interface of, 175
    Location control, 175
    SMS, 176
    Telephony actions, 175
    Telephony status, 175
  file transfers
    deletion, 167
    host machine to target
      machine, 163
    target machine to host
      machine, 167
  process management
    designation, 170
    Eclipse, 168
    emulator, 169
    List of, 170
  screen capture, 171
Dalvik virtual machine (DVM), 133
  vs. ART, 232
  vs. JVM, 231
Debugging
  breakpoint setup, 112–113
  cross-debugging, 57
    adb debugger, 58
    software environment, 58
  tools, 57
  Eclipse IDE, 115–116
  Log.X function, 117
  program execution techniques, 116–117
  source code editing, 110

Debugging (*cont.*)
  system simulators, 55
    analog peripherals, 55
    AVD interface, 56
    two uses on one machine, 56
    types, 55
  terminate button, 123
  variable observation, 121
  warning dialog box, 114
  Watch command, 121
Design applications
  multiple activities
    explicit match, 271 (*see also* Direct
      intent triggering mechanism)
    implicit match, 271
    implicit match, 271 (*see also*
      Indirect intent triggering
      mechanism)
Development environment, Android
  cross-development, 48
  programming languages, 49
Development process, Android, 51
  construction stage, 52
  debugging and optimizing stage, 54
  deployment stage, 53
  encoding, 52
Dialog boxes
  activity's dialog theme
    AlertDialog class, 323
    dismissDialog() function, 323
    onCreateDialog() function, 322
    onPrepareDialog() function, 323
    ProgressDialog class, 323
    showDialog() function, 322
    toast reminders, 323
  AlertDialog.Builder class, 326
  application interface, 324
  code implementation, 324
  DialogInterface class, 327
  OnKeyDown response function, 327
  setPositiveButton function, 327
Digital signal processing (DSP), 9
Direct intent triggering mechanism
  without parameters
    activity class, 277
    application interface, 273
    callee activity, 272, 280
    class-name modifiers, 280
    constructor, 280
    drag-and-drop layout, 276
    final configuration, 276

    layout configuration, 279
    layout file, 274–275
    reflection, 273
    setContentView() function, 278
  with parameters
    application interface, 282
    callee activity, 281
    executing application, 283
    Intent.setClassName()
      function, 286
    layout design, 284, 288
    layout file, 289
    onActivityResult function, 287
    property-value data pairing, 286
    set result function, 291
Dynamic frequency scaling (DFS), 447–448
Dynamic voltage and frequency
    scaling (DVFS), 448
Dynamic voltage scaling (DVS), 448

■ E

Embedded OS
  modes of, 192
  principle of, 191
Embedded systems, 1, 203
  advantages, 11
  android devices *vs.* desktop
    computers, 204
  application layer, 17
  basic architecture, 6
  characteristics, 11, 17
  comparison of RISC and CISC, 10
  computer architecture, 7
  consumer electronics and
    information, 3
  debug, 5
  feature, 17
  four layers, 15
  general-purpose, 3
  hardware abstraction layer (HAL), 16
  hardware architecture, 6
  Harvard architecture, 8–9
  integrated hardware and software, 5
  Intel Atom processor, 2
  limited resources, 4
  macro operation/macro-op, 11
  microprocessor architecture, 9
  MIPS architecture, 12
  mobile phones, 3
  OS layer, 16

power constraints, 5
PowerPC architecture, 13
real-time aspect, 4
robustness, 5
SoC-based hardware
    system structure, 14
software architecture, 15
SuperH (SH), 13
system on chip (SoC), 14
system service layer, 17
target machine, 18
typical hardware structure, 13
Von Neumann architecture, 7–8
x86 architecture, 12
x86 instruction fusion, 11
Emulator
    APIs, 184
    creation, 186
    DDMS interface, 98–99, 102
    Eclipse interface, 97
    event command, 187
    geo command, 187–188
    gsm command, 188
    home page, 100
    IDE interface, 104
    initial page, 103
    installation, 184
    Intel HAXM, 97
    kill command, 188
    MainActivity application, 100–101
    message box, 96
    network command, 189
    power command, 189
    redir Command, 189
    runtime configuration, 95
    scale command, 190
    sms command, 190
    Telnet command, 186
Engineering and Technology (IET), 4
Enhanced Intel SpeedStep
    Technology (EIST), 25

■ F

Field-programmable gate
    array (FPGA), 15

■ G, H

Garbage collector, 50
GNU development tools, 61–62

Graphical User Interface (GUI) design
    embedded systems (see Embedded
        systems)
    system service layer, 17
GuiExam application, 248
    activity state transition
        active states, 235
        finish function, 239
        inactive states, 236
        onCreate function, 237
        onDestroy function, 239
        onPause function, 238
        onRestart function, 238
        onResume function, 238
        onStart function, 238
        onStop function, 238
        paused states, 235
        schematic representation, 236
        stopped states, 236
        triggers, 239
    applications and activities, 247
        application interface, 268
        DDMS view, 269
        finish function, 266
        ImageView, 266
    buttons and events, 259
    code implementation, 251
    Context class
        activity context, 241
        context wrapper/direct context
            methods, 242
        dialog constructor, 240
        offspring classes, 241
        subclasses, 241
    design layouts
        interface structure, 255
        text-edit widget, 254
        text property, 253
        user interface, 254
    file structure, 249
    ID attribute, 257
    ImageView, 262
    inner class listener, 260
    intent, 243
        action test, 245
        category test, 246
        components, 244
        data test, 246
        explicit matching/direct intent, 244
        implicit matching/indirect
            intent, 245

GuiExam application (*cont.*)
    mechanism, 245
    roles, 244
  interface, 250
  setContentView function, 255
GUiExam project
  interface of, 311
  touchscreen input
    code implementation, 306
    constructor function, 308
    setStyle function, 308
    View.onDraw function, 308

■ I

Indirect intent triggering mechanism
  built-in activity
    ACTION constants, 296
    Activity.startActivityForResult()
      function, 292
    application interface, 293
    constructor function, 295
    layout file, 294
  custom activity
    application interface, 297
    Intent.ACTION_EDIT, 304
    layout design, 299
    layout file, 301
Intel architecture-32 (IA-32), 12
Intel architecture-64 (IA-64), 12
Intel Atom processor
  architecture, 20
  64-bit architecture
    advantages, 32
    memory and CPU register size, 33
  chipset
    computer system
      architecture, 29
    integrated graphics chip, 30
    North Bridge chip, 30
    PCI and ISA, 30
    South Bridge chip, 30
  description, 19
  high performance, 25
    floating-point-intensive
      applications, 26
    Intel HT Technology, 27
    Intel VT, 27
    multi-core technologies, 27
    SIMD, realization procedure, 27
    vector data, 26

IMVP-6, 25
integer execution area, 21
low power consumption, 25
reference platform (*see* Reference
    platform)
Silvermont microarchitecture
  advantages, 22
  benefits and features, 24
SIMD/floating-point
    execution area, 21
small form factor, 24
System on Chip (SoC), 30
  Bay Trail, 32
  Medfield, 31
technologies
  burst mode, 28
  enhanced data pre-fetch
    technology, 28
  low cost, 28
  Power-optimized FSB, 28
  Smart cache, 28
Intel Atom processors
  backpack journalism, 44
  learning, 44
  portable video recording, 44
  RFID tags, 44
  wireless sensor networks, 43
Intel C++ Compiler (Intel ICC), 125
Intel embedded chipset
  computer system architecture, 29
  integrated graphics chip, 30
  North Bridge chip, 30
  PCI and ISA, 30
  South Bridge chip, 30
  variations, 29
Intel Galileo development board, 35
Intel Graphics Performance Analyzers
    (Intel GPA), 126
  on Android
    application cross development, 341
    MoveCircle application, 346
    MoveCircle operation, 345
  installation, 344
  interface monitoring, 342
  System Analyzer, 341
  windows and toolbar, 343–344
Intel Integrated Native Developer
    Experience (Intel INDE)
  AVD (Emulator) creation, 79
  Eclipse configuration, 77
  environment setup, 72

host machines, 73
installation
download screen, 75
install window, 76
launch process, 77
setup process, 76
setup, 75
tools and libraries
compiling, 74
compute code builder, 74
threading, 74
Intel Integrated Performance Primitives
(Intel IPP), 426
Intel Mobile Voltage Positioning
(IMVP)-6, 25
Intel NUC Kit DE3815TYKHE, 34
Intel's Silvermont microarchitecture, 22
Internet of Things (IoT), 34
Inter-process communications (IPC)
functions, 132

■ J, K

Java Native Interface (JNI)
AOT, 391
ART, 391
C/C++ function, 392
Dalvik virtual machine, 391
host platform, 391
Java methods and C Function, 394
Java *vs.* C/C++
correspondence, 395
Java array processing, 397
resource release, 397
uses, 396
local platform, 391
scenarios, 392
system level approach, 392
System.loadLibrary() method, 393
System.load() method, 393
workflow, 392
Java Thread Programming Interface, 356
Java virtual machine (JVM), 50

■ L

Large-scale integration (LSI), 1
Lenovo K900 smartphone
DDMS, 139
drop-down menu options, 136
four-leaf clover design, 134

menu interface, 136
mobile device menu, 138
multiscreen interface, 136
parameters of, 138
Web browser, 139
Linux commands and operations
Android file-operation
commands, 144–145
cd command, 143
change command, 141
check command, 141
clear command, 142
executable file path, 147
File/Directory
permission-modification, 145
find command, 144
grep command, 148
Linux ping command, 149
ls command, 143
su command, 142
uname command, 149
Linux power-control mechanism
PowerTOP, 455
Tickless idle, 454
Log.X function, 117
Low-power design, 445
in application, 459
data acquisition and
communications, 463
event-driven programming, 462
fast algorithm, 460
hardware, types of, 460
periodic operations reduction, 462
polling method, 460
power-aware program, 463
processor and peripherals, 459
dynamic power dissipation, 446
linux power-control mechanism
PowerTOP, 455
Tickless idle, 454
mobile device, 446
power consumption control
technology
ACPI, 451
Advanced Power
Management (APM), 451
Clock gating, 449
DFS, 447–448
DVS, 448
EIST, 450
hibernate mode, 453

Low-power design (*cont.*)
  Intel SpeedStep, 450
  Sleep mode, 453
  standby mode, 452
  ULV processor, 449
  power-optimization aids, 456
  static power consumption, 446

M

Macro operation/macro-op, 11
Mobile phone settings, 85, 130
  android application development
    (*see* Android application
    development)
  debugging
    breakpoint setup, 112–113
    Eclipse IDE, 115–116
    Log.X function, 117
    program execution
      techniques, 116–117
    source code editing, 110
    terminate button, 123
    variable observation, 121
    warning dialog box, 114
    Watch command, 121
  host and target machines, 88
  Lenovo K900 smartphone, 85
  USB driver installation, 85
MoveCircle application
  Analyzable application list, 349
  CPU loads, 354
  document framework, 346
  Intel GPA, 346
  Internet write/read access, 347
  OpenGL metrics, 354
  operation interface, 345
Multithreaded optimization
  Intel GPA, 373
    SerialPi app interface, 374
    ThreadPi user interface, 381
  principles
    hyperthreading/multi-core
      support, 372
    start/scheduling, 372

N

Native Development Kit (NDK), 397
  ABI, 400
  Android API, 399

Android application files, 398
application projects, 399
benefits, 397
CDT installation, 401
command line, 403
  APP_ABI parameters, 410
  classpath, 406
  command parameters, 406
  jnitest project, file structure, 404
  libs and obj, 410
  LoadLibrary function, 405
  LOCAL_SRC_FILES variable, 410
  stringFromJNI local
    function, 408–409
compiler optimizations, 419
  anotherCCodeTask function, 436
  anotherCCodeTask prototype, 440
  CCodeTaskThread class, 439
  command options, 441
  Original Application
    Accelaration, 437
  SSE instructions, 442
  System.loadLibrary function, 441
components, 398
dynamic libraries, 398
integrated optimization
  C/C++ native library function, 427
  CCodeTaskThread, 432, 434
  JavaTaskThread class, 435
  MyTaskThread class, 434
  NdkExp layout, 429
  System.loadLibrary function, 435
Intel Processor-Related Compiler
    Switch Options, 422
  01 optimization level, 424
  gcc command options, 425
  gcc-march parameters, 423
  -march option, 423
  -mtune option, 423
  SSE instructions, 425
Java native library files, 398
library file, 411
loop unrolling, 421
machine independent compiler
    switch options, 420–422
performance optimization, 428
workflow analysis
  .apk file, 417
  Eclipse Logcat window, 418
  project file structure, 417
Next Unit of Computing (NUC), 34

■ O

Original device manufacturers (ODMs), 5

■ P, Q

Performance optimization
    combined value principle, 336
    compiler optimization, 338
    efficacy principle, 335
    equal value principle, 335
    execution frequency, 336
    faster instruction selection, 336
    GPA tool, 338 (see also Intel Graphics
        Performance Analyzers
        (Intel GPA))
    high-performance libraries, 339
    instruction-level parallelism, 337
    machine-dependent, 338
    machine-independent, 338
    manual optimization
        assembly-language level, 340
        compiling-instruction level, 340
        source-code level, 340
    reducing instructions, 336
    register cache
        high-speed cache, 337
        locality principle, 337
        space locality, 337
        temporal locality, 337
    user optimization, 340
Personal computers (PCs), 1
Power optimization, 463
    PollLast application
        CPU frequency analysis, 466, 468
        creation, 464–465
        definition, 464
        interface, 464
        layout of, 465
        processor computing
            resources, 466
    SleepLast application
        CPU frequency analysis, 471–473
        creation, 470–471
        try-catch statement block, 471
    timer method
        CPU frequency analysis, 477–479
        creation, 475–476
        MyTaskTimer class, 477
Programmable logic device (PLD), 15

■ R

Radio-frequency ID (RFID), 44
Recent platform
    cloud computing, 43
    in-Vehicle Infotainment (IVI)
        systems, 42
    robotics, 43
    smartphones, 36
        Lenovo K900, 37
        Vexia Zippers phone, 38
        ZTE Grand X2, 38
    tablets, 39
        Acer Iconia A1-830, 41
        ASUS MeMO Pad FHD 10, 41
        Dell Venue 7/8" tablet, 40
        Samsung Galaxy
            Tab 3 10.1, 40
Reduced instruction set
    computer (RISC), 9
Reference platform
    Intel NUC Kit DE3815TYKHE, 34
    Internet of Things (IoT), 34–35
    IoT, 34
Robotics, 43
ROM package/image
    creation, 196
    data\app directory, 197
    development process, 193
    embedded system, 194
    files and folders, 195
    file structure of, 195
    Java environment, 198
    Lenovo K900 Website, 197
    process of, 196
    system\app directory, 197
    system\bin directory, 197
    system\media directory, 197
    zip packages, 198

■ S

SerialPi app interface, 375
Silvermont microarchitecture, 22
Single instruction, multiple
    data (SIMD), 21
Streaming SIMD Extensions (SSE), 27
System on Chip (SoC), 30
    Bay Trail, 32
    Medfield, 31

System simulators, 55
analog peripherals, 55
AVD interface, 56
two uses on one machine, 56
types, 55

■ **T**

Thermal design power (TDP), 446
ThreadPi user interface, 382
Tool chains
aapt.exe, 71
adb.exe, 71
aidl.exe, 71
android.bat, 71
android.jar, 68
build manager, 63
by companies and organizations, 61
in command-line format,
    Android SDK, 66
command line toolsets, 61
compiler and linker, 62
ddms.bat, 69
debugger, 63
dx.bat, 71
full-screen editors, 62
GNU toolsets, 61, 65
gproof, 64
IDEs, 61
Intel tools, 66
libraries, 66
line editors, 62
Makefile, 63
sqlite3.exe, 71
types, 60
Touchscreen input
application settings
    applying properties, 329
    icon dialog box, 332
    menulist, 328
    screen resolutions, 329
    target device, 328
dialog boxes
    activity's dialog theme, 322
    AlertDialog.Builder class, 327
    AlertDialog class, 323
    application interface, 323
    code implementation, 324

DialogInterface class, 327
OnKeyDown response
    function, 327
ProgressDialog class, 323
setPositiveButton function, 327
toast reminders, 323
display framework
    application interface, 309
    code implementation, 309
    fill mode parameters, 308
    GuiExam project (*see* GUiExam
        project)
    onDraw function, 305
    setContentView function, 306
drawing framework
    application interface, 311
    code implementation, 311
    invalidate function, 310
    postInvalidate function, 310
    View.onDraw function, 310
    View.onTouchEvent, 310
keyboard input
    application interface, 318
    code implementation, 319
    keyCode parameter, 321
    onKeyDown function, 317
    virtual machine, 319
multi-touch code framework
    application interface, 314
    code implementation, 315
    getx/gety functions, 313
    onDraw function, 317
    touch event class, 313

■ **U**

Ultra-low voltage (ULV)
    processor, 449
Universal asynchronous
    receiver/transmitter (UART), 14

■ **V**

Very-large-scale integration (VLSI), 1

■ **W, X, Y, Z**

Wi-Fi communication, 463